WHEN CHILDREN BECAME PEOPLE

WHEN CHILDREN

The Birth of Childhood in Early Christianity

BECAME PEOPLE

O. M. BAKKE

Translated by Brian McNeil

FORTRESS PRESS
MINNEAPOLIS

WHEN CHILDREN BECAME PEOPLE
The Birth of Childhood in Early Christianity

Cover art: Detail of children playing games from a Roman relief from sarcophagus of
a child. Kunsthistorisches Museum, Vienna, Austria. Photo ©Erich Lessing /
Art Resource, N.Y.

Cover and interior design: Zan Ceeley

Library of Congress Cataloging-in-Publication Data
Bakke, Odd Magne, 1962–
When children became people : the birth of childhood in early Christianity /
O. M. Bakke.
p. cm.
Includes bibliographical references and index.
ISBN 0-8006-3725-9 (pbk. : alk. paper)
1. Children (Christian theology)—History of doctrines—Early church, ca. 30-600.
2. Christian children—Religious life—History—To 1500. 3. Children—Rome—
Social conditions. I. Title.
BR195.C46B35 2005
270.1'083—dc22
2004029375

Manufactured in the U.S.A.
09   08   07   06   05   1   2   3   4   5   6   7   8   9   10

CONTENTS

ACKNOWLEDGMENTS

M ost of this book was written while I was a visiting scholar at Luther Seminary in the academic year 2001–2002. I am grateful to Profes- sor Todd W. Nichol for his hospitality and friendship during that time, not least because he read parts of my manuscript and was a good dialogue partner. I also wish to thank the Lee, Bosell, and Moen families, who did so much to make my time at Luther Seminary so valuable for my whole fam- ily. I also wish to thank the governing body of the School of Mission and Theology in Stavanger for allowing me to spend one year doing research on this subject, without other academic obligations.

I also wish to thank the staff in the library of the School of Mission and Theology, Turid Helgeland, Trine Olsen Lande, and the Reverend Arne Samuelsen, for excellent service.

My colleague, Professor Thor Strandenæs, suggested the idea of study- ing children in the early Christian world. I am sure that, if he had not begun the research project into children and theology at the School of Mission and Theology, this book would never have seen the light of day!

I am grateful to Fortress Press for publishing this book.

Last but not least, I wish to thank Dr. Brian McNeil for translating my manuscript from Norwegian with accuracy and skill (with the exception of Chapters 1 and 3, where he revised my English text). In the interests of accessibility, we have foregone reproducing the many Greek texts in the original manuscript, and we have used transliterated Greek terms. I am confident that the extensive citations in the notes will lead scholars and other interested readers to the full original sources.

This book is published with support from the project "Christian Man and Woman: The Construction of New Identity in Antiquity" in the Nor- wegian Research Council's Program for Classical Antiquity.

I dedicate this book to our three children, Helena, Maria Yun, and Bjarte Woo. They have caused their parents many sleepless nights and much worry, and have made our lives very busy. But most of all, they are a source of joy and gratitude, and make our lives meaningful.

ABBREVIATIONS

The text of the New Testament is K. Aland et al., *Novum Testamentum Graece*, 27th ed. (Stuttgart: Deutsche Bibelgesellschaft, 1993). Quotations in English are taken from the *New Revised Standard Version*, Anglicized Edition (Oxford: Oxford University Press, 1995). Abbreviations of biblical, apocryphal, and early patristic writings follow those listed in the *Journal of Biblical Literature*'s "Instruction for Contributors" (Membership Directory and Handbook [1993], 386–88). Abbreviations of other patristic writings follow those listed in G. W. H. Lampe, *A Patristic Greek Lexicon*.

Abbreviations of Philo and Josephus follow S. M. Schwertner, *Abkürzungsverzeichnis, Theologische Realenzyklopädie*.

References to classical texts follow the abbreviations listed in N. G. L. Hammond and H. H. Scullard, *Oxford Classical Dictionary*. Where texts are not found in that list, the lists in H. G. Liddell and R. Scott, *A Greek-English Lexicon*, and in P. G. W. Glare, *Oxford Latin Dictionary*, are used. Classical texts are cited according to the text and translation of the Loeb Classical Library editions. Text editions from well-known series are not listed in the bibliography, but they are identified in the notes. The following abbreviations are used:

ACW	Ancient Christian Writers
AFNTC	The Apostolic Fathers: A New Translation and Commentary
ANF	*The Ante-Nicene Fathers*
CCL	Corpus Christianorum Latinorum
CSEL	Corpus Scriptorum Ecclesiasticorum Latinorum
FC	Fathers of the Church: A New Translation
FCh	Fontes Christiani
GCS	Die griechischen christlichen Schriftsteller der erste Jahrhunderte

LCL	Loeb Classical Library
NPNF	*Nicene and Post-Nicene Fathers*
PG	Patrologia graeca. Edited by J.-P. Migne. 162 vols. Paris, 1857–1886
PL	Patrologia latina. Edited by J.-P. Migne. 217 vols. Paris, 1844–1864
SC	Sources Chrétiennes
TDNT	*Theological Dictionary of the New Testament.* Edited by G. Kittle and G. Friedrich, translated by G. W. Bromiley. 10 vols. Grand Rapids, Mich.: Eerdmans, 1964–1976
WSA	The Works of Saint Augustine: A Translation for the Twenty-first Century
WUNT	Wissenschaftliche Untersuchungen zum Neuen Testament

1
INTRODUCTION

～～

How did Christians in the ancient world deal with children? What was it like to grow up in a Christian household? What did Christians in antiquity think about children? To what extent did children participate in the life of the church? Did they have any specific roles? What influence did Christianity have on how adults thought about children and how children were treated? By asking such questions, I intend to draw as clearly as possible a picture both of the theology of children and of the social history of children during that formative period in Christian history.

The main focus of the present volume is children in early Christianity (c. 100–450 C.E.). By children I mean real children, not children used as a metaphor for adults as in the common designation of adult Christians as children of God. By children I mean human beings who not yet had become grown-ups. It was customary in the classical period to follow Hippocrates, the father of medical science, in his division of the human lifespan into eight chronologically successive phases. The first three of these were (1) *paidion*, the small child (until the age of seven); (2) *pais*, the child (from seven to fourteen); and (3) *meirakion*, the young person (from fourteen to twenty).[1] In keeping with this way of understanding the life cycle, "child/children" in the present book refers to human beings from birth to the age of about twenty.

GROWING ATTENTION TO CHILDREN IN SOCIETY AND RESEARCH

Never before in the history of the Western countries, and probably also in other parts of the world, have the situation of children and issues related to childhood been so much in the focus of public life as they are now. It should come as no surprise then that I, as a Norwegian living at

1

the beginning of the twenty-first century, am interested in this subject. Besides the fact that I am the father of three children, I am a product of a culture that is increasingly concerned with children. Our society is deeply concerned that children experience the love and care that they need for healthy physical and mental development. People of many professions discuss how one can best deal with the serious problems too many children are facing, such as sexual abuse, divorce, and poverty. The quality of schools and day care services, and whether parents should have a real, that is, affordable option to stay home with their children have been hot issues in election campaigns in many locales. There is perhaps no clearer expression of the fact that children and their condition have become a part of the public agenda than the United Nations' declaration of the year 1979 as the year of the children. It is not my task here to consider whether this public interest in issues related to children has improved their general situation.

At the same time, and no doubt because of this widespread concern about children in public life, there has been an increasing interest in topics related to children and childhood in a growing range of academic disciplines. A striking expression of the growing interest in children is the fact that fields other than those that traditionally focus on children, such as education and child psychology, have recently begun to devote attention to children.[2] For instance, during the last two decades, several studies in the field of philosophy have been published focusing on among other things philosophical conceptions of childhood and on children's cognitive and philosophical capacities.[3] In the field of sociology, an immense number of books discuss the effects on children of changing family structures, particularly with respect to divorce and single-parent households.[4] Other disciplines that have traditionally focused on children (for example, psychology) have reinforced this focus. During the two last decades, books dealing with the "classical" theme of the moral development of children have been published; others discuss in a more narrow sense the religious perceptions and faith development of children.[5]

In the field of history, the publication of Philippe Ariès's study in 1960 was fundamental.[6] His thesis, that it was not until after the Renaissance that one started to consider or realized that childhood constituted a particular stage in the development of a human being, has rightly been disputed.[7] In spite of this, a lasting value of Ariès's study is its contribution to shaping awareness of the fact that historical periods of the past could have had totally different presuppositions about childhood than our own, and that it is of vital importance to uncover these in order to give an adequate interpretation of the conception of children. His book represented the starting point for a number of studies that explicitly explored the history of childhood in the West. Many of these focus on the time from the middle ages to the nineteenth century.[8] More important with respect to the present work is the publication of several studies of various aspects of children and childhood in the Greco-Roman world.[9] As will become clear below, I will draw to a great extent on these works in my picture of children in the wider cultural environment of the ancient Christians, that is, non-Christian Greco-Roman antiquity.

[margin handwriting: Draw from non-Xian Greco-Roman antiquity]

Children and childhood have tended to be a neglected theme in most theological disciplines in modern times.[10] It appears that New Testament studies is the only traditional theological discipline that represents the exception to the rule. The passages of the Gospels dealing with Jesus' attitude toward children have, of course, been discussed in standard commentaries. Several monographs have also been published. The first of these, by Simon Légasse, was published as early as 1969.[11] Only three years later, a book by H. H. Schroeder that deals with children and parents in Jesus' proclamation emerged.[12] These books were followed by a major study by Peter Müller in 1992,[13] and the recent monograph by Peter Balla on the child-parent relationship in the New Testament (2003).[14] Besides the works of these scholars, various aspects of children in the New Testament are dealt with in a number of articles and parts of books, several of them published during the last decade.[15]

In the field of systematic theology, Dawn DeVries has remarked, in an article published in 2001, that "until very recently" this theological discipline "in the twentieth century has been largely silent on the question of children."[16] Her article contributes to a systematic discussion of children, and suggests lines for further studies.

In the field of church history, the situation is somewhat better. Though much work remains to be done on the images and ideas of children in the history of the church and the treatment of children, a number of highly valuable works have appeared. A major recent publication is the collection of seventeen essays, *The Child in Christian Thought*, edited by Marcia J. Bunge; according to the series editors, this book "fills an enormous gap in contemporary family studies."[17] The other major publication is *The Church and Childhood*, edited by Diana Wood (1994), a collection of thirty-two papers read at two meetings of the Ecclesiastical History Society. These vary more in approach and topic than the essays in *The Child in Christian Thought*, and several emphasize more social-historical perspectives. The strength of this collection is that it makes visible the ambiguity of Christian ideas and images of children and childhood through the history of Christianity. However, its strength tends also to be its weakness; the diversity of themes and approaches makes it sometimes difficult to discern a unifying theme, except that all of them in one way or another deal with children in the history of Christianity. Both of these works demonstrate that children and childhood have been a neglected topic in the field of church history, and, as *The Child in Christian Thought* makes particularly clear, theologians of the past have had more to say about issues related to children than we often have supposed.

Children and Childhood in the Early Church

A number of books and articles deal with issues related to the question of children and childhood in the early church, for examples on *expositio* (exposure of children), orphans, infant baptism, and upbringing.[18] However, only a few publications focus on the way in which children were understood and how they were treated in general. The fact that nearly all these studies were published in the last decade is a clear indicator, as suggested above, of growing scholarly interest in this subject.

The monograph *Die Familienerziehung in der Alten Kirche* by Michael Gärtner (1985) is an exception to the rule. The first part of the book offers a relatively extensive analysis of the upbringing of children in the four first centuries, while the second part is a translation and commentary on John Chrysostom's treatise *De Inani Gloria et de Educandis Liberis.*[19] Gärtner demonstrates that the early church was indeed concerned with the proper upbringing of children, and explores its goals and methods. Although Gärtner's is the major monograph on this topic, as the title indicates, the book is rather narrow: it focuses primarily on the upbringing of children and does not attempt to give a general picture of how early Christians thought about children nor of the ideals and practice governing the treatment of children in the early church.

The next published studies on this topic are two essays in *The Church and Childhood*. Though she touches upon several aspects by children and childhood, Gillian Clark ("The Fathers and the Children") deals mainly with the adult-child relationship.[20] Clark introduces her essay by referring to a couple of stories told by patristic writers in which adults are admired for leaving their children for the purpose of practicing a religious life, or where adults commit children to a strict religious life. Contrasting this behavior with apparently positive attitudes toward children in Christian teaching (that Christ the savior was born as a child and used children as paradigms of the proper way to receive the kingdom of God), she asks the following question: "Did Christian teaching transform inherited ideas about children, and consequently the experience of childhood?" To answer this question Clark focuses mainly upon parents' concern for children and how this concern was expressed, roles and structures of the household, and child rearing. Clark concludes that "for most children, life was not very different" from what it was before Christianity emerged.[21]

In the essay "Childhood in Eastern Patristic Thought," G. Gould focuses on the nature of childhood within the context of theological anthropology.[22] Here he explores three interrelated issues: (1) "the development of a child's soul in terms of its possession, or lack, of faculties such as reason and desire"; (2) "the extent to which a child's soul is open to the same temptations, desires, or passions as that of an adult"; and (3) "the extent to which children are capable of understanding religious ideas and precepts or may be held to deserve reward or punishment for their action."[23] In this instructive essay, Gould traces the idea in Eastern patristic theology (Clement of Alexandria, Origen, John Chrysostom, Basil of Ancyra, and Jerome) that from birth, passions are absent in children, and also explores what these writers say about the development of passions as the child grows up.

William A. Strange's *Children in the Early Church* (1996), at 123 pages, represents the only monograph-length publication with a relatively comprehensive approach. However, a relatively large part of this book focuses on children in the Greco-Roman world, in Judaism, and on what the New Testament says about children. Only approximately thirty pages are directly devoted to patristic understanding of children; Strange's main focus is on the issue of children's participation in the sacraments, and especially the question of infant baptism. In my opinion, he argues convincingly for the view that infant baptism, as well as infant communion, was a common practice in the first three centuries of the church. He argues that it was Tertullian, and others who opposed the practice of baptizing infants, who attempted to introduce a new practice in the church. Other aspects related to children and childhood that Strange includes in his discussion are sexual abuse, child exposure, and the education of the young, though these topics are treated very briefly. Certainly, Strange's work represents a useful introduction to children and childhood in the early church. He deserves credit for putting the issue on the agenda, and for including several aspects related to children and childhood in order to paint an overall picture of what it meant to be a child at that time in history. Nevertheless, I have some critical comments. First, and most significantly, Strange virtually ignores the discussion of the anthropology of children—for example, the extent to which children possess or lack faculties such as reason and desire. Given that Strange intends to answer the question "what did people at the time think about their children," it is striking that anthropological matters are neglected. Second, he does not distinguish between children in the thought of the fathers, that is, how people understood children and childhood, and how children were treated in society, or what we could call the social history of children. Third, several topics are treated only very briefly. Finally, Strange does not provide a summary of his investigation; the closest he comes to doing so is the last chapter, "Contemporary Reflections." The main focus of this chapter is, however, of a more practical nature: it discusses the relevance of the view of children and childhood in the New Testament and the early church for our contemporary view of children in general, and children in the church in particular.[24]

While Strange's study is the only monograph published on children in the early church, there is also an unpublished doctoral thesis from 1993 by Sarah Currie, which deals with certain aspects of children in early Christianity.[25] Currie states that the "thesis is a study of the interaction between children and ritual practices of antique Christianity" and concludes by stating that "the child" was placed "at the centre of Christian practice, both in its making of symbols and in its everyday reproduction of a community."[26] A significant part in her argumentation is the way the church fathers used the gospel commands to present children as symbols for appropriate Christian behavior, and how the early church used the metaphor of children in Christian formation and in the construction of Christian identity. It is, however, questionable whether Currie's conclusions are adequately supported by the metaphorical use of children, and of children as examples for adults. She does not distinguish carefully enough between children as metaphors and symbols, and the place of children in social life.

The article "Appealing to Children" by Blake Leyerle focuses on children in the writings of John Chrysostom.[27] In the first part of the article Leyerle presents material that sheds light on "Children's lives in fourth-century Antioch and Constantinople" in general. Among other things she deals with parents' attachment to their offspring, breastfeeding and weaning, toys, play, clothing, child rearing, and children at schools. In the second main part, "Children in Chrysostom's Thought," Leyerle notes that Chrysostom frequently refers to children's behavior in his attempt to transform or change Christian adults. This does not mean, however, that he valued it: in general, he uses children and childish behavior as negative paradigms. According to Leyerle, Chrysostom "saw exhibited in children the 'natural' state of every person unimproved by virtuous restraint. . . . The characteristic actions and affects of children . . . serve as perfect illustrations of the foolishness of adults."[28] These characteristic actions include uncontrolled anger and covetousness. However, the nature of children is corrigible. "A strong believer in the possibility of change, Chrysostom insists that despite the 'natural obstinacy' of children, they are still malleable."[29] Virtues are not an innate quality that children possess from birth, but are qualities that must be learned. Leyerle notes that Chrysostom, in fact, holds such a positive view of the possibility of molding children that he believed that a period of two months was enough time to implant good habits in them. At the end of her article, Layerle observes that a few examples of the use of children as positive paradigms occur. For example, babies (unlike adults) stop eating when they are full; and they are not concerned with wealth and status. Leyerle emphasizes that such positive evaluation of children represents an exception to the rule, and suggests that it is prompted by scriptural passages that portray children in a positive way (for example, Matthew 19:4 and 1 Corinthians 14:20).

Vigen Guroian, in his essay "The Ecclesial Family," emphasizes other aspects of children and childhood in the thought of John Chrysostom, namely the importance and responsibility of parents to socialize and train their children into a Christian life.[30] The focus of Guroian's essay is not primarily on children, but on Chrysostom's understanding of parenthood. However, since the question about the nature of parenthood and the evaluation of children are obviously interrelated, Guroian also touches on several elements relevant to Chrysostom's evaluation of children. Among other things, he investigates the theological motivation behind Chrysostom's prominent concern for proper Christian parenthood. His understanding of the duty of Christian parents is based on moral principles drawn from the New Testament, the most important of which is love of neighbor. This moral principle requires that one be concerned about one's neighbor's salvation, because the ultimate expression of love of neighbor is to show active interest in his or her eternal destiny. Besides the fact that children are the parents' closest neighbors, they belong to the weakest and most defenseless members of society. Consequently, the imperative of loving one's neighbor "is that much stronger in the parent-child relationship."[31]

In general, the picture Guroian draws of children in the thoughts of Chrysostom tends to be more positive than that drawn by Leyerle. When dealing with the theology of childhood, Guroian emphasizes the great value Chrysostom attributes to children, as full human beings insofar as they are created in the image of God, while Leyerle deals more with the social history and the way in which the appeal to children in Chrysostom's argumentation emphasizes the negative evaluation of the nature of childhood and childish behavior. References to children function (with only a few exceptions) as negative examples for adult Christians. In my opinion, these works mutually complement each other, and show that we must consider both the more fundamental theological teaching about children and childhood (as Guroian does), and how the concrete behavior of children is valued.

The final work I include in this survey is an essay on Augustine by Martha Ellen Stortz, "'Where or When Was Your Servant Innocent?'"[32] Taking its starting point in the controversy with the Pelagians (420–430) over anthropology and infant baptism, the bulk of Stortz's essay deals with Augustine's view on the nature of childhood. In this connection, the key issue is whether a child is innocent. Stortz argues that Augustine advocates a third position between these alternatives, which we might call non-innocence. "Any innocence in childhood resided in physical weakness—that is, in being unable to harm anyone else."[33] However, the habit of concupiscence is present in newborn babies. Augustine considered the fact that a baby could grasp for the breast after it had been fed, or that it cried because of jealousy after being fed, when it saw another baby at a nurse's breast, as a symbol of the habit of concupiscence. Because of its lack of language and understanding one should not punish the infant; it would not understand the rebuke. As the child gets older and its physical strength and the ability to talk and reason develops, it assumes greater responsibility for its actions. "Language introduced the difference between obedience and disobedience, for which a child was accountable."[34] When the child reached puberty, *adulescentia*, and the faculty of reason further developed, "a youth faced even greater accountability for his or her behavior."[35] With respect to the question of baptism, Augustine draws the conclusion that infants also need to be baptized, because they were corrupted by original sin. The above-mentioned behavior of infants manifests the one mass of sin into which all of Adam's descendants were born: "the sin of Adam penetrated all of human nature, even the newborn baby."[36] Though their physical weakness prevented infants from harming anyone else, they were "non-innocent." Hence they need the forgiveness of sins that is mediated through baptism.

Why This Volume?

As the history of research shows, studies on children and childhood in early Christianity are beginning to see the light of day. However, though the studies published up to now provide illuminating discussions of various aspects of this topic, only the work by William A. Strange, and partly the essay by Gillian Clark, combine several perspectives, and thus seek to give a general account of how Christians in the early church thought about children and how children were treated. I have already expressed my substantial agreement with these findings, but I have pointed out that many important aspects related to children and childhood receive only a superficial treatment, while some go virtually unmentioned in these works; besides this, only a relatively brief section of Strange's book deals explicitly with the post–New Testament period. This means that we still need a book offering a comprehensive examination of children and childhood in early Christianity.

The present work aims at comprehensiveness by including a large number of relevant aspects, in order to achieve as nuanced as possible a picture of children and childhood. The breadth of the approach I have chosen makes it, however, impossible to enter here into detailed discussions of every interesting question brought up by our source material. I am convinced that a broad approach is necessary, if we are to get adequate answers to the following two main questions: (1) What did Christians think about children and about the nature of children, and what qualities did they ascribe to children? (2) What did they say about the treatment of children, and how did they treat children de facto?

The first question deals primarily with theological anthropology and the mentality associated with children. Here, I focus on how selected church fathers thought about the nature of children and the qualities they attributed to children. Their discussions of Jesus' statements about children in the Synoptic Gospels are significant. Jesus used children as positive examples for the appropriate attitude of the members of the kingdom. In the Synoptic Gospels children are presented as paradigms of the proper response to Jesus' proclamation of the kingdom of heaven. Certain church fathers' discussions of why Jesus used children as examples and the way in which they function as positive examples for adult Christians are of great interest in our context because the question of the nature of the child is involved. Here we get a glimpse of the characteristics or qualities church fathers attributed to children. Other kinds of material in which the issue of the nature of children is involved, for example, Augustine's controversy with the Pelagians (420–430), will be considered. Besides these discussions of the theological anthropology of childhood in a more narrow sense, I find it fruitful to pay attention to patristic appeals to childish behavior in the fathers' strategy of transforming adult Christians. What aspects of childish behavior are emphasized, and how is this behavior evaluated? By asking these kinds of questions, I hope to widen the perspective, enabling us to get some glimpses of the mentality associated with children. Hence our first main question investigates what the fathers thought about the nature of children, and what characteristics and qualities they attributed to them.

This central part of the study must be complemented by other perspectives. When the aim is to draw a picture of children in late Christian antiquity, it is not sufficient to study theological discussions on the nature of children, or to note what qualities were associated with children. It is of equal importance to focus on social-historical perspectives, that is, how children were treated in social life. From the perspective of a child, the decisive factor is how adults treated children in practical life, not so much what they thought about children. It is reasonable to assume that there is a connection (perhaps more or less visible) between the nature and qualities associated with children, and how one dealt with them in the social fabric of life.

Accordingly, in my investigation of the second main question, I shall deal with topics that are fundamental for children's experience of life, such as abortion, the exposure of children, infanticide, sexual relationships with children, and the upbringing and education of children—including the goal and method of upbringing. Religion was organically integrated into life in the ancient world. In a book written by a church historian, it is natural also to include a chapter dealing with the participation of children in Christian worship. To what extent did people think that children needed, or ought to have, access to the spiritual nourishment given to adults in the form of baptism and holy communion? And did children play any specific role in liturgical actions?

The basic interest and focus of the present study is children in early Christianity. However, an important issue that will be considered throughout the study is the extent to which Christianity made any impact on what adults thought about children and how they treated children in social life. Thus, this study intends to function as a contribution to the classic question regarding the relationship between Christianity and ancient culture in general: Did Christianity make any difference?

TEXTS AND REALITY

As indicated above it is important to distinguish between a "thought" level, that is, how the church fathers *thought* about the nature of children and what qualities they ascribed to them, and a social history level, that is, how one *dealt with* children in social life. In view of the nature of the sources, however, this approach raises a fundamental methodological challenge, namely the relation between text and reality. The majority of the sources can be called argumentative texts, that is, texts in which the author exhorts or attempts to persuade the readers to follow a certain pattern of behavior. The majority of the sources are prescriptive, not descriptive. The sources present certain ideals of behavior or attitudes that the author aims to persuade his readers to follow. A further complicating element is the fact that, virtually without exceptions, our authors represent the higher social strata among Christians, and in many respects could be considered "elite" Christians. The crucial question is the extent to which the ideals advocated in the sources reflected the actual behavior and attitudes among Christians in general, and thus, ultimately, the measure of correspondence between the ideal of the texts and the way one dealt with children in social life.

In many cases, the nature of the sources does not allow us to draw any certain conclusions regarding this question. On the one hand, the fact that a certain author finds it needful to admonish the readers to behave in a certain way indicates that he believed that they did not live sufficiently in accord with his ideals. On the other hand, for the argumentation of a text to have an effect on the readers, the advocated ideals must not been out of touch with the readers' reality. This kind of common sense reasoning is the closest I come to a general answer regarding the question about the relationship between text and reality. In the course of this volume, this question will confront us several times.

Throughout our investigation, the term "ideal" will be used (for example, the ideal of upbringing), because we must distinguish between the prescriptions of the texts and the behavior of Christians in their social life. We must be cautious when we move from analyzing the textual level to the level of social life. Sometimes it is difficult to decide to what extent the ideals proposed by the fathers reflect real life, or whether their teaching had any impact on the way children experienced life. Nevertheless, in keeping with the second main question formulated above (What did Christians say about the treatment of children, and how did they treat children de facto?), I have included such texts in my discussion of children in society. A broad definition of "social life" or "social history" allows us to include significant sources, such as John Chrysostom's discourse on the correct way for parents to raise their children.[37] This means that I deliberately include material in the social history section that, strictly speaking, deals with children and childhood in Christian thought.

A further problem is that it is sometimes difficult to decide how to categorize a source: Is it dealing with the nature and qualities of children, or with children in social life? Take, for example, the condemnation of child exposure by some patristic writers. On the one hand, this obviously concerns a reality of social life. Since many children who were exposed suffered death, the parents' attitude toward *expositio* (child exposure) could be of vital importance for a newborn baby, determining whether the little child had the possibility to grow up at all. On a somewhat less dramatic level, it could determine whether a child got the possibility to grow up together with his or her relatives, or if she or he grew up as a slave and/or a prostitute, as was the fate of the majority of those exposed children who were picked up by strangers. On the other hand, patristic criticism is relatively often based on arguments that directly or indirectly ascribe a theological value to children as a creation of God. Hence, this issue could be subsumed under both the "thought" level and the social history level. For the sake of convenience, I have decided to included all issues related to children's social life in the part that deals with social history.

This investigation has a clearly diachronic perspective, since a wide range of sources spanning from the first to the fifth century will be consulted. As a rule, I begin with the oldest sources that deal with the actual topic under discussion and move chronologically through the others. This means that the study applies the combination of a thematic and a chronological approach. I hope that this chronological approach will allow the texts themselves to be heard clearly; this is why I quote the sources relatively often, so that the reader can have direct contact with them. In other words, my analysis takes its starting point in texts that, in many cases, will be quoted and discussed. Another advantage of the chronological approach is that it allows us to trace developments over time.

One disadvantage of a purely chronological approach is that it would entail far too many repetitions. It is indeed impossible to avoid these entirely, but I have sought to keep them to a minimum.

When one considers a specific phenomenon in early Christianity, it is usually wise to see it in the context of its wider cultural environment of the church, for example, Judaism and, in particular, the Greco-Roman world. The latter tradition is of particular importance when dealing with the church fathers. Most of them received the classical *paideia* or upbringing of this tradition at school, and both they and their addressees lived in societies heavily influenced by Greco-Roman culture in general. Since this study relies to a large extent on scattered statements about children and childhood in sources that primarily deal with other subjects, it is of even greater significance that these be read in the context of their wider cultural environment. On the one hand, paying attention to children and childhood in Judaism and, in particular, the Greco-Roman world can shed light on and complement the information offered by Christian sources. This perspective presupposes a kind of continuity, whereby associations related to children and childhood are taken over by Christianity. On the other hand, reading Christian sources against the backdrop of the Greco-Roman traditions enables us to see the differences, and it allows us to ask if Christianity made any difference to the evaluation of children and their place in society in the Greco-Roman era. For this reason, a relatively extensive chapter studies children and childhood in the Greco-Roman tradition, before we move on to the main topic, namely, children in the Christian tradition. After considering the nature and qualities of children we shall see how one dealt with children in social life.

FINDING CHILDREN IN THE FATHERS

Given the general attitudes toward children and their place in society in the cultural environment of Christians in antiquity, it would have been remarkable if the church fathers in general had had a heavy focus on children in their writings.[38] There are, in fact, no writings that introduce concern for children and their needs as a subject on the theological agenda. John Chrysostom's treatise, *De Inani Gloria,* comes closest to having children and their needs as a main theme. Chrysostom provides advice on child rearing, emphasizing the parents' grave responsibility to bring up their children in the Christian faith and socialize them into a proper, Christian way of life. However, this treatise, together with sections of a couple of other writings by the same author, is almost unique in its focus on children. As a rule, we have to make use of incidental comments about children and childhood in material from this period. In this respect, research on children in the early church faces the same challenges that confronted studies about women in early Christianity. Neither the role of women nor children's place in society and the church were topics discussed on their own. Because no systematic accounts are provided by ancient sources, modern scholars have to rely on more or less accidental references in the literature.

The present volume is based almost exclusively on literary sources. The most important are church orders, letters, and treatises of the church fathers. Inscriptions and iconographic material are left to other studies. I have already noted the difficulties associated with the literary Christian sources: (1) by and large, they are written by male elite Christians belonging to the upper strata of Christians; and (2) most of the texts are argumentative, in the sense that the authors attempt to persuade the readers to practice certain ideals of behavior. Consequently, one must be careful not to draw hasty generalizations, nor to infer from text to reality in social life. However, when used with care, these sources provide information that helps reconstruct the understanding of children, at least among the Christian elite, and of children's place in social life.

Furthermore, the evidence available is not sufficient to reconstruct how Christian children viewed the world. We have neither sources that report how children experienced life (the only exception would be the *Confessiones* by Augustine), or that attempt to imagine how life was from the perspective of children. The sources always reflect adults' view of children and the place adults assigned to children in their conception of social life. Consequently, this work deals with what adult Christians thought about children, how children were treated, and what adults said about the treatment of children in social life. The results of this investigation do, however, allow us to attempt to grasp how children themselves experienced life.

2
CHILDREN IN THE GRECO-ROMAN WORLD

We have distinguished between children on the level of ideas—that is, the question how people *thought* about children—and the actual *treatment* of children and their living conditions in society. It is however neither possible nor desirable to make this distinction too sharply. In many cases, the boundaries between the level of ideas and the level of social history are fluid, and we should expect a certain measure of interaction between the way people thought about children and the way they treated them. Still, this approach offers a satisfactory basic structure for our investigation. I begin with the level of ideas: What does the philosophical tradition say about children and about their characteristic qualities?

Children's Nature and Qualities according to the Philosophical Tradition

From Plato, Aristotle, and Stoicism onward, anthropological debates centered on speculations about the composition and function of the human person and the human soul.[1] Here, the concept of *logos* (word, speech, reason) plays a central role. There was a broad consensus in the Greek philosophical tradition that the city-state was held together, despite serious conflicts of interest, by the *logos* that was employed to resolve these conflicts in a peaceful manner. It was the free male citizens who possessed the *logos* that was the presupposition for rational thought. Women and older men possessed it to some extent, or more correctly, they had the potential for *logos,* while slaves and barbarians definitely lacked it. Not surprisingly, children were classified along with this last group.[2] The child symbolized the absence of *logos,* something reflected in the etymology of the word that designated children: *nêpioi* in Greek and *in-fantes* in Latin, that is, "not speaking." Children's lack of the ability to communicate in an adult manner meant that they were defined as standing outside the rational world of adults.[3]

The idea that children lack reason occurs in many sources from the time of Homer to that of Cicero.[4] In view of the great importance Plato ascribes to true knowledge as a presupposition for correct ethical development, it is not surprising that it is precisely this philosopher who has most to say about the various ways in which children's lack of reason finds expression. He claims that children have little knowledge; they are "gullible" and easily persuaded, they are able to understand only the simplest things, they talk nonsense and make unreliable judgments.[5] When children yield to their wishes and desires, they give yet another proof of their limited possession of *logos*. Along with slaves, women, and members of the lower classes, children form that group of human beings in whose lives desires, pleasures, and pains have the greatest place. Plato writes about "the mob of motley appetites and pleasures and pains (*epithumai kai hêdonai te kai lupai*) one would find chiefly in children and women and slaves and in the rabble of those who are freemen in name."[6] These "pleasures" include music and sweet things—he notes that you can get a baby to stop crying by putting a piece of honeycomb in its mouth.[7] All young creatures are by nature "fiery, they are unable to keep still either body or voice, but are always crying and leaping in disorderly fashion."[8] Similarly, Aristotle claims that children are more quick-tempered, greedy, and wrathful than adults. Childhood is that stage in life where the appetite for "pleasure" is strongest. These manifestations of children's lack of *logos* led the classical philosophers to find a comparison with animals appropriate; indeed, Plato asserts that of all animals, it is the child who is "the most intractable; for in so far as it, above all others, possesses a fount of reason that is as yet uncurbed, it is a treacherous, sly and most insolent creature."[9]

Plato frequently groups children together with other marginal actors in classical society: women, slaves, and animals.[10] Aristotle does the same, emphasizing that there is a physical similarity between women and children in that neither of them has semen; that animals have the same relationship to human beings as children do to adults; and that both animals and children are inferior to adults, in the same way that stupid and foolish men are inferior to good and wise men. One consequence of such ideas is that the opinions of children were seen as of no more consequence than those of animals.[11] No human being in possession of his rational faculties would choose to live with the limited capacity for rational thought that one finds in a child, or to return to childhood once one had left it behind.[12]

One of the most popular Greek adages says: "Old men are like children once more." This reference to old persons' mental incapacities reflects the very common association of children with the lack of reason.[13] Similarly, children and childish conduct—as in the phrase, "Not even a child would deny that!"—were used as symbols of foolish and irrational opinions and conduct: other people's behavior and attitudes were criticized by being called childish.[14] In rhetoric, calling someone a "boy" was perceived as a grave insult. Antony called Octavian a "boy" when he fought on the side of the senate in the civil war in 43 B.C.E., and this wounded Octavian so profoundly that he issued a decree forbidding anyone to speak of him in this way. When Cicero defended Octavian against this and other charges, he said: "That is certainly a word which we apply to a particular age-group, but hardly to be used by someone who makes a boy a present of his own stupidity as a source of glory."[15] Children were associated with stupidity: *pueritia amentia*.[16]

We find similar attitudes in other thinkers influenced by Stoicism—for example, Marcus Aurelius and Seneca. Children were employed above all as a symbol of the irrationality to be found in adults who had not studied philosophy, on the grounds that children were not capable of discovering by means of reasoning that which is ethically right, and at most could learn by heart a basic ethical principle or rule. Seneca writes: "That is why we give to children a proverb, or that which the Greeks call *Chria*, to be learned by heart; that sort of thing can be comprehended by the young mind, which cannot as yet hold more." And when he discusses the difference between natural things that are neither good nor bad in a moral sense, and natural things that have a positive value, he says: "A person, once a child, becomes a youth; his peculiar quality is transformed, for the child could not reason, but the youth possesses reason (*Ille enim inrationalis est, hic rationalis*)."[17]

A number of theories offered explanations of why children, like women and barbarians, did not share in *logos* in the same way as free men. Clearly, it was taken for granted that the norm, or normality, was free men's rationality. The Epicureans saw a certain connection between adults' rationality and children: they held that the irrational conduct typical of children at that period had once been typical of all adults, in the earlier historical period when humanity was at an animal, pre-societal stage. They also suggested that children had within themselves a germ or seed that could flower into virtues such as gratitude, intelligence, wisdom, and courage.[18]

According to Thomas Wiedemann, the commonest view linked the absence of *logos* to some imbalance in one of the four humors of the body. This physical explanation broadly implied that the lack of reason was caused by an illness. In the fifth century B.C.E., the physician Diogenes of Apollonia argued that irrationality was due to an excess of the wet humor; this was a standard explanation of what was seen as a defect of reason in women.

Children were not only considered to be weak in the sense that they lacked *logos*. The Romans held that they were physically weak, particularly vulnerable, and exposed to sickness. When we bear in mind the high mortality rate among children, this view is not surprising. Our sources often mention sick children; they refer to a number of remedies and give advice on what to do when babies and children get sick. We need not go into detail here about this advice and the ideas it implied.[19] It suffices to note that children were regarded as physically weak, because they were especially vulnerable and exposed to the risk of illness. Children were, in fact, a symbol of the human person's physical weakness.

One aspect linked to children's physical weakness was their lack of courage: children are more easily frightened than adults. In connection with war and the risk of war, our sources often contrast the men who serve as soldiers with the weak group consisting of children, women, and old persons. Like the two latter categories, children also are seen as symbols of human fear.[20]

Children's weakness and helplessness was a topic among philosophers,[21] as we see in a text by Pliny the Elder. He begins his discussion of animals' inferiority to human beings by describing the weakness that characterizes the human person as a newborn baby:

> But man alone on the day of his birth she [Nature] casts away naked on the naked ground, to burst at once into wailing and weeping, and none other among all the animals is more prone to tears, and that immediately at the very beginning of life; whereas, I vow, the much-talked-of smile of infancy even at the earliest is bestowed on no child less than six weeks old. This initiation into the light is followed by a period of bondage such as befalls not even the animals bred in our midst, fettering all his limbs; and thus when successfully born he lies with hands and feet in shackles, weeping—the animal that is to lord it over all the rest, and he

initiates his life with punishment because of one fault only, the offence of being born. Alas the madness of those who think that from these beginnings they were bred to proud estate![22]

Pliny obviously finds it paradoxical that the creature who is to rule over the other creatures should begin his life in a state of weakness and help-lessness, and he does not attempt to conceal his contempt and lack of esteem for this phase in human life. Naturally, his reflections imply that the child has the potential to grow out of the weakness and those other qualities that he regards as negative. Aristotle says that a child is not complete and whole, but attains this state only when it grows up and is formed in keeping with conduct appropriate to noble adult behavior.[23] Cicero made the well-known observation that it is difficult to find any reason to praise a child for its inherent qualities. It deserves praise only on account of the potential it has to become something in the *future*, that is, an adult human being with the qualities characteristic of adulthood: "The thing itself cannot be praised, only its potential."[24] Although these words refer in context to the child's capabilities as a rhetorician, we can in many ways take it as a general expression of the way classical antiquity saw and evaluated children's qualities.

This statement reflects first and foremost the negative assessment of children and childhood found in antiquity as a whole; at the same time, however, it implies the idea of a development from a stage undeserving of praise to a praiseworthy stage at which the child is capable of acquiring behavioral patterns that can be seen as positive. Cicero himself observes that small children are interested in learning new things.[25] Seneca the Younger can excuse children's unsuitable and unacceptable conduct by pointing to their limited measure of reason; he presupposes that they have the potential to develop into rational individuals.[26] Puberty was seen as a decisive phase in the child's development, since it brings not only a physical change or development, but also a fundamental change in the intellectual sphere. In this period, the *logos* emerges, with the consequence that the presuppositions for distinguishing between right and wrong, and between good and bad conduct, are now present.[27] The fact that puberty was seen as a transition from childhood to adulthood—at least in the sense that, at this stage, the child has developed its potential for rational thinking—does not of course mean that no attempt had been long made before this point to teach and bring up the child in keeping with current ideals of good conduct. Plato, to take one example, describes children as soft and malleable, both in the physical and in the intellectual sense. He compares a child with a "wax tablet" (perhaps the most important pedagogical instrument in the school of that period), and emphasizes that what children encounter while they are small is particularly important, since their tablet is still fresh and new at that time.[28] This idea is also reflected in Quintilian, who says that one who teaches children is making an imprint on an unformed mind.[29] Referring to Plato, Pseudo-Plutarch also employs the image of the wax tablet to emphasize how important it is that the correct formation of a child's character begins at an early stage. Indeed, this begins from the moment of birth, through the choice of wet nurses and servants:

> For youth is impressionable and plastic, and while such minds are still tender lessons are infused deeply into them; but anything which has become hard is with difficulty softened. For just as seals leave their impression in soft wax, so are lessons impressed upon the minds of children while they are young.[30]

The decisively new element introduced by puberty is that the child itself is now able to work out by reasoning what is right and what is wrong. Instruction, especially moral formation, must begin while children are still small, for their wax tablet is soft at that age, and more malleable than when they are older.

The image of the wax tablet implies that children are considered as imperfect raw material that must be transformed into something noble by means of upbringing and instruction. Another image drawn from agriculture and applied to the effects of education on pupils makes the same point: if the soil is to produce a good harvest, both the earth and the seed must be good, and there must be a farmer to cultivate and take care of the growth. This implies a comparison of the teacher with a farmer or gardener, while the children are the earth that is to receive the right seed.[31] It also implies a strikingly passive view of children's role in the educational process, while the teacher plays the active role by sowing knowledge of the correct virtues in his pupils.[32] The idea of children as raw material also underlies Quintilian's image of the teacher as an artist who shapes (*formanda*) the pupil into a statue; he emphasizes that no child is too small to be an object for the right moral formation.[33] In another passage, he calls the pupils *formandos . . . tantummodo*, "purely to be formed."[34]

I limit myself here to a few remarks about the methods used in instruction. Logically enough, the view of the pupil as a kind of raw material requiring cultivation led to a pedagogy where imitation, repetition, and memorization were central; and this required the pupil to be obedient to the teacher.[35] Bearing in mind the fact that the philosophical tradition commonly grouped or compared children with animals, we are not surprised to find an approach we today would call authoritarian and brutal, with frequent use of physical force. Although we do find examples of critical voices, the sources in general confirm that corporal punishment was accepted and regarded as a necessary instrument in the work of education.[36] One spokesman for this view is Seneca, who writes that the wise man will admonish one who has behaved unjustly toward him:

> just as if they were children, he will admonish them and inflict suffering and punishment, not because he has received an injury, but because they have committed one, and in order that they may desist from so doing. For thus also we break in animals by using the lash, and we do not get angry at them when they will not submit to a rider, but we curb them in order that by pain we may overcome their obstinacy.[37]

This is not a question of the chance employment of physical force in a moment of rage. This text expresses the conscious conviction that blows are an appropriate instrument to obtain the desired result. This view may be linked to the idea that it is meaningless to speak reasonably to individuals who lack reason, or have only a limited measure of reason: since instruction by means of words has no hope of succeeding, one must employ physical punishment to check children and slaves.[38]

Although children's qualities tended to be portrayed in negative terms, that is, as a counterpart to the positive qualities associated with the free male urban citizen, we do find examples of positive descriptions of children too. Sometimes, they are described as "sweet."[39] We also note a tendency, especially in Greek antiquity, to think that small children represent a natural state of innocence, since they have performed neither good nor bad actions.[40] However, as we shall see, this characteristic of children attracted much less interest and attention among pagans than in the Christian tradition. Nor were children used as positive paradigms in order to persuade adults to imitate this quality.

The main tendency is perfectly clear: in the philosophical tradition, children were portrayed, along with other weak groups, as the negative counterfoil to the free male urban citizen. Children lack reason, or at best have a limited measure of reason. They also lack the physical strength and courage that are typical of men (or at least of the ideal man). This means that children are portrayed as negative symbols or paradigms for adult conduct. According to Aristotle, children are not complete human beings. If they are interesting and possess a positive value, this is because they have the potential to develop those valuable characteristics and qualities that were associated with free men. As we have seen, this is explicitly affirmed by Cicero. If we apply a model of center and periphery, where the free male urban citizen is the center of power and of interest, children are located on the periphery among the marginal actors of society, or indeed are excluded altogether. I believe that Thomas Wiedemann is correct to summarize the situation as follows:

> In the Mediterranean city of the classical period—republican Rome as well as Greece—the adult male citizen was at the centre of activity. Hence those who were not adult male citizens were in various respects "marginal." Sometimes these groups are discussed by intellectuals who are interested in objectively describing them; but far more frequently they are mentioned, not for their own qualities (positive or negative), but because they symbolise the absence of certain qualities thought to be typical of the adult male citizen. Children frequently appear as one such symbol; others are the old, women, and slaves.[41]

A Social-Historical Perspective on Children and Childhood

Hygienic and Sanitary Conditions

It is exceedingly difficult for those who live in the Western world in the twenty-first century to imagine the hygienic and sanitary conditions under which most people lived in the classical period. This is not the place for a detailed discussion; it suffices to mention a number of facts that show that the situation was abysmal. In the cities, people lived in close proximity to one another—far closer than is usual in today's big cities.[42] For sanitation, people in antiquity were dependent on chamber pots and on holes in hills that functioned as latrines; the contents had to be emptied into open sewers, into which other domestic rubbish also was thrown. In many cases, however, people could not be bothered to do this, and simply emptied their chamber pots out of the windows during the night.[43] Ventilation in the apartments was ineffective, so that they were often full of smoke from the fireplace, especially in wintertime, when people burnt wood for fuel and closed the windows (which were holes in the wall) with pieces of cloth or animal skins to keep the cold out. As Rodney Stark says, "The smell of sweat, urine, feces, and decay permeated everything." He points out that things were not much better out of doors on the street: "Mud, open sewers, manure, and crowds. In fact, human corpses—adult as well as infant—were sometimes just pushed into the street and abandoned."[44] Although the Romans' public baths and aqueducts were impressive in many ways, and were tremendous innovations in their time, the simple fact that the public baths had no soap (to say nothing of anti-bacterial additives in the water) made it inevitable that they helped spread infectious diseases. Naturally, all this meant that illnesses and epidemics of various kinds had excellent breeding grounds, and the risk of infection was high.[45] This was all the more deadly, in that knowledge of bacteria was minimal, and effective medicines were barely available. The high concentration of population in the cities made their inhabitants especially vulnerable to plague and illnesses. One indication of this is the fact that the cities in the Roman empire were so dependent on a high level of immigration in order to offset the numbers who died, that the population of the country villages declined.[46] The average life expectancy for city dwellers was low, although it is not possible to determine it exactly. Nevertheless, although scholars who have attempted to estimate the average life span on the basis of epitaphs arrive at different conclusions, there is general agreement that it was under thirty years.[47] In societies with a high mortality rate, the general state of health of the populace is poor.[48]

Although what I have written here about the sanitary, hygienic, and health situation relates to the cities, it is likely that the situation was not significantly better among those who lived in the country villages. Another factor with great significance for life and health is the food people eat. Poverty and periods of famine meant that very many people in classical antiquity did not have enough to eat. This means that children were born into societal situations that represented a threat to their life and health from the very outset.

All this means, not surprisingly, that child mortality was high. Studies of funeral inscriptions and other sources have concluded that perhaps as many as 50 percent of all children died before their tenth birthday.[49] Accordingly, one gloomy aspect of being born into the ancient world was the high risk that the child would die young. Undernourishment and generally bad living conditions meant that this affected the children of poor parents worst, but our sources suggest that the rate of mortality was high even among the children of better-off parents.[50]

Children as an Investment for the Future

It follows that, if parents wanted to ensure that they had heirs—a fundamentally important concern—they had to have several children. The primary purpose of getting married in the Roman world was to produce children. The wife's duty to obey and help her husband included the duty to help him have heirs. These were essential if one of the basic functions of the family was to be realized, namely ensuring that valuables and property could pass in an unbroken chain from one generation to the next.[51] This is reflected in legislation, where most of what is said about children is related to questions about inheritance and inheritance law.[52]

We should note, however, that the next generation did not only inherit concrete and visible valuables such as houses, slaves, land, businesses, and other objects: one essential part of the inheritance consisted of "intangible" valuables such as the family's name and honor. These entailed obligations to carry on the family cult, and rituals intended to keep alive the memory of individual members of the family such as parents, aunts, and uncles were particularly important.[53]

In addition to producing heirs, one central reason for having children was the need to ensure that one would find support and help in one's old age. We find many examples of this viewpoint in sources from Homer down to the time of Cicero.[54] I quote one text from Euripides' *Medea*. When her two children are to die, she expresses her disappointment about expectations that will not be fulfilled:

> It was all for nothing—those years in which I reared you, my cares, my aches and exhaustion, and the sharp pain when I gave you birth. I once built many hopes on you. I imagined that you would care for me in my old age, and that you yourselves would prepare my body for burial when I was dead.[55]

We can therefore argue that children were seen as an investment for the future.[56] It was above all the poor who needed their children's help and support in the quest for food, care, and other basic needs of life; and while the rich could indeed buy welfare and material care from slaves or relatives, they also expected their children to give them a worthy funeral and to keep alive their memory in the appropriate manner. However, although the desire to ensure one's own future was undeniably a prominent motivation for having children—in order words, children were a kind of investment in a pension fund—we should not exaggerate the difference between this attitude and the attitudes we find in modern Western societies. There may be relatively few parents today who are dependent on their children to supply their fundamental needs for food, housing, and health in their old age; but when we bear in mind the loneliness and broken relationships that are characteristic of our society, it is clear that in reality, the wish to have someone "look after us" when we are old is still an important reason why many people choose to have children.[57]

The dominant motivation for having children in the ancient world was the desire to take care of one's future, both here on earth and after death, when one could expect one's children to bury one with honor and to keep one's memory alive in a worthy manner. Another aspect of having children is the satisfaction and joy felt by parents (especially fathers) at seeing the traits of their own personalities in their children. According to Dio Cassius, this argument was employed by Augustus when he attempted to persuade well-off Romans to have children:

> Is it not a joy to acknowledge a child who possesses the qualities of both parents, to tend and educate a person who is both the physical and the mental mirror of yourselves, so that, as he grows up, another self is created? Is it not a blessing, when we leave this life, to leave behind as our successor an heir both to our family and to our property, one that is our own, born of our own essence, so that only the mortal part of us passes away, while we live on in the child who succeeds us?[58]

At the same time, these words reflect the idea that children who live on after their parents' death offer a consolation in face of the mortality of human beings: even if the parents die, their character traits live on in the children, who thus make possible a kind of immortality.[59]

As I have mentioned, Augustus's words are prompted by a situation where aristocratic women did not wish to have children. Their economic position allowed them to decline the health risk of giving birth with the medical equipment and knowledge available at that time, and they probably saw the responsibility for children as something burdensome. The practice of these upper-class women confirms the idea that one main reason for having children was to take care of one's own future: their wealth permitted them to lead a childless life, and it seems that such attitudes were so widespread that it became difficult to recruit candidates for those official positions and jobs that had to be occupied by aristocrats. In order to resolve this problem, Augustus appeals to these women's sense of responsibility to contribute to the necessary supply of recruits.[60] This brings us to another aspect of the motivation for having children: a child was seen as an individual who was to carry out particular functions and role not only in the family, but also in society as a whole. The procreation of children was a necessary presupposition for the continuing existence of the Roman empire, and was generally seen as a duty incumbent upon the citizens. Just as the child was an investment that would give its parents security in the future, so the child was also an investment on behalf of the larger society, primarily as one who would protect land and people in case of war, but also one who would carry out necessary work.[61]

Since a child played such an important role with regard to the future security of its parents (at least in the great majority of cases), the loss of a child entailed much more than a merely personal grief and sorrow. When a child died, a part of one's hope and security for the future died too. Suzanne Dixon summarizes this as follows:

> it was a tragedy to be predeceased by a child of any age. Apart from any sense of loss, of missing the child as an individual, it represented the dashing of hopes and, to an extent, the reversal of the natural order. . . . Like Greeks before them, Romans lamented on the tombstones of their children that they were—unnaturally—performing the very office for their children that the children ought to have performed for them. This sentiment is so common as to be abbreviated to a code. Like Medea, they grieved for the loss of the many services the children would in the normal course of events have performed for them.[62]

Abortion and the Exposure of Children

Although children represented security and hope for their parents, to have many children was not an unmixed blessing. On the one hand, they were an investment for the future; but on the other, since most people were poor, it could be difficult to cope economically with the requirements of a large number of children, and this led to various methods for limiting their number. Apart from abortion, various kinds of medicines with a supposedly contraceptive effect were employed. Abortion was the subject of debates focusing not (as often in modern discussions) on the value inherent in the fetus itself or on a woman's right to make decisions about her own body and the situation in which she wishes to live, but rather on the husband's right to make decisions about the woman and about the fate of the fetus.[63]

The instruments employed were often extremely dangerous to the woman's health, and such operations led, in many cases, to her death; it has been claimed that complications in connection with abortions were one of the commonest causes of female death in the Greco-Roman world, and this would imply that abortion was a very widespread practice.[64] This view presupposes that the literary sources that speak of abortion largely reflect historical facts, an interpretation called into question by a recent study by Suzanne Dixon,[65] who points out that a number of sources associate abortion with infidelity and a generally loose moral life: abortion is portrayed as a means to conceal infidelity, thus avoiding shame for the woman and her husband. One aspect of this picture is the abortions performed for upper-class women because they feared that pregnancy and birth would have a negative effect on the shape of their bodies: male writers in the classical period present such attitudes as symptoms of moral decadence and contrast them with the women in the "good old days" who were virtuous and good wives and mothers. A traditional theme in antiquity was to portray the moral decline of one's own days by comparing them with an idealized past when everything was much better. One of Dixon's main points is that abortion and infidelity posed a threat to the traditional power of the husband over his wife, her body, and their children—a power that our sources consider wholly legitimate. This means that we should read the references to abortion as expressions of an ideological agenda where men are attempting to maintain or reestablish traditional structures and patterns of power between the sexes, not as information about historical realities.[66]

One need not necessarily agree with all her conclusions, but Dixon's approach certainly urges us to be cautious in our estimate of how widespread abortion was. I think that we can at least note the following points: the spectrum of sources indicate that the phenomenon was universally known, and if the references in these sources to abortion were to have argumentative power at all, they cannot *only* be a literary construction (as Dixon tends to suggest), but must to some extent mirror the historical situation. A further piece of evidence is the very detailed instructions given by the celebrated Roman medical writer Aulus Cornelius Celsus in his *De Medicina* (first century c.e.) on how various kinds of medical instruments are to be used in abortion; this can be interpreted as evidence that the operation was relatively common,[67] for why else would it have been necessary to provide guidance in a book?

Another indicator of the relative frequency of abortion is the fact that legislation began to criminalize abortion from the second century c.e. onward. A rescript of emperor Septimus Severus (193–211), later confirmed by Antonius, laid down that women who had abortions should be punished by a temporary exile, "for it would appear shameful that she could with impunity deprive her husband of children."[68] The prominent Roman jurist Paul asserts that those who give a woman poison to drink, intending to cause an abortion, give a bad example; the penalty for those poisoners who belong to the lower classes is banishment to the mines, while more prosperous criminals are banished to an island and part of their property is confiscated. If the pregnant woman dies, however, they are to receive the death penalty.[69] We know nothing about the influence such legislation had on the number of abortions. We should note that the criminalization of abortion is not prompted by the value of the fetus per se, or by the idea that it is a human being: rather, it is the father's interests that must be protected. We should also note that abortion is not described as anything worse than a "bad example."[70]

Expositio (*ekthesis*), the exposure of children, was another way of limiting their numbers. Scholars in the nineteenth century devoted considerable attention to this subject, and it has recently returned to the center of interest, partly as a consequence of the growing interest in the family in classical times.[71] Central questions have been what were the historical periods and geographical areas in which *expositio* was practiced, what was the extent of this phenomenon, what motives led people to expose their children, what was the extent to which such children died or were taken care of by others, what happened to those who survived, and whether girls were exposed more frequently than boys. There can be no doubt that the frequency of *expositio* and the consequences for the children varied in the different periods and regions, and this makes it dangerous to use simplified generalizations in speaking of *expositio* in the classical period.[72] Nevertheless, I believe that we can make some general affirmations about this phenomenon, adjusting our picture to make allowance for particular circumstances.[73]

Scholars disagree about the extent to which children were exposed in the Greek *polis* (city-state) in the classical age, but we need not pursue this question here, since there seems to be a consensus (even among scholars who hold that this practice was rare in earlier centuries) that *expositio* was widespread in many Greek societies in the period after Alexander the Great.[74] The sources indicate that the exposure of children was common in the Greek region of the Roman empire in the first centuries B.C.E. and C.E. The same is true of Egypt.[75] In the western regions of the empire, the sources have much less to say about *expositio*, especially in the late republican period.[76] In the first two centuries of the Common Era, however, *expositio* is mentioned so frequently, both directly and indirectly, that William V. Harris can claim "an array of texts makes it obvious that exposure of infants was widely practised in the high Roman Empire,"[77] although he may be going too far when he asserts: "Child-exposure appears in every Greek and Latin author of the second and third centuries who could reasonably be expected to mention it."[78] He may be exaggerating the extent of this phenomenon, but there is no doubt that our source material shows that the practice of exposing children was both well-known and socially accepted. This is also emphasized in a recent study by Mireille Corbier. Although she is much more cautious than Harris on the question of the extent of *expositio,* Corbier concludes as follows:

> So, to the question of how common and wide-ranging the practice of exposure was, we can only respond as follows: over the centuries, whatever its precise legal basis, the exposure of newborn babies in Rome was perfectly legal and socially acceptable. Even after that ceased to be the case, exposure apparently continued to be practised. But nobody can state its extent.[79]

To sum up, children were exposed in both the western and the eastern parts of the Roman empire, but it is difficult to be specific about the extent to which this occurred, especially in the western regions. We stay within the limits of known facts, if we follow Corbier in stating that *expositio* was both legally permitted and socially accepted; we may also choose to follow Harris in affirming that a phenomenon mentioned so often in sources from the first two centuries of the Common Era must clearly have been "widely practised." Naturally, we cannot say anything about percentages, but we are probably on safe ground if we say that, as far as the eastern region of the Roman empire was concerned, *expositio* was socially accepted and widespread from the time of Alexander the Great onward.[80]

In this context, the "child" was normally a newborn baby. In a Roman family, the father (*paterfamilias*) had the legal right to decide the life and death of the other members of the family, and it was he, at least in the final instance, who decided whether a child should be accepted into the family or exposed. The critical phase was the first eight to nine days,[81] during which this question was decided. The acceptance of the child as a family member was celebrated ritually in the home on the so-called *dies lustricus* ("day of purification") in the presence of the immediate family and relatives. It was then that the child was given its name. This ceremony was held for boys on the eighth day after birth, for girls on the ninth day, and it marked the child's social birth, as opposed to its biological birth. The registry office was to be informed only after the child had received a name and been socially accepted into the family; this shows that social birth was more important or considered more fundamental than biological birth.[82] In the period before its social birth, the child did not have the status of a juridical person as it did afterward. This seems to be because the child was not yet perceived as a full human being.[83] Plutarch, for example, holds that a child who has not yet lost its umbilical cord—something he believes happens normally on the seventh day—is "more like a plant than a human being."[84] The decision made by the parents, especially the father, in the interim period of eight or nine days after birth, when the child had not yet become part of the social fellowship, sealed its future fate.[85] Accordingly, if the child was exposed, this normally happened before it was eight or nine days old.

As I have mentioned, poverty was the commonest reason for the exposure of children. One more mouth to feed might all too easily mean taking food from family members who already suffered hunger.[86] Naturally, the definition of poverty varies, and it is not surprising that our sources tell of cases where parents claimed that poverty had led them to expose their children, although they had in fact far more than the absolute minimum.[87] There are even sources that suggest that prosperous Romans practiced *expositio*.[88] Here, such actions cannot possibly be explained or understood by pointing to social distress or poverty.

Another reason for the exposure of children was their illegitimacy, which entailed social humiliation and brought shame on the mothers. We also find cases in which parents exposed their children after receiving omens of doom that made them afraid. According to Suetonius, one of Augustus's freedmen claimed that the Senate had issued a law in 63 B.C.E. because of an "evil portent," forbidding parents to raise the boys born in that year.[89] One specifically Roman phenomenon was the *expositio* of children as a kind of protest against the gods, in response to events that people felt were gravely unjust: Suetonius relates that when news spread of the death of Germanicus, the popular crown prince and father of Caligula, some parents reacted by exposing their children.[90] If this did, in fact, occur, it may perhaps be interpreted "as a social suicide in response to a situation of 'anomy.'"[91] In the rhetorical tradition, we find a view that the frequency of *expositio* was related to how the emperor ruled: "It is a sign of a good emperor, in the universe of the rhetoricians, when parents want to raise up children; under a tyranny they expose them."[92] Such an attitude may involve an element of protest, but its primary message is that living conditions and future prospects among the populace in general played an important role in the choice parents made about whether to expose a child. As I have just pointed out, poverty was the commonest reason for *expositio*.

Finally, children with obvious physical deformities were usually prevented from growing up. Seneca the Younger indicates that in his day, such children were commonly drowned; sources from the early imperial period also mention drowning as a means of killing babies. However, it is more probable that the midwives examined the newborn children and eliminated those they thought unfit to live; it is also probable that some were exposed. According to Seneca, not only children with deformities were killed, but also those considered weak. The physician Soranus gives a long list of the criteria (some of them rather strict) a child must satisfy in order to be considered healthy enough to be allowed to grow up. We do not know to what extent his criteria were actually employed, but at any rate they show that it was societally acceptable to lay down criteria entailing that many babies would have been refused the right to grow up.[93]

It is reasonable to assume that more girls than boys met with such a fate.[94] Such a view is supported, though not definitively affirmed, in our sources, and many factors point in this direction. Since the firstborn boy was the (principal) heir, it was important to "ensure" that a couple had a son. As we have seen, the center/periphery model made the free male citizen the center in classical society. Since characteristics and qualities associated with men functioned as the norm for the evaluation of other groups in the population, this naturally led to a higher esteem for boys than girls. Boys were considered more useful. The words of an Egyptian man in the first century B.C.E., in a letter to his wife who was soon to bear a child, have become well-known: "If you chance to bear a child, and it is a boy, let it be; if it is a girl, expose it."[95] Obviously, this unparalleled utterance, taken by itself, does not entitle us to draw far-reaching conclusions; a group of inscriptions from Delphi are more important in the search for representative texts. Scholars maintain that we can reconstruct six hundred families on the basis of this material, and only six of these families had more than one daughter.[96] The simplest explanation of this disproportion seems to be that the parents got rid of female babies.

Some of those who exposed their children did so in places that may suggest a hope that someone would take care of the baby and rescue it—at a street corner, near a temple or another public building, or at particular spots outside the city or village that were known to be used for this purpose.[97] Some sources assume or indicate that a number of these children were in fact rescued and looked after by other adults.[98] Many were rescued at periods when there was a great demand for slaves, and most foundlings in fact ended up as slaves, and frequently also as prostitutes.[99] Although adoption was common in classical antiquity, especially among childless couples in the higher social classes for whom it was an instrument to achieve economic and political goals, it appears that foundlings were not adopted. Nevertheless, they could benefit from some of the advantages available to foster children, such as a certain measure of positive affection on the part of other family members, and they could look forward to receiving a small part of the family inheritance.[100] Scholars disagree about how many died and how many were rescued; some hold that almost no children died,[101] while others hold that the majority perished.[102] This is a complicated question, but my own impression is that those who argue that hardly any babies died do not do justice to the sources that point in the opposite direction, or indeed overlook these sources altogether. William V. Harris presents and discusses a broad spectrum of source materials that indicate that many of those exposed did in fact die.[103]

As mentioned above, the killing of children with deformities and of children who were considered weak was accepted by law and society in the same way as *expositio* was accepted. I do not intend to discuss the extent of this practice here; I limit myself to one brief quotation from an article in which Lawrence E. Stager relates what he and his colleagues found during excavations in a villa in Ashkelon. This *may* be archeological evidence of the practice of infanticide. They made

> a gruesome discovery in the sewer that ran under the bathhouse. . . . The sewer had been clogged with refuse sometime in the sixth century A.D. When we excavated and dry-sieved the desiccated sewage, we found [the] bones . . . of nearly 100 little babies apparently murdered and thrown into the sewer.[104]

These observations on infanticide and *expositio* should not lead the reader to suppose that these practices received universal assent. The hellenized Jew Philo was the first to offer an explicit critique, affirming that it goes against the divine law. Next was the Stoic philosopher Musonius Rufus, who criticized these practices on several counts: he points to the need for recruits to public positions, and says that one must show respect for the legislators whose laws were intended to ensure precisely this recruitment. Interestingly enough, we also find a religious element here, namely, the exhortation to respect the gods, especially Zeus, the protector of the family.[105] Stoics such as Epictetus and Hierocles maintained that it goes against nature to refuse to bring up one's own children.[106] At the close of the first century of the Common Era, the historian Tacitus also criticized this practice.[107] At about the same time, the governing authorities in some Italian regions changed their attitude to *expositio,* and the so-called imperial *alimenta* (all the necessities of life) were set up at the beginning of the second century. The drop in population had negative consequences for recruitment to a number of positions in the empire, and the authorities decided to offer poor parents economic aid, primarily in the form of low-interest loans, so that they would have the necessary resources to produce and bring up a larger number of children.[108] The intention expressed by the *alimenta* presupposes criticism of every form of birth control, and according to Pliny, *expositio* is the most easily controlled form. This means that there was an unambiguous opposition to *expositio* on the part of the governing authorities in some parts of Italy at the beginning of the second century c.e. We should note that this stance had nothing to do with ideology or religion: it was based on pragmatic considerations, namely, the desire to ensure a supply of workers. The *alimenta* program demonstrates that "by the time of Nerva" (that is, 96–98) "criticism of child-exposure had spread from philosophers and moralists to leading Romans of more pragmatic mentality."[109] Despite this, no law was promulgated against *expositio* until the reign of Emperor Valentinian, in 384. The fact that it took so long for legislation to make the exposure of children a criminal offense, despite the fact that many emperors resorted to making laws to get parents to produce future workers, indicates the enduring, traditional strength of this phenomenon in the classical world. It is impossible to know how effective the prohibition of *expositio* was, but much evidence suggests that the practice continued, with fluctuations depending on local traditions and changing economic circumstances.

Social Roles, Upbringing and Instruction, and Sexual Relationships with Children

As I have mentioned, the social birth of a child and its acceptance by the family were ritually marked on the *dies lustricus.* What kind of upbringing did the child then receive? In connection with the current growing interest in the family in classical times, scholars have paid considerable attention to the social relationships between various groups within the family. Here, I limit myself to some aspects that directly concern children, especially the relationship between parents and their children, and that shed light on what it was like to grow up as a child in a family in antiquity.

Let us, however, begin by asking who belonged to the family. In our modern Western culture, the term "family" evokes for us the picture of parents with one child or more—the so-called nuclear family. But neither Greek nor Latin has a technical term for a corresponding societal unit. The Greek noun *oikos* or household was frequently employed in two distinct senses: (1) referring to the material possessions that belonged to the master of the household; and (2) referring to all the members of the household who were subject to the master's authority, namely, wife, children, other relatives, and slaves and servants. Similarly, the Latin noun *familia* could refer both to things and possessions, and to persons; in the latter sense, it could include all those subject to the authority of the master of the household (the *paterfamilias*): wife and children, foster children (if any), as well as slaves and all those descended on the male side from a common ancestor. The noun *domus* or house was applied most frequently to the household, and designated husband, wife, children, slaves, and other persons who lived in the house; it could however also have a broader meaning, covering whole groups of descendants, including those on the wife's side.[110]

When I speak of the "family" here, I refer to the societal unit dwelling in the same household, that is, husband, wife, and their unmarried descendants, with other relatives living under the same roof, as well as slaves and other persons. It was not necessarily only the upper classes who had slaves and servants, but it is clear that having servants presupposed a certain measure of prosperity.[111] Our sources mostly apply the terms *oikos, domus,* and *familia* to larger households of well-off persons, and this means that what they have to say about family life and household structures refers primarily to the higher societal strata. We have much less direct information about poor households, but it is reasonable to suppose that the basic social structures and patterns governing relations between the spouses and between parents and children were relatively similar. Since the Greco-Roman world was a "shame/honor" culture, where relationships between persons and groups were largely determined by conventional ideas of what brought honor and what entailed disgrace, it is highly likely that relationships between groups in the household were much the same, whether those involved were rich or poor.[112]

Most Romans lived for most of their lives in so-called "nuclear households,"[113] but this does not mean that they necessarily spent all their life in the same household. This is particularly true of women and children. Because the husband was usually about ten years older than his wife when they married, many women became widows; and this, in addition to the high divorce rate, meant that second marriages were common, making the remarried woman part of a new household. If her new husband had children from an earlier marriage, these had now to relate to a new maternal figure, a stepmother. According to the law, it was the husband who had the right to decide whether he wished to keep the children after a divorce, and this was usually the case.[114] If the husband died, the wife kept the children; if she remarried, the children too became members of her new household. Since remarriage was so widespread, relatively large numbers of children grew up with half-siblings of roughly their own age. In general, groups of siblings were small: it was unusual both in the republican period and in the imperial age for a family (whether rich or poor) to have more than two or three children.[115] Harsh economic conditions could lead to the separation of young children from their parents, either because the children had to go elsewhere to work, and became members of a new household, or because the parents had to leave their children in order to find work.[116] Accordingly, the household in classical times was an open and flexible unit whose central element was the nuclear family (the couple and their unmarried children), but which often included many other members. This meant that children had a much larger range of adults to relate to in their immediate vicinity than is the case in most of today's Western urban, nuclear families.

When we ask what life was like for a child in a household in the period we are studying, we must inevitably generalize: just like children today, children in the past had very different experiences of what it meant to grow up in a family. Demographic variations are one factor here, but even where the external framework was the same, children were treated in a variety of ways by other family members. Nevertheless, we can identify some characteristic aspects of the treatment of children and of the social interaction between children and others.

Let us first consider the relationship between mother and child. Wet nurses have been a favorite subject for both comedians and moralists down through history, and mothers have been criticized for neglecting their maternal duty by letting others look after their babies.[117] The same is true of classical antiquity. Criticisms might vary somewhat, but in general they reflect the ideal that mothers should be closely involved in the first years of their children's life, as well as the view that the milk, the morality, and the Latin of wet nurses were suspect. Despite this, it was normal for the higher social classes in Rome to employ wet nurses.[118] It is harder to be more precise about the situation in other societal strata, but some inscriptions suggest that persons other than the mother may have reared and fostered children from the lower social classes too.[119] This means that many children had more contact with other adults than with their mothers. Quintilian, for example, assumes that the nurse is the person with whom a little child has the most contact. He mentions her in the list of those who play important roles in the life of his five-year-old son, together with the grandmother and other persons whom he does not identify precisely, but who were probably slaves.[120] Since the nurse was the person with whom the child spent the greatest amount of time right from the moment of its birth, it is reasonable to believe that many children formed stronger emotional bonds to their nurses than to their own mothers. This seems to have been the accepted view in the period we are studying; at any rate, Quintilian writes that a child will usually have the strongest ties to the woman with whom he has had most contact.[121] In many cases—and certainly for the majority of the children in the prosperous classes—this woman was not the mother, but a nurse. Favorinus's critical attitude toward nurses is based, in part, on the fact that a child has stronger emotional bonds to them than to its own parents; indeed, he claims that a child displays signs of affection to its parents as an expression of politeness, rather than as a spontaneous act![122] This does not mean that the mother (and father) took no part in caring for the child during its first years—the relatively extensive medical literature offering advice on the rearing of children indicates that they certainly were involved in this. These texts were written for well-off circles, where the household always included a nurse,[123] and perhaps we should picture the mother as a kind of "supervisor" with overall responsibility, while the nurse performs the practical activities entailed in looking after the child. When authors as diverse as Cicero, Quintilian, and Tacitus speak of the mother-child relationship, they neither envisage nor argue that the mother ought to have an intimate emotional relationship to her children;[124] bonds of this kind tended to be formed with the nurse and other servants. We should note, therefore, that even if a mother did not give her child the physical closeness and attention that we today consider essential for the further development of the child, there were other adults who did so. The evidence presented in this paragraph should not be taken to mean that the mother was absent. Rather, it is assumed that her role is as a model of cultivated discourse, one who implants the correct virtues in the child once it is old enough: "The implication of the texts is that upper-class women in general did not involve themselves very closely with the physical care of small children. This does not really seem to have been expected of them, although an overseer role in their moral education was vaguely hoped for and, if given, praised extravagantly."[125]

As these words indicate, this task was not reserved to mothers. On the contrary, our sources show that the practical upbringing and education of the child was primarily the task of slaves and servants.[126] The pedagogue (*paidagôgos*) was the central figure here. In addition to his involvement in upbringing and education at home, it was his responsibility to follow boys to and from school and to keep an eye on their activities throughout the school hours. These *paidagôgoi* were often educated persons, and several sources say that high standards are to be required of them in their behavior, language, and pedagogical abilities.[127] The tasks of nurses and pedagogues overlapped, but it seems that the nurses were mainly responsible for looking after the needs of babies and very young children, while the pedagogues were responsible for educating and forming children in accordance with prevalent ideals, once they had become a little older.[128]

Once again, this does not mean that mothers were not involved in their children's lives; but it is clear that they tended to spend more time with their children as they grew older. To quote Suzanne Dixon: "Even maternal supervision of children's training seems to have been stronger once they had passed beyond early childhood. Where we tend to see that part of the life cycle as at home with Mother, then at school with Teacher, Romans saw it as spent with nurses, then with teachers and parents."[129] Although our sources do not spell this out, it is a reasonable assumption that in addition to the moral education mentioned above, mothers played a central role in teaching their daughters domestic tasks, both through instructions and exhortations and through their own example.[130] The upbringing and formation of daughters largely aimed at equipping them to become good wives, once they themselves married. When the time came, the mother was involved in the choice of husband.[131] It was expected that she would exercise control over her daughter, who was expected to tell her mother almost everything, even after her marriage. The mother's authority over her daughter was connected in part with her access to economic resources, which benefited the daughter; in fact, the relationship between a mother and a teenage daughter is not unlike the patron/client relationship, since the mother owed her daughter assistance and support, including a part of the family fortune, and the daughter repaid this in the form of visiting her mother and obeying her. Although the sources indicate that many Roman women enjoyed a good education and that some girls attended a public school, at least at the primary stage, it is probable that this was accessible to a larger proportion of boys than girls,[132] and it is at any rate certain that far more boys than girls continued their studies beyond the elementary level. This meant that mothers in general had less contact with their sons than with their daughters. Nevertheless, it was expected that a mother would be involved in the choice of her son's education and career, even if her husband was still alive, and she could also have strong views about the choice of a wife for her son. Naturally, we find examples of conflicts between mother and son, but this relationship is "conventionally depicted as a happy one founded on mutual esteem."[133]

The father's role and function in upbringing seems in many ways to have been parallel to that of the mother, in that he was expected to become more involved as the children grew older; however, the sources assume that it is he who has the ultimate responsibility for their upbringing, especially for teaching them the correct virtues and a cultivated use of language.[134] Some texts display an awareness of the importance of the parents' role in the development of a child's character, positing a connection between instruction in particular virtues and the way the child turns out as an adult.[135] However, we should note that Cicero refuses to blame fathers for the mistakes their sons make, and that biographers seem to assume that a person's character is not primarily the result of his upbringing, but is something that gradually emerges as the result of an internal biological development.[136]

The father's ultimate responsibility must be seen in the context of his role and status as the head of the family (*paterfamilias*).[137] He was the definitive authority in the household; although his juridical right to decide on the life and death of the other members of his household had been limited in the first century B.C.E., he retained (as mentioned above) the right to decide the fate of a newborn child. From the very instant it entered the world, the child was under his power (*potestas*); the mother possessed no legal control or rights with regard to her children. Children and slaves were the father's property, just like material objects. To a very large extent, he could treat his wife, his children, and other household members as he pleased, without any fear of legal consequences. His *potestas* meant for example that he had the unrestricted right to make decisions regarding divorce (which was easy to get), not only in the case of his own marriage, but also in those of his children or of other persons in his household.

In the fourth and fifth centuries of the Common Era, legislation gradually restricted his absolute power over the other household members,[138] stipulating for example that the wife should retain her rights over the property she had brought into the marriage, that the father lost his property rights over things his children had inherited from relatives on the mother's side, and that legitimate children should inherit the whole of the father's fortune (to prevent him from giving all or part of the inheritance to his illegitimate children). In another fundamentally important change, (adult) children were allowed to bring lawsuits against their father. Despite these legal changes, most of which were introduced toward the end of the fifth century, a father could still expect that all the other household members would show him obedience and respect. A child who rebelled against his parents, especially his father, in the presence of other people impaired the family's honor and brought shame on them.

This kind of hierarchic-patriarchal structure opened the door to what we today would call abuse of power; indeed, it legitimated this. We should however note that the *paterfamilias* did not always actually exercise the power to which he was theoretically entitled by virtue of his *patria potestas* (power of the father). Two moderating factors were important: first, there existed an ideal picture of the good father (*bonus paterfamilias*) as opposed to the bad father (*malus paterfamilias*),[139] with an implicit code of socially acceptable behavior. Fathers were expected to treat their children with a certain measure of respect and justice, and to show moderation in the use of corporal punishment.[140] Secondly, the traditional family council (*consilium*) functioned in practice as a limitation on the father's exercise of power. It seems that both sexes were represented, with participation depending on who was involved in the matters under discussion. In cases involving kin, only family members could attend, but if the case involved other household members such as slaves, it had a broader composition, where slaves, friends, and other persons could be represented. The *consilium* was not a formal institution with legislative and executive power; it was convoked when required. Although the *paterfamilias* had the last word, he was certainly expected to take into account the views of the members of his family council.[141]

The existence of these moderating elements does not contradict the basic fact that the *paterfamilias* was the definitive authority in the household, and that children—like the other members of the household—were expected to submit to his will. This is true of all societal strata.[142] It was common to employ physical force in order to compel children to do what was desired, but Richard P. Saller has argued that parents were reluctant to use physical force on their children;[143] beatings and kickings were associated with the punishment of slaves. It was a grave matter to beat a free person, since this was considered an attack on his *dignitas* (dignity). Saller concludes that although children might be beaten, this was seen as inappropriate conduct, which provoked criticism.

It is possible that Saller is correct to affirm that the ideal *paterfamilias* was one who displayed moderation in the treatment of his children, one who made a distinction between the disciplining of his own free children and that of his slaves. He can point to the proverb that states "Youth ought to be curbed by reason, not violence,"[144] and to the many classical authors who exhort fathers to be patient and to speak with their children before inflicting punishment on them.[145] To what extent were such ideals translated into practice? This is hard to say, given that a number of texts either assume or state explicitly that children were beaten and harshly disciplined by their parents.[146] At the same time, we should note that our sources associate corporal punishment with pedagogues and teachers rather than with parents, which may indicate a certain measure of correspondence between ideal and reality in the case of the disciplining of children.[147]

In an educational context, violence against children was societally accepted, a part of everyday life. Thomas Wiedemann correctly notes: "Just as the whip was a symbol of the master's superiority over his slave . . . so the schoolteacher's rod came to symbolise the master's authority over his irrational child pupils. That association between beating and schooling . . . remained constant throughout antiquity. . . . It is hardly surprising that we should find occasional references to children physically attacking their teachers in return."[148] When Augustine looks back to his time as a student and compares his teachers to torturers, his words indicate how widespread and accepted physical violence was in schools.[149] A few critical voices were raised: the best known is Quintilian's affirmation that physical violence against pupils was poor pedagogy, which created a slave mentality in the children.[150] We are also told that Cato himself taught his son, so that he would not be beaten on the head by a Greek slave, that is, by a professional teacher.[151] However, we should not overestimate the significance and effect of such criticism. In our sources, it is striking how rarely we meet critical attitudes to the use of physical violence—often, it is simply taken for granted, and indeed the critical attitudes of a Quintilian or a Cato are themselves evidence of how common corporal punishment was in an educational context.

Here we should remember that only a small part of the populace attended school; the overwhelming majority of families, more than 90 percent, could not afford to send their children to school, and their children had to work in order to contribute to the family's income as soon as they could make themselves useful.[152] For the approximately 90 percent who lived in the countryside, this meant taking part in the running of farms. In the cities, the children of lower-class parents such as craftsmen and tradesmen were usually trained in these jobs at an early age, so that they could help support the family.[153] It was customary for moderately well-off

families to keep slaves, and much of what I have said about the way prosperous parents treated their children is relevant here too.[154] However, since
the slaves in the household were fewer in number, and the children helped
run the farm or helped their fathers in their work from an early age, such
children spent more time with their parents, especially with their fathers;
this applies to all those who were so poor that they could not afford slaves
and servants.

A large section of the populace were slaves.[155] What was life like for
their children?[156] Slaves born in a household (*vernae*),[157] became the master's property. Naturally, they were valuable in economic terms; in the imperial period, children of slaves were an important source for new slaves.
In some instances, they took on a role as substitute for the master's own
children, or as a kind of appendage to these children, and accordingly enjoyed far better conditions than most slaves. In most cases, the *vernae* did
not take on a role like that of a foster child, but even so, they could expect
to receive better treatment than other slaves.[158] This can help explain why
some formed strong ties to the household: even after they had been given
their freedom, they could continue to form part of the household. Some
sources indicate that children of slaves were reared in groups, perhaps after
being separated from their mothers.[159] If he found it advisable, the master
of the household could sell such children while they were still small; in
many cases, the mother and siblings were not sold at the same time, and
this meant that the child was separated from its closest relatives.

In view of what we know in general about the treatment of slaves in
classical antiquity, we have good reason to believe that the majority of
their children lived under extremely harsh conditions, where arbitrary
violence (or the fear of such violence) was a constant reality. This applies
above all to those children who were bought as slaves, but also to those
who became a part of the household into which they had been born, despite the custom of treating these better than other slaves: they were the
master's property, and he could treat them as he pleased. We do indeed
find the idea that a master who used excessive violence against his slaves
was displaying a lack of self-control,[160] but there is no doubt that beatings
and kickings were common, and expressed the inferiority of the slave in
relation to his master. And what I have written about attitudes to the corporal punishment of children and slaves in general implies that children
who grew up as slaves had to endure a brutal existence.

This brings us to another aspect of growing up that a modern reader will
tend to call abuse, namely, sexual relations between children and adults.
Lloyd de Mause, for example, paints a somber picture of the situation when

he writes: "the child in antiquity lived his earliest years in an atmosphere of sexual abuse. Growing up in Greece and Rome often included being used sexually by older men."[161] He is certainly correct to state that many men initiated sexual relationships with boys and that this was societally accepted, but his conclusions require some nuances.

First of all, we must emphasize that de Mause and other readers who operate within the framework of a modern Western sexual discourse are quick to evaluate as sexual abuse conduct that the moral code of antiquity viewed as normal and natural. In his book on homosexuality in ancient Greece, Kenneth Dover shows (1) that most homosexual activity among free urban citizens in Greece took the form of pederastic relationships between adult men and boys aged twelve years and over; (2) that such relationships were considered normal and natural; (3) that neither ethics nor legislation forbade or penalized this form of sexual activity, as long as certain regulations governing propriety were observed; and (4) that this form of homosexual activity was seen as noble, as a natural part of growing into adulthood, and as mentally and spiritually more estimable than heterosexual intercourse. In the "grammar school" (*gymnasion*), it was customary for friendship to be established between an older pedagogue and a young pupil, and this often involved a sexual relationship.[162] In other words, sexual activity that is condemned today as pedophilic was not only accepted in Greece, but viewed as honorable and natural.

This is because pederasty was not considered on the lines of our modern dichotomy between homosexual and heterosexual, but in terms of an understanding of sexuality where the fundamental antithesis is active/passive: one partner is to be active and dominating, the one who penetrates, while the other partner is to be passive and submissive, the one who is penetrated.[163] Not only women but also boys belonged to the latter category. Hence, the criterion of normal or natural sex is the extent to which one acts in accordance with the role one has been assigned, as the active or the passive partner. An adult free man's sexual conduct was "normal" as long as he was the active, dominating, and penetrating partner. Consequently, sexual activity in which a free adult man was passive was unacceptable, and this is why a free citizen was forbidden to prostitute himself. On the other hand, a sexual relationship between an adult and a boy in which the boy took the passive role was normal, and widespread. In other words, sexual behavior was understood in terms of a hierarchical pattern of power relationships. As long as these were reflected in sexual behavior, it was considered legitimate and normal. We should however note that sexual activity with under-age children was not accepted societally, although it was relatively common.[164]

The Romans thought in the same categories:[165] here too, the fundamental dichotomy was between active and passive. There is however one difference that is significant in our present context: the Romans found the Greek practice of pederasty disgraceful. The problem for Romans was that it meant a free adult entered a sexual relationship with freeborn boys who would one day attain the same status he had. This has been emphasized by C. A. Williams in his important study of Roman homosexuality. He summarizes the greatest difference between Greek and Roman attitudes to sexual behavior as follows:

> The Greek tradition of pederasty, whereby citizen males might openly engage in romantic and sexual relationships with freeborn adolescent males who would one day be citizens, in Roman terms was *stuprum*; it was a disgraceful, illicit behavior. Thus a situation like that obtaining in Athens, where a statuary group of the pederastic couple Harmodios and Aristogeiton was erected in the agora in recognition of their role in overthrowing the last tyrant of Athens, would be impossible in Rome. Yet this was not because the couple was male but because both parties were freeborn.[166]

It must be emphasized that the Romans criticized the Greek form of pederasty because they saw it as a threat to the hierarchical social order that was presupposed by the active/passive dichotomy. This may help understand why the Romans attempted to protect free under-age children from sexual abuse. The rape of under-age children was punished harshly, but it seems that the seduction of children was viewed more leniently.[167] The fact that sexual relationships between freeborn under-age children and boys and adult men were not socially accepted must mean that children who belonged to this category were less frequently exposed to abuse. On the other hand, we should note that sexual relations between boys and men were so widespread that they posed a problem to Pseudo-Plutarch, who found it difficult to decide whether fathers should allow men to have sexual relationships with their sons: "But in regard to the topic now to be introduced I am of two opinions and two minds . . . whether boys' admirers are to be permitted to associate with them and pass their time with them, or whether, on the contrary, they should be kept away and driven off from association with the youth."[168] The most important point here is not the answer he gives, but that he undoubtedly takes it for granted that such relationships exist.

Our sources do not give a clear indication of the extent to which free Roman under-age boys were involved in sexual activity with adults. This is partly true of other groups of children too. For example, Suetonius condemns Tiberius because he "taught children of the most tender years, whom he called his *little fishes,* to play between his legs while he was in his bath. Those which had not yet been weaned, but were strong and hearty, he set at fellatio."[169] As de Mause correctly points out, the decisive point is not the degree of truth there may be in this story, but the fact that Suetonius clearly thought his readers would find it credible. Brothels staffed by boys existed in many towns. Intercourse with castrated boys is often described as especially exciting, and we know that babies were castrated so that they could work in brothels later on.[170] One reason why people bought small children as slaves was in order to have sex with them. Musonius Rufus poses the question whether a boy can be called disobedient if he objects to being used sexually in such a relationship: "I knew a father so depraved that, having a son conspicuous for youthful beauty, he sold him into a life of shame. If, now, that lad who was sold and sent into such a life by his father had refused and would not go, should we say that he was disobedient?"[171] Most of the children who were rescued after being exposed became slaves, and it is easy to imagine that many of these—boys and girls alike—were exploited sexually by their masters. Justin Martyr confirms that this was the case, when he writes that almost all exposed children, both girls and boys, come to be used as prostitutes.[172] Clement of Alexandria describes how boys who were to be sold as slaves were "beautified," to make them more attractive to potential buyers.[173]

Although a relatively wide range of texts certainly assume that sexual relationships between children and adults were well-known among the Romans, it is difficult to say anything definite about the extent of this practice. Many sources pose questions, or directly criticize such relationships, even when slave children were involved. This makes our sources somewhat ambiguous: on the one hand, they take it for granted that slave children were sexually exploited and that child prostitution was a universal phenomenon, while on the other hand, the critical attitude in many sources shows that this practice met with opposition. Accordingly, we cannot accept de Mause's conclusions at face value, especially in the case of freeborn children in the Roman context. In the case of other groups of children, in both the Greek and the Roman spheres, it appears that sexual relationships between children and men were societally accepted, and it is reasonable to suppose that they were relatively common—or, as we would put it today, that many children were sexually abused by men.[174]

Were Parents Positively Emotionally Involved with Their Children?

My remarks on abortion and *expositio,* the physical and sometimes emotional distance between parents and their small children, the use of corporal punishment in children's upbringing and education, and sexual relationships between children and adults paint a very gloomy picture of the basic living conditions of children. There is no doubt that children were treated in a very rough way, and relatively many of them were exposed to what we today would call violence and sexual abuse. This prompts the question whether the parents and other persons close to children actually loved them. Were they emotionally involved with children?

Many scholars have studied this question. Ariès put forward the hypothesis that parents in a society with a high infant mortality did not commit themselves emotionally to their children until these had reached a certain age, and this is why they did not grieve at the death of small children.[175] His book led to an extensive discussion of this aspect of classical antiquity.[176] There has been a clear tendency to clarify nuances of Ariès's picture, but our sources do not permit us to draw a definitive conclusion. Cicero says that it is not common to grieve over dead babies, and claims that it is inappropriate to do so.[177] He himself displays a striking lack of interest in the premature death of his grandchild, referring to the dead girl as "a thing."[178] We find the same point of view in a letter written by Seneca to a man whose young son had died.[179] It has been argued that such views are confirmed by the study of epitaphs. Although one might have expected (in view of the high rate of infant mortality) that inscriptions dedicated to dead babies would account for a high proportion of all epitaphs, they are in fact rare.[180] This disproportion need not mean that babies were not commemorated at all; perhaps their commemoration did not involve inscriptions on their graves. This, however, is a matter of speculation, which may perhaps never be confirmed by our sources.[181]

On the other hand, the fact that Cicero finds it necessary to call grief over a dead baby inappropriate does in fact tell us that there were parents who grieved in such situations. Likewise, Seneca's exhortations are addressed to a man who (in the author's eyes) was displaying excessive grief at the loss of his baby. Another interesting point is his opening remark that the letter is written to a man who "was reported to be rather womanish in his grief." He does not criticize *women* for grieving, and this description of the man's reactions as "womanish" suggests that it was customary and socially accepted for mothers to grieve when their babies died.[182] This agrees with what Plutarch wrote to console his wife after they lost their only daughter:

> And I know what great satisfaction lay in this—that after four sons the longed-for daughter was born to you, and that she made it possible for me to call her by your name. Our affection for children so young has, furthermore, a poignancy all its own: the delight it gives is quite pure and free from all anger or reproach. She had herself, moreover, a surprising natural gift of mildness and good temper, and her way of responding to friendship and of bestowing favours gave us pleasure while it afforded an insight into her kindness.[183]

This daughter was two years old when she died, and can therefore no longer be considered a baby. Nevertheless, this quotation is interesting, because it shows that not only the mother, but also the father had positive feelings toward a little child. As I have said, the sources are open to various interpretations. At any rate, the literary sources imply that both father and mother grieved at the deaths of small children, even if this was not in accord with the ideal promoted by authors influenced by Stoicism, especially as far as fathers were concerned.[184]

In the case of older children, from five years upward, our sources are easier to interpret. A number of epitaphs from the first three centuries of the Common Era express profound grief over dead children, on the part of parents and of other relatives.[185] Here, however, there is an over-representation of older children from about fifteen to thirty years of age, reflecting the fact that "the typical focus of tragic or untimely death is the young adult."[186] Here we must recall that parents were dependent on their children and expected that they would help them in old age, provide for their burial, and keep their memory alive. When the children had reached their late teens and twenties, parents expected that their children would outlive them and carry out their filial obligations.[187]

Studies have shown that a large number of inscriptions and literary texts are aware that children were different from adults, and that these differences were prized.[188] Children are referred to in affectionate terminology, and adjectives such as *dulcis* (sweet) or *mellitus* (honey-sweet) are applied to them.[189] Suzanne Dixon interprets this "sentimental interest in young children and enjoyment of their childish qualities" against the background of "a general ideological stress on the domestic comfort of the conjugal unit which emerges in Latin art and literature from the first century B.C."[190] She claims that this ideal of the family as the space for emotional closeness, affirmation, and intimacy resembles in many ways the idea of the family as a "haven in a heartless world" in nineteenth-century Europe, and gives examples of this ideal in texts from Lucretius and Cicero. The former quotes (in order to criticize) a "common lament of mourners" for a young man who has died: "No more, no more will your happy house welcome you, nor will your excellent wife. No more will your sweet children run to greet you with kisses and cling to your chest in sweet silence."[191] Cicero writes to Atticus that he felt so desolate when he lacked the company of his brother or his best friends that he found no joy in all the hangers-on who gathered around him every day. His only joy was in the time he spent with his wife, his daughter, and his little son Cicero.[192]

I agree with Dixon that inscriptions and literary sources from the first century B.C.E. reflect a "sentimental ideal of the Roman family" and that the parents' delight in their children is an essential element in this picture. I am more hesitant in interpreting the increased appearance of children as motifs in various forms of art and on coins as an expression of this general ideal of the family, and more specifically as an expression of a growing focus on children and a positive interest in them. I do not wish to deny any connection here, but it seems indisputable that much of the iconographic material featuring children has primarily a political motivation: it was part of the imperial propaganda, aiming to win popular support either in general terms or for some specific aspect of the emperor's policies.[193]

Children and Religion

Finally, let us look briefly at children as religious actors. What place and function did they have in the domestic cult and in public festivals? And what implications might this have for the perceptions of children and of childhood?[194] The domestic cult was an important element in daily life in both Greek and Roman households. Unsurprisingly, it centered on the worship of the gods who watched over the storehouse and had the task of ensuring a sufficient supply of food, and sacrifices were offered to them. In the Greek context, Zeus was the most important, while the *Penates* or household gods were central in the Roman sphere, but honor was also paid to other gods associated with the family. In Roman households, for example, gods known as the *Lares* (probably spirits of the ancestors) were honored. Literary sources allude to sacrifices to these gods, and a number of household shrines have been found in niches in the dining room or kitchen, as well as free-standing shrines in the atrium or the garden.[195]

These gods were often joined by the figure of Fortuna or the *genius* of the family.[196] Drawings show the *paterfamilias* surrounded by *Lares* as he carries out the sacrificial rite, while our sources indicate that other family members, too, could offer daily gifts of incense or wine.[197] We may therefore say that the domestic cult had two functions: it united the living branch of the *paterfamilias* with his deceased ancestors, and it was intended to ensure the supply of food.

As I have written above, part of the Roman "inheritance" consisted in continuing the practice of domestic worship, and there is every reason to believe that children were socialized into this cult from a very early age. Both pagan and Christian sources attest this.[198] Here, I quote only one text, from the fourth-century Christian author Prudentius, who gives a vivid portrait of the "vain superstition" that has found expression in the pagan domestic cult "through a thousand generations one after another." He writes:

> Children in their infancy drank in the error with their first milk; while still at the crying stage, they had tasted of the sacrificial meal. . . . The little one had looked at a figure in the shape of Fortune. . . . Then, raised on his nurse's shoulder, he too pressed his lips to the flint and rubbed it with them, pouring out his childish petitions, asking for riches from a sightless stone, and convinced that all one's wishes must be sought from thence.[199]

According to this description, children were present at domestic worship from a very early age and were involved in its rituals, learning to pay the necessary honor and respect to the appropriate deities.[200] But they were not only present while the adults acted. Although our source materials are scantier than we would wish, it appears that children exercised cultic functions in some contexts. In his commentary on the *Aeneid*, Servius (fifth century C.E.) writes that it was the children who had to say whether the house gods were satisfied when the *paterfamilias* offered sacrifice in the course of the meal.[201] Here, they were intermediaries between the adults and the gods whose task it was to ensure a sufficient supply of food, the *Penates* mentioned above.

In this context, it is interesting to read what Columella (first century C.E.) writes about children's role in connection with the preparation of food. There was no clear-cut distinction between the sacred and the profane in the household, and the way food was handled had religious overtones. Columella writes that among the Greeks, Carthaginians, and

Romans, many believed that those who had to prepare food should refrain from sexual intercourse. This meant that children were given a central role: "Equipment should only be handled by a child. . . . They thought that it was essential for this work to be done by a boy or girl, who would distribute each day's supplies."[202] Here, children's religious function in domestic worship seems related to the idea that they are sexually pure (or, to put it differently, sexually inactive).

From the reign of emperor Augustus onward, children had specific cultic functions in public festivals. The Romans adopted (or perhaps more precisely, continued) the ancient Greek tradition of having children sing at various public festivals and ceremonies. Perhaps the best known of these ceremonies was held when Augustus established the "Secular Games" in 17 c.e. An inscription gives a fairly detailed account of what took place: "After the completion of the sacrifice, a hymn was sung by twenty-seven (= 3 x 3 x 3) chosen boys, all with their father and mother still alive, and the same number of girls. This was on the Capitol. The hymn was composed by Q. Horatius Flaccus."[203] We know that similar choirs of girls and boys from well-off Roman households took part in public ceremonial occasions as late as the third century.[204]

Children could have other functions too. Boys assisted some priests in the sacrifices. Dionysius of Halicarnassus, a contemporary of Augustus, desired to demonstrate that the role the emperor gave children in public ceremonies had its model in Greek tradition. Irrespective of how we evaluate his argumentation on this point, his remarks about children's function as assistants are so interesting that it is worth presenting an excerpt:

> And because some rites were to be performed by women, others by children whose fathers and mothers were living, to the end that these also might be administered in the best manner, he ordered that the wives of the priests should be associated with their husbands in the priesthood; and that in the case of any rites which men were forbidden by the law of the country to celebrate, their wives should perform them and their children should assist as their duties required; and that the priests who had no children should choose out of the other families of each *curia* the most beautiful boy and girl, the boy to assist in the rites till the age of manhood, and the girl so long as she remained unmarried.[205]

Dionysius goes on to describe these child acolytes as *camili*. It is not completely clear from the sources whether this term refers to the child assistants of every Roman priest or college of priests, or whether it should be understood more narrowly as a reference to the child assistants in specific rituals. In our context, this is not so important; what matters is that we can affirm that in the first two centuries of the Common Era, "child acolytes were present at a wide range of social occasions. . . . [They were] carrying and holding vessels of food or water at sacrifices, religious processions, and weddings."[206] It follows that children were a visible presence at public ceremonies in the early imperial period, thanks to the cultic functions assigned to them.

Another important dimension is children's function as intermediaries between the divine world and the societal world of adult citizens: we have relatively many examples of children's utterances being interpreted as a prophecy or an omen concerning the future.[207] In his discussion of children's religious functions in the Greco-Roman world, Thomas Wiedemann frequently affirms that such functions did not mean that children were equal in rank to adults: on the contrary, children (like women and slaves) were a marginal group on the periphery of human society, with few or no opportunities to influence the future course of events. The only way they could look after their own needs was to appeal to the gods. Since children were weak and vulnerable, they were particularly dependent on the protection and help of the gods. Like other marginal groups, the child was in a kind of intermediate position between societal human fellowship and the divine sphere, and Wiedemann claims that their closeness to the gods and dependence on them made children suitable to exercise cultic functions.[208]

I do not believe that this statement can be accepted as it stands. First, none of the sources to which Wiedemann refers gives explicit support to his interpretation. On the contrary, we have seen the explicit expression of another view—the idea that children have certain cultic functions because they are sexually inactive; this is expressly stated in connection with the correct handling of food. It is surely not unreasonable to see their function as mediators between the gods (who ensured a sufficient supply of food to the household) and adult household members in the light of the same idea, and Wiedemann himself points out that when adults prepared themselves to carry out religious ceremonies, it was expected that they would abstain from sexual intercourse. At the same time, he rejects any connection between this fact and children's cultic function, although he does not offer any arguments in support of his own view. Another problem with his hypothesis is that if it were really true that children's marginal position in human society meant that they were closer to the divine sphere, we should have expected them to have more (and more central) cultic functions than they in fact seem to have had. If we prescind from the link made in the sources themselves between children's cultic functions and their sexual inactivity, it is difficult to offer any certain explanation of why they were assigned these functions at all, unless we are to interpret this as one reflection of the general process whereby children became more visible in the imperial period—a process largely due to political strategies, since the underlying motive was to get the Romans to produce more children in order to ensure a stable recruitment to various functions in the empire.

CHILDREN IN PAGAN ANTIQUITY

We may sum up as follows: children in antiquity were born into harsh living conditions, and infant mortality was high, thanks to appalling sanitary, hygienic, and health provisions, as well as to the lack of food. Perhaps as many as 50 percent of all children died before their tenth birthday.

But children were at risk from dangers other than death from sickness. In the course of a child's first week of life, the parents decided whether or not to expose it. We do not know what percentage were in fact exposed, but there is no doubt that *expositio* was well-known and societally accepted in both the eastern and the western regions of the empire. There is no consensus among scholars about what happened to these children; some were rescued and looked after, and most of these ended up as slaves, but the sources also indicate that a relatively large number of such children died. A number of reasons led parents to take this step. Mostly, poverty was the cause of *expositio,* but we know of instances where even wealthy Romans exposed their children. Other common reasons were illegitimacy or a handicap, though it was probably more common to kill children born with deformities, or those judged not strong enough to grow up. It is also reasonable to assume that more girls than boys were exposed. A few voices were raised in criticism of this practice, primarily Stoic philosophers who sometimes claimed that child exposure was against nature. From the second century of the Common Era onward, there was vigorous opposition to *expositio* on the part of the governing authorities in several Italian cities, thanks to the need to ensure a supply of workers—in other words, a pragmatic opposition rather than one based on ideological or religious grounds. It was only under Emperor Valentinian in 374 that legislation made *expositio* a crime.

During a child's earliest years, its daily needs were usually looked after by wet nurses and other caregivers. This is certainly the case with children of well-off families, but it seems that many children of relatively poor families were likewise cared for on a daily basis by persons other than their parents. The parents, especially the mother, became more involved as the child grew older, but here too, it was primarily servants and slaves who were responsible for the practical side of rearing and education. In addition to the nurse, the pedagogue played an important role. He was charged with upbringing and instruction in the home, and it was also his task to follow the child to and from school and to keep an eye on him throughout the school hours. This meant that in many wealthy families, the children had stronger emotional bonds to other adults in the household than to their mothers. This does not mean that the mother was absent; along with the husband, the mother had overall responsibility for the child, but this was more a supervisory role. Naturally, things were different in poor homes where the parents could not afford slaves.

As *paterfamilias,* the father was the definitive authority in the household, and he could expect respect and obedience from all the other household members. Anyone who put up resistance to the father's will in the presence of outsiders brought shame both on the father and on the rest of the household. Despite the ideal that a good father should display moderation in the use of force against his own children, a number of sources indicate that parents beat their children and disciplined them harshly; blows and other forms of violence against children were, however, more often associated with pedagogues and teachers. Physical violence, or the fear of this, was a part of children's everyday life, all the more so in the case of slave children, whether born in the household, foundlings, or children bought from slave dealers.

Another aspect of childhood in antiquity was that a relatively high number—mostly boys—had sexual relations with adult men. This was because the basic dichotomy in sexual discourse at that time was active/passive, not homosexual/heterosexual. A free adult citizen's sexual conduct was considered normal or natural, as long as he was the active and dominant partner. Sexual relationships between a boy and a man where the boy took the passive role were normal and widespread. Sexual intercourse with under-age children was not societally accepted, but it seems to have been relatively widespread. It was not uncommon to find brothels in the cities where both girls and boys offered their sexual services. Many foundlings were forced to work as prostitutes.

Most parents saw their children as an investment: children had to help their parents at work as soon as they were old enough to make themselves useful. More importantly, parents could expect to be helped and support-ed by their children when they were old; their children would ensure that they were buried with dignity, and children would continue the domestic cult and commemorate the dead in an appropriate manner. These expec-tations, and this dependency of parents on their children, help explain why parents grieved more over children who died as teenagers or adults than over those who died when they were still very small—for in the for-mer case, they had a realistic hope that their children would outlive them. The high mortality rate among small children may be one reason why they were not formally commemorated, and why parents who grieved openly over the death of small children were criticized. To lose small children was simply part of life, something most parents experienced. Another factor may be the idea that the social birth, ritually marked on the *dies lustricus,* was more fundamental in terms of the child's societal relationships than its physical birth; this may mean that children who died in the first week of their lives were not commemorated.

The domestic cult was an important element in family life in antiquity. Children took part in this from a very early age, and were thereby socialized into the symbolic universe that found expression in these acts of worship. In addition to taking part in the rituals in the same way as other house-hold members, children were assigned specific cultic functions. When the *paterfamilias* offered sacrifice, their task was to say whether the domestic gods were satisfied—in other words, children functioned as intermediar-ies between the divine sphere and the societal world of the adults. There are also indications that children had certain tasks in connection with the handling of food—tasks with religious overtones. From the time of emperor Augustus onward, children had specific liturgical roles in public festivals and ceremonies. Until the third century C.E., choirs of children took part in various public ceremonial occasions, and children were the priests' assistants in sacrifice. They also took part in religious processions. Their ritual functions both in the domestic cult and in public ceremonies seem in part to have been motivated by their sexual purity, since it was thought that persons who had to carry out ritual ceremonies ought to ab-stain from intercourse for a certain period beforehand. Their visible pres-ence at public ceremonies may, however, also reflect the general process from the early imperial period onward whereby children became more visible, thanks to the political situation—children were needed in order to ensure recruitment to various functions in the empire. But however their participation and their specific roles in worship are to be interpreted, we can at any rate say that children were integrated into religious life, both in the household and in public ceremonies.

When we hear about children's nature and qualities in ancient sources, the emphasis lies on their lack of *logos*. They do not possess the necessary presupposition for rational thinking. Children were associated with the lack of reason, and were employed as symbols of irrational behavioral patterns and attitudes: one criticized other adults by calling their conduct "childish." Here, children functioned as negative paradigms for adults. Their lack of reason was expressed in their moral incompetence: they yielded to desires and passions more readily than adults, and in the philosophical tradition, they were compared to animals that had to be tamed. It is possible that the widespread use of physical violence in children's education reflects the idea that children lacked reason. They were also perceived as weak and timorous. There was a clear tendency to prize children, not because of their childlike qualities, but because they had the potential to acquire one day those qualities and characteristics that would make them good Roman citizens. Children were interesting, not primarily for their character as children, but because of something they would become in the future.

This chapter has painted a generally somber picture of what it was like to be a child in classical antiquity, implying a negative view of children and childhood. However, this picture must be supplemented by brighter colors: from the early imperial period onward, we find sources that reflect an ideal of the family as a sphere of emotional closeness, intimacy, and affirmation, as for example when children's qualities are described in positive terms, when they are called "sweet," and when parents express happiness at being together with their children. There is every reason to believe that parents at that period, just like parents today, loved their children and wanted the best for them. However, it is clear that no contradiction was felt to exist between this basic attitude and the way in which children were treated de facto in the household and in classical society in general. Hence it is interesting that Dixon, the most decided spokesperson for "the sentimental ideal of the Roman family," should sum up children's existential situation in antiquity as follows:

> Most children who died young were not formally commemorated, and parents who did openly grieve for them were commonly

rebuked by their peers (even by the other parent) for such excess. The great cultural emphasis was undoubtedly on children as progeny who were able to continue the family name and cult, supply labor, and supply them with proper funeral rites....

The modern concern for child welfare had no real equivalent in the ancient world. Depending on their social standing, young children were routinely apprenticed, put to heavy labor, sexually exploited, or beaten by schoolteachers. Roman law made certain concessions to youthful ignorance and the need to provide guardians for orphaned children, but the main emphasis was on the preservation of family estates rather than the protection of the individual child.[209]

3

PATRISTIC TEACHING ABOUT THE NATURE
OF CHILDREN AND THEIR CHARACTERISTICS

Early Christian writers—the so-called patristic writers or fathers of the church—wrote extensively on children and children's nature and qualities. How did they view children? What characteristics and typical traits did they attribute to children?

I use the conceptual pair "nature and qualities" in a relatively broad sense here. Besides including classical anthropological questions such as the extent to which children are driven by desire, passions, or (original) sin, whether or not the child is innocent in a moral sense, and whether children undergo a development in this sphere, the word pair "nature and qualities" refers also to concrete conduct and behavioral patterns. We shall investigate how our sources portray children's conduct and the characteristics and attitudes typical of children. This pair of concepts also refers to their potential for acquiring knowledge. Accordingly, our investigation of patristic ideas about children's nature and qualities entails a concentration on anthropology in the traditional sense, on the conduct and behavioral patterns associated with children, and on what the fathers say about children's potential for assimilating Christian ideals. Naturally, this last point involves the patristic understanding of education and instruction, the subject of Chapter 5. Nevertheless, I wish to integrate some aspects of this topic into the present discussion, since this will show more fully how Christians in that period thought about children's qualities.

The primary question that we shall investigate concerns the child's nature in a moral sense. Is the child innocent or not? This emphasis is dictated by the simple fact that the source material, especially from the close of the fourth and the beginning of the fifth centuries, concentrates on this problem. At the heart of the Pelagian controversy lay the question of original sin, which obviously also entails theological reflection on the nature of small children. However, this issue was in turn intimately linked to other theological topics, not least to the doctrine of God's righteousness. I shall devote a considerable amount of space to the Pelagian controversy, precisely in order to show how reflection on the nature of children was interwoven with other theological questions. I shall also consider in some detail Gregory of Nyssa's treatise on the death of small children, which is interesting not only because it reflects one particular view of children's nature, but also because this text shows that this view implies complex questions of what we might call "normal theology." When an infant dies, what awaits it on the other side of the grave? An underlying question that occurs in the course of our discussion and will be treated in our closing section is whether the qualities that the fathers attribute to children allow us to draw any conclusions about how they evaluated children in general and how the appeal to children's behavioral patterns functions in the context of their argumentation.

CHILDREN AS PARADIGMS FOR ADULTS

A good starting point for an investigation of what the church fathers thought about children is their discussion of the biblical metaphor of childhood as a designation of the Christian life. How do they interpret the logion of Jesus (Matthew 18:1-4 and 19:13-14) where adults are exhorted to become like children? In their interpretation of this metaphor and the way they apply it to contemporary Christians, we may expect them to disclose their understanding of what particular elements (if any) constitute the nature and qualities, in moral and religious terms, which differentiate children and the mature.[1]

When patristic writers deal with the implications of the affirmation that adults are the children of God, what aspects of children and childhood do they emphasize? Obviously, they are not speaking here about real children in particular social contexts. Instead, they construct an ideal child or an ideal picture of childhood in ways that suit their argumentative strategy. For this reason, one might suspect that the patristic writers are selective with regard to the qualities they ascribe to children, that is, that certain aspects are played up while others are underplayed. However, assuming that they were in some sense persuasive, we may assume that their constructed pictures of childhood related to or reflected points of connection with real images of childhood. It is reasonable to assume that the qualities they ascribe to children are not much different from those their audience associated with children.[2]

Clement of Alexandria

The patristic writer who offers the most extensive discussion of the implications of the biblical metaphor of childhood is Clement of Alexandria in the late second century.[3] Of special interest here is his *Paedagogus*.[4] While Books II and III provide instructions on how to behave in particular social contexts, Book I deals more broadly and in principle with the author's understanding of what it means to be a Christian. He makes heavy use of developmental and educational language where he portrays the "process of becoming a Christian as analogous to the process of conception, embryonic development, birth, and growth."[5] The title of this work refers to Christ as the pedagogue who guides the little ones in their steps in the process of spiritual growth.[6] Its addressees have generally been thought to be Christian catechumens or the newly baptized, though some scholars have argued in recent years that the treatise may have been written for a broader audience.[7]

Chapters 5 and 6 of the first Book constitute a unity that begins with this introduction: "That education (*paidagogia*) is the training (*agon*) given children (*pais*) is evident from the very name. It remains for us to consider who the children are as explained in the Scriptures and, from the same Scriptural passages, to understand the Educator. We are the children" (*Paed.* 1.5.12). A basic element in the following section is the attempt to prove the thesis that "we [the Christians] are the children" by referring to a large number of passages of both the Old and the New Testaments, in which the people of God are depicted either explicitly or implicitly as "children." Clement's biblical evidence for the view that it is fitting to describe Christians as children reaches its climax when he underscores that the Lord himself is called a child (*Paed.* 1.5.24). Clement's comments on certain passages of scripture reveal his view of what it meant and what it did not mean to be a child.

The first comment sets the tone and shows what Clement considers a fundamental aspect of the nature of children. He refers to Jesus' rebuke of his disciples when they tried to prevent parents from bringing their children to him. Parents should not hinder them "for of such is the kingdom of heaven."[8] Then Clement, in order to explain the meaning of this statement, quotes another saying of Jesus concerning children: "Unless you turn and become like little children, you shall not enter into the kingdom of heaven."[9] He opposes a spiritual interpretation of this logion, which would interpret it as referring to some kind of regeneration. Jesus is talking about real children. Then Clement briefly explains why Jesus uses children as positive paradigms for adults by referring to one particular quality children possess: they function as paradigms because of their simplicity.[10]

Clement frequently attributes this quality of simplicity to childhood. (1) Among the many passages of scripture he quotes to demonstrate that Christians are children is the statement of Jesus: "'Let My lambs stand on My Right.'" Clement argues that "lamb" refers not to adults, but to children, "the simple." If Jesus had adults in mind he would have used the word "sheep." Later on in the same chapter, he associates simplicity with the lamb (child): Isaiah "uses the more innocent class of sheep, lambs, as a figure for simplicity."[11] (2) Clement notes that in scripture the people of God is once referred to as a collection of young birds (chickens), "a name which graphically and mystically describes the simplicity of soul belonging to childhood." He goes on to list various names of the people of God in scripture, all of which directly or indirectly carry the connotation of childhood. He also refers to a passage that says God's servant will be given a new name. His definition of what is meant by a "new" name is interesting: "one that is different and everlasting, pure and simple, suggestive of childhood and of candor."[12]

Clement attributes a number of other qualities to children, some of them closely associated with simplicity. A statement that occurs in a context where he discusses the etymology of the term *nêpios* (infant) is illuminating. After having argued that the word is composed of the prefix *ne-* (new), and the adjective *epios* (gentle), he presents a passage of Paul (1 Thess 2:7): as scriptural proof: "St. Paul obviously suggests this when he says: 'Although as the apostles of Christ we could have claimed a position of honor among you, still while in your midst we were gentle,'[13] as if a nurse were cherishing her own children." On the basis of this line of thought, Clement draws an inference with respect to the nature of childhood, listing many qualities that he associates with infancy or qualities he wished his readers to associate with this stage of the development of human beings. He says: "A little one is thus gentle and for that reason decidedly amenable, mild and simple, without deceit or pretense, direct and upright of mind. Childlikeness is the foundation for simplicity and truthfulness."[14]

Another quality Clement attributes to children is their loyalty and obedience to their fathers. In order to convince his readers that this behavior is in concert with what is "natural" he uses analogies from parent-child relations among animals.[15] For example, he anthropomorphizes and applauds the relationship between foals and their fathers. After having pointed out that scripture figuratively calls us foals unyoked to vice, he emphasizes that foals run only to their father, "not stallions 'who whinny lustfully for their neighbor's wife, beasts of burden unrestrained in their lust.' Rather, we are free and newly born, joyous in our faith, holding fast to the course of truth, swift in seeking salvation, spurning and trampling upon worldliness."[16] Like foals that naturally run to their father and thereby obey him, it is natural that human children show obedience and express loyalty toward their father.[17]

This attitude is clearly expressed in another passage in Chapter 5. Besides underscoring the significance of children's obedience to their father, this passage also reflects other important qualities the author associated with childhood. For this reason I quote the first passage at some length:

> Really, then, children are those who look upon God alone as their father, who are simple, little ones, uncontaminated, who are lovers of the horn of the unicorn. To these, surely, who have matured in the Word, He has proclaimed His message, bidding them not to be concerned with the affairs of this life and encouraging them to imitate children and devote themselves to the Father alone. So it is that He says to those who have some possessions: "Do not be anxious about the morrow; for tomorrow will have anxieties of its own." Here He commands us to lay aside the cares of life and give our whole mind and heart to the Father alone. Whoever fulfils this command is a little one, indeed, and a child, both before God and the world: to the world, in the sense of one who has lost his wits; to God, in the sense of one dearly beloved. (*Paed.* 1.5.17)

Obviously, Clement uses children here as a metaphor for adult Christians. It is individual adult Christians who should "look upon" God and "devote themselves" to him alone. However, Clement explicitly states that when adult Christians do so, they are imitating children. In other words, Clement uses children's obedience toward their earthly father as a positive paradigm for adults' relationship to their heavenly Father.

Another positive quality Clement ascribes to children here is that they are not "concerned with the affairs of this life." A similar expression occurs when he describes the praiseworthy behavior of the foal or child: the foal treads and stamps underfoot the things of the world.[18] These expressions refer most likely to what Clement perceived as children's indifference to things associated with wealth and social status. Furthermore, the anecdote about the foal suggests that he ascribes an additional positive characteristic to children. Although it is not emphasized in other parts of Clement's authorship, the fact that he contrasts the exemplary behavior of the foal or child with the sex-crazed behavior of the stallion or adult man suggests that he considered children's lack of sexual desire a laudable quality.[19] Hence, it is reasonable to assume that sexual purity is included when he depicts children as simple and guileless.[20] This does not imply, however, that Clement advocates sexual renunciation within the framework of marriage, as do several more ascetic church fathers later on.[21]

Clement pays attention to viewpoints held by others on childhood that he does not want his readers to accept. In this connection his comments on why Jesus used the little child as an example of the ideal member of the kingdom of heaven are interesting. As we have noted above, a basic idea associated with children in the Greco-Roman world was their lack of the faculty of reason. Therefore we can understand why Clement attempts to underplay precisely this quality of childhood when he applies the metaphor of childhood to Christians: when Jesus talked about a little child he was referring, not to "one who has not reached the use of reason because of his immaturity," but to the innocence and simplicity of children. These qualities are not, however, the same thing as stupidity. Christians are not "children" in the sense that they crawl on the ground like snakes; instead, their feet barely touch the ground while they live a life that represents holy wisdom, though this wisdom appears to evil persons to be foolishness. Clement attempts to transform negative aspects of the commonly held view of childhood in order to make the metaphor of childhood better express the proper way of Christian life. Although I do not agree with the opinion that "Clement counters views that children are stupid . . . or earthly,"[22] it reasonable to affirm that he reflects a positive evaluation of childhood.

Clement's introduction to the discussion of the words of Jesus about children in 5.16 summarizes in an illuminating way this positive attitude. He writes that there is no doubt that people "call the most excellent and perfect possessions in life by names derived from the word 'child' (*pai*), that is, education (*paidagogia*) and culture (*paideia*)." This is a remarkable statement, if we take into account the generally negative view of childhood in pagan antiquity. Here, as a matter of fact, Clement associates the most valuable features in the Greco-Roman world with childhood! Of course, it was no novelty for the educated reader that *paideia* and *paidagogia* were derived from *pai*. The striking point is how Clement makes use of this etymology in his argumentation. It is beyond doubt that it serves to link children with fundamental elements of culture and thereby increases the status and the value of children. This is an other example of how Clement constructs or transforms traditional conceptions of childhood for the purpose of his argumentation. When Christians are exhorted to be like children, Clement draws what he considered to be a positive picture of children, a picture that expresses his idea of what it means to be a Christian. However, at the same time, it expresses a fundamentally positive attitude toward real children. It is hard to imagine that he would have proposed positive associations with children if he held a basically negative view of children and childhood.

Clement's fundamentally positive attitude toward children is also mirrored in other texts. When he argues for the legitimacy of marriage under the rule of *logos or the principle of reason* he refers to what he apparently believed to be the experience of many people: that "childlessness is the most grievous experience of all."[23] For Clement it is self-evident that marriage was the only legitimate framework in which men and women should attempt to realize the deeply rooted desire to become parents. In subsequent argumentation Clement provides an explication of Matthew 28:20,[24] asserting, among other things, that "God through his Son is with those who responsibly marry and produce children."[25] Similarly, in another context where he discusses the goal and the law of marriage,[26] Clement condemns men who "escape from partnership in life with wife and children." This is, in fact, a sign of weakness that annuls God's will for future generations. One can argue for the obligation to give birth to children from different perspectives, as do several representatives of the Greek philosophical tradition to whom Clement refers. For Christians, however, it is regarded as sin against the Creator not to produce children. He argues that children represent a blessing to their parents, quoting with approval those Greeks who say that "the loss of children is one of the gravest evils." Clement then draws the conclusion that "the acquisition of children is a good thing."[27] Even the apostles Peter and Philip were married and produced children.[28] Although Clement's stress on the duty incumbent on married people to produce children must be seen as an expression of obedience to the will of God, as well as a concern for the nation as a whole, his references to other people's desire for getting children, and the way these are used in the argumentation, leave us with the impression of a positive attitude toward children.

All this makes it is clear that Clement applies the metaphor of childhood to Christians. With Christ as their *paidagôgos*, the life of religious discipleship is depicted in terms of imitating behavior associated with childhood.[29] Children, or behavior Clement associates with childhood, function as positive examples for adult Christians. Although Clement paints a picture of the child that emphasizes qualities fitting his program of transforming people to what he considered the proper understanding of Christian life, the very fact that he so frequently uses children as positive paradigms is striking. It is even more remarkable when we take into account the marginal position of children and the qualities associated with childhood in his cultural environment. Clement's positive use of children in his argumentation represents a novelty in the ancient world, where childish behavior was commonly used as a negative example.[30]

Origen

In general, Origen (185–253) adopts and develops the thinking of Clement. This is also true of the qualities he associated with children in his discussion of how children function as positive examples for adult Christians, although the metaphor of childhood and appeals to children do not play nearly so important a role in Origen's writings as in those of his predecessor at the catechetical school in Alexandria. In fact, the only writing in which Origen deals with the topic is his commentary on the Gospel of Matthew.

Like Clement, Origen explores the meaning of Jesus' words about becoming like a child. Clement asserts that children possess freedom from irrational desires, but this aspect is more emphasized by Origen. The basic characteristic of childhood is its lack of desire and this is why Jesus presented children as paradigms for adults. His first reflection on the subject is illuminating:

> If any who is a man mortifies the lusts of manhood, putting to death by the spirit the deeds of the body, and "always bearing about in the body the putting to death of Jesus," to such a degree that he has the condition of the little child who has not tasted sensual pleasures (*aphrôdisiôn*), and has had no conception of the impulses of manhood (*andrikôn kinêmatôn*), then such an one is converted, and has become as the little children. And the greater the advance he has made towards the condition of the little children in regard to such emotions, by so much the more as compared with those who are in training and have not advanced to so great a height of self-control, is he the greatest in the kingdom of heaven.[31]

We note that when the author here explores what distinguishes children from adults he first turns to lack of sexual desire. The expressions "sensual pleasures" and the "impulses of manhood" obviously refer to desires associated with sexuality. It is a child's freedom from sexual desire or its condition as an asexual human being that made it suitable to function as a positive paradigm for adults. It is scarcely by chance that he first focuses on children's lack of sexual desire: this reflects an increasing asceticism, which advocates the renunciation of sexual pleasure and marriage.[32]

After stressing the lack of sexual desire, Origen goes on to widen the perspective. What is true with respect to children's lack of sexual desires is also true of "the rest of the affections and infirmities and sicknesses of the soul, into which it is not the nature of little children to fall, who have not yet fully attained the possession of reason."[33] In subsequent statements the author explicitly names the actual desires absent in the soul of a child: anger and fear. Regarding lack of grief, he notes that a child "laughs and plays at the very time that his father or mother or brother is dead." However, one gets the impression that Origen feels somewhat ambiguous about the validity of his argument. After once more emphasizing his fundamental views on the condition on of children—that "no passion is incident to little children," including fear—he admits that children can express something corresponding to passions. But these are "faint, and very quickly suppressed, and healed in the case of little children."[34] With respect to fear, or more precisely what might be conceived as fear, he has observed that children show "a forgetfulness of their evils at the very time of their tears, for they change in a moment, and laugh and play along with those who were thought to grieve and terrify them, but in truth had wrought in them no such emotion."[35]

Another reason why Jesus exhorted his disciples to imitate children is because of their indifference toward status and wealth, things that adults "thought to be good, but are not." Children up to three or four years of age do not pay attention to the birth or the wealth of others when they relate to each other. Origen commends Jesus' disciple for having humbled himself like a little child: he writes that he was "not being exalted because of vainglory, nor puffed up on the ground of wealth, or raiment, nor elated because of noble birth."[36] Obviously, the lack of desire for status and wealth is one quality that distinguishes children from adults who not have yet been transformed into true Christians, that is, adults who still suffer from the "infirmities and sicknesses of the soul."

Origen's observation that lack of concern in matters related to status and wealth is limited to children of a certain age is interesting. Apparently, the condition of children is seen in a perspective of development from one stage to another. At birth, the child does not suffer from desire, and it continues to live in an existence free from desire until a certain age. The development of reason is analogous to the development of desire. The assertion that children "have not yet fully attained to the possession of reason" occurs once more in the course of Origen's discussion.[37] Obviously, both desires and reason, providing the ability or the choice to resist desires, are thought to develop as the child grows older.[38]

Does Origen hold that the faculty of reason is wholly absent in a little child, by analogy to its freedom from desire? G. Gould has rightly argued that this is improbable, because it would contradict the basic feature in Origen's anthropology that "the rational mind (*nous*) is the ontological core of the human person which pre-exists its entry into the body. The sense of the verb *pleron* must be the complete development, or complete manifestation, of something previously unexercised or hidden."[39]

At which age or period does the faculty of reason begin to manifest itself in children's life? At which age does the possession of desire arise? Origen does not consider this question in detail. However, the observation that children under three to four years are not subject to desire for wealth and status provides a hint. Normally, children who are three to four years old have learned to speak quite fluently. This suggests that Origen sees a connection between the development of the faculty of reason and the appearance of desire and the development of speech.[40]

OTHER EVIDENCE FROM THE FIRST TO THE THIRD CENTURY

The Apostolic Fathers

The association of children with simplicity and innocence also appears in the apostolic fathers, primarily in the Shepherd of Hermas. In *Mandates* 1-5 the author exhorts the readers to practice the virtues of faith, simplicity, fear of the Lord, and restraint. In this context he uses the nature of children as a positive paradigm: "He [God] said to me: 'Have simplicity and be innocent and you shall be as the children who do not know the wickedness that destroys the life of men.'"[41] Though the author is not speaking here of real children, the qualities he associates with children are interesting. He depicts the child as being free of evil, in contrast to the condition of adults. When he then elaborates the implications of this for the life of his readers, he emphasizes that they must abstain from slander and give to needy people.

In *Similitudes* 9.29.1–3 the author of the Shepherd of Hermas depicts his vision of an ideal church. Its members behave "as innocent babes," which implies that "no evil enters into their heart, nor have they known what wickedness is." Far from defiling the commandments of God, they have remained constantly in childlike innocence. He goes on to state that the members of his ideal church "shall live without doubt in the kingdom of God, because by no act did they defile the commandments of God, but remained in innocence all the days of their lives in the same mind." In the subsequent statement Hermas once more exhorts his readers to be as babes:

> All of you, then, as many as shall continue and shall be as babes, with no wickedness, shall be more glorious than all those who have been mentioned before, for all babes are glorious before God, and are in the first place by him. Blessed then are you who put away evil from yourselves, and put on guiltlessness, for you shall be the first of all to live to God.[42]

Obviously, when using the metaphor of childhood, Hermas reflects a view that associates childhood with a state of freedom from evil, of not behaving in opposition to God's commandments. He draws a picture of the nature of infants that underscores "the complete absence of any evil tendency in their hearts."[43] In positive terms, infants are described as simple and innocent, terms that also play a significant role expressing the ideal religious-moral character of the Christian.[44] Unlike the double-minded, those who are simple and innocent do the will of God with their whole heart.[45] In line with the use of the virtue of simplicity in the Septuagint and other Jewish writings, the term designates here the righteous ones who observe the commandments of God and have no other concern than to do his will.[46]

Accordingly, there are some basic similarities in the use of the metaphor of the childhood and the qualities associated with children between Clement of Alexandria and Origen on the one hand, and Hermas on the other. They all appeal to their readers to behave like children, whose nature or condition they present as free from evil. Though Hermas does not explicitly state that children are free from desire or passion, this is more or less implied in the conception of simplicity. We should note, however, that a focus on passion related to sexual behavior, characteristic for Origen, is not found in Hermas.[47] Furthermore, there is nothing in this writing that would indicate any interest or awareness of the question of the extent to which children share in *logos*.

The *Epistle of Barnabas* is also interesting here. When dealing with the relationship between the people of the old and new covenants he states, among other things: "Since then he made us new by the remission of sins he made us another type, that we should have the soul of children, as though he were creating us afresh."[48] We note that the author describes the renewal of the human being, thanks to the remission of sins, in terms of having the soul of a child. The context indicates that the "soul of a child" expresses the *imago dei* or image of God in the human being.[49] Does this text reflect the view that the child's soul is free from evil and desire? This may be reading too much into the text. There is, however, no doubt that the author makes a connection between renewal and the soul of a child.

The Gospel of Thomas

If we turn our attention to the Gnostic writing called the Gospel of Thomas (ca. 100–110)[50] we discover that it reflects a use of the metaphor of the child like that of Clement and Origen. In reply to the disciples' question about when Jesus will reveal himself, Jesus says that this will take place "When you disrobe without being ashamed and take up your garments and place them under your feet like little children and tread on them."[51] It is not clear how one should understand the different elements of this saying, but I find plausible the interpretation that the disciples are exhorted to transcend themselves by trampling underfoot the sinfulness of the old Adam.[52] This seems to imply among other things sexual abstinence or sexual purity,[53] thus reflecting the ascetic nature of the Gospel of Thomas in general.[54] If this is correct, the function of the metaphor of the child as a positive paradigm is associated with sexual purity. Further, Howard Clark Kee argues that the aspect of children's sexual innocence is implied in logion 4 as well, where Jesus says: "The man old in days will not hesitate to ask a small child seven days old about the place of life, and he will live. For many who are the first will become last, and they will become one and the same." Kee comments that such a little child is living in the perfect week, before the fall of Adam. According to this reading, Jesus exhorts adults to change into a condition of childlike asexual innocence, that is, into the prelapsarian existence of Adam.[55]

The Apologists

Aristides of Athens wrote an apology under the reign of Hadrian (117–138).[56] After a polemic against the religions of the barbarians, Greeks, and Jews in the most extensive first part of the *Apology* (1-14), in the shorter second part (15-17) he presents the Christian faith and way of living in contrast to such traditions. One element that distinguishes Christians is that "when a child (*parvulus*) has been born to one of them, they give thanks to God (*deum laudant*); and if moreover it happen to die in childhood (*naepion*), they give thanks to God the more, as for one who has passed through the world without sins (*sine peccato per mundum transivit*)."[57]

It has been argued that Aristides always uses the phrase "thanks to God" to describe Christian rites, and hence this is a reference to baptism. Consequently, the expression "without sin" would refer to the forgiveness of sins granted in baptism.[58] I find it more plausible, however, to understand it as a part of the polemic against pagans. In chapters 7 to 13 the author focuses on aspects of the behavior of Greek gods that he considered dreadful. Among other things he notes that Heracles became mad and killed his own children (10) and that the worshipers of Chiun (Saturn) practice the sacrificing of children and that "they burn some of them alive in his honour." A basic point in Aristides' argument is that the behavior of the gods serves to set the example for their worshipers, though this is not said explicitly with regard to the killing of children.[59] There is, however, no doubt that the killing of children is included among the outrageous actions of Greek gods and their worshipers. The widespread practice of exposure of children may also function as a backdrop to his statements. I believe that it is within this context we should understand his comment that Christians thank God for their children. In contrast to pagans who do not care for, and even kill, children, Christians value children and consider them a gift from the Creator. This implies that the reference to infants' sinlessness should be understood literally, that is, as referring to their innocent nature. Aristides presupposes that infants are in a state free from sin.[60]

Another Christian apologist from the second century seems to hold a similar point of view. In his treatise *De Resurrectione Mortuorum*, Athenagoras discusses the interrelation between the resurrection and a future judgment, and states that if the cause of the future resurrection is limited to a just judgment, "it would of course follow that those who had done neither evil nor good—namely, very young children—would not rise again"(14).[61] The fact that all are going to rise again, including "those who have died in infancy," functions as the ultimate proof for his argument that resurrection does not take place primarily for the purpose of future judgment, but will occur due to God's purpose "in forming men" (14). The point to note here is that the author depicts the moral condition of infants as neutral: they are neither evil nor good. It is implied that the infant is free from sin.

Irenaeus, Tertullian, and Cyprian

Irenaeus operates with a similar association between childhood and innocence. Dealing with the nature of Adam and Eve prior to the fall, he explains their absence of shame over their nakedness by referring to their "innocent and childlike" thoughts. This implies that "they had no conception or imagination of the sort that is engendered in the soul by evil, through concupiscence [literally 'pleasurable desires'], and by lust. . . . They *were not ashamed*, as they kissed each other and embraced with the innocence of childhood."[62] Though it is not correct to include Irenaeus among the ascetic writers of the early church, he obviously connects the innocence of children with their freedom from sexual desire.

Tertullian's objections to infant baptism in his homily *De Baptismo* (c. 200) are well-known.[63] In a key passage where he interprets Jesus' words that one should not forbid the children to come to him, he writes as follows:

> Let them "come," then, while they are growing up; let them "come" while they are learning, while they are learning whither to come, let them become Christians when they have become able to know Christ. Why does the innocent period of life (*innocens aetas*) hasten to the "remission of sins?" (*De Bapt.* 18)

Although Tertullian does not go into detail about the meaning of *innocens*, it is clear that he presupposes that infants have not sinned. This, however, does not entitle us to assert that Tertullian did not believe in original sin. In other contexts he is not hesitant to speak about the impact of Adam's fall on all mankind. J. N. D. Kelly has noted that "he is more explicit and outspoken about this sinful bias [of a vitiated nature] than previous theologians."[64] For example, in one passage in the treatise *De Anima,* he asserts that every soul is impure (*immunda*) until it is reborn in Christ.[65] It is not easy to grasp accurately the implications of this concept, but it appears to involve "a transmitted natural infection by sin." Hence, when he refers to the *innocens aetas* or innocent age he probably has in mind the infant's "lack of sins of his own commission."[66]

According to Tertullian, children's lack of sexual desire is a manifestation of innocence. This is evident from a passage in his treatise *De Monogamia*[67] where he refers to Christ's life and teaching in order to demonstrate the need both to teach and to practice chastity. In the first reference to his teaching, he quotes the logion that the kingdom of heaven is for children, and states that Jesus associates "with those who, even after marriage, are as children."[68] It is not clear which logion Tertullian has in mind here; perhaps it is an allusion to Matthew 19:12, which speaks of those who have "made themselves eunuchs for the kingdom of heaven."[69] It is, in any case, beyond doubt that Tertullian's use of the metaphor of childhood has a paradigmatic function because of their sexual innocence, or their absence of sexual desire.[70]

An African bishop of an unknown see, Fideus, questioned the practice of baptizing newborn babies. The case was discussed in a council of African bishops in the spring of 253. Cyprian wrote a letter in the name of the bishops, saying that he expresses the unanimous opinion of those who participated in the council.[71] According to this text, Fideus understood baptism as an analogy to the Jewish practice of circumcision, which took place when a boy was eight days old. Consequently he argued that the baptism of infants should be delayed until eight days after their birth. In addition to this theological argument against the current custom of baptizing newborn babies, he obviously thought that an infant was impure in the first days after its birth, which made people shudder to kiss it. He found it disgusting to perform the baptismal kiss required by the liturgy. We do not know whether others shared his view. At any event, the council of bishops objected to his position. The interesting point here is not primarily the fact that the letter confirms that infant baptism was an established practice in the North African church in the mid-third century, but the way in which the argumentation reflects opinions about the nature and value of childhood.

First, against the postponement of baptism because of the alleged analogy to circumcision, the letter emphasizes that "the mercy and grace of God must be denied to no man born (*nulli hominum nato misericordiam Dei et gratiam denegandam*)" (64.2.1). The subsequent argumentation is interesting. Cyprian refers to Jesus' words in Luke 9:56, "The Son of Man did not come to destroy men's life, but to save." He infers from this logion that the duty of the church is to be an instrument for the salvation of all souls, including those of newborn babies. Further, he provides a theological argument for this viewpoint: "For what is lacking to him who has once been formed in the womb by the hands of God? . . . Whatever things have been made by God have been perfected by the work and majesty of God, the Maker." The point is that because newborn babies are made perfect by God the Creator, one should not exclude them from God's gifts of mercy and grace. Cyprian develops this idea by affirming that the scriptures demonstrate the equality of the divine gifts given to both infants and older persons.[72] Because it is characteristic of the argumentation of the letter, I quote the conclusion at some length:

Thereby is expressed the divine and spiritual equality because all men are alike and equal since they have been made once by God (*illic aequalitas diuina et spiritalis exprimitur, quod pares atque aequales sint omnes homines, quando a Deo semel facti sunt*), and our age can have discrimination according to the world in growth of body, but not according to God, unless, indeed, grace itself as given to the baptized is considered greater or lesser according to the age of those who receive it, since the Holy Spirit offers to all, not according to measure, but according to love and fatherly mercy equal for all. For God does not make such distinction of person or of age since He offers Himself as a Father to all to obtain celestial grace with balanced equality.[73]

Cyprian's stress on the equality of infants and adults here is striking. It is self-evident that in social life there are differences between these groups of people, but this does not affect their fundamental equality. Rooted in the theology of creation, Cyprian depicts infants as complete human beings. His intention is to make clear that since the gifts of God—including baptism—are for all human beings, there is no reason for postponing the baptism of infants.

Cyprian's response to Fideus's refusal to kiss a newborn baby because he finds it unclean reflects a similarly strong theology of creation. No one ought to shudder at what God has decided to make. This is particularly true with respect to the newborn because it so clearly reflects God's creative work. Indeed, Cyprian says in embracing the freshly made creation of God, we kiss in a certain manner the hands of God himself.[74] It would be hard to find a stronger expression of the view that the newborn baby is a complete human being! In brief, infants and adults stand on the same level with regard to their ability to receive salvation. As David F. Wright puts it, "age makes no difference at all in the equality of the divine grace."[75]

In Cyprian's thinking, infants and adults are perceived as equal before God; they are all the objects of his salvific gifts. Thus we can speak of an equality between infants and adults at the vertical level. But what about equality on a horizontal level, that is, among human beings? Cyprian does not explicitly state that he regards infants as equal in value to adults in the social fabric of life. Furthermore, he does not elaborate on the consequences of his theological thinking about the place and role of children in society. Though one might regret this lack, it is understandable when we keep the purpose of the letter in mind. Nevertheless, embedded in the way he incorporates the state of infants into his theology of creation is the implication that infants and adults are of equal value. It must be underscored that this is the case on the level of theological or anthropological principles. There is no necessary connection between this principle and the question of how infants and children were treated in society. The only logical implication of Cyprian's argument is that he does not distinguish between the value of infants and adults. Both groups are seen as complete human beings designed by God.

As we have seen, Cyprian's theological mentor, Tertullian, used the innocence of childhood as evidence to oppose the practice of baptizing infants. What position does Cyprian take regarding the question of an innocent nature in children? On the basis of his strong support for baptizing newborn babies, one might expect that he did not share Tertullian's views on this point. Although Cyprian in fact basically shared Tertullian's opinions regarding the nature of children, he employs this position in a totally different manner in the discussion of infant baptism. He clearly takes it for granted that a recently born infant has not committed any sins on his or her own account. According to this opinion, the child is innocent. However, because the infant is "born carnally according to Adam, he has contracted the contagion of the first death from the first nativity" (Ep. 64.5). In other words, the newborn child is affected by the fall of Adam. It is not unreasonable to assume that Tertullian would have approved Cyprian's thinking that infants are affected by Adam's fall. What distinguishes them sharply is that Cyprian links belief in original sin with the perception of the innocence of infants and, as indicated above, employs this position as an argument against postponing the baptism of children. Because it is not the infant's own sins that are to be remitted in baptism but another's, he or she receives forgiveness "more easily." Arguing from the greater to the lesser, Cyprian reasons that infants should be taken to baptism no less than "the greatest sinners and those sinning much against God, when afterward they believe, the remission of their sins is granted and no one is prevented from baptism and grace" (Ep. 64.5).[76]

Later Writers, Especially John Chrysostom and Augustine

We have seen how Christian authors from the first to the third centuries provide some material that reveals the qualities or characteristics they associate with the nature of childhood; the most frequently discussed topics are children's innocence and their lack of desire. In the following two centuries, the question of the innocence of children continues to be a key issue among Western writers. This was certainly a major point in Augustine's controversy with the Pelagians. It is well-known that he argued that the original sin of Adam is transmitted through birth, that is, that the newborn baby inherited original sin. For this reason the baptism of infants was a necessary condition for salvation.

Although one can find indications of interest in the nature of the child, including attention to the question of innocence, there is a striking lack of interest in the subject among the Eastern church fathers. The focus in Clement of Alexandria and Origen upon the paradigmatic function of children, and the qualities they associated with children, appears almost idiosyncratic. The reason for this is obscure, but the lack of interest may be connected to the fact that Eastern theologians were not particularly concerned about infant baptism in general, and did not link infant baptism with the question of the nature of the child in particular.[77] This does not mean, however, that our sources lack any information relevant to our topic. As a matter of fact, it was in this period that writings primarily related to children and childhood emerged for the first time in the history of Christianity. Although the focus has changed, the sources contain material relevant to our topic. As indicated in the introduction, among the Eastern fathers it is John Chrysostom who provides the most extensive and relevant discussion for our purpose; for this reason it is natural that I pay most attention to him. However, I shall begin with one of his contemporary theologians, Gregory of Nyssa (died c. 395).

Gregory of Nyssa

In his treatise *De Infantibus qui Praemature Abripiuntur* Gregory of Nyssa deals with the problem of evil from one particular angle, namely what one is to make of the premature death of infants.[78] A central issue is what happens to them after their death, and why God accepts their deaths or even causes newborn babies to die. Gregory is struggling with the classical problem of combining belief in divine justice with the idea that everything that happens is dependent on God's will. What is one to make of the fact that, in a world where everything happens in accord with the divine will of a righteous God, the lives of some human beings are prolonged into old age, while others suffer and die as infants, "the moment of whose birth almost coincides with that of their death,"[79] without having any possibilities to share in any of life's pleasure?[80] In view of the high death rate of infants, it is not surprising that Gregory felt challenged to reflect theologically upon this issue.

Gregory considers this question in the framework of a general understanding of the nature and destiny of the human being. Made in the image
of God, human beings are destined to participate in the nature of God.
He writes: "In our partaking of God there should be some kinship in the
constitution of the partaker with that which is partaken of."[81] All creation
is divided in two parts, an intelligible or immaterial (*noetos*) sphere and a
sensible or a material (*aisthêtos*) sphere. Angels and other spiritual beings
belong to the first category. Human beings are unique among all God's
creatures in the way that they belong both to the immaterial and the material world. Their ultimate purpose, shared with all immaterial beings, is to
glorify the Creator. Gregory writes: "The design of all that is being born,
then, is that the Power which is above both the heavenly and the earthly
universe may in all parts of creation be glorified by means of intellectual
natures, conspiring to the same end by virtue of the same faculty in operation in all, I mean that of looking upon God."[82]

In this life, however, human beings find that the soul has become
clouded by ignorance of the true good, so that they lose sight of the basic
purpose of life. Though Gregory is very reluctant to attempt an explanation of the origin of this ignorance,[83] he is more explicit when he describes
its grave consequence. Ignorance is the reason the soul no longer par-
takes in God, so that it ceases to live, a condition described as "the worst
of evils."[84] There is, however, still a possibility open to a human being to
achieve participation in God and accomplish its purpose in keeping with
the will of the Creator. A human being faces the fundamental option of
either devoting himself to the painful struggle to achieve virtue in order
to purify himself of ignorance, or of being overpowered by the pleasures.
Those who choose the first alternative will receive life in God, while those
choosing the latter are denied a share in the divine life. The thought that
God is going to recompense the individual human being in the future
judgment plays a fundamental role in this treatise. Gregory emphasizes
that one's eternal fate depends on the individual's effort to live a virtuous
life in accord with the teaching of the Gospels. "There [the Master] says,
the acquisition of the Kingdom comes to those who are deemed worthy of
it, as a matter of exchange. 'When ye have done such and such things then
it is right that ye get the Kingdom as a reward.'"[85] A presupposition for
such thinking is that human persons possess free will. We may indeed say
that free will constitutes the basic feature of what it means to be created in
the image of God.[86]

In his application of this line of thought to individuals who had died
as infants, Gregory faced difficulties. For an infant who dies cannot have

done either good or evil that would deserve any reward or punishment in a future life. Those who died in infancy were not capable of laying "in this life any foundation, good or bad" that could be an object for God's retribution.[87] This presupposes that the infant is innocent in the sense that it is free of sin.[88] Gregory presents four interrelated objections to the view that those who died in infancy will receive from God the same reward as those who have struggled to live a virtuous life in agreement with the will of God.[89] (1) This would be against justice. "How is justice apparent in such a view?" Here justice might refer to both justice in general and the justice of God in particular. When the premise is that the kingdom of God is for those who deserve to enter it on the basis of a life lived in accordance with the utterances of the Gospels, it is not consistent with the justice of God to include those without such qualifications. (2) If those who died in infancy received the same reward as those who had laid a good foundation, it would be a happier thing to die in infancy than to live a longer life, since the latter always involves facing the hard struggle to purify the soul from its pollution of evil and to achieve virtue, or else facing judgment by God after death on the basis of a life of sin. (3) If those who died in infancy are included among the good or the blessed, it necessarily follows that "a state of unreason is preferable to having reason." We note that Gregory here reflects the view that infants lack reason, and that he presumes that a person's potential for moral and religious behavior is connected to the possession of reason. It seems that the absence of the faculty of reason is one reason why he depicts infants as neither bad nor good. Unfortunately but understandably, he does not provide any further hints about his understanding of the development of reason in a child. (4) The fundamental objection, implied in the others, runs as follows: "virtue will thereby be revealed as of no value: if he who has never possessed it suffers no loss, so, as regards the enjoyment of blessedness, the labour to acquire it will be useless folly."[90] The acceptance of the view that infants are classified among the good is, in other words, a serious threat to a basic element in Gregory's entire theological thinking.

After having opposed the view that those who die in infancy are to receive the same reward as the good, Gregory presents his suggestion regarding their eternal fate. Because infants had neither the time nor the capacity to live a life of virtue or of sin, they must expect to be classified in a position between the good and bad. "In the future life they must be content with a gradual growth in knowledge of and participation in God until they are ready to receive the full reward."[91] Gregory emphasizes, however, that this existence is much preferable to that of those who have lived their

life in sin, since for these sinners "the chastisement in the way of purgation will be extended into infinity."[92] Though Gregory here and elsewhere
talks about eternal punishment and an eternal estrangement from God,
this should be understood as an overstatement serving to emphasize his
argument. Like Origen, he advocated the doctrine of *apokatastasis*, that is,
that a universal restoration will take place at the end.[93]

This relatively long detour has permitted Gregory to establish a theological framework. Now he returns to his original question: Why do some
pass away in their infancy while others are allowed to grow up? One thing
is self-evident: because everything that happens in this world is made necessary by God's will, everything must have a purpose and a deeper meaning.[94] It is not those cases where infants are done away with by evil parents,
that is, infanticide or *expositio* (child exposure), that causes the problem:
God will surely punish such "unholy deeds." The problem emerges when
infants whose parents have nurtured and taken care of them die. Why
does this happen? Gregory's answer is that God in his foreknowledge sees
what is best for the infant. More precisely, certain infants have an particularly strong evil disposition, and in his love for humanity, including the
infant, God withdraws them from life before they are able to carry out
their sinful deeds. The "far-seeing Providence of God curtails the immen-
sity of sins in the case of those whose lives are going to be so evil."[95] This
implies that the infant's soul is put in a far better position in the future life
than would have been the case if God had allowed it to grow up. The early
death is an expression of God's love and care. Also, this solution of the
problem is consistent with Gregory's fundamental theological axiom that
God's ultimate purpose in the creation of human beings, and thus their
true good, is that they are to participate in him. In other words, the death
of infants ought to be understood as an expression of God's care for their
souls.

It appears that Gregory believes that there is a connection as a rule
between the lives of parents and the moral disposition of their offspring.
He argues that scripture clearly teaches "us that the tender care shown
by God to those who have deserved it is shared in by their successors."[96]
Experience, however, shows that parents who live virtuous lives may lose
their offspring in infancy. This implies that the infants of good parents
could be born with a disposition to sinful lives. Though Gregory admits
that "our reason in this matter has to grope in the dark," he plainly states
that even if there is no evil among the ancestors, "it is not unreasonable to
conjecture that *they* [those who die in infancy] would have plunged into a
vicious life with a more desperate vehemence than any of those who have

actually become notorious for their wickedness."[97] Besides the fact that an infant's death is best for the child itself, Gregory argues that this also expresses God's kindness to pious parents. The logic is obviously that it is a lesser burden to lose a child than to see and realize its wickedness as it matures. Correspondingly, Gregory explains the fact that God allows the wicked offspring of ungodly parents to live by stating that he does not show the same kindness to them.[98]

Gregory clearly deals with the question of infants within a wider theological context. I have attempted to present here the main features in this theological framework and show how the particular issue of the treatise is related to it. What can we deduce from this with regard to the theme of our present investigation?

First, we note the simple fact that Gregory includes the topic of the death of infants in a theological treatise. Why? I believe that one reason is that the loss of newborn children occasioned grief and sorrow, and that his treatise should partly be viewed as an response to this experience. Although the thought that God permits some infants to die out of kindness to good parents appears harsh to a modern reader, it contains an element of comfort if one shares Gregory's presuppositions. In his foreknowledge, God provides what is best for the child with respect to its eternal destiny. There is nothing in the treatise that indicates a failure to empathize with and share the grief of parents. However, the primary reason for writing the treatise was the theological difficulties or challenges caused by the death of infants.

Second, on the level of creation, Gregory does not distinguish between infants and adults. All human beings are created in the image of God. God is concerned about the salvation of infants as well as adults. Though Gregory does not explicitly draw this conclusion, it is inevitably implied that in the sight of God, infants are basically equal in value to adults.

Third, Gregory does not discuss the extent to which children have passions, nor matters related to their moral development. This is understandable when we keep in mind that that the treatise is a response to difficulties caused by the death of newborn infants.[99] Nevertheless, a few statements are of interest for our purposes. He obviously reflects the view that infants are neither good nor bad. This implies that they are free from sin and innocent, presumably in the sense that they have not committed any sinful deeds. The "neutral" moral condition of infants presupposes that they have not inherited original sin from birth.

Finally, Gregory clearly condemns infanticide and may also intend to rebuke the practice of exposure of children.

John Chrysostom

As indicated earlier, John Chrysostom is the Eastern father who provides
the richest material on topics related to children. After he returned from
his life as a hermit in a desert cave to become first priest in Antioch and
then bishop in Constantinople, the highest episcopal see in the Christian
East, he devoted his care to the family and the domestic life of his congregation. Inspired by the ideal of monastic discipline, he attempted to
transform the life of Christians who lived in the city, insisting that the
highest Christian virtues were not limited to the life of monks but were
binding upon all Christians.[100] The formation or socialization of children
into a genuinely Christian life constituted a basic element in this transformation. His concern for the formation of children is especially reflected in
the educational treatise *De Inani Gloria*, in which he discusses how Christian parents living in the city ought to raise their children.[101] The treatise *Adversus Oppugnatores Vitae Monasticae* also contains much relevant
material, as do certain of his homilies.[102] Although a great deal of what
Chrysostom says is related to the upbringing and education of children
and will thus be dealt with in a later chapter, these writings also contain
information of peculiar value with respect to the nature and qualities of
children.

In one homily, Chrysostom expounds Jesus' words about the kingdom
and the children in Matthew 19:14. In what respects were children exemplary? He affirms:[103]

> And wherefore did the disciples repel the little children? For dig-
> nity. What then doth He? Teaching them to be lowly, and to tram-
> ple under foot worldly pride, He doth receive them, and takes
> them in His arms, and to such as them promises the kingdom;
> which kind of thing He said before also.
>
> Let us also then, if we would be inheritors of the heavens, pos-
> sess ourselves of this virtue with much diligence. For this is the
> height[104] of true wisdom; to be simple with understanding; this
> is angelic life; yes, for the soul of a little child is pure from all
> the passions. Towards them who have vexed him he bears no re-
> sentment, but goes to them as to friends, as if nothing had been
> done; and how much soever he be beaten by his mother, after
> her he seeks, and her doth he prefer to all. Though thou show
> him the queen with a diadem, he prefers her not to his mother
> clad in rags, but would choose rather to see her in these, than the
> queen in splendor. For he useth to distinguish what pertains to

him and what is strange to him, not by its poverty and wealth, but by friendship. And nothing more than necessary things doth he seek, but just to be satisfied from the breast, and then he leaves sucking. The young child is not grieved at what we are grieved, as at loss of money and such things as that, and he doth not rejoice again at what we rejoice, namely, at these temporal things, he is not eager about the beauty of persons.

Therefore He said, "of such is the kingdom of Heaven," that by choice we should practise these things, which young children have by nature.

This interpretation comes close to that of Clement of Alexandria and Origen. Children are exemplary because they are free of passion. Chrysostom does not, however, focus on sexuality, as Origen in particular did. When Chrysostom gives examples from his observation of children's behavior, he emphasizes that they are uncorrupted by worldly values. This is manifested in their indifference toward status, wealth, and poverty. Even though a child is beaten by a mother dressed in rags, it prefers to go to her instead of to a queen dressed in the most splendid clothes. Small boys do not, as he states in De Inani Gloria, "fight for wealth or glory." Children are moderate and not greedy. They let go of the nipple when they are full. When he explores why they function as positive paradigms, it is no coincidence that he emphasizes precisely children's lack of concern about matters of status and wealth. He regarded the quest for status and wealth, or for vainglory as he called it, as the root of the moral and social evils of society at large. He was also of the opinion that these vices represented a threat to the community life of the church. Vainglory, he says, is "bringing ruin on the entire body of the Church," and he thus exhorts parents to teach children "what is at the base of all evils, inculcate in them what are the most tyrannical lusts, I mean the love of money and—what is even more wicked—the love of vain and empty glory."[105] Children's lack of passions mean that they are unconcerned about issues related to status and wealth; hence they are paradigms of the Christian life. I must underscore that Chrysostom is thinking here of little children. Although we cannot draw any precise conclusion regarding their age, he obviously refers to babies who are breast-fed. It is more difficult to guess what he thinks about the upper limit of their age, but the description of their reaction suggests that the children he describes have reached a physical and mental development associated with children around one year old.[106]

Does Chrysostom assume children to be without sin? This seems to be the case; and this is confirmed elsewhere in his writings, most explicitly in the third catechetical lecture on baptism. Dealing with the benefits of baptism, he states: "Although many men think that the only gift it confers is the remission of sins, we have counted its honors to the number of ten. It is on this account that we baptize even infants, although they are sinless."[107] This passage was used by Julian of Eclanum to argue that John Chrysostom denied the existence of original sin. On the other hand, Augustine argued that the plural "sins" referred to personal sins (*propria peccata*); consequently, there would be no cogent reason to assert that Chrysostom denied original sin.[108] Although this argument in itself is reasonable, the wider context indicates that Augustine is wrong. In the preceding paragraph, Chrysostom has enumerated ten gifts of baptism including the forgiveness of sin. When he goes on to talk about the benefits of baptism for small children he does not mention deliverance from sins. The reason for this omission is that small children have no sins to forgive.[109] A statement in one of the homilies on the Gospel of Matthew also appears to presume that infants are without sin. He opposes the popular view that the souls of little children killed by sorcerers become the dwelling places of demons. Instead he says that the souls of the just are in the hands of God, and if this is the fate of the souls of the just, this is also the case for the souls of children, "for neither are they wicked."[110]

This does not imply that the descendants of Adam are unaffected by the consequences or penalties of his sin. Chrysostom interprets the "fall as an inheritance essentially of mortality rather than sinfulness, sinfulness being merely a consequence of mortality."[111] This understanding of original sin reflects a consensus among the Greek patristic writers and is to a great extent rooted in a reading of Romans 5:12, where, speaking of the Genesis story, Paul writes, "As sin came into the world through one man, and through sin, death, so death spread to all men *because all men have sinned*."[112]

While the theological interpretation in the Latin West, with Augustine as its major voice, underscored that sin and guilt are transmitted by Adam to all humankind, Chrysostom and the other Eastern theologians emphasized death as the penalty for Adam's sin, which is transmitted to all his descendants; sin is the inevitable consequence of death.[113] This understanding "presupposes a cosmic significance of the sin of Adam, but does not say that his descendants are 'guilty' as he was, unless they also sin as he sinned."[114]

It is within this theological context that we must see Chrysostom's reference to small children as free of passions and of sin. Infants and small children, who have not committed any sins, are not guilty of anything. Consequently, he can present their behavior as paradigmatic for adults. This might indicate a positive evaluation of children and childhood, where behavior associated with children is generally admirable. This is not, however, the case. As already noted, it was infants and small children he had in mind when he referred to the praiseworthy qualities of children's behavior in his interpretation of Jesus' logion about the children. Although the structure of the text quoted above is somewhat difficult to grasp, it appears that Chrysostom asserts that the child is not an example of the angelic life, which presupposes reason, "not just single-mindedness and freedom from distraction by desires. The unreasoning child is innocent; the adult must use reason to recover innocence."[115]

Chrysostom emphasizes the fact that children lack reason, and his reference to childlike behavior serves in general to illustrate the foolishness of adults.[116] A striking element in his *Homilia in Col.* 4 is his comparison of the behavior of the Israelites with the behavior of children, and the way he blames the conduct of the members of his audience by terming it childish. Their lack of reason means, among other things, that children are eager to take revenge and that they are moved by anger. "For nothing is so eager to revenge as a childish mind. For seeing it is a passion of irrationality, and there is much irrationality, and great lack of consideration in that age, no wonder the child is tyrannized by anger."[117] He then goes on to give evidence for this position. When children fall after having stumbled against a piece of furniture, their first reaction after having gotten up again is to "smite their knee for passion" or overturn the footstool. Obviously, the child has already learned to walk, but perhaps its stumbling indicates that it has not developed good skills in walking. However, children who have reached the age of about five might also accidentally stumble against a piece of furniture and respond angrily. He gives other examples elsewhere. Children strike adults passionately as if they were taking revenge.[118]

Another consequence of the lack of reason is that children are easily frightened. "For as with children, when having been frightened at anything not frightful, such as either a lock of wool, or any other thing of like sort, they are suddenly alarmed."[119] In order to cure this timidity, Chrysostom suggests that parents or the nurse should bring the thing to the child in order that he or she might touch it and learn that it is not dangerous.[120]

In brief, due to the lack of reason "all the passions are tyrannous in children (for as yet they have not that which is to bridle them [that is, reason]), vainglory, desire, irrationality, anger, envy."[121] Chrysostom draws a picture of children driven by strong, uncontrolled passions. Because he held that adult members of his congregation, especially wealthy ones, were driven by desire for honor and glory, he employed children in his argumentative strategy as negative paradigms for adults, and called the behavior of the adults childish. Clearly, this reflects a negative evaluation of children, or at least of their behavior.[122]

How should we then understand this attitude in relation to the positive attitude to children reflected in his interpretation of Jesus' logion about children? It might seem that he operates with two contradictory pictures of children, and this apparent ambiguity has caused B. Leyerle to assert that the positive evaluation "is at odds with the dominant tenor of Chrysostom's remarks."[123] According to her, we are presented with two basically different portraits of children, one positive and one negative. Taking into account the great number of writings from Chrysostom's pen, and the range of time over which they were composed, one should not be surprised if inconsistencies occur. The question is whether the positive and negative evaluations of behavior associated with children are mutually exclusive. In my opinion, it is imperative to consider the extent to which Chrysostom distinguishes among children of different ages. When he considers Jesus' logion about children and explores their positive paradigmatic function, he clearly has small children in mind, that is, babies; he seems also to envisage here those who have reached the age of at least a year. When he refers to children as negative examples, however, the behavior he cites indicates that he is thinking of somewhat older children, who cannot be classified as infants. In other words, though all categories of children lack reason, it appears that he distinguishes between infants and other children when it comes to the question of passion. Infants are free from passion, older children are not. Hence, Chrysostom does not present two contradictory pictures of the nature or qualities of children. Instead, he differentiates, on the one hand, between his portrait of the nature of infants and, on the other hand, his description of the nature and qualities of somewhat older children. The infant is free from the passion and the desire that are at the root of the inappropriate behavior of adult members of the church; accordingly he finds little children suitable as positive examples. He evaluates the nature and qualities of older children negatively, because they are driven by the same passions found in the adults who pose a threat to the community life of the church.

Chrysostom assumes a development from the admirable condition of innocence to a state in which older children are driven by passion.[124] He does not, however, explore the actual steps involved in such a development, nor does he state at which age passions and desire emerge. In *De Inani Gloria* 22 he suggests that desire takes root at about the age of fifteen, but in this context the term refers to sexual desire, that is, to a physical rather than to a psychological development. At the end of the treatise, it is said that desire, whether or not this refers to sexual desires exclusively, affects boys more than girls. The latter are more prone to "love of finery and excitement."[125]

Nor does Chrysostom explicitly discuss the emergence of reason in children. Clearly, however, he holds certain assumptions about the age at which children are intellectually mature enough to understand different kinds of religious ideas. In a homily on Ephesians 6:1-4, Chrysostom explores how Paul takes the intellectual level of children into account when he addresses them.[126] First Chrysostom notes that the "passage is very short, since children have a short span of attention."[127] Then, with respect to the content, he says that Paul does not speak about the kingdom to come because this is a subject too difficult for children; he restricts himself to speaking about what the child's soul wants to hear: "how to have a long life." Paul "simply gives them the Old Testament commandments . . . because he addresses the children on their own level."[128] Children have a limited level of reason, but those at a certain age are capable of understanding the notion of reward.[129]

What age does he have in mind? In *De Inani Gloria* 22 Chrysostom provides us with some indications. Among other things, he encourages parents to teach their children Bible stories that implant the idea of rewards at an early stage in the process of Christian formation. Obviously Chrysostom felt that reason had emerged to such an extent that children had the capacity to grasp the notion of reward. He does not mention an actual age, although clearly he has young schoolchildren in mind. This is evident from what he writes later on regarding the appropriate age for introducing certain subjects of the Christian faith, as well from his encouragement to lead the child by hand in church.[130] Among other things, he retells the story of Cain and Abel and gives advice about what aspect of the story parents should emphasize, as well as about which particular points children are to learn from it. Parents must attempt to make the "stories agreeable that they may give the child pleasure and his soul may not grow weary."[131] Because the terminology and the language of scripture could be difficult for children to understand, parents are recommended to retell the story in simpler language.[132] The Cain and Abel story teaches the children that God receives and honors those who bring him gifts and that he punishes those who offend him. Chrysostom advises parents to elaborate on the matter of punishment. "And do thou relate the punishment with much intensity and not simply that he heard God say: 'Groaning and trembling thou shalt be on the earth'; for the child does not understand this yet. But say: 'Just as thou, when thou art standing before thy teacher and art in an agony of doubt whether thou art to receive a whipping, thou tremblest and art afraid, even so did he live all his days, because he had given offense to God.'"[133] Clearly, Chrysostom believed that children of a certain age possess sufficient reason to let them understand the notion of reward. They can also learn the story of the raising from the dead. The fact that God raised Abel from death and received him into heaven gives parents the opportunity to teach the resurrection of the dead.

When the child has learned this story, the parents should introduce the story about Jacob and Esau. From this story the children are supposed to "learn to reverence and honor their fathers, when they see so keen a rivalry for the father's blessing," and to "despise the belly"—since the greed of the belly caused Esau to betray the advantage of his birth.[134] After the child has grown older he is ready for more fearful tales. Parents are recommended to teach "whatever stories are full of divine punishment" at the age of ten or eight, or less, but the child should not be introduced to the idea of hell before he is fifteen. An understanding of the New Testament and grace also belongs to this stage of development. From this it follows that children who are intellectually ready for the Cain and Abel story belong to the age group of six to eight. Furthermore, Chrysostom assumes that children are capable of devotion and that they can "pray with great fervor and contrition."[135]

The view that children are driven by passion does not imply a negative view of the possibility of change. Chrysostom is, in fact, a strong believer in the possibility of changing and molding children in a positive direction.[136] Positive development presupposes that parents pay sufficient attention to implanting desirable behavior in them, that is, to training the child's soul in virtue. Just as artists create paintings and statues, the task of parents is to "care for these wondrous statues of ours. . . . Sculptors, too, working in marble . . . remove what is superfluous and add what is lacking."[137] I shall return to the parental task of molding children in a later chapter. Here I confine myself to observing that the nature or condition of a child is malleable. The child is a statue in the hands of its parents. Another expression for his optimistic view of molding children is Chrysostom's comparison of the child's soul to a recently founded city.[138] Because the inhabitants have not grown up under the influence of a bad constitution, they are "very easy to direct." Therefore it is imperative for the rulers to establish appropriate laws and not least to give appropriate punishments if these are transgressed. So also with children: they are "very easily guided."[139]

Several times Chrysostom notes that the soul of the child is tender, and that the younger the child, the more tender it is.[140] Precisely this tenderness allows the child to be molded. Hence, he exhorts parents to discipline their sons "from the first." It is important to inculcate good precepts at an early age, because what is set firmly in this period of life will not be destroyed.[141] For this reason he exhorts parents: "Make use of the beginning of his [the child's] life as thou shouldst."[142] Unlike lawmakers, who are not concerned with instilling fear in people before they have grown up, but only after they have already been perverted, parents should begin to educate and mold the child from the earliest age.[143] Chrysostom never mentions any specific age at which the process of molding should begin, but one gets the unequivocal impression that he is speaking about young children. I suggest that he primarily has schoolchildren in mind. This appears to be the case in *De Inani Gloria*.[144] However, expressions such as "from the first" and "from the beginning" may indicate that a deliberate molding of the child should begin to take place from a considerably earlier stage.

In any event, it is beyond doubt that Chrysostom holds that children are receptive to formation and that they are easily influenced by good habits.[145] Children are so malleable that if the mother, tutor, and servant all pay attention to the child, it will take no more than few months to inculcate virtue. I quote the statement that reflects his remarkably optimistic view:

> And do not, I pray, think that this takes a long time. If from the first thou dost firmly lay on thy behests and threats and dost appoint so many guardians, two months suffice, and all is in good order and the habit is firmly established as his second nature.[146]

This firm belief in the possibility of correction is theologically related to the thought that all human beings are created in the image of God. In his homily on Ephesians 6:1-4 dealing with the responsibility of parents to educate their children in the discipline and instruction of the Lord, Chrysostom says that to implant Christian virtues in the children is to "reveal and beautify His royal image (for man is the image of God)." When parents educate their children in virtues that are attributes of God—such as gentleness, readiness to forgive, generosity, and love—they "reveal the image of God within them."[147] As I noted above, death is perceived as the punishment of the fall of Adam and sin is the inevitable consequence of death. This does not imply that the essential image of God is destroyed, but that the likeness to God and the potential to grow in this image have been considerably weakened.[148] However, Jesus Christ has healed and restored the human existence. "Christ by the very nature of being fully God and fully human invites a synergy of grace and human striving to purify the image and bring humanity into communion with the divine life."[149] Although the habit of sin still affects human existence and the individual human being, our capacity to reflect or reveal the divine likeness has fundamentally changed because of the life and work of Jesus. It seems, therefore, that Chrysostom's optimistic view of the possibility of correcting children and molding them in a way consistent with his Christian ideal presupposes his theological anthropology, in which the doctrine of *imago dei* is a basic element.[150]

Jerome

Jerome was asked to give his advice on the upbringing of girls dedicated to a life of virginity. His answer is contained in two well-known letters, to Laeta and to Gaudentius.[151] Here he touches on matters related to the nature and quality of children. By pretending to write to the little girl and not to her relatives, he states it is difficult to write to one he does not know, and who does not have the capacity to understand what he says. Jerome does not believe that "a child who is eager for cakes, who babbles on her mother's knee, and to whom honey is sweeter than any words" is able to grasp the teaching of the Bible and practice the virtue of self-control.[152] For this reason, he suggests that the girl (Pacatula) must read the letter when she gets somewhat older.

This does not mean, however, that the little girl lacks the capacity to learn other things. She has the capacity to learn the alphabet, grammar, spelling, and syntax (*Ep.* 128.1). Jerome also provides pedagogical hints and advice on how to teach small children these things. The girl should be given a set of little letters made of boxwood or of ivory (*Ep.* 107.4). After she has arranged them, the adult should disarrange them, and let her begin all over again. When she has done well one should offer her rewards of cakes, mead, or sweetmeats. She will work better if she hopes to get some bright bunch of flowers, some glittering bauble, or some enchanting doll. When she has finished the lesson she might relax by "hanging round her mother's neck, or snatch kisses from her relations" (*Ep.* 128.1). He does not mention the age of the child he is talking about, but seems to have a girl of four to five in mind.[153]

When she grows a little older and the faculty of reason has further developed, the girl must follow her parents to church (*Ep.* 107.7). Jerome does not mention any particular age, but later on he seems to imply that he thinks of a child of tender age (*Ep.* 107.8). In *Ep.* 128.3a he is specific about the age of the child. Here he states that "as soon as she is seven years old" she should begin to memorize and read the scriptures. At this age the child is capable of an extensive devotional life. She must rise in the night to recite prayers and psalms; she must sing hymns in the morning; at the third, sixth, and ninth hours she ought to participate in the prayers. Reading must follow prayer and prayer must lead to reading (*Ep.* 107.9). Jerome also recommends a certain order in which the child should study the scripture. She must begin with the Psalter, and then "gather rules of life out of the proverbs of Solomon" (107.12). Then she should gain the habit of despising the world by reading Ecclesiastes, before she turns to Job in order to learn the virtue of patience. She should go on with the Gospels, "never to be laid aside when once they have been taken in hand" (*Ep.* 107.12). Then she should read the Acts, the Epistles, the Prophets, the Heptateuch, Kings, Chronicles, Ezra, Esther. When all this is done, but not before, she may read the Songs of Songs, for then she will understand the spiritual meaning behind the fleshly words (*Ep.* 107.12). Obviously, at this age Jerome believes that reason in the girl has risen to a level that makes her capable of understanding the message of scripture, of integrating its commandments and prescriptions into her own life, and of practicing Christian virtue.

Although he does not emphasize this as strongly as Chrysostom, Jerome believes in the possibility of changing and molding children. "One of soft and tender years is pliable for good or evil; she can be drawn in whatever direction you choose to guide her" (*Ep.* 128.3a). It is therefore important to implant desirable behavior in the child when it is malleable. In this context, it seems that Jerome has in mind children seven years old. Nevertheless, the formation of children should begin earlier. When dealing with children of four to five, he emphasizes that the parents must not permit any lack of moderation that the child would need to renounce later on, for example, with respect to clothes and adornment.[154]

In these letters, we find no categorical statements about the nature of children and the qualities associated with children. The only exceptions to this are the already mentioned references to children of seven as capable of

good or evil. However, Jerome's advice on upbringing indicates that he assumes that small children must be guided to resist their desires, and habits
of restraint must be inculcated from earliest childhood. In this respect, he
echoes the position taken by Chrysostom, but not the latter's view on the
innocence of infants. Jerome seems to assume that infants are baptized
on account of sin.[155] When he teaches that parents are responsible for the
actions of their children, whether good or bad, he opposes the view that
"the children of Christians are liable for their own sins (reos . . . peccati)"
if they are not baptized, and "that no guilt (scelus) attaches to parents who
withhold from baptism those who by reason of their tender age can offer
no objection to it" (Ep. 107.6). It seems that Jerome indicates that infants
are baptized for their own sin, but in cases where baptism is withheld
from them, their parents become accountable for their sins.[156] However,
he restricts himself to the positive statement: "The truth is that, as baptism ensures the salvation of the child, this in turn brings advantage to the
parents" (Ep. 107.6). Here he reflects the view, stated even more firmly by
Chrysostom, that one's own virtue is not sufficient for salvation, but salvation depends also on the virtues of one's relatives.[157]

An interesting statement is found at the beginning of the letter to Gaudentius. Complaining over the difficulties of writing to a little girl who
cannot understand what he is going to say, Jerome quotes a famous statement of Cicero: spes in ea magis laudanda sit, quam res ("The potential in
her is to be praised, rather than the present reality").[158] Certainly, one must
remember that the little girl was dedicated to virginity and that Jerome is
discussing how to mold her in accord with the ascetic ideals associated
with this state of life; nevertheless, his words imply a negative evaluation
of childhood. The child is not valued for what she is, but is regarded as a
kind of raw material that has to be molded and shaped in way consistent
with certain adult ideals. His attitude toward children mirrors the opinion
that the child is valuable to the extent that it has potential to develop and
socialize into the adult world.

Augustine
Children in the Confessions
The Confessions (the most probable date is 397 C.E.) and writings related to the controversy with the Pelagians provide the richest evidence for
Augustine's view on children and childhood.[159] In the Confessions, he describes his own journey to God and considers his life in retrospect. He
tells his history, calls to mind and places before God certain events and
circumstances of his life that led him to God. Although it is written in the

form of a confession to God based on his personal experience, Augustine also includes material that he assumes to be universally true of the existence of human beings. He

> searches the human heart and exposes the predicament of weak, sinful, sensual, vacillating, hopeful, graced human beings, evoking their valiant and passionate search for truth, their fascination with beauty, their disintegration when they yield to temptation and sink back to their native darkness, their longing for happiness that will be found only in the satisfaction of the questioning mind and restless heart in God.[160]

By recalling particular events and circumstances in his own life that led him to Christianity, Augustine also intends to say something universal regarding the life of human beings in this world. This is particularly the case when he deals with his earliest years. Several times he comments that what he has been told about his earliest years by those who knew him then has been confirmed from his observations of babies and small children.

Following a common classical trope, Augustine divides the life cycle of human beings into six stages.[161] The first is the stage of infancy, which extended from birth until the child has learned to talk. He states that he does not know about the origin of his soul,[162] but he knows that he was welcomed by a tender care provided by God through his parents. They are seen as instruments of God's love and care, since "they wanted to pass on to me [Augustine] the overflowing gift they received from" him.[163] Tenderly he describes the very beginning of his life. He "knew only how to suck and be deliciously comforted, and how to cry when anything hurt my body, but no more."[164] When he had grown a little bit older he began to smile, at first in his sleep and then when he was awake. At first this fact seems banal, but we miss its meaning unless we realize that it was a commonplace in the ancient world that laughter distinguished human beings from animals.[165] As the months passed he started to express his needs by screaming and crying. When people did not obey him, either because he was misunderstood or because they did not want to be his servants, he "would take revenge on them by bursting into tears."[166] His remark that he has learned this by observing babies, from whom he has learned more what he was like in infancy than from his nurses, is a part of the strategy of establishing a universal conception of the nature of babies. He also emphasizes that he was made by God, and praises his Creator for his earliest days and infancy (*Conf.* 1.6.10). The statement that babies take revenge when they experience that their inappropriate wants are not satisfied is the first indication that, in spite of his tenderness toward babies and in spite of the fact that he praises God for his infancy, he thinks of babies as sinners.

Augustine explicitly expresses this view by quoting Job 14:4f. as biblical support for this opinion. Then he gives evidence from his own infancy. Because he cannot remember the actual sinful deeds, Augustine refers to his own observation of babies. Was the sin "that I cried so greedily for those breasts? . . . I have watched and experienced for myself the jealousy of a small child: he could not even speak, yet he glared with livid fury at his fellow-nursling. Everyone has seen this" (1.7.11). His greed for food in adulthood is taken as evidence of the fact that he sinned when he was an infant. Obviously, he sees his sins in adult life as anticipated in infancy. He emphasizes that there is no fundamental difference in the gravity of the sin with respect to whether it is committed by an adult or an infant. Such sins deserve equal rebuke. Since the infant is not able to understand anyone who reprimands him, "neither custom nor common sense" allows any scolding to be given (1.7.11). Without reason and language, little ones lack the prerequisites for understanding. Another reason for condoning the sinful behavior of babies cheerfully is that everyone knows that they will give these things up when they grow up. "This is clear from the fact that those same actions are by no means calmly tolerated if detected in anyone of more mature years" (1.7.11). This suggests that Augustine ascribes more accountability to the child as it grows older. Notwithstanding this insight, the basic conviction that "the minds of infants are far from innocent" endures. He elaborates this point when he concludes the passage dealing with the first stage of his life by applying to himself the words of the Psalmist that he was conceived in iniquity and his mother nourished him in her womb with sin (Psalm 51). Then he rhetorically asks: "Where was I, your servant, ever innocent? Where, Lord, and when?" The only sense of innocence in an infant is related to its physical weakness—that is, its inability to harm others (1.7.11). Perhaps Augustine alludes to the literal meaning of the term *innocentia*, "not harming."[167] The idea that the innocence of infants is limited to their lack of physical ability to commit evil deeds is reflected later on in his argument with the Pelagians, for example, when he states that although they are captured by the power of the devil because of original sin, "little ones have committed no personal sin in their own life."[168]

Although the main line of thought in Augustine's argumentation in the section dealing with the condition of infants is plain, there appears to be a certain inconsistency or obscurity about whether or not infants commit personal sins. On the one hand, due to their physical weakness they are unable to harm others. On the other hand, Augustine uses their greed for the breast and their jealousy to demonstrate their lack of innocence. Although well fed, they react with screaming anger at their fellow-nurslings who are in the greatest need of food. Perhaps this is merely symptomatic of their sinful dispositions. This did not eventuate in sin, because they were not able to carry out their purposes.

From the point of view of a modern autobiographer, the information Augustine provides about his infancy is strange. Instead of paying attention to what was particular to him, he mentions facts that the readers certainly will know are to be true about all babies. This banal observation reflects, of course, his aim of depicting the universal nature of infants from the earliest observable moment.[169]

The second stage of the life cycle is childhood, inaugurated by the achievement of speech. Or to say with Augustine, "I was no longer an infant who lacked the faculty of speech, but a boy who could talk" (1.8.13). This stage was considered to last until the child was fifteen years old. The ability to communicate his own wishes and to understand others introduced him to a rational world where he was increasingly accountable for his behavior. Now he would wade "deeper into the stormy world of human life" (1.8.13). His experience of harsh treatment and punishment at school, which he characterizes as torture, is an expression of this "stormy world" and reflects the view that language and reason increased the responsibility of the child to behave according to rules set by adults. For example, because he found no meaning in learning letters or because he simply preferred to play, his laziness was strictly punished. He does not question that "we were blameworthy, because we were less assiduous in reading, writing and concentrating on our studies than was expected of us" (*Conf.* 1.9.15). Apparently, he takes it for granted that the faculty of speech and the increasing development of reason made children capable of responding adequately to the rules set by adults and also made them responsible for their deeds. He was now a sinner who deserved punishment. To use the words of Mary Ellen Stortz, "With childhood came rebuke and punishment as the child trespassed boundaries created by language and policed by adults. The non-innocence of infancy that resided in a grasping insatiability beyond all physical need phased into increased accountability. Language introduced the difference between obedience and disobedience, for which a child was accountable."[170]

Although he accepted that children needed punishment, Augustine obviously found the punishment meted out to him too harsh and brutal. He and his classmates were as terrified of it as of torture. His introductory comment to the passage dealing with his experience from school could be taken as a heading for the whole section: "Ah, God, my God, what wretchedness I suffered." He also notes that adults operated with a double set of standards regarding punishments; this point signals his critical attitude. Adults punish school children while behaving in the same fashion themselves:

> We were punished by adults who nonetheless did the same themselves. But whereas the frivolous pursuits of grown-up people are called "business," children are punished for behaving in the same fashion. . . . Moreover, was the master who flogged me any better himself? If he had been worsted by a fellow-scholar in some pedantic dispute, would he not have been racked by even more bitter jealousy than I was when my opponent in a game of ball got the better of me? (*Conf.* 1.9.15)

In another writing, Augustine comments that while sins, thefts, lies, and false oaths are common in childhood, children should not be punished as severely as adults.[171] Besides its implicit disapproval of the harsh punishment of children, this passage is interesting because of the reason he gives for this view. He asserts that "as reason begins to take hold" the capability to understand God's precepts relating to salvation increases as well as children's willingness to obey them. Clearly, Augustine presumes a potential for a positive development in children with respect to their ability and willingness to obey the will of God. This is linked to the faculty of reason, which enables more mature children to see the rationale behind the precepts. This may underlie his criticism of harsh punishment of children, although this is not explicitly expressed. In the *Confessions*, Augustine stresses the sinfulness of children, and it does not serve his argument to include any positive expression of belief in the moral development of children. In fact, as we shall see later on, he underscores that the gravity of sins will increase as the child grows up to adulthood.

Augustine's attitude toward study changed during his time at the secondary level, the so-called "grammar school." Augustine was about twelve when he started this study in Thagaste, and was about fourteen when he went on in the neighboring town of Madaura (2.3.5). When he started to read books and practice the art of rhetoric, he began to love his studies and threw himself into them deeply, though there was no change with respect to the harsh discipline. He was an excellent student, and reports that he got a lot of praise and was admired for his rhetorical skills (1.17.27). From the perspective of his later Christian position, he does not value this positively. Although he does not discredit the usefulness of learning words and rhetorical skills, the pagan contents of the readings and exercises made this empty and even corrupting.[172] As a matter of fact, Augustine's commitment to the goal of such study, that is to say, to educate the students for success and honor in this world, and his great efforts to gain praise from his teachers, are now regarded as "the whirlpool of disgraceful conduct" far from the Lord's sight. According to Augustine, in God's eyes no one could be more debased than he was (1.19.30).

The very people whom Augustine attempted to please disapproved of him, because of the many sins he committed against them. He mentions his countless lies to the slave who took him to school, to his parents and teachers, and his stealing from his parents' kitchen. He tended to dominate when he played with other boys because he himself was dominated by a vain urge to excel. He refers to his unwillingness to excuse things he severely condemned in others, and the tendency to lose his temper. Presumably the world regarded these things as childish peccadilloes, which need not be taken seriously because nothing of great value was at stake.[173] However, Augustine is of the opposite opinion. "Is this boyhood innocence?" His answer is emphatic: "Lord, it is not; hear me, dear God, it is not." He emphasizes that the gravity of the sins will increase as the child grows up to adulthood:

> The same sins grow worse as we grow older: first it is offenses against pedagogues and teachers, or cheating over nuts and balls and sparrows; then later it is crimes against prefects and kings, and fraud in gold and estates and slaves, just as a schoolboy's canings are succeeded by heavier punishments. (1.19.30)

In other words, there is a continuity of desire between children and adults. The only difference is a change of objects, that is, in which ways the desire is manifested in actual sins.[174] Augustine's main purpose seems not to be to mark disapproval of the sins of his adult readers, although of course this is involved, but to amplify the point that children are sinners. Although the actual sins committed by adults and children are different, it is the same nature, the same desire, that causes these sins. When it comes to the question of nature there is no difference between children and adults. No one is innocent. "The child who cheats at a game to win some marbles does the same thing, according to the capacities of his age, as does the adult who cheats his fellow out of a vast estate."[175]

In line with this understanding, Augustine interprets Jesus' words about children by limiting their paradigmatic function to their physical condition. "It was only the small stature of a child that you mentioned with approval as a symbol of humanity, O Lord our king, when you declared that of such is the kingdom of heaven" (1.19.30). This reference to Jesus and the children is rather abruptly introduced. In view of the traditional understanding of this passage that ascribes innocence to children, he presumably feels a need to clarify that his argument does not imply any inconsistency with the words of Jesus. When he restricts children's paradigmatic function to their physical weakness and powerlessness, he gives this biblical passage a new interpretation without identifying it as such.[176]

In spite of this, he concludes the section dealing with his childhood by giving thanks to God for being created in his image. Even then he (1) had being (*eram*), (2) had life (*vivebam*), and (3) was capable of experience (*sentiebam*). These were understood as created images of God's trinitarian nature.[177] Each of these interrelated goods sought its own proper good.[178](1) He had an instinct to keep himself safe and sound, an instinct for self-preservation. (2) He had an inner sense that watched over his bodily senses. (3) Even in the little things that occupied his thoughts he found pleasure in the truth. He did not like to be wrong, he had a good memory, he was acquiring the command of words, he enjoyed friends, and he shrank from pain, ignorance, and sorrow. Augustine highly values these boyhood qualities. "In a living creature such as this everything is wonderful and worthy of praise" (1.20.31). He would owe his Creator gratitude even if it had been his will that Augustine should not survive his childhood. He thanks God for all the good gifts that made him what he was, even as a boy. However, Augustine misused the gifts of God. Instead of seeking the proper good in God who had made both him and his gifts, he sought pleasures, beauty, and truth in himself and other creatures. This misdirected search, his orientation toward created things instead of the Creator, the *summum bonum* or highest good, constitutes Augustine's fundamental sin (1.20.31).

The next stage of the life cycle according to the traditional division is *adolescence*, the stage from puberty until early adulthood. Augustine deals with this stage of development in the second book. He recalls the pride of his father, Patricius, when he observed clear signs of Augustine's virility at the baths when he was sixteen years old. He was happy to tell his

wife about it, but for her it was alarming news. She feared unchastity.[179]
Augustine speaks quite frankly about his sexual awakening and desires,
which caused him to break God's law. He sets the tone in the introduction: "Now I want to call to mind the foul deeds I committed, those sins
of the flesh that corrupted my soul. . . . There was a time in adolescence
when I was afire to take my fill of hell. I boldly thrust out rank, luxuriant
growth in various furtive love affairs; my beauty wasted away and I rotted
in your sight, intent on pleasing myself and winning favor in the eyes of
men" (2.1.1.).[180] Instead of being overpowered by sexual desires, he argues
that man must overpower and control these desires, either by restricting
their outlet to legal marriage for the purpose of producing children only,
or by total chastity.[181] As an adolescent he did the opposite: "I swept across
all your laws. . . . Where was I, and how far was I exiled from the joys of
your house in that sixteenth year of my bodily age, when the frenzy of lust
imposed its rule on me, and I wholeheartedly yielded to it? As lust it was
licensed by disgraceful human custom, but illicit before your laws" (2.2.4).
When he considers this period of his life in retrospect, Augustine focuses
on his unregulated sexual desires and emphasizes that this lack of control
was sin. This does not mean that youth is captured by fleshly desires. If he
had listened more attentively to the Word of God in scripture, he might
have found the strength to resist. Furthermore, his criticism of his parents
for allowing him to behave as he did implies that Augustine believes that
an adequate Christian upbringing contributes to the restraint of sexual
desires.[182] These facts suggest that a youth has the capacity to control his
sexual drive, provided he receives the right guidance.

It is not, however, sexual desires and sexual sins that Augustine is most
concerned about when dealing with his adolescence, but such an apparently trivial thing as a theft of pears. One night Augustine and some friends
went to a pear tree close to his parents' vineyard and stole some of its fruit.
He reports that they took a great number of pears, not to eat themselves,
but to throw them to the pigs. This story serves as a starting point for a
lengthy discussion of the gravity of this sin and what caused him to commit it. Among other things, he asserts that it brought him to "abysmal
depths" and even implies that the theft of pears was worse than the cruel
crimes of the Roman patrician Catiline, who, according to Sallust's history, tried to set fire to Rome and initiate rebellion throughout Italy just for
the purpose of acquiring an office and money to pay off his debts.[183] There
was thought to be no proportion between his deeds and his aim. Hence
Sallust considers Catiline to be, by preference, vicious and cruel without
reason,[184] and by Augustine's day Catiline was regarded as the archetype

of vicious and blind cruelty. Some see the comparison with Catiline as an expression of Augustine's hyperbolic style. "Rum thing to see a man making a mountain out of robbing a pear tree in his teens."[185] This, of course, presumes that the incident was insignificant. It is quite natural and common for boys to do such things for the sake of excitement. Augustine would certainly disagree with this: it is precisely because it is natural, and not commonly regarded as serious by people in general, that Augustine includes it in his *Confessions*. It serves his purpose of illustrating not only his own moral condition, but the moral condition of people in general. Another reason for choosing the theft of fruit as a starting point for his deliberation on the moral condition of man is the apparently intentional allusion to the fall in Genesis 3.[186]

What does the pear-tree episode reveal about Augustine's moral condition in his adolescence? He emphasizes that it was not hunger or lack of food that caused him to rob the pear-tree; nor did he seek any advantage from it. It was because he felt satisfaction from the theft itself. In the introduction to this incident he writes: "I already had plenty of what I stole, and of much better quality too, and I had no desire to enjoy it when I resolved to steal it. I simply wanted to enjoy the theft for its own sake, and the sin" (2.4.9). When he goes on to discuss the motive and his understanding of the incident he returns to this idea and emphasizes it several times. Normally, he says, when there is an inquiry to discover why a person has committed a crime, one is not satisfied until it is clear that the motive is related either to the desire of gain or to the fear of losing things considered to be good. Even the evil deeds of Catiline had a purpose, according to Augustine, since he intended to use the crime for the training of his young conspirators. He did not love crime for crime's sake, but for the advantage he aimed to gain by committing this evil deed. In contrast, Augustine stole the pears with no purpose of gaining any advantage in the future. He stole the fruit because he loved the sin itself. "I feasted on the sin, nothing else, and that I relished and enjoyed" (2.6.12).[187] This knowledge led him to see this apparently trivial incident as implying such tremendous consequences that he burst out: "What rottenness, what a misshapen life! Rather a hideous pit of death" (2.6.14). Naturally, this harsh judgment implies that he broke the divine law,[188] but he also broke "the law written in human hearts" (2.4.9). The latter implies that though he did not pay attention to the Christian teaching at that time, he and his friends knew that they were doing wrong. They deliberately disobeyed a divine law present in man as a part of his very nature. Because adolescents know the difference between right and wrong even before they are told about it by adults, and possess the reason to behave properly, young people bear greater responsibility for their behavior.[189] In his adolescence, Augustine was a sinner who needed to repent and find rest for his soul.[190]

Infants in the Pelagian Controversy

A basic concern for Augustine in the two first books of the *Confessions* is to argue that the child is a sinner from the day of his birth. This issue constituted a central element in the controversy with the Pelagians, which broke out in the second and third decades of the fifth century. During this controversy Augustine was challenged to consider, among other things, the anthropology of infants in more detail. Although his basic position, as found in the *Confessions*, remains unchanged, it is of interest to trace the main lines in this controversy to get a fuller picture of his theological anthropology of children, and of the theological concerns that were at stake.

The debate centered on the relation between God's justice, power, and goodness and human freedom. A main concern for Pelagius and his companions was to construct a theology that avoided all forms of divine determinism, in particular Manichaeanism.[191] God has given free will to human beings, including the possibility of fulfilling his commandments. Pelagius argues that if one holds that God imposes upon human beings commandments that they are not capable of bearing due to their weakness or sin, this means ascribing injustice to the Just One. A passage from his letter to *Demetrias* illustrates his theological thinking on this point.[192] It is also characteristic of his struggle against determinism.

> It is God himself . . . who sends us his holy scriptures and the writ of his own commandments truly worthy of our worship, and yet we fail to receive them at once with joy and reverence. . . . On the contrary, with a proud and casual attitude of mind, in the manner of good-for-nothing and haughty servants, we cry out against the face of God and say, "It is hard, it is difficult, we cannot do it, we are but men, we are encompassed by frail flesh." What blind madness! What unholy foolhardiness! We accuse God of a twofold lack of knowledge, so that he appears not to know what he has done, and not to know what he has commanded; as if, forgetful of the human frailty of which he is himself the author, he has imposed on man commands which he cannot bear. And, at the same time, oh horror!, we ascribe iniquity to the righteous and cruelty to the holy, while complaining, first, that he has commanded something

impossible, secondly, that man is to be damned by him for doing
things which he was unable to avoid, so that God . . . seems to
have sought not so much our salvation as our punishment! . . . No
one knows better the true measure of our strength than he who
has given it to us . . . nor has he who is just wished to command
anything impossible or he who is good intended to condemn a
man for doing what he could not avoid doing.[193]

We may not water down the capacity granted to every human being to
choose between good and evil, since a compromise on this point would
be at odds with the justice of God. Pelagius admits that the sin of Adam
affected the whole human race and not merely Adam alone, since we follow Adam's example; he opposes, however, any idea of the physical transmission of original sins, partly because of his understanding of Romans
5:12. The Latin translation he used read that "sin came into the world
[*introire*]" through one person. The literal meaning of *introire*, "to come
into," enables him to argue that sin "came to the world" (*advenire*) through
Adam and passed on to his descendants "by example or pattern."[194] Thus,
babies are not born with sin,[195] though they are not in same state as Adam
before the fall, because, unlike Adam, they do not posses the faculty of
reason.[196] If humans let themselves be guided and strengthened by the law,
by the examples of the holy men in the Bible, and by Christ, they will be
capable of willing and doing what is good.[197] Pelagius emphasizes several
times that this capacity for doing good reveals the goodness of human
creation.[198] Furthermore, he was a strong believer in the transforming and
re-creating power of baptism, which brings to perfection the gifts humans
have been given in creation and by revelation, and makes them capable of
living without committing sins.[199]

The issue of the transmission of sin and its effect on children was
pressed by Caelestius[200] and in particular by Julian of Eclanum, "the
sharpest opponent he [Augustine] had ever confronted."[201] Unfortunately,
Julian's two major theological works are preserved only as fragments in
works by Augustine. Like his Pelagian predecessors, Julian was concerned
to refute all varieties of "Manichaean profanity" and determinism.[202] Julian argued that those who advocated the doctrine of original sin pre-
sumed the hypothesis of Traducianism—that soul is begotten from soul
as body from body, thus linking the soul to the male seed.[203] This, Julian
claims, resembles the teaching of Mani.[204] Against the view that the soul
is associated with the sperm, Julian advocates a creationistic position: the

soul is created by God and then united with the body. The implication is, of course, that the baby is born without inherited sin.[205]

Julian stresses that the doctrine of original sin, which holds that it is transmitted to newborn babies, jeopardizes belief in God's justice. Is not God unjust if he condemns a baby "though it was created by him, [when] it contracted another's sin, without either knowing or willing it, from those parents whose sins had been forgiven [through baptism]"?[206] The thought that God should condemn innocents angers Julian, for it would imply that God is a criminal.

> Which God then do you accuse of this crime? . . . God himself, you say . . . is such a judge; he is the persecutor of the newborn; with bad will he hands over to eternal fire little ones who he knows could not have either a good or a bad will. After this statement which is so heinous, so sacrilegious, so lamentable, if we had sound judges, I ought to demand nothing but your excommunication. . . . You have abandoned religion, learning, and even the common sensibilities to the point that you regard your God as a criminal—something a barbarian would hardly do.[207]

A few years earlier, Pelagius had rejected Augustine's belief that infants who died without being baptized were not saved. Against this view, he maintained that he does not know where infants who die unbaptized go, but he is sure that they do not go to hell.[208] Those advocating the doctrine of original sin hand over the baby to the devil.[209] This doctrine is contradictory to a fundamental characteristic of God, his justice. In fact, Pelagius affirms that it is more foolish to believe in an unjust God, than it is to deny his very existence.[210]

Augustine's interpretation of Romans 5 constituted a basic element in his understanding of the human nature. His interpretation of Romans 5:12 was especially important. Against the view of the Pelagians, Augustine argued that this passage says that through Adam sin not only "came into" the world, but "penetrated it." The different interpretations are partly due to the fact that Augustine used a different Latin text. According to his version, Romans 5:12 says that "sin penetrated [*intrare*] the world." This reading suggests a radical view of the impact of Adam's sin on his descendants. Further, he argues that the phrase *in quo omnes peccaverunt*—in whom all have sinned—implies a physical transmission of original sin from Adam to his descendants. "Paul meant that all sinned in that man

[Adam], because, when he sinned, all were in him."[211] Although the little ones have not committed any personal sin due to their "great weakness of mind and body, their great ignorance of things, their utter inability to obey a precept, the absence in them of all perception and impression of law, either natural or written, the complete want of reason to impel them in either direction,"[212] they are corrupted by original sin, "by which they are held captive under the power of the devil." Consequently, it is imperative to baptize infants in order that Christ the redeemer might set them free from sin and incorporate them into his body.[213]

According to the Pelagians, this position jeopardizes human freedom and God's justice. Augustine was also much concerned about these issues, but he approached the problem in quite a different way. For him, the doctrine of inherited sin did not jeopardize God's justice. On the contrary, this doctrine was a precondition for upholding God's justice. Augustine argues that if infants were free of sin, one would have no way of accounting for their sufferings.[214] The logic is that sin leads to death and misery.

In Augustine's first anti-Pelagian writing, this argument is applied in the following way: "If the soul is not propagated, where is the justice that, what has been but recently created and is quite free from the contagion of sin, should be compelled in infants to endure the passions and other torments of the flesh, and, what is more terrible still, even the attacks of evil spirits?"[215] This argument reoccurs and is reinforced in his later anti-Pelagian writings. In the treatise *Contra Iulianum,* Augustine accuses his adversary of not taking seriously the many evils almost all infants suffer in this world and of having no reasonable explanation for the miseries of the little ones. If one does not ascribe original sin to infants, the inevitable inference is that God is not just. Suffering "would certainly not be imposed upon God's image under the just and omnipotent God, if those infants contracted no evils deserving punishment from their parents."[216] Augustine also includes birth defects in this scheme. He asks rhetorically, "Tell me, then, because of what wrong are such innocents [as infants are according to Julian] sometimes born blind and other times deaf?"[217] Later, he gives the following answer, which summarizes his thinking on this point: If the little ones "did not contract any evil from their origin, they would never be born with defects, even with those of the body." In other words, birth defects function as proof of original sin. The underlying premise of his reasoning is the idea that because God is just and good he would not punish anyone that did not deserve it.[218]

Augustine insists that the Pelagian position fails to explain the sufferings of infants because it does not ascribe sinfulness to babies. Or to make the same point in positive terms, the sinfulness of newborn babies is necessary, in order to offer a reasonable explanation of why they deserve to suffer. If they suffer without deserving it, the implication is that God punishes them without any reason. That is to say that God is unjust. This is exactly what Augustine accuses Julian of doing: "When you say that these miseries happen to the little ones without any sin, you really make God unjust."[219] However, this position is impossible because only justice and goodness can be ascribed to God.[220]

Augustine is concerned with the salvation of the little ones, and emphasizes that Christ died for them too.[221] He refers to several passages of the New Testament which say that Christ's salvific work was intended for all human beings. For instance, after having quoted the words of Paul that God demonstrated his love toward us by the fact that Christ died for us when we were sinners (Romans 5:8-9), he argues that if the little ones are not fettered by sin, then Christ did not die for them. The premise is that all those for whom Christ has died are guilty, otherwise there would be nothing from which to save them.[222] According to Augustine, the Pelagian position implies that little ones do not benefit from the death of Christ.[223] Similarly, if the little ones are not affected by original sin, there is no need to baptize them, since baptism provides remedies for sins. The grave consequence would be that they are excluded from the kingdom of God. "Why do you exclude from the kingdom of God so many images of God in little ones if they are not baptized, since they have done nothing evil?"[224] In fact, if one denies the existence of original sin, one exposes little ones to serious harm. Consequently, Augustine asserts, it is not he who is cruel to infants (as the Pelagians alleged because of his view that little ones who died without being baptized were not saved) but the Pelagians themselves.[225] Instead of leaving them in the power of the devil, Augustine exhorts his audience to

> speak for the babies all the more mercifully, the less they can do it for themselves. The Church habitually comes to the assistance of orphans in watching over their interests; let us all speak for the babies, all of us come to their assistance, lest they should lose their heavenly inheritance. It was for their sakes too that their Lord became a baby. How can they not be included in his liberation, seeing that they were the first who were found worthy to die for him?[226]

In spite of his attempt to convince his readers that it is his own position that in the deepest sense takes care of little ones who die unbaptized,

Augustine felt troubled by his conclusion. Early in the debate he speculated that they would suffer only "the mildest condemnation of all."[227] He does not discuss how a milder form of punishment might differ from a "normal" punishment, nor does he return to this question in other writings. This may be because it is difficult to combine the idea of different levels of condemnation with his criticism of the Pelagians' distinction between different levels of salvation for unbaptized infants. Given their position on the innocence of babies, the Pelagians asserted that babies are not to be baptized for the sake of obtaining salvation and eternal life, but for the kingdom of heaven. Against this position, Augustine argued that there is no intermediary place between the kingdom of heaven and eternal damnation.[228]

At one point Augustine wrote a letter to Jerome asking for advice on the possibility of combining belief in original sin with the creationist position he imputed to Jerome. Though what Augustine says is related to this particular position regarding the origin of the soul, the offense he felt at the view that little ones were condemned by God is apparent. "What kind of justice is it that so many thousands of souls should be damned because they departed from their bodies by death in infancy, without the grace of the Christian sacrament . . . when He [God] certainly knew that each one of them by no fault of its own would leave the body without the baptism of Christ?"[229] Jerome never answered.

Augustine explicitly states his uneasiness about his view in *Sermon* 294. He admits that the question is profoundly difficult and recognizes that his "powers are not sufficient to get to the bottom of it. . . . I cannot find a satisfactory and worthy explanation; because I cannot find one." His interpretation of scripture led him to the conclusion that unbaptized babies go to damnation, and he felt obliged to maintain this. He could not "condemn divine authority" and quotes Romans 11:33-36 as he often does when he faces a question that goes beyond the limit of his reason: "Oh the depths of the riches of the wisdom and knowledge of God! How inscrutable are his judgments, and untraceable his ways!" Ultimately, the damnation of unbaptized children is a mystery, and therefore cannot be given a logical explanation. However, because Augustine was convinced that his view on this matter was in agreement with God's revelation in the Holy Scriptures, he maintained it. Although he apparently felt that this doctrine was harsh, he never wavered from the view that little ones who died unbaptized were punished by God.

In addition to theological arguments, Augustine refers to the practice of the church. Infants, like adults, underwent the *exsufflatio*, a rite of exorcism conducted before the baptism took place. This implies that little ones, like adults, needed exorcism to be rescued from the darkness of the devil. "What does my exorcism work in that babe, if he be not held in the devil's family?" Augustine asks rhetorically.[230] His point is, of course, that infants are afflicted with original sin and need remission of sins through baptism in order to be reconciled with God.[231] He also takes the crying and struggling of babies when they are baptized as an expression of their original sin. Due to their condition, they resist grace.[232] He even takes the hurrying of mothers to church with their babies to baptize them as an argument that children need to be redeemed from the power of the devil.

We have seen that Augustine draws an ambiguous picture of childhood. On the one hand, he emphasizes that the child is from birth a sinner. Against the Pelagians, who asserted that the little ones are innocent with respect both to actual sins and to their nature, Augustine ascribed to infants an original sin inherited from Adam. In Augustine's boyhood, this universal human condition is manifested in behavior and deeds that seek pleasures, renown, and truth in things that belong to the created world instead of in the Creator. In his adolescence, this was manifested by unrestrained sexual desire and by the committing of sin without the purpose of gain, illustrated by the theft of pears. Though the infant has not committed any personal sin, Augustine tends to take babies' greed for the breast and their jealousy as manifestations of their sinful nature. It is hard for a modern reader to agree with his explanation and evaluation of children's behavior. What we tend to regard as signs of development, Augustine takes as evidence of the sinful nature of the child.[233] His view that assigns little ones who die unbaptized to eternal punishment also sounds harsh to modern readers, and might be invoked (as the Pelagians did) as evidence of a hostile attitude toward children.

On the other hand, Augustine's apparently negative view is balanced by an attitude that acknowledges the value of children, in whom Augustine finds that "everything is wonderful and worthy of praise." Although this appraisal is related to the fact God has provided children with the gifts that enable them to seek and find him, so that they thus realize the ultimate purpose of life, it also reflects a striking recognition of the value of children. Likewise, the description of infants and children in his *Confessions* reflects warm sympathy with how they experience life. Perhaps more importantly, Augustine's deep concern about the salvation of children, for which baptism was a precondition, indicates that he regarded children as full and worthy religious beings who need the same spiritual nourishment as adults. However, I can find no connection between this expression of concern for the well-being of the child's soul and the status and role of children in social life.

Furthermore, Augustine considers children as subjects with responsibility for their moral behavior. He depicts an increasing accountability as they mature and their abilities to speak and to reason develop. Because babies lack speech and the faculty of reason, there is no point for adults to rebuke them. But when they reach the age when they learn to speak and reason develops, the conditions for knowing and understanding what is right and wrong gradually emerge and children become increasingly responsible for their moral behavior. When children reach adolescence, their abilities to speak and reason are so developed that they are fully accountable for their deeds.[234] Augustine assumes that children are capable of behaving according to his moral ideals, if they receive a proper Christian upbringing.

INNOCENCE, PASSION, AND SIN IN CHILDREN

Our source material is far from furnishing a complete picture of how Christians in late antiquity viewed children's nature, characteristics, and qualities, but we can reconstruct certain aspects of this picture. We have seen how Jesus' saying about the child as paradigmatic citizen of the kingdom of God was interpreted. According to the fathers, Jesus used small children as examples because they are simple, innocent, and pure in a moral sense. This means that they are not sexually active; they have not yet developed sexual desire; they are not plagued by anger and grief; and they are indifferent to the wealth and positions that are associated with honor and status in this world. Besides this, children obey their parents. It is primarily in the Eastern fathers—Origen, John Chrysostom, and especially Clement of Alexandria—that we find such ideas, but we also find in Tertullian the idea that the child is taken as a model because it is not plagued by sexual desire.

We must, however, emphasize that the fathers attribute such qualities to *small* children. As they grow older, the passions take shape. According to Clement of Alexandria and Origen, this development is analogous to the emergence of the reason and of speech (*logos*). At the same time, the reason is a necessary presupposition, if one is to be able to choose and to resist desire. It is not clear at what age the child leaves behind an existence of simplicity and purity, but it appears that Origen believes that something happens to the child when it reaches the age of four or five, while John Chrysostom limits the phase of innocence to the first years of a child's life.

As I have indicated, Clement and Origen presuppose a connection between the emergence of the reason (*logos*) and the growth away from innocence, while also affirming that, if desire is to be overcome, reason is the necessary instrument. We also find a connection between reason and desire in John Chrysostom, but his approach is different, since he believes that the passions are present in the child before the reason emerges, and that the child is tyrannized by "all the passions (*pathos*)" precisely because it lacks rationality. This is why he normally employs children and their characteristic qualities as negative paradigms, unlike Clement, who generally reflects a positive evaluation of children's qualities and invariably employs children and the conduct associated with them as positive examples.

The idea that infants are innocent, or morally neutral, is found consistently in all the patristic material I have studied, until a clear break occurs among Western theologians at the beginning of the fifth century. Although Eastern theologians agreed with the Western tradition, which emphasized that Adam's sin had consequences for his posterity, and some even came close to affirming, or at least implicitly presupposing, the idea of original sin, this was asserted with much greater vigor by Augustine. In the course of the Pelagian controversy, where the fundamental issue concerned anthropology, Augustine elaborated a theological defense of the doctrine of original sin and underlined that children enter this world with a nature already marked by original sin. Children are not innocent! Although Augustine does emphasize that physical limitations make it impossible for newborn children personally to commit sins, he claims that they are guilty because they are born with original sin. This sinful nature can be seen in the infant's greed for its mother's breast and in the jealousy it shows when other children lie at the mother's or wet nurse's breast. Accordingly, Augustine claims that when Jesus speaks of children as positive examples, he is referring only to their physical weakness, which makes it impossible for them to perpetrate sinful actions. The importance of the doctrine of original sin was that it allowed Augustine to make sense of the idea of God's righteousness. His main argument is that if a child is without original sin and hence is innocent, God would be unjust when he punishes it by means of sufferings. Punishment presupposes guilt. It follows that the child must be guilty, that is, must be born with original sin, for otherwise God would be afflicting an innocent person. That, in turn, is unthinkable, since God's righteousness is one of his fundamental qualities.

The church fathers see children as moral subjects. They are moral individuals who bear responsibility for their actions. This is particularly clear in Augustine, who affirms that the degree of responsibility grows in proportion to the child's intellectual development. It appears that he holds children to be fully responsible for their actions once they are about sixteen years old.[235]

The fourth- and fifth-century fathers in East and West may differ on the question of original sin, but they agree that children are driven by passions or desires. At the same time, they emphasize the child's potential to be molded in keeping with Christian ideals, and John Chrysostom has an especially optimistic view of the possibilities of forming children, whom he compares with sculptures in the artist's hand. Chrysostom goes so far as to hold that it takes as little as two months to transform a child in accordance with Christian ideals. The premise for such a positive view of the possibility of change is the idea that the child is created in God's image. When the parents educate their child in virtues that reflect God's own being, for example, kindness and forgiveness, they uncover God's image in the child. We are not told explicitly what level of maturity must be reached before a child can internalize the Christian virtues, but it is clear that the process is in full swing by the time the child begins its schooling. Chrysostom exhorts parents to discipline their children "from the first," since it is easier to form a child's soul while it is still small. This indicates that the formation must start before the child begins school. Jerome assumes that a child of four or five has the necessary presuppositions for learning moderation.

The study of the Bible was a central element in Christian education. According to Jerome, a seven-year-old child should read the scriptures and learn them by heart. The order that Jerome proposes for reading the individual books reflects his awareness that it is easier for children to absorb material related to rules of conduct and morality than more abstract theological texts. We find the same awareness that one must begin with children's own presuppositions in John Chrysostom, who exhorts parents to teach their children biblical narratives from the beginning of their schooling. He assumes that seven-year-olds have reached the level of intellectual maturity necessary to grasp the relationship between rewards and merits and that they are able to relate the biblical material to their own lives.

Education requires one to see children as religious individuals who must develop their own individual relationship to God. Parents are urged to take their children with them to church while they are so small that it is still natural to hold their hands. According to Jerome, seven-year-old children should participate in a comprehensive and regular life of piety. In other words, children are religious subjects who must live their relationship to God both as individuals and in fellowship with adults.

This, however, does not mean that the moral and religious individuality of children is acknowledged as something positive or valuable per se. It is a means toward the attainment of a future goal. The children's moral and religious life attracts the church fathers' attention primarily because the correct input in this area lays those foundations that allow the child at some future date to become an adult who believes and who lives in accordance with particular Christian ideals. Children are seen as "raw material" that must be worked on, so that they can be "attractive products" later on—adult persons who have internalized the Christian faith and its consequences for a virtuous life. We find this line of thought more or less explicitly in all the patristic writers of the fourth and fifth centuries whom I have studied, but it finds its clearest expression in Jerome, who quotes Cicero's explicit affirmation that a child deserves praise not so much because of what it now is, but rather because of what it will become.

Our modern Western thinking, influenced by the insights of child psychology, may be inclined to say that such affirmations imply a negative view of children's qualities and characteristics. This impression seems confirmed by the idea that children are tyrannized by passions which must be tamed (John Chrysostom) or that they are born with original sin (Augustine), since such notions supply the premise for the picture of children as "raw material." It is, however, anachronistic to apply such a criterion to the fathers' attitudes and their understanding of children's nature and qualities. They must be read and interpreted against the background of their own period, and in this context it is reasonable to see the idea of children as unformed raw material as a reflection and continuation of conventional ideas in pagan Greco-Roman culture.

Besides this, the apparently negative attitude toward children must be nuanced by other factors, such as the intensity of the debate about the salvation of children. Gregory of Nyssa composed a theological treatise that discusses why God permits the death of small children and what awaits them on the far side of the grave. Augustine emphasizes that Jesus died for babies too. His controversy with Pelagius about which of them represented the more "child-friendly" theology of the salvation of children is a clear indication that theologians were concerned about children's eternal happiness. Children were seen as individuals with a dignity and a nature that made them (just as much as adults) the recipients of God's salvation.

A second factor, linked to this, is the emphasis that children are created in God's image. In Eastern theology, represented by Gregory of Nyssa, this implies that the child shares in God's life and that the goal of education is to sow the virtues in the child, so that its soul will be cleansed of the consequences of the fall, and it can truly achieve that degree of sharing in God for which it was created. In a similar manner, John Chrysostom holds that when parents educate their child to a virtuous life, they uncover God's image in it. Although Augustine goes further than the Eastern fathers in the dramatic consequences for the child's nature, which he ascribes to the fall, he too emphasizes that the child is created in God's image. The acknowledgment of this fact and of its implications for his own existence and life as a boy lead him to strikingly positive affirmations: "In a living creature such as this everything is wonderful and worthy of praise." Even if it had been God's will that he should not outlive his own childhood, Augustine would still owe him profound thanks. This fundamentally positive evaluation is connected to Augustine's belief that God has created children in such a way that they can seek him and find him, but this does not diminish the strikingly positive character of his attitude to children and to their qualities, especially in the light of prevalent attitudes in his period. This means that Augustine combines the idea of original sin and of the child as a sinner with a basically positive assessment of children, based on the theology of creation.

Third, the life and existence of babies had such a significance and dignity that theologians reflected on their suffering in the form of deformity, sickness, and death. Both Gregory of Nyssa and Augustine discuss the suffering and death of small children in relation to the idea of God's righteousness. Their approaches to this question and the answers they offer may differ, but the very fact that these patristic writers devoted specific attention to the suffering of babies, and related this topic to fundamental characteristics of God's own being, demonstrates that they thought the lives and fates of small children a matter worthy of their concern.

I find no evidence that the Greco-Roman pagan tradition ever regarded the sufferings of small children as so problematic that moral-philosophical treatises were devoted to this question. On the contrary, writers such as Cicero and Seneca criticize parents and especially fathers for grieving over the deaths of their small children. As I noted in the previous chapter, our sources do not give an unambiguous answer to the question whether parents did, in fact, grieve over their dead babies, but the fact that representatives of the intellectual elite express the view that small children are not worth their parents' grief tells us clearly what kinds of reaction were regarded as conventional.

This means that the church fathers apparently had a different attitude to the worth of babies than that found in the pagan moral-philosophical tradition. Although our sources are not explicit on this point, it is reasonable to believe that this positive assessment of the worth of babies is connected with the idea that all human beings, even small children, are created in the image of God. Whereas pagans thought that a newborn baby was not a human person in the full sense, patristic thinking implies that the newborn possesses the fullness of human dignity. I quote Cyprian's words once more: "For what is lacking to him who has once been formed in the womb by the hands of God?" (*Ep.* 64.2). This means that the newborn has a soul and can receive the gifts of divine salvation, and that the church is the instrument that is to mediate these gifts even to the smallest children. The idea that babies are created in God's image, and hence are the recipients of divine salvation, thus leads to a focus on babies and an interest in them that was unknown in pagan antiquity.

This patristic interest in babies, however, does not entitle us to draw conclusions about how children were treated and were evaluated in social life, as they gradually grew up to adulthood. What I want to emphasize here is simply that babies were considered complete and whole human persons from their birth onward, and that this naturally affected reactions to and reflections on their suffering and death.

4

ABORTION, INFANTICIDE AND *EXPOSITIO,* AND SEXUAL RELATIONS BETWEEN CHILDREN AND ADULTS

This chapter begins with an examination of early Christian attitudes to abortion, infanticide, and *expositio* (child exposure). In my discussion of *expositio* in pagan antiquity, I pointed out that not all children who were exposed actually died. This would appear to argue against the link between *expositio* and infanticide in the title of the present chapter. One might indeed defend it by recalling that many such children did indeed die, although (as we shall shortly see) many Christian sources criticized *expositio* for reasons other than that it led to the child's death. I deal with these subjects under one single heading partly because the sources themselves often do so, and partly because the attitude to abortion and infanticide often decided whether the fetus or the newborn child was allowed to grow up. Since my primary interest is attitudes to children and the living conditions of children, my main focus here is on infanticide and *expositio.*

The second part of the chapter focuses on Christian attitudes to sexual relations between children and adults.

Abortion, Infanticide, and *Expositio*

Judaism

It is obvious that the early Christians adopted Jewish ideas on this subject. Before we look at Christian texts, let us therefore see briefly how the Jewish tradition regarded abortion, infanticide, and *expositio.* Many scholars distinguish two main schools of thought within Judaism with regard to abortion and the fetus—the Alexandrian and the Palestinian schools.[1]

Despite a variety of emphases and lines of argumentation, both schools held a very restrictive position on abortion, which they accepted only in an emergency situation where the mother's health was at stake; abortion was not envisaged as a possible means of limiting the number of one's children.

The most important point of controversy was whether or not the fetus should be attributed legal personhood, and (if the answer was positive) at what point in its development this status was acquired. This question was usually discussed in the framework of a juridical context: what punishment should be imposed on one who by a mishap hurt a pregnant woman so that she lost her child? One important scriptural passage here was Exodus 21:22-25. The Hebrew text says that if a man strikes a woman so that she miscarries, but without herself being hurt, the guilty one is to receive the punishment that the woman's husband demands; if however the blow hurts the woman, the principle of "a life for a life" is to apply. The Palestinian tradition interpreted the "hurt" as referring to the woman, while the Septuagint translated the Hebrew word *asôn* (hurt) as "form," which was taken as a reference to the fetus and to the stage of its development. This implies a distinction between an unformed and a formed fetus. The severity of the punishment depended on whether or not the fetus had acquired human form.[2]

This way of thinking about a fetus clearly reflects early influence from Aristotle's distinction between the fetus before and after its "vivification" (which was held to occur after forty days for boys, and after ninety days for girls), and represents a stance midway between Plato, who claimed that life began with conception, and the Stoics, who held that life began at birth.[3] The Alexandrian school, with a minority in the Palestinian school, held that the fetus acquired the juridical status of a human person at one particular point in time, while the Palestinian majority held that the fetus and the mother were one, so that the fetus on its own had no legal existence. This latter point of view entailed that abortion was allowed, or indeed even demanded, in certain situations.[4] We must, however, emphasize that the Palestinian school discussed abortion almost exclusively in relation to "the problem of the legal and cultic status of the fetus, especially in miscarriages and certain necessary (and usually late) abortions. Abortion in the early stages of pregnancy, 'on demand' or as a means of birth control 'is very likely not even contemplated in the Mishnaic law.'"[5]

The primary concern was not to determine the stage in pregnancy at which the fetus acquired the form and status of a human being, in view of potential judicial proceedings. Rather, the main point of these discussions was to emphasize the profound immorality of killing a fetus, irrespective of the stage of its development: this action was classified as murder. Where the fetus died, not through an unlucky miscarriage, but by means of an intentional *abortus provocatus,* this was regarded with particular gravity, and it is not by chance that Philo discusses the legal status of the fetus in the context of his exposition of the commandment "Thou shalt not kill."[6]

It is natural, if we assume that *expositio* leads to the death of the child, that this critical position vis-à-vis abortion would also entail a critical position vis-à-vis the exposure of children. Hence, it is not surprising that Philo, after condemning abortion, goes on to condemn *expositio* as well, calling it "a sacrilegious practice which among many other nations . . . has come to be regarded with complacence." Parents who expose their children are guilty of "the worst abomination of all, murder of their own children." The only difference between infanticide and *expositio* is that the parents kill their children with their own hands in the former case, whereas they hand them over to wild beasts in the latter.[7] Philo is aware that parents say they hope that their children will be rescued, but he affirms that they are in reality exposing their children to the worst possible fate: "For all the beasts that feed on human flesh visit the spot and feast unhindered on the infants, a fine banquet provided by their sole guardians, those who above all others should keep them safe, their fathers and mothers."[8]

Two other texts from the Alexandrian tradition criticize abortion and *expositio* in a way that indicates a logical continuity between these two phenomena. The *Sentences of Pseudo-Phocylides* is a Jewish sapiential writing, a collection of ethical maxims or rules of conduct for daily life composed probably between 30 B.C.E. and 40 C.E.[9] In the section devoted to sexuality, marriage, and the family, the author writes: "Do not let a woman destroy the unborn babe in her belly, nor after its birth throw it before the dogs and the vultures as a prey."[10]

The context shows that the author is concerned for the fetus and the newborn child, and that he has a very positive attitude toward human reproduction—an idea typical of Jewish writings, and often based on Genesis 1:28 and 2:24. In other words, the obligation to procreate children seems to be one element in the criticism of abortion and *expositio.*

A similar condemnation of abortion and *expositio* is found in the *Sibylline Oracles.* This text, as we have it today, is the result of a long process of composition; internal and external indications suggest that the passages that interest us come from the second century B.C.E. (Book 3) and the second century C.E. (Book 2).[11] The *Oracles* employ motifs obviously drawn from apocalyptic literature: the author includes those who "aborted what they carried in the womb" and those who "cast forth their offspring unlawfully" among the wicked who will be punished by God on the day of judgment.[12] Like wizards and witches, adulterers, impure persons, and those who oppress the poor and widows, such persons will taste God's wrath in Gehenna. Another passage describes infanticide as sinful: "Rear thine own offspring and slay it not: for the Eternal will surely be wroth with him who commits these sins."[13] In the case of abortion, we note that these authors are not in the least interested in the legal aspects or in technical considerations of the stage of development of the fetus, although it is highly probable that they were acquainted with such questions. Within an ethical framework, they emphasize the immoral aspect of abortion.

We find similar points of view in Palestinian Judaism. Philo's contemporary Josephus affirms: "The Law orders all the offspring to be brought up, and forbids women either to cause abortion or to make away with the fetus; a woman convicted of this is regarded as an infanticide, because she destroys a soul and diminishes the race."

These words raise a number of questions. In other passages, Josephus distinguishes between a formed and an unformed fetus, and holds that the fetus is not a person in the legal sense.[14] How does this fit in with what he says here about the fetus and abortion? The most important point in our present context is that—however we are to understand the relationship between these somewhat contradictory affirmations—here, in an ethical context, Josephus strictly rejects abortion and condemns it as murder.

Further, it is not clear what "the Law" means here, since there is no explicit prohibition in the Old Testament or in other Jewish writings that speaks of the phenomenon Josephus condemns. However, since he speaks of *expositio* and abortion as murder, and juridical aspects play no role in what he says about abortion, it is certainly possible that he is thinking of the Decalogue here. If this is the case, we would have a parallel to Philo, who (as I mentioned above) discusses abortion, *expositio,* and infanticide in the context of his exposition of the commandment not to kill.

This critical attitude to abortion, infanticide, and *expositio* is not based exclusively on the commandment not to kill. It must also be seen in the context of a very positive attitude to procreation, which is also reflected in the text quoted from Josephus. This in turn is certainly a reflection of the injunction in the creation narrative to establish the human person's rule over the earth; it is also born of the necessity for the Jews to survive as a people, thus ensuring God's presence on earth. Another factor contributing to this critical attitude is a general aversion to blood and the shedding

of blood.[15] Besides this, abortion, *expositio,* and infanticide are often condemned in the context of the condemnation of infidelity and other sexual
sins. This may mean that the criticism of these actions should be understood as one element in the critique of sexual sins in general.

This does not however mean that *expositio* was unknown in Jewish society. The Talmud clearly reflects the existence of this practice, when it
determines whom foundlings were allowed to marry. The rabbis concede
that one who marries a foundling risks committing incest; nevertheless,
since the likelihood was so small, they permitted foundlings to contract
marriage.[16] The rabbinic tradition also emphasizes that even if there is
no law which establishes a legal obligation for parents to look after their
children, they bear a moral responsibility for doing so. When he was asked
whether the law that a "man must maintain his sons and daughters while
they are young" was in accord with a resolution promulgated by an earlier rabbinical synod,[17] Rabbi R. Hisda answered: "The raven cares for its
young but that man (father) does not care for his children."[18] Accordingly,
parents have a moral responsibility to look after their children; the fact
that they are not legally obliged to do so is a concession made to the poor.
This implies that the reason why children were exposed was the poverty
of their parents; in the case of well-off parents, it is reasonable to demand
that they take care of their own children and bring them up.[19]

Christian Sources
The Pre-Constantinian Period
We begin by noting that none of the New Testament writings directly
speaks of abortion, infanticide, or *expositio.* It is possible that the employment of terms related to *pharmakeia* (drugs) at Galatians 5:20 and Revelation 9:21; 18:23; 21:8; and 22:5 imply a critical attitude to abortion,
since they were associated with abortion both in pagan writings and in
later Christian texts.[20] These matters are, however, mentioned explicitly in
other early Christian writings.

The first text to deal with this topic is the *Didache,* which was given its
present form at the beginning of the second century.[21] It consists of four
main sections.[22] The first section, the one that interests us here, consists
of ethical instructions based on the Jewish and oral tradition about the
"two ways,"[23] which sets out a contrast between the path to life or light
and the path to death or darkness. The author of the *Didache* adopts and
transforms this tradition so that it fits a Christian context. The tradition
about the "two ways" was used frequently in the early church, especially
in connection with the instruction of candidates for baptism.[24] The question

of the relationship between the *Didache* and other Christian texts that employ the tradition of the "two ways" is complicated, and need not detain us here.[25]

In his introduction, the author of the *Didache* affirms that there are two paths, one to life and one to death, and he emphasizes that there is a great difference between these paths. When he describes the good path, his starting point is the double commandment to love, and part of his exposition of the commandment to love one's neighbor as oneself is cast in the form of a list of prohibitions ("you shall not . . ."). The model for this formulation is clearly the Decalogue, and some of the prohibitions are direct quotations from the biblical text. First, we find prohibitions of such actions as murder, adultery, sodomy, fornication, theft, and magic. Then follows the prohibition of abortion and infanticide: "Do not murder a child by abortion, nor kill it at birth."[26] We note that the author speaks of the fetus as a "child." The fact that he does not distinguish between the various phases of the fetus's development—that is, between an unformed and a formed stage—means that, from an ethical perspective, he equates abortion with infanticide. It is difficult to say with certainty how far the commandment not to kill children also implies the prohibition of *expositio*. As we have seen in the preceding section, Jewish texts with the same basic ethical attitude to abortion and infanticide as the *Didache* associate infanticide with *expositio*. It is therefore reasonable to assume that the prohibition of killing children also implies that it is forbidden to expose them.[27]

The author returns to this subject later on, when he is describing the path of death. Life along this path is characterized by a long list of vices; among those who take this path are "murderers of children, corrupters of God's creation."[28] We note that the word for "child" in this passage was used in *Didache* 2:2, quoted above. This suggests that it refers here too to the unborn child.[29] The immediate context of this affirmation is interesting. Immediately before these words, the author claims that it is typical of those who carry out such actions that they show no mercy to the poor, nor do they work "on behalf of the downtrodden." And his words about those who kill children are immediately followed by a focus on sins against the poor and needy: "turning away from the needy, afflicting the oppressed; advocates of the rich, lawless judges of the poor."[30] This indicates that the author regards the situation of children as like that of adults who are suffering in need and must be taken care of. It is also interesting to note that he not only forbids the killing of children, but also describes those who do so as "corrupters of God's creation," since this means that his position has

a theological foundation, even if this is not developed in detail: from the
fetal stage onward, the child is God's creation.[31] The implicit idea seems
to be that, since children are created by God, their life must be protected.
This is the first example of an early Christian writer basing his opposition
to abortion and infanticide on creation theology.

We find the same prohibition of abortion and infanticide in *Barnabas*.
It has not yet proved possible to establish precisely the date or the geographical provenance of this writing; most scholars date it to the early second century, and it is difficult to identify the place of composition more
precisely than the eastern Mediterranean region.[32] It can be described as a
Jewish-Christian writing; one of its author's main concerns is to show that
Christ is the fulfillment of the prophecies in the Old Testament, so that
it is the Christians who offer the correct interpretation of the Old Testament. The doctrine of the "two ways" is a central element in this text too
(18:1—21:9), and it is in this section of the letter, which has much material in common with the *Didache*, that we find the prohibition of abortion
and infanticide.[33] The author employs almost the same formulation as the
Didache. Those who walk on the path of light are not to "murder a child
by abortion, nor, again, destroy that which is born" (*Did.* 19:5), and those
who take the path of darkness are called "murderers of children, corrupters of God's creation" (*Did.* 20:2).

Here too, the immediate context is interesting. The prohibition in 19:5
follows directly on the commandment to love one's neighbor more than
oneself.[34] This means that the child—both unborn and born—is considered as a "neighbor," as an individual who is to be loved. As in the *Didache*,
the prohibition of killing children is found in a passage where the author
condemns the oppression of the poor and needy. The formula "you shall
not" in the prohibition of abortion and infanticide is highly reminiscent
of the commandment in the Decalogue not to kill. Bearing in mind the
high status this formula has in these early Christian writings, it should
probably be understood as subordinate to the biblical prohibition, which
it seeks to make explicit.[35]

It is important to note that it is precisely in these writings—in their
doctrine of the "two ways," catechetical material that helped shape the
early Christians' perceptions and attitudes—that we find such an intense
opposition to views on abortion and infanticide that were common in
Greek-Roman antiquity.

We find similar attitudes to abortion and infanticide in the *Apocalypse of
Peter*, which may be contemporary or somewhat later. Internal and external evidence suggest that the author lived in Egypt. This writing circulated

in the western and eastern regions of the Roman empire; its diffusion and authority are attested by the fact that Clement of Alexandria attributed to it the status of a canonical writing, while the Muratorian Canon, the oldest Western list of the writings in the New Testament, included it (even if only in the category of texts whose status was disputed).[36] The author draws a vivid picture of hell, probably under the influence of oriental and Orphic-Pythagorean eschatology. Here, women who have had abortions and parents who have killed their children receive their punishment. The description includes the following scene:

> And near this flame there is a great and very deep pit and into it there flow all kinds of things from everywhere: judgment (?), horrifying things and excretions. And the women (are) swallowed up (by this) up to their necks and are punished with great pain. These are they who have procured abortions and have ruined the work of God which he has created.[37]

We see that this author, like the *Didache* and *Barnabas*, anchors his condemnation of abortion in creation theology: the fetus is God's creation. Even if it is not made explicit, there appears to be a link between this idea and the equation of abortion with murder. It is clear that he considers abortion to be murder, since when he describes the fate awaiting those who have had abortions, he does so in a section of his work that begins with these words: "And the murderers and those who have made common cause with them are cast into the fire."

The author of the *Apocalypse of Peter* moves directly from his condemnation of those who have had abortions to his description of the harsh fate awaiting those women and men who have killed their children. They will meet them again, when they themselves are in hell—but now, their children are their accusers:

> Other men and women stand above them naked. And their children stand opposite to them in a place of delight. And they say and cry to God because of their parents, "These are they who neglected and cursed and transgressed thy commandment. They killed us and cursed the angel who created (us) and hung us up. And they withheld from us the light which thou hast appointed for all." And the milk of the mothers flows from their breasts and congeals and smells foul, and from it come forth beasts that devour flesh, which turn and torture them for ever with their

husbands, because they forsook the commandments of God and killed their children. And the children shall be given to the angel Temlakos. And those who slew them will be tortured for ever, for God wills it to be so.[38]

In addition to the vigorous condemnation of abortion and infanticide, we should note what the *Apocalypse of Peter* says about the fate of the children who were killed: they will be taken care of by an angel. This implies that God looks after these individuals, and that they will be saved together with all the others he has chosen. This means that small children who were killed (a category that may also include unborn children who were aborted) are seen as individuals on whom God will bestow immortality.

The idea that aborted unborn children and dead children will be taken care of by an angel is not unique to the *Apocalypse of Peter*. In his *Eclogae*, a commentary on early Christian writings, Clement of Alexandria quotes the *Apocalypse of Peter* with approval, when he writes that both children who were exposed and unborn children who were aborted will be looked after and helped by an angel.[39] Similarly, Methodius of Olympus, a teacher who lived in Asia Minor in the second half of the third century, claims that all children who were killed by *expositio* are entrusted to a protective angel. Methodius, too, draws on the *Apocalypse of Peter*, and refers to the scene where the children accuse their parents of having killed them and thereby despised the commandments of God.[40]

Clement of Alexandria touches on our subject a few times in other writings, always in a context of polemic against all forms of luxury, vanity, and sexual excesses. One argument he employs is that the intention of Christian marriage is procreation; he rejects all sexual activity that does not have this goal. In this context, Clement writes:

> If we should but control our lusts at the start and if we would not kill off the human race born and developing according to the divine plan, then our whole lives would be lived according to nature. But women who resort to some sort of deadly abortion drug kill not only the embryo but, along with it, all human kindness.[41]

As we have seen above, Stoic philosophers too argued that abortion is against nature. In the present context, the criticism of abortion is a subsidiary argument supporting Clement's main concern—that sex detached from procreation is illicit. This may indicate that his opposition to abortion does not have a fundamental theological basis in the scriptures, and that it was not an important issue for him. On the other hand, however, we should note that he calls abortion murder and claims that it is incompatible with "all human kindness."

When he writes about *expositio*, Clement argues more in terms of fundamental theological principles. He attempts to demonstrate that the law of Moses is the source of all ethics; the positive elements found in Greek ethics reflect the influence of Moses. He claims, among other things, that Pythagoras was taught by the biblical exhortations to show mercy: this is why he and the other Greeks have compassion on newborn animals, by not separating them from their mothers. The paradox in Clement's eyes is that they do not display the same merciful attitude toward newborn babies, and he criticizes them for treating animals better than human beings: "Let the Greeks, then, feel ashamed, and whoever else inveighs against the law; since it shows mildness in the case of the irrational creatures, while they expose the offspring of men."[42] In other words, Clement roots his opposition to *expositio* in the law of God. There may be reasons to separate newborn animals from their mothers, but there is no legitimate reason to practice *expositio*, which makes one a murderer of children.

In this same passage, he criticizes a sexuality detached from the procreation of children: "For the man who did not desire to beget children had no right to marry at first; certainly not to have become, through licentious indulgence, the murderer of his children." But here, his criticism of *expositio* is not subordinate to some other agenda: it does not function primarily as a argument in support of Clement's views of the place sexuality ought to have in marriage. The primary point here is the condemnation of *expositio*, which Clement anchors in the law of Moses. When he remarks that one who does not wish to have children ought not to marry, these words serve to explain why people get into a situation where they wish to expose their own children. The same is true of his observation that the luxurious life of parents leads them to murder their children: he wishes to affirm that the priority of such persons is their own prosperity, although they could have used their material resources and their energy to care for their children.

When Clement calls those who expose children murderers, he gives the impression that it was normal for children who were exposed to die. This, however, seems to contradict another passage where, in connection with his polemic against the sexual licentiousness of the pagans (which includes prostitution), he claims that such activities often mean that parents have sex with their own children—who had been exposed when they were infants. He takes for granted the existence of brothels where women sell their services, and also assumes that "boys are taught to renounce their own natures and play the role of women."[43] This can lead to fathers having intercourse with their own sons and daughters: "a father, not recognizing the child he had exiled by exposure, may have frequent relations with a son turned catamite, or with a daughter become a harlot, and the freedom with which license is indulged may lead fathers into becoming husbands [of their children]."[44] If the reader is to find such an argument at all credible, this presupposes that so many exposed children survived that unintentional incest was a genuine possibility. On the other hand, it is reasonable to suppose that Clement is employing the rhetorical device of exaggeration here, in order to portray pagan behavior in the worst light possible—since pagans, too, regarded incest as morally reprehensible.[45] Clement is ambiguous about whether exposed children actually did survive. We should note, however, that (unlike Justin, as we will see below) Clement does not use the risk of incest as an argument against *expositio*. This strengthens my argument that his opposition to this practice is based on his understanding of the law and of Christian ethics: it does not function "merely" as a supporting argument in his endeavor to make it clear that sexual intercourse must be limited to reproduction.[46]

The writings to which I have hitherto referred were addressed primarily to Christian communities or groups. Although they clearly contain polemical elements that criticize pagan behavior, their primary intention is to form Christians in accordance with particular ideals, thus contributing to the construction of a Christian identity. As Christianity gradually took root and became better known, tensions arose in relation to the pagan environment, partly because Christian circles consciously broke with pagan religiosity and behavior, and partly because the new religion was misunderstood. In order to counter the criticism and accusations leveled by the society in which they lived, a number of apologetic writings were composed from the mid-second century onward. Several of these are relevant to our present investigation.

The *Letter to Diognetus* has traditionally been included among the "apostolic fathers," but its contents make it more appropriate to classify it among the apologists. No precise date has yet been established for this letter; in the present context, it suffices to date it to the second half of the second century. It may have been written in Alexandria.[47] In one passage where the rhetorically gifted author is describing the similarities and differences between Christians and pagans, he emphasizes that Christians follow the local laws and customs in many spheres. He portrays them as good citizens, who are not dramatically different from their surroundings. Nevertheless, there are some important differences. For example, all marry and have children, but "they do not expose their offspring."[48] He does not offer any theological justification for this stance, nor for any of his other examples; he merely points out what Christian practice is, and this gives his text the character of a summary. Nevertheless, it is interesting that the *Letter to Diognetus* should specify *expositio* as one thing that distinguishes Christians from their pagan surroundings. His reference to Christian practice on this point is part of his argument that the pagans themselves ought to regard Christian behavior as good.

Another interesting text is the *Legatio* of Athenagoras, addressed to Marcus Aurelius and his son Commodus, and probably composed in 177. After relating the widespread pagan accusations of atheism, cannibalism, and incest levied against Christians, the author takes up each of these charges and attempts to show how unjustified they are. In order to demonstrate how absurd the accusation of cannibalism and murder is, he points to the fact that, since Christians hold that "women who practice abortion are murderers and will render account to God for abortion," it would be meaningless to accuse them of killing their children after birth. Similarly, it would be illogical to forbid the exposure of children on the grounds that those who do so are murderers, and then to kill the same children at a later date, once they had been weaned. Athenagoras confirms the critical attitude to abortion and *expositio* that we have found in other early Christian texts: both are called murder. The interesting point is not simply that he relates what Christians believe on these questions, but that he offers a fundamental theological argument in favor of his position: "The same man cannot regard that which is in the womb as a living being and for that reason an object of God's concern and then murder it when it comes into the light."[49] From the fetal stage onward, the child is regarded as a living being who is taken care of by God. We would press the text too far if we were to claim that Athenagoras implies here that the fetus possesses full human dignity from the moment of its conception, but it is certain that he bases the Christian opposition to abortion on the idea that God looks after his creatures. This line of thought implies a critical attitude to *expositio*, where it is presupposed that this leads to the death of the exposed children; Athenagoras seems to take this for granted.

Although Justin Martyr shares Athenagoras's fundamentally critical position on *expositio*, his argumentation is different. He seems to presuppose that most of those who are exposed survive: they are picked up and taken care of, with the expectation that they will work as prostitutes when they are older. "And as the ancients are said to have reared herds of oxen, or goats, or sheep, or grazing horses, so now we see you rear children only for this shameful use."[50] Justin condemns sex with prostitutes in harsh words, as "the godless and infamous and impure intercourse." Even worse is the possibility that one who resorts to a prostitute "may possibly be having intercourse with his own child, or relative, or brother." Justin makes a much more active use of the argument about incest than Clement was later to do; the future prostitution of the foundlings, with the inherent possibility of incest, furnishes his main argument in favor of the view that *expositio* is a sin against God.

This, however, is not the only reason why Christians reject the exposure of children. Since it is not at all certain that all those who are exposed will be picked up by other persons, this means that some will die—and in that case, those who have exposed the children become murderers. Justin mentions this only in passing; this is not one of his main arguments. It is nevertheless clear that he assumes that one reason why *expositio* is morally reprehensible is that it can lead to murder.[51]

Justin's main argument against this practice is that adults use foundlings for sex, and not least that this involves the risk of incest; this must be understood against the background of the accusations that the Christian fellowship indulged in sexual orgies and promiscuity—accusations generated by misunderstandings of the Christian *agape* or love meal. Justin employs the argument about incest as a countermove against such charges. His point is: you pagans do much more abominable things than you accuse us Christians of doing, since you even commit incest! I believe that this context helps explain why he offers this particular justification of the Christians' opposition to *expositio*. We may also suspect that Justin is exaggerating when he asserts that almost all exposed children survive: his intention would be to increase the statistical likelihood of incest.[52] He does in fact use rather vague language when he says that Christians fear that not all children are picked up. Since Christians were also accused of cannibalism and murder, we might have expected him to counter by emphasizing the point that *expositio* made parents murderers, if he really had believed that exposed children usually died. Since he does not do so, it is probable that he believed that most exposed children were picked up and ended as prostitutes.

We meet the argument about incest once again in Tertullian's *Apology*, written in 197 and addressed to Roman provincial governors and to Emperor Septimus Severus.[53] The context is accusations of incest. On the basis that attack is the best form of defense, Tertullian argues that, on the contrary, it is the pagans who are involved in "incestuous unions."[54] The first point in his argument that interests us is that the identity of the children who are picked up "by some passerby out of the pity of a stranger's heart" will gradually disappear, entailing the risk of unintentional incest.[55] Clearly, Tertullian assumes that some exposed children are rescued. Like Justin, he may be exaggerating the frequency of such cases so that he can charge his opponents with incest. He charges his pagan opponents with killing babies in a wicked manner by drowning them or exposing them "to cold and starvation and the dogs."[56] Tertullian may be exaggerating the extent of infanticide and *expositio,* but his main point is that all forms of killing are prohibited for Christians. It is also interesting to note that he sees abortion and the killing of a newborn child as basically the same action:

> But with us, murder is forbidden once for all. We are not permitted to destroy even the fetus in the womb, as long as blood is still being drawn to form a human being. To prevent the birth of a child is a quicker way to murder. It makes no difference whether one destroys a soul already born or interferes with its coming to birth. It is a human being and one who is a man, for the whole fruit is already present in the seed (*Homo est et qui est futurus; etiam fructus omnis iam in semine est*).[57]

In the *De Anima,* composed between 210 and 213 after he had embraced Montanism, Tertullian argues theologically, philosophically, and empirically that the fetus has a life of its own.[58] Technically speaking, the fetus is not a human being before it is fully developed, but since it is God who forms the fetus in the mother's womb, it is to be regarded as a human being.[59] This view contrasts sharply with Roman law, which laid down that the fetus was not a person, but a part of the mother.[60] Although the fetus is dependent on the mother, Tertullian regards it as far more than merely a part of her. This means that he anchors the status of the fetus as a human being in creation theology. The logic implicit in his thinking is that abortion is contrary to the law of Moses: "The law of Moses, indeed, punishes with due penalties the man who shall cause abortion."[61]

Tertullian presents here an argument, based on theological principles, about the status of the fetus as a human being, which entails that both abortion and *expositio* (in cases where the child dies) are classified as murder. When he writes that they are a breach of the prohibition of murder that Christians have received once and for all, it is natural to assume that he is referring to the relevant commandment in the Decalogue.[62] This means that, although Tertullian makes use of the incest argument in his reply to accusations that Christians are promiscuous, he is arguing on primarily theological and ethical lines in support of his critical attitude to both abortion and *expositio*. From the fetal stage onward, the child is God's creature, a human being, and it accordingly enjoys the same protection from the prohibition of murder in the law of Moses as other groups in society.

We find a similarly critical attitude to abortion and infanticide in Municius Felix, who wrote the *Octavius*, an apology for Christians in dialogue form, in Rome during a time of persecution in the first quarter of the third century.[63] He rejects accusations that Christians kill babies, and denies that Christian rites of initiation include drinking the blood of infants. His first argument is that it is completely unthinkable that anyone should take the life of a "tender and so tiny" baby. Here, he attacks those who have dared to formulate such an idea; he claims that the only people who would in fact be capable of doing such an abominable deed must be those whose lurid imaginations have conjured up such images.[64] His next step is to relate what he himself has seen and heard of infanticide by pagans:

> And, in fact, it is a practice of yours, I observe, to expose your very own children to birds and wild beasts, or at times to smother and strangle them—a pitiful way to die; and there are women who swallow drugs to stifle in their own womb the beginnings of a man to be—committing infanticide (*parricidium*) before they give birth to their infant.[65]

Municius Felix does not offer any justification for his unambiguous condemnation of *expositio* (which leads to death at least in some cases) and of infanticide; perhaps it is unreasonable to expect such a justification here, where his point is that such things are done by the pagans. We should note that the term used for infanticide, *parricidium*, is a technical term in Roman law for intentional murder, especially the cruel murder of one's near relatives.[66] This indicates that although he does not regard the fetus as a complete human being (*homo*), but rather as a future human being (*futurus homo*), nevertheless it has the value of a human person: abortion is just as grave a crime as the murder of a newborn child.

We have now examined a number of Christian writings, which come from both the western and the eastern regions of the empire and span the period from the beginning of the second century to the beginning of the third, and we have seen their critical attitude to abortion, *expositio,* and infanticide. Although the authors use a variety of arguments, there is a clear tendency to root this attitude in creation theology and to anchor it ethically in the law of Moses. Even at the fetal stage, the child is God's creature, and God cares for it and protects it. Since both the fetus and the newborn child have the status of a human being, they are protected by the prohibition of murder in the Decalogue. One who kills a child—irrespective of the way in which this is done—will be punished by God. The critical attitude toward *expositio* in this argumentation is based on the premise that it leads to the death of the child.

This way of thinking clearly reflects influence from Judaism. Indeed, early Christian texts such as the *Didache* and *Barnabas* incorporate the Jewish tradition about the "two ways," where abortion and *expositio* are condemned as murder. It is difficult to overestimate the importance of the fact that the doctrine of the "two ways" condemned abortion, *expositio,* and infanticide: this tradition became an integral part of catechetical instruction and thus helped form early Christian attitudes.

We can therefore say that by the beginning of the third century, there was a well established critical attitude to all forms of the murder of children—whether abortion, *expositio,* or other methods of killing. "Critical" is really too mild a word: these practices were utterly condemned. There already existed a certain measure of opposition to these practices among Roman moral philosophers, and some forms of the limitation of the number of children (including *expositio*) were rejected by the ruling authorities in some Italian cities, as is reflected in the *alimenta* program mentioned above. Nevertheless, the early Christian attitude represents a considerable intensification of this criticism. The Christian writers go much further in backing up their arguments by means of fundamental principles; we also perceive a greater zeal and commitment, since they understood this question, theologically and ethically, as a matter of living in accordance with the will of God. On the deepest level, the question of refraining from murder was a question of salvation or damnation. I therefore find it difficult to see the Christian critique of *expositio* as nothing more than an echo and development of other critical voices in contemporary society. The intensity and extent of the Christian critique represents an intensification of existing criticism of Roman praxis and legislation in these fields.[67]

What about praxis? Here it is more difficult to make confident affirmations: we cannot simply assume that the attitudes of the Christian authors I have presented reflect actual practice, especially when we bear in mind that their wish is to form Christian readers in keeping with particular ideals, and that they themselves assuredly belong to an elite group that made generally high demands of their fellow Christians. We must also bear in mind that the apologists portray Christians in the most favorable light possible. On the other hand, if the apologists' arguments are to have any genuine power, there must be at least *some* correspondence between what they write about Christian behavior and what was in fact the case, at any rate in the case of a visible action such as the exposure of children, which was open to empirical observation. If Christians had in fact practiced *expositio* to any great degree, this would have been so well-known in local society that the apologists' argument would have been completely implausible; and the fact that the exposure of children does not feature in polemic *within* the church indicates, at the very least, that this was not very widespread practice.[68] No source in the time before Constantine tells us that Christians practiced the exposure of children. This does not allow us to infer that it never happened, but it suggests that it was a rare occurrence.

The situation with regard to abortion was somewhat different. Abortion is more hidden, and this means that it can be employed by the apologists without there being any necessary agreement between the text and the societal reality. And, in fact, we possess Christian texts addressing members of the church from the first half of the third century that indicate that Christians did practice abortion. One of the leading theologians in the Roman church, Hippolytus (c. 170–c. 236), complains that the church is influenced by Roman morality and praxis, while its leaders fail to raise their voices in criticism. Callistus, the bishop of Rome, had accepted a Roman law about concubine marriages, although this often resulted in unwanted pregnancies. Hippolytus writes about the results of this papal leniency:

> Whence women, reputed believers, began to resort to drugs for producing sterility, and to gird themselves round, so as to expel what was being conceived on account of their not wishing to have a child either by a slave or by any paltry fellow, for the sake of their family and excessive wealth. Behold, into how great impiety that lawless *one* has proceeded, by inculcating adultery and murder at the same time![69]

Since these accusations against upper-class women who allegedly have abortions are one element in Hippolytus's polemic against Callistus, we must be cautious about drawing too-definite conclusions from it: Hippolytus is painting an exaggerated picture of immorality in order to portray Callistus in the worst possible light. We may also wonder how he came to know about these abortions, although it is of course possible that a cultured and highly educated man like Hippolytus had close links to prosperous Christian circles in Rome, and was informed about current rumors (whether or not these were true). Similarly, it is possible that elements of pagan morality and conduct were becoming more influential in the church at a period when its numbers were increasing among the Roman populace; and it is not unreasonable to believe that concubine marriages did in fact lead to unwanted pregnancies, so that abortion became for a larger number of women (with or without their husbands' consent) a real alternative to bearing the child.

The main point here, however, is that Hippolytus calls abortion murder, as does Cyprian. Like Hippolytus, Cyprian takes it for granted that there is a connection between heretical doctrine and immorality: for example, he accuses the schismatic Novatian of having caused his wife to have an abortion by kicking her in the belly.[70]

Our sources do not allow us to demonstrate any direct link between the critical attitude toward abortion among the church's main spokesmen and the first Roman laws that criminalized it, but it is not unreasonable to suppose that there was some connection. It is at any rate striking that the laws issued under Septimus Severus (193–211) and Antonius Caracalla (211–217) came so soon after the apologetic writings of Athenagoras and especially Tertullian, who had addressed their texts to Roman governors and emperors. These may not themselves have read the Christian apologists, but there is every reason to believe that they were familiar with Christian attitudes in this area.[71] On the other hand, the need for recruits to the army and concern for the interests of the *paterfamilias* may equally well have motivated this legislation.

Before we turn to the period after Constantine, let us note the presence of the same critical attitude to infanticide and *expositio* in Lactantius, at the beginning of the fourth century. His *Divine Institutes* (305–310) contain apologetic sections that reject a number of accusations against Christians, including murder. Like the apologists before him, Lactantius claims that the opposite is true: it is the pagans who are guilty of such abominable deeds. He points to the practice of killing newborn children, which he calls "an especially great impiety."[72] He also points out that some parents prefer to expose their children, but says that this is a "false piety," since children thrown to the dogs lose their lives in a much more cruel manner than if their parents had killed them. In other words, he equates infanticide and *expositio*, both of which contradict God's commandment not to take life. But he does not base his opposition to infanticide and *expositio* exclusively on God's commandment: like many before him, he makes a connection to the idea of creation. "It is always wrong to kill a man whom God has intended to be a sacrosanct creature."[73] All human life, including the newborn child, is sacred and inviolable, because it is created by God.

Although he affirms that *expositio* means a cruel death for the child, he is also aware that some children are in fact rescued. This, however, does not legitimate the exposure of children, for they may end up as prostitutes—with the ensuing risk of incest. However, although Lactantius, too, employs the incest argument, it is clearly subordinate to his argument that *expositio* contradicts the commandment not to take life.[74]

Lactantius is the first church father to say that parents are driven by poverty to expose their children, and that they hope that other people will look after them; but he displays no sympathy with such parents, nor does he in any way accept that poverty legitimates infanticide. His own solution is that one who "really cannot support children because of poverty" should "abstain from relations with his wife" rather than "undo the work of God with guilty hands."[75] In other words, this author on the threshold to the age of Constantine confirms and develops the basic position that Christian writers in the second and third centuries had taken on these questions.

The Constantinian and Post-Constantinian Periods

What happens to the church's thinking and Christian practice with regard to abortion, *expositio*, and infanticide after Christianity receives legal tolerance under Emperor Constantine in 311 and later becomes the only "licit religion" in the Roman empire under Theodosius I (379–395)? As Christianity acquired ever greater privileges in the course of the fourth century, huge numbers of people joined the church. Did this lead to a watering-down of the clear Christian opposition to abortion, *expositio*, and infanticide, by means of a conscious or unconscious assimilation of pagan attitudes? We can formulate the same question in positive terms: did the encounter with a new ecclesial reality pose new, large-scale challenges that demanded a different theological approach and a mitigation of the unambiguous positions taken in an earlier period?

Let me answer this question at once. The basic thinking remains the same as far as theological principles are concerned, but some nuances are introduced, above all on the issue of *expositio*. Since an increasing number of Christian parents were poor and found it difficult to look after their children, the theologians were forced to take into account this situation and to reflect anew on the question. This made it possible to take a more tolerant attitude toward poor people who exposed their children. As I have said, however, the basic thinking did not change; this is why I limit myself in this section to a brief overview of the discussion.

Let us begin with the question of abortion. Our starting point is two councils. Ninety Spanish bishops gathered in Elvira in southern Spain in the first decade of the fourth century to discuss the attitude the church should take toward those who had fallen away from the faith during persecution or who had committed other grave sins, and to lay down the penalty for the individual transgressions; this varied from penances lasting for several years to exclusion from Holy Communion for the rest of the person's life. Most of the canons deal with sins related to sexuality; it has been argued that this is the result of pagan influence.[76] Canons 63 and 68 are interesting in our present context. Canon 63 stipulates that if a woman becomes pregnant after infidelity while her husband is absent, and takes the child's life after this sin (*idque post facinus occiderit*), she "shall not be given communion even at the end, since she has doubled her crime."[77] And canon 68 says that if a catechumen becomes pregnant after committing fornication and then causes the death of the child (*si per adulterium conceperit et praefocaverit*), her baptism is to be postponed until the end of her life. The wording in these decrees does not allow us to decide with certainty whether they are speaking of abortion or infanticide (or both).[78] One indication that canon 63 includes abortion is the fact that the council of Ancyra in 314 probably refers to this text and interprets it as a reference to abortion; a similar indication is the inclusion of this text in later collections of canons dealing with abortion.[79] This, together with the clause noting that the husband was absent when his wife commits adultery, makes it plausible that the conciliar decree refers to an abortion carried out in order to conceal illicit sexual activities, and I base my following remarks on this interpretation.

Although the context of this condemnation of abortion (and perhaps of infanticide too) is sexual sins, it is not these actions as such, but rather *murder* that is the main subject and determines the extent of the penalty to be meted out. In canon 63, the harsh penalty is motivated by the fact that the woman "has doubled her crime." The council says nothing about women who become pregnant within marriage and then have an abortion, but since the basis for the calculation of the penalty seems primarily to be abortion per se—rather than the sexual act that resulted in the woman's pregnancy—it is reasonable to claim that canon 63 at the very least implies the condemnation of such cases.[80] It is of course true that the council fathers associated abortion with illicit sexual activities, and this may explain the harsh penalty for abortion. We should note, however, that the penalty for individual acts of fornication was much milder—five years of penances (canons 47 and 48). Exclusion from Holy Communion for life, which canon 63 prescribes for the combined sins of infidelity and abortion, is prescribed in canon 71 for promiscuity. The bishops who took part in the council, like the great majority of early Christians, had no desire to impose the death penalty for this or for other sins.[81]

I have mentioned that the council which met in Ancyra, the capital of the province of Galatia in Asia Minor, probably referred to canon 63 of Elvira. The council of Ancyra was attended by representatives of churches in Asia Minor and Syria, and thus had a wider geographical composition than Elvira. Here, too, the focus was on ecclesiastical discipline: how was the church to deal with those who had committed apostasy during the persecutions, and those who had committed immoral actions under the influence of paganism? The council laid down the following guidelines for the punishment of abortion and infanticide: "Women who prostitute themselves, and who kill the children thus begotten, or who try to destroy them when in their wombs, are by ancient law excommunicated to the end of their lives. We, however, have softened their punishment, and condemned them to the various appointed degrees of penance for ten years."[82] The "ancient law" referred to here is probably canon 63 of Elvira.[83] This Ancyra decree stipulates a much milder penalty for abortion than the Spanish bishops had made, but if we compare this with the penalties imposed for other sins, there is no doubt that abortion was still considered a highly immoral action. For example, the penalty for unintentional killing and for fornication was various forms of penance for five to seven years, while intentional murder was punished with excommunication for life. In other words, abortion was considered a more serious action in the juridical sense than unintentional killing, but not so serious as intentional murder.[84]

We should note that neither Elvira nor Ancyra distinguishes between the various stages of the fetus, that is, between a formed and an unformed fetus. Morally speaking, *abortus provocatus* was classified as murder. The decree of the council of Ancyra about ten years' excommunication for abortion is important, since it remained in force until well into the Middle Ages.

As I have indicated, the church fathers maintained this critical and condemnatory attitude toward abortion in the second half of the fourth century and on into the fifth: *abortus provocatus* is the destruction of a life that God has created and that he looks after. This fundamental respect for the life God had created did not, however, rule out a variety of approaches to this issue, especially on the fundamentally important question whether or not the fetus was a human person, or possessed human dignity, from the moment of conception onward. Unlike the Western tradition, the Eastern fathers seem to have tended to avoid any explicit or implicit distinction between the formed and the unformed fetus. It is perhaps Basil of Caesarea (c. 330–379), one of the Cappadocians, who is the clearest spokesman for the Eastern thinking. In reply to Bishop Amphilochius of Iconium,[85] who had asked for advice on a number of questions concerning church order and moral problems, Basil has the following to say about abortion:

> A woman who deliberately destroys a fœtus is answerable for murder. And any fine distinction as to its being completely formed or unformed is not admissible amongst us. For in this case not only the child which is about to be born is vindicated, but also she herself who plotted against herself, since women usually die from such attempts. And there is added to this crime the destruction of the embryo, a second murder—at least that is the intent of those who dare these deeds. We should not, however, prolong their punishment until death, but should accept the term of ten years; and we should not determine the treatment according to time but according to the manner of repentance.[86]

Basil is obviously aware of the problem of the distinction between the unformed and the formed fetus, but dismisses this as irrelevant. In his eyes, the fetus is a life, independently of the stage it has reached in its development, and this is why he classifies the destruction of the fetus as murder. He does not need to point out to his correspondent Amphilochius that abortion is therefore a breach of the injunction in the Decalogue not to take life.

About ten years after Basil wrote these words, the *Apostolic Constitutions* were composed in Syria. Both in content and in form, this writing has links to the *Didache* and *Barnabas*. It consists of a church order and of regulations for the conduct of the Christian life.[87] In the context of his condemnation of a number of forms of immorality, including illicit sexual relationships, the author writes, "Thou shalt not slay the child by causing abortion, nor kill that which is begotten; for 'everything that is shaped, and has received a soul from God, if it be slain, shall be avenged, as being unjustly destroyed.'"[88] It is possible that the author makes a distinction in the second half of this sentence between the unformed and the formed fetus, but his words can equally well be understood as affirming that both the born and the unborn child are created by God, who bestows a soul on the child.[89] In any case, he anchors his critical attitude to abortion in the idea of God as creator.

Although he does not state this explicitly, John Chrysostom presupposes a similar idea in a homily on Romans 13:11-14, when he condemns abortion in severe words and calls it murder:

> Why sow where the ground makes it its care to destroy the fruit? Where there are many efforts at abortion? Where there is murder before the birth? For even the harlot thou dost not let continue a mere harlot, but makest her a murderess too. You see how drunkenness leads to whoredom, whoredom to adultery, adultery to murder; or rather to something even worse than murder. . . . Why then dost thou abuse the gift of God, and fight with His laws, and follow after what is a curse as if a blessing, and make the chamber of procreation a chamber for murder, and arm the woman that was given for childbearing unto slaughter?[90]

The fact that this vigorous condemnation of abortion is uttered in the course of an attack on drunkenness and fornication, and that Chrysostom accordingly associates abortion with sexual immorality (like many before him in the early church), does not lessen the significance of what he is saying in this passage. His opposition to abortion is rooted in the theological principle that the fetus is a gift from God. He does not explicitly speak of it as a human being, but since he calls abortion murder—indeed, "something even worse than murder"—it is clear that he attributes human dignity to the fetus. He disregards the technical discussion of the stage at which the fetus takes on human form, and hence human dignity: ethically speaking, abortion must be considered murder, irrespective of when it occurs. This means that one who takes abortion "fights" against God's laws—against the commandment not to take life.

Chrysostom's Western contemporary, Jerome (342–420), is equally passionate in his condemnation of what he sees as moral decadence among

Christians. He accuses unmarried women members of the church of imitating pagan conduct by drinking poison in order to become sterile, by practicing fornication, and by provoking abortion by means of poison. He calls this the murder of an unborn child.[91] Unlike the theologians in the Eastern church, however, he makes a distinction between the formed and the unformed fetus. Since the fetus must have reached a certain stage of development before it can be called a person, one cannot speak of abortion as "murder" before that stage. Thus only the abortion of a formed fetus is classified as murder.[92]

Of all the church fathers, it is Augustine (354–430) who speaks most frequently of abortion and presents the most detailed discussions of the nature and status of the fetus. This is a fruit of his lifelong concern and theological wrestlings with the questions of the origin of the soul, and when and how the fetus receives a soul. He discusses a variety of solutions: (1) the soul is pre-existent; (2) the soul is created by God at the moment of conception; (3) like the body, the soul comes from the parents; (4) the soul is infused at a particular stage in the development of the fetus. As I have mentioned in an earlier chapter, he never found a satisfactory solution to this question. He frequently makes a distinction between the unformed and the formed fetus; the latter term refers to the fetus who has received a soul. We find one example of this distinction in the treatise *De Nuptiis et Concupiscientia,* when Augustine condemns sexual intercourse detached from reproduction: "At times this lust-filled cruelty or cruel lust goes so far that it even procures drugs to cause sterility, and if they are not effective, it somehow extinguishes and destroys within the womb the fetus already conceived, desiring that its own offspring perish before it begins to live. Or, if it was living in the womb, it desires that it be killed before it is born."[93] Naturally, this distinction presupposes that the fetus receives a soul at one particular stage in its development; the consequence of this idea, which he shares with Jerome, is that only the abortion of a formed fetus that has received a soul can be classified as murder.[94] This becomes clear in the *Quaestiones in Heptateuchum* 2.80, where Augustine refers to the Septuagint version of Exodus 21:2 and following and argues that the abortion of an unformed fetus is not murder, since one cannot say whether it already had a soul at that stage. Although the abortion even of an unformed fetus is morally reprehensible, the punishment for this act is limited to a fine.[95] On the question whether the embryo is to be defined as a part of the mother's body, Augustine breaks with Stoic thinking and Roman law, which affirmed that this was not the case.[96]

We should also note the reason for his critical attitude regarding abortion. We have seen that abortion was often associated with infidelity and with sexual laxity in general, and that abortion is employed as one element in polemic against these practices. The same is true in Augustine's writings too, but his primary reason for condemning abortion, along with contraception and medicines which result in sterilization, is that this frustrates the purpose of marital intercourse—the production of children.[97] In other words, his opposition to abortion is based first and foremost on his understanding of the function of sexuality within marriage—which he limits to reproduction—and to his theology of marriage, which defines its primary goal as the production of children. Since Augustine emphasizes in other passages that children are created in the image of God, and that this is the basis of their dignity and greatness, it is striking that his criticism of abortion does not mention creation theology or God's care for his creatures.[98]

Let us now look briefly at the questions of *expositio* and infanticide. We find a universally critical attitude toward the latter; in view of the attitude toward abortion, anything else would have been astonishing. Here, I limit myself to referring to the above-quoted text from *Apostolic Constitutions* 7.3.[99] The criticism of infanticide is here based on theological principles: it is God who created the child. The formulation of this prohibition suggests that we should interpret it as an application of the commandment in the Decalogue not to take life. We find an equally categorical rejection of infanticide in several other church fathers.[100]

As I have indicated, there is also a considerable degree of continuity between the attitudes of the church theologians and leaders of the pre-Constantinian and the post-Constantinian periods toward *expositio*. Let us first note that the emperors Constantine and Valentinian issued laws which sought to limit or abolish *expositio,* although Constantine's decrees are not unambiguous on this point. On the one hand, his law of 331 stipulated that parents had no right to demand the restitution of children whom they had exposed, and who had subsequently been taken care of by other persons: the one who rescues the child owns it, and can himself determine whether the child is to grow up as a slave or as his own child.[101] It had been illegal since the first century C.E. to sell free-born children as slaves, irrespective of how poor and needy their parents might be. The sale of children did in fact occur, especially in times of acute need and poverty; nevertheless, free-born children who were sold retained their original status as free citizens. Similarly, the father retained his legal power (*patria potestas*) over such children, and this made it possible for him at a later date to demand the children back. This, too, was changed under Constantine, in his law of August 18, 329 which stipulated that extremely poor parents were entitled to sell their children, and that the purchaser was allowed to use them as slaves, or even sell them on to another person in order to pay his debts. This law also states that if the one who sold the child subsequently wishes to have it back, he must either pay the market price or else offer a new slave in exchange.[102]

We can readily imagine that parents' demand for the restitution of their children, after other persons had looked after them for a shorter or longer period, could lead to antagonism and conflicts. The law responds to a juridically unclear situation, and appears to legitimate the practice of *expositio,* while granting the concession that poor parents might sell their children for money. On the other hand, this law may also imply a somewhat critical attitude, since it makes it clear to the parents that they lose the possibility of changing their minds, once they have, in fact, exposed their child.[103]

Other laws are less ambiguous: here, there is no doubt that they are seeking to limit the extent of *expositio* and the sale of children. In response to acute economic distress in Italy and Africa, two decrees state that parents are to receive help, so that they may not be forced by their penury to expose or sell their children. The first decree, issued in 322, says: "If any parent should report that he has offspring which on account of poverty he is not able to rear, there shall be no delay in issuing food and clothing, since the rearing of a newborn infant will not allow any delay."[104] The second, probably from 329 and referring to Africa, begins by noting that the emperor has "learned that provincials suffering from lack of sustenance and the necessities of life are selling or pledging their own children." It goes on to lay down what is to be done to avoid this situation: "Therefore, if any such person should be found who is sustained by no substance of family fortune and who is supporting his children with suffering and difficulty, he shall be assisted through Our fisc before he comes a prey to calamity."[105] Nothing indicates that these measures reflect the same kind of wide-reaching, long-term commitment to help parents look after children as the *alimenta* program: rather, they seem to have been a response to specific situations of acute need.[106] These decrees do not explain why it should be fundamentally desirable to avoid the exposure and sale of children, but it is likely that Constantine was influenced by the Christian opposition to *expositio.* Not only is it probable that he was acquainted with the Christians' attitude to murder, their sexual ethics, and the attitudes they took on moral questions in general; we should bear in mind that Lactantius was the tutor of Constantine's son Crispus, so there were personal relations between the imperial family and one of the most explicit Christian critics of *expositio* and infanticide. We should also note that Lactantius dedicated the *Divine Institutes* to the emperor, and we have seen above that this work expresses criticism of pagan practice on these points. It is reasonable to assume that the emperor knew this work.[107]

On March 5, 374, Valentinian, together with his co-regents Valens and Gratian, issued an edict which made *expositio* a criminal offense: "Let everyone give nourishment to his progeny. If, however, anyone thinks of exposing it, he will be subject to the statutory punishment" (*quod si exponendum putaverit, animadversioni quae constituta est subiacebit*).[108] It is clear that this law forbids *expositio*, but we do not know what the penalty for infringing this prohibition was. It is possible, but not at all certain, that the words *quae constituta est* refer to an edict issued the previous month which laid down the death penalty for infanticide.[109] If this is the case, then the edict of March 5 would entail that parents who exposed their children were liable to the death penalty.[110]

In my view, however, several factors raise a question about this interpretation. First, the decree that inflicted the death penalty for infanticide was a new law, and was not well-known. If the law against *expositio* had this decree in mind, therefore, we should have expected to find an explicit reference. Second, no later laws equate infanticide and *expositio*.[111] This may show that this law did not stand the test of reality, since *expositio* was so widespread that the legislation could not affect established practice.[112] At any rate, it is clear that this law did not succeed in putting an end to the praxis of exposing children.[113]

The formulation of his law tells us nothing about why Valentinian criminalized *expositio*. It is of course possible that this reflects the influence of Christian morality and ideas; in view of the fact that he made Christianity the religious basis of the Roman empire, we must certainly assume that Valentinian was acquainted with the fundamental elements in Christian theology and ethics. On the other hand, the fact that this law was issued ten years after he had assumed the reins of government suggests that it was not based on any strong moral conviction, for in that case, he would surely have promulgated it earlier.[114] Besides this, it is not unlikely that the idea behind the *alimenta* program also provided motivation here, that is to say, the need to ensure a supply of recruits for various tasks that had to be carried out in the Roman empire. Perhaps it was a combination of impulses from Christianity and the need to maintain the level of population that led to the criminalization of *expositio*.

While the church fathers in the fourth and fifth centuries remain true to the basic critical attitude toward *expositio,* they tend to be much more vigorous in their condemnation of the rich and prosperous than in the case of poor parents. Although they do not actually defend this praxis, they show a large measure of understanding and express sympathy with the plight of poor parents who lack the means to look after their children.[115] This development is well illustrated in Basil of Caesarea. Like earlier church fathers, he too begins by regarding *expositio* as a very grave sin. In a letter written in 375, Basil says that if a woman abandons "her newborn child uncared-for on the road, if, although she was really able to save it, she disregarded it, either thinking in this way to conceal her sin or scheming in some entirely brutal and inhuman manner, let her be judged as for murder."[116] It is not clear whether he classifies *expositio* here as murder, or means that this crime is to be punished with the same severity as murder; in either case, it represents a gravely immoral action. It is interesting that this applies to women who are capable of looking after their children, since this denotes a more nuanced approach than in the pre-Constantinian period: now, the situation of the parents and the motives that lead them to expose their children are taken into consideration. Basil finds no extenuating circumstances in the case of parents prosperous enough to care for their children, and here he condemns *expositio* as utterly immoral. However, he goes on: "If she was unable to protect it and the child perished through destitution and the want of the necessities of life, the mother is to be pardoned."[117] In his *Hexaemeron,* Basil writes critically of parents who expose their children "under the plea of poverty," but without mentioning any form of penalty inflicted on such persons.[118] His language here indicates that there are some who use poverty as an excuse for not taking care of their own children, although in reality they are led by quite different motives to expose them.[119] In another passage, however, he describes in moving terms and with considerable empathy the torments suffered by a poor man when he feels himself compelled to sell one of his children.[120]

Thus, although Basil undoubtedly condemns *expositio* as a gravely immoral act, he recognizes that poor people can find themselves in a situation where they have no real choice. They are acting in self-defense when they expose or sell their children, and they cannot be reproached for this.

Ambrose, bishop of Milan from 374 to 397, takes a similar approach. When he exhorts parents to take care of their children, he uses the way crows treat their chicks as a positive example, then makes the following negative contrast:

Those who are very poor expose their infants and refuse to lay claim to them when they are discovered. Even the wealthy, in order that their inheritance may not be divided among several, deny in their very womb their own progeny. By the use of parricidal mixtures they snuff out the fruit of their wombs in the genital organs themselves. In this way it is taken away before it is given.[121]

Ambrose uses much harsher language against the rich who have abortions for economic reasons than against poor people who expose their children. The rich have no excuse! This however does not mean that he simply accepts the fact that poor people practice *expositio*, for if that had been the case, he would not have spoken of this as a contrast to the positive examples from the world of birds.[122] A little further on, Ambrose refers to the "kindly traits" of the fenh, a waterfowl that adopts the eaglet, which its mother has kicked out of the nest, and brings it up with its own brood, ensuring that it receives food and nourishment exactly like its own chicks. He then draws a contrast between the behavior of this bird and the *expositio* of children: "The fenh, therefore, supports an alien brood, whereas we show excessive cruelty when we abandon our own children. Rather, she does not acknowledge them to be such, but considers them to be base-born. Our procedure is worse. We renounce what we acknowledge to be our own."[123] Here, he does not distinguish between the motives that lead the poor and the rich to get rid of their children, and we are therefore justified in reading his words as a general criticism of *expositio*.

Although Ambrose takes a critical attitude to this praxis, however, he concedes that poor people have no real choice. He himself has seen how difficult things can be for parents. By mentioning the concrete example of a father who sold his son at an auction, he integrates into his argument and develops what Basil had earlier written about the torments suffered by parents whose poverty leaves them with no other option than to sell one of their children.[124] Ambrose feels sympathy with this father, and does not express any moral indignation at what he does: this is reserved for the rich who refuse to give any help.

In *De Nuptiis et Concupiscientia*, Augustine calls the exposure of children a sign of their parents' "cruelty" (*crudelitate*)[125] and defines this as sin. But we should note that he regards this primarily as a confirmation (or prolongation) of the sin the married couple had committed by having intercourse without the intention of producing children. This is also why Augustine condemns contraception and abortion, which he appears to regard as more serious sins than *expositio*.

In another context, where Augustine is arguing that it possible for other persons than the parents to bring orphans for baptism, he writes: "Foundlings whom heartless parents have exposed in order that they may be cared for by any passer-by . . . are presented for baptism by these persons [who picked up the children]."[126] He is content to mention this practice; he does not make any moral judgments about the parents who exposed the children, perhaps because this was not relevant to the subject he was discussing. On the other hand, if he had had strong moral objections to *expositio*, he would surely have used a more negative formulation when he spoke of this praxis. In any case, it is wrong to infer from these words that Augustine saw the exposure of children as something quite unproblematic; rather, like Basil and Ambrose, he saw that poor people had no real choice in this matter.

The negative attitude toward abortion, *expositio*, and other forms of limiting the number of children is connected to the generally positive evaluation of procreation by the church's theologians. The fundamental purpose of marriage is to bring children into the world, and children were considered a gift from God. Aristides is one of many who reflect this positive attitude to procreation. In his *Apology*, he says that one expression of the Christian love of neighbor is that "when a child has been born to one of them, they give thanks to God."[127] We find a beautiful expression of a similarly positive basic attitude toward children, rooted in creation theology, in Cyprian's response to Bishop Fideus, who had refused to kiss newborn children in the course of the baptismal liturgy, on the grounds that they were impure. Cyprian writes on behalf of the North African bishops that, when one kisses a creature who has just been created by God, one is in a real sense kissing God's own hands.[128] When Clement of Alexandria discusses marriage, he expresses his solidarity with those who hold that one of the worst things that can happen is to lose a child by death: to have children is a good thing.[129] Ambrose explicitly calls the fertility of parents a gift from God.[130] For Augustine and many other fathers, concupiscence is evil, but sexual intercourse is licit and free from sin when a married couple intend to produce children.[131] In the course of a description of our life here on earth, so unstable and full of dangers, he exclaims: "What joy a newborn child brings to people, and immediately they are all fearful they may be mourning it as they carry it out for burial!"[132]

THE CHURCH'S ATTITUDE TOWARD SEXUAL RELATIONS
BETWEEN ADULTS AND CHILDREN

We noted in chapter 2 that sexual relations between young boys and free men were socially accepted and a widespread phenomenon in the Greek cultural sphere, where they had a long tradition and were regarded as a normal or natural form of sex. This must be seen in the light of a pattern of sexuality where the fundamental dichotomy is not homosexual/heterosexual, but the active/passive or dominant/passive; the "male" was associated with the active role, the "female" with the passive, and boys were considered as belonging in the same category as women, that is, as the passive partner in the sexual act. The Romans too shared this pattern of sexuality, but here we find a critical attitude toward sex with free-born boys, since these would later attain the status of free citizens. However, in both the Greek and the Roman cultural spheres, intercourse between men and children (both boys and girls) of lower societal status was seen as legitimate, normal sex. This applies first and foremost to sexual relations between men and slave-children, or between men and prostitutes.

Did the Christian religion introduce any changes in this area? Did Christianity have any significance for the extent of sexual relations between boys or minors and adult men? If we begin by looking only at the doctrine and ethical thinking of the church fathers, that is, their ideals of correct morality, and at the decrees of early councils, the answer is unambiguous: they consistently upheld the condemnation of sexual relations between children and adults. The doctrine of the "two ways" in the *Didache* and *Barnabas* includes the prohibition of corrupting boys.[133] Like adultery and fornication, this a sexual sin from which one who takes the path of life must abstain. In the *Didache*, these sins are prohibited in the context of the exposition of the second half of the double commandment to love. The same sexual sins are mentioned in a catalog of vices in *Ad Autolycum,* a text composed by Bishop Theophilus of Antioch c. 180. In the course of his comparison of pagan and Christian morality, he writes:

> Do you, therefore, show me yourself, whether you are not an adulterer, or a fornicator, or a thief, or a robber, or a purloiner; whether you do not corrupt boys; whether you are not insolent, or a slanderer, or passionate, or envious, or proud, or supercilious; whether you are not a brawler, or covetous, or disobedient to parents; and whether you do not sell your children; for to those who do these things God is not manifest.[134]

Clearly, Theophilus links pederasty with idolatry, as does Athenagoras in his defense of the Christians against pagan accusations. Polemic against the homosexual conduct of pagans is one important aspect in his portrait of the infinite gulf that yawns between Christian and pagan morality:

> For those who have set up a market for fornication, and established infamous resorts for the young for every kind of vile pleasure,—who do not abstain even from males, males with males committing shocking abominations, outraging all the noblest and comeliest bodies in all sorts of ways, so dishonouring the fair workmanship of God . . . these men, I say, revile us for the very things which they are conscious of themselves, and ascribe to their own gods, boasting of them as noble deeds, and worthy of gods. These adulterers and pæderasts defame the eunuchs and the once-married.[135]

In his interpretation of the story of Sodom (Genesis 19), Clement of Alexandria writes that apostasy from God revealed itself precisely when men directed their sexual desires to other men and boys: "The Sodomites having, through much luxury, fallen into uncleanness, practicing adultery shamelessly, and burning with insane love for boys."[136] Sexual intercourse between persons of the same gender—whether between women, between adult men, or between men and boys—is regarded as bestial and contrary to nature, since this sexuality does not serve the goal of procreation.[137]

Elizabeth A. Clark does complete justice to our sources when she writes: "Homosexual activity, especially pederasty, was strongly condemned by early Christian writers."[138] This condemnation found expression in the penalties that gradually came to be imposed for homosexual praxis, including pederasty. Canon 71 of the Council of Elvira (306) lays down that one who seduces boys is to be excommunicated for the rest of his life. Not surprisingly, there were divided opinions about how severe the punishment should be, or how long it should last. Some decades later, Gregory of Nyssa says that the punishment should be limited to nine years of penance.[139] In our context, it is not the precise calculation of penalties that is interesting, so much as the fact that ecclesiastical councils and theologians considered pederasty a sin that entailed exclusion from the Christian community.

A number of facts influenced the early church's negative attitude to all forms of sex between persons of the same gender, including pederasty. While the Christian religion saw sexuality within a much more restricted

framework than the Greco-Roman world, one fundamental reason was its
Jewish roots: homosexual acts are rejected both in the Old Testament and
in Hellenistic Judaism, where male and female homosexual activity was
seen as a conscious break with God's order of creation, and as linked to the
Gentile ethos from which the Jews wished to mark their distance. The tendency to relate homosexual activity to idolatry intensified in Judaism in
late antiquity,[140] and there is every reason to believe that the relatively few
New Testament authors who touch on this subject (and who all condemn
homosexual activity) were strongly influenced by Jewish thinking.[141] Many
scholarly studies have been devoted in recent years to the question of the
type of homosexual relations that are condemned—for example, cultic
prostitution, pederasty, men who also have sex with women, or stable relationships where the persons involved have a fundamental homosexual
orientation—and the presuppositions that underlie this condemnation
in the New Testament.[142] Naturally, these questions are highly important,
when we try to determine the relevance and weight of the biblical critique
of homosexual activity for our own contemporary church debates about
homosexual partnership and about the possible ordination of practicing
homosexuals and lesbians to the ministry, but I cannot discuss such issues
here. Nor is this necessary; in the context of our present investigation, it
suffices to note that the early Christian writers employed the biblical material in their polemic against homosexual activity.

This employment of the biblical material, and the fathers' negative attitude toward homosexuality, must also be seen in the light of general
attitudes to sexuality, marriage, and celibacy. We can trace a tension as
early as the New Testament between living in marriage and living in sexual
abstinence.[143] Although sexual desire and passions in general were something to be held under a tight rein, the theologians accepted that they were
necessary for the sake of procreation. For example, Clement of Alexandria held that marriage was licit and that intercourse should be allowed,
provided the intention was to procreate children.[144] At the same time, he
emphasizes that the sexual act should be carried out with self-control, and
without passion.[145]

From the beginning of the third century, more radical Encratite ideals
began to gain wide acceptance in the church. We may say that a new epoch
begins with Origen (d. 256), who in many ways laid the foundations of
the monastic movement that was to become an important factor in the
church from the beginning of the following century. His ideal was celibacy
and total chastity. Sexuality, like everything else that contains earthly joy
and pleasure, is threatening because it distracts the human person from

the spiritual life.[146] We must emphasize that the hermits and ascetics were a spiritual elite. Nevertheless—or perhaps precisely for that reason—their views of the ideal virtuous Christian life had a formative influence on "ordinary" Christians too. The view of sexuality that came to predominate can be seen as a compromise between radical ascetic ideals and a concession to those who were unable to live in celibacy: the only legitimate framework for sexual intercourse is marriage. But not even this gave the green light for sexuality, since the only admissible purpose of intercourse was procreation.

We find this view of sexuality in the great fathers of the fourth century, both in the Latin tradition—represented by theologians such as Ambrose, Augustine, and Jerome—and in the Greek tradition—represented by figures such as Athanasius of Alexandria, John Chrysostom, Basil of Caesarea, Gregory Nazianzen, and Gregory of Nyssa. Although marriage was an institution ordained by God, the fathers considered it an emergency solution, or the lesser of two evils. As Jostein Børtnes writes, it was "a concession to the fallen human being, and a place of refuge for those who did not succeed in living in celibacy. But there is no doubt that sexual abstinence was the Christian fathers' ideal. The highest form of the Christian life was virginity, the struggle to preserve one's body pure and virginal. Through chastity and abstinence, the individual Christian was to shape his sinful body anew so that it became God's temple."[147]

Naturally, the consequence of such an ethic was the condemnation of all forms of homosexual activity, including sexual relations between men and boys.[148] The idea that the only legitimate context in which sexual desire may find expression is procreation, is a basic premise for the way in which the fathers read and employ the biblical texts that condemn homosexual acts. Such a view of sexuality implies not only the rejection of the ancient Greek tradition of sexual relations between men and boys; it also entails the condemnation of every extramarital sexual relation, including every context where children are involved. We do, nevertheless, find traces of the "active/passive" dichotomy in the formulations and approaches of the fathers. It has, for example, been demonstrated that John Chrysostom reads Paul's condemnation of sexual intercourse between men in Romans 1:26-27 "against the background of the pagan, pre-Christian categorization of men who have sex with men. Like Paul, he divides them into active and passive partners, and transfers this category to a Christian context, while at the same time condemning these forms of sexual intercourse in a way different from the customary Roman view of the normative and natural sexual praxis of men and boys."[149]

There can therefore be no doubt that the early Christian moral tradition condemned all forms of sexual activity between children (of whatever
age) and adults. The Christian sexual ethic which the patristic theologians
present was a clear break with the view of sexual relations between adults
and children in the Greco-Roman tradition. On this point, Christian theology and ethics are crystal clear.

But what of praxis? These ethical ideals were largely formed by a theological elite, who were influenced by asceticism; did they win acceptance
among Christians in general? The very fact that the Council of Elvira issued a canon about the penalty to be imposed on those who had sex with
boys indicates that this did in fact happen among Christians; otherwise,
it would not have been necessary to deal with such problems in a special canon. John Chrysostom's condemnation of sexual relations between
Christians of the same gender in Antioch is also interesting here. In his
Adversus Oppugnatores Vitae Monasticae, he calls sexual relations between
men "the greatest of the evils" and "the chief catastrophe." According to
Chrysostom, sex between men is so widespread that "womankind is in
danger of being superfluous when young men take their place in every
activity." He continues:

> Even this is not so terrible as the fact that such a great abomi-
> nation is performed with a great fearlessness and lawlessness
> has become the law. No one is afraid, no one trembles. No one
> is ashamed, no one blushes, but they enjoy a good laugh. Those
> who are self-controlled are thought to be crazy, and those who
> admonish are considered fools. . . . No benefit comes from law
> courts or laws or pedagogues or parents or attendants or teachers.
> Some are corrupted by money, others are concerned only about
> their pay. Some are more moral and pay attention to the salva-
> tion of those entrusted to them; but these are easily deceived and
> tricked, or else they fear the power of the unchaste. For it would
> be easier for a suspected tyrant to save himself than it would be
> for someone who tried to rescue [the youth] from these vile men
> to escape their hands. Thus, in the middle of the cities, as if in a
> great desert, males perform shameless acts with males. . . .
>
> These persons who . . . have had the benefit of divine instruc-
> tion, who say to others what should be done and what should
> not be done, and who have heard the scriptures which have come
> down from heaven—these men have intercourse more fearlessly

with young boys than with prostitutes! And as if they were not human, as if the providence of God did not exist to judge events, as if darkness were all around and no one could see or hear what they do, thus they commit all these reckless deeds in utter madness.

But the parents of the children who are being violated bear it in silence; they do not bury themselves in the earth along with their children, nor do they think of some remedy for that evil. If it were necessary to take children to a foreign land to save them from this sickness, or to the sea, or to the islands, or to an inaccessible land, or to the world beyond us, should we not do and suffer all things so as not to allow these defilements?[150]

It is not clear whether the first half of this quotation refers to sexual activities involving boys, or to sex between adult men; but the fact that Chrysostom says that parents and teachers do not do what they can to prevent such immorality indicates that boys are the object of the sexual activities of adults. In the second section, it is clear that he is speaking about boys, and if we read the first section in the light of what follows, it is reasonable to assume that he is speaking of pederasty there too. If this is the case, Chrysostom's description of sexual relations between men and boys refers to the most common form of sex between persons of the same gender in Greek antiquity.

It is not easy to determine the extent to which Chrysostom intends to describe the general situation in Antioch, or more precisely the situation in the church; perhaps he does both. However, when Chrysostom speaks explicitly of pederasty, he is referring to Christians—for those who commit such shameless deeds have received Christian instruction and are acquainted with the Christian writings, and this makes their conduct all the worse in Chrysostom's eyes. When he writes that such persons "say to others what should be done and what should not be done," it is not likely that he is referring to church leaders.[151] It is more probable that those he has in mind took part in a more general manner in discussions and debates with other Christians, using the opportunity to put forward their own views. In any case, however, the picture he paints of the situation among Antioch's Christians is perfectly clear, as far as pederasty is concerned: it was very widespread. And this picture has been used by scholars as evidence that, although the early Christian theologians and teachers condemned pederasty, they could not exercise control over the ordinary members of the church, who followed other norms.[152]

This conclusion may at first sight seem obvious. But I believe that it presupposes an uncritical equation of what the text says (on the one hand) and societal reality (on the other). To begin with, we must not forget that the aim of the *Adversus Oppugnatores Vitae Monasticae* was to defend the monastic life against general criticism, and to persuade Christian fathers to send their sons to the monks, so that they could receive a higher education and, above all, moral instruction.[153] This suggests that we should read his remarks about pederasty among church members as a rhetorical exaggeration intended to amplify the contrast between the monastic life and life in the city: he exaggerates the moral degeneracy among urban Christians in order to frighten fathers into sending their sons to the monks where (it is implied) they will not become victims of adult men's sexual desires and will receive a moral formation that prevents them from attempting to seduce boys when they themselves have grown up. Second, we should remember that this text was composed at a period when Chrysostom was a zealous adherent of ascetic ideals and held that all Christians could and should choose this form of life. It is reasonable to assume that this colors his description of the moral standard of those who did not choose the monastic way of life. Finally, Chrysostom saw a very close link between pederasty and the Greek *paideia* or education.[154] This makes his condemnation of pederasty part of the general onslaught on Greek culture and morality that runs throughout this text and has left its mark on many of his other writings too.[155]

This suggests a need for caution against reading Chrysostom's words in *Adversus Oppugnatores Vitae Monasticae* 3.8 as an account of a real situation. I am not suggesting that pederasty never occurred, but rather that we have good reasons to assume that Chrysostom's rhetorical goal leads him to exaggerate his description. He certainly seems to have believed that pederasty did in fact occur, as we see from a homily on Matthew 23:14, where he attacks men whose "curiosity is kindled by boys' flowering youth."[156]

I have suggested that when Chrysostom attempts to persuade fathers to send their sons to the monks for further education and moral instruction, he implies that the boys will not fall victim to adult sexual desire in a monastic community. This, however, was not always the case. It is not difficult to imagine that the colonies of hermits and the monasteries which came into existence from the closing years of the third century onward had a special attraction for persons with a clearly homosexual orientation; and such environments could also promote homosexual praxis, since this was the only form of sexual intercourse available there. Understandably, our sources do not speak clearly on this matter, but we do find some hints. In his biography of the hermit Antony, who lived from the late third century to the mid-fourth, Bishop Athanasius of Alexandria describes how one who has decided to lead an ascetic life in chastity is exposed to temptation by sexual desire and by pleasure in general. He describes the various strategies employed by the devil in his attempt to seduce the hermit. First, he appears to the holy man as a woman; when this is unsuccessful, he appears to Antony in the form of a young black boy. In other words, Antony is being tempted to commit pederasty. The point that the boy is black is a racist element in the narrative: the incarnate devil's mind corresponds to the color of his skin:

> And as if succumbing, he no longer attacked by means of thoughts (for the crafty one had been cast out), but using now a human voice, said, "I tricked many, and I vanquished many, but just now, waging my attack on you and your labors, as I have upon many others, I was too weak. . . . I am the friend of fornication. I set its ambushes and I worked its seductions against the young—I have been called the spirit of fornication. How many who wanted to live prudently I have deceived! How many of those exercising self-control I won over when I agitated them! . . . I am he who so frequently troubled you and so many times was overturned by you." And Antony gave thanks to the Lord, and responding boldly to him, said: "'You, then, are much to be despised, for you are black of mind, and like a powerless child. From now on you cause me no anxiety. . . .'" Hearing these words, the black one immediately fled, cowering at the words and afraid even to approach the man.[157]

Although this narrative is a stereotype, there is reason to believe that it reflects genuine temptations in the hermit colonies and monasteries.

Toward the end of the fourth century, Basil offered practical advice on how monks should avoid being tempted sexually by their confrères. His words show that he believed there was a real danger that older monks would be sexually attracted by younger brethren:

> It is frequently the case with young men that when rigorous self-restraint is exercised, the glowing complexion of youth still blossoms forth and becomes a source of desire to those around them. If, therefore, anyone is youthful and physically beautiful, let him

keep his attractiveness hidden until his appearance reaches a suitable state.

Sit in a chair far from such a youth; in sleep do not allow your
clothing to touch his but, rather, have an old man between you.
When he is speaking to you or singing opposite you, look down
as you respond to him, so that you do not by gazing on his face
take the seed of desire from the enemy sower and bring forth har-
vests of corruption and loss. Do not be found with him either
indoors or where no one can see what you do, either for studying
the prophecies of Holy Scripture or for any other purpose, no
matter how necessary.[158]

Our sources show that boys could represent a sexual temptation for men
in the hermit colonies and monasteries, but they do not tell us that pederasty actually occurred. On the contrary, Athanasius emphasizes that
Antony withstood the devil's temptation. We should not, of course, expect anything else in a biography that seeks to portray Antony as a holy
man and an example of the virtuous ascetic life; but it is reasonable to
assume that the advice given by Basil to his monks was prompted not only
by awareness of the sexual temptations that monks might encounter, but
also by the knowledge that they did sometimes yield to the temptation to
have sex with boys.[159] Similarly, we may assume that Athanasius knew that
pederasty occurred in the hermit colonies, and wished to present Saint
Antony as an example of one who resisted such temptations. It is impossible to estimate how widespread sexual relations between men and boys
were; but only a tiny percentage of Christian boys entered monastic life
and thereby became potential temptations for the adult monks.

We may sum up as follows: the theologians and leaders of the early
church are unanimous in their condemnation of all forms of sexual activity between persons of the same gender, but our sources indicate that
sexual relations between men and boys did occur among Christians. Nevertheless, there is no reason to doubt that the normative Christian sexual
ethic, which held that marriage was the only legitimate context for sexual
intercourse and that the intention thereby should be procreation, did in
fact lead Christians to adopt a pattern of sexuality different from that
of the Greco-Roman tradition; and precisely the area of sexual relations
between children and adult men shows that this was the case. Only one
council, that of Elvira, discussed pederasty and stipulated the penalty to
be imposed upon Christian men who were involved in such activity, and

this is surely a clear sign that pederasty was *not* a common phenomenon among the members of the church. This is also indicated by the fact that, with the exception of the text of John Chrysostom discussed above, pederasty is not one of the subjects of polemic within the church. And this means that the Christian religion had consequences for children in the sphere of sexuality. Children—especially boys—were much less involved in sexual relations with adults in a Christian context than was the case in pagan antiquity.

Emerging Christian Standards and Practice

We have concentrated in the first half of this chapter on abortion, the exposure of children, and infanticide. From the *Didache* and *Barnabas* onward, our Christian sources throughout the pre-Constantinian period reject these phenomena and condemn those who practice them. Here, the Christian texts adopt Jewish thinking, as is especially clear in the *Didache* and *Barnabas*, whose authors have incorporated the tradition of the "two ways" into their own ethical instruction. The commandment not to kill children, either in the womb or after birth, is seen in connection with the obligation to love one's neighbor. Like adults, children are regarded as individuals who must be taken care of. It is interesting to note how in these early Christian writings the opposition to abortion, *expositio*, and infanticide is rooted in the idea of God as creator: since the children are created by him, one must not destroy their lives, but must look after them. We encounter this argument in various forms in most of the writers who condemn abortion, *expositio*, and infanticide in the first three centuries: the *Apocalypse of Peter*, Methodius of Olympus, Athenagoras, and Tertullian. Other writers, such as Clement of Alexandria, Justin Martyr, and Lactantius, are equally harsh in their condemnation, but do not argue so clearly on the basis of creation theology. Clement's critique of abortion functions as a subsidiary argument against having sexual intercourse without the intention of procreation; he argues more in terms of theological principles when he rejects *expositio*, since he appeals here to the law of Moses. He also points to the risk that fathers may unintentionally have sexual intercourse at some later date with the children whom they are exposing—many of the children who worked in brothels were foundlings. Nevertheless, Clement makes far less use of the incest argument than Justin Martyr, who argues that *expositio* is a sin against God primarily because of such children's future fate as prostitutes, with the inherent possibility of incest. This line of argument must be understood against the background of pagan accusations that the Christian assemblies involved sexual orgies and promiscuity. Justin rejects such accusations and insists that the pagans who make such charges are in fact themselves guilty of much more abominable actions. Lactantius claims that *expositio* and infanticide break God's commandment not to take life. Although some Roman moral philosophers criticized abortion and *expositio,* the Christian critique and condemnation of these phenomena were significantly harsher.

This basic criticism and way of thinking about abortion and *expositio* was continued in the Constantinian and post-Constantinian periods, as we see among other things in the conciliar decrees of Elvira and Ancyra, which imposed heavy penalties for abortion. Theologians such as Basil of Caesarea, John Chrysostom, Jerome, and Augustine condemned abortion. One important fundamental difference between Eastern and Western thinking was that Western theologians made a much greater distinction than Eastern fathers between the formed and unformed fetus. Abortion was morally reprehensible in the eyes of the Westerners too, but it was only when the fetus had acquired its full form (that is, when it had received its soul) that abortion was regarded as a breach of the commandment not to kill.

Although we find the same basic critical attitude to *expositio* in the church fathers of the fourth and fifth centuries, their criticism is more nuanced, in the sense that they take into account the actual conditions of people's lives. Several of them go far in expressing compassion and understanding with regard to poor parents who are not able to look after their children; but their condemnation of prosperous parents who expose their children is just as categorical as that made in earlier centuries.

Naturally, we cannot simply assume that the ideals reflected in the Christian texts corresponded totally to praxis among Christians. If, however, the fathers' arguments were to be convincing at all, there must have been some measure of coherence between what they said about the Christian life and how people did in fact live—not least in the case of visible and easily demonstrable phenomena such as the exposure of children. Abortion is more hidden, and it is therefore more difficult to make a serious assessment of actual praxis. If, however, there was in fact some correspondence between ideals and reality, we may say that abortion occurred more rarely among Christians than among others.

The second part of this chapter dealt with Christian attitudes to sexual relations between adults and children. Here, we have seen that the early Christian moral tradition proclaims unanimously that marriage is the only sphere within which sexuality can be lived legitimately, though this does not give a green light for sexual pleasure, since sexual activity is meant to be restricted to the goal of procreation. The consequence of such a restrictive sexual ethic was the prohibition of all forms of homosexual activity, including the sexual relations between boys and adult men that had a long tradition in the Greco-Roman world. Such a view of the place and function of sexuality entails the condemnation of all other forms of sexual relations between adults and children. On this issue, Christian sexual ethics broke in a very obvious way with the Greco-Roman tradition.

This sexual ethic was elaborated by an ascetic elite in the church, by men who tended to set high standards for Christian praxis. To what extent did Christians in general accept these ideals? The council of Elvira and texts by John Chrysostom and monastic writers show that pederasty did occur among Christians; however, the fact that only one council mentioned this problem, and that John Chrysostom is the only father to speak of this topic in his polemic against other Christians, indicates that it was not widespread. It is also reasonable to believe that Chrysostom exaggerates the extent of pederasty among Christians in Antioch for the purposes of his rhetoric. It is impossible to guess how widespread sexual relations between boys and adult men in monasteries were. The texts that describe or hint at the temptations boys represented for the adult monks are credible, however, when we bear in mind that homosexual activity was the only form of sex possible within such communities, and that it is far from improbable that the hermit colonies possessed a special attraction for men with a clearly homosexual orientation. But irrespective of how often pederasty did in fact occur in the hermit colonies, it must be emphasized that only a tiny percentage of Christian boys actually entered such an environment. I believe therefore that we may safely conclude that the Christian sexual ethic brought a dramatic decline in the number of children—especially boys—who were involved in sexual relations with adults.

5
MAKING "ATHLETES OF CHRIST": UPBRINGING AND EDUCATION OF CHILDREN

The main focus in this chapter is on the upbringing of children in the household. What do our sources say about the parents' responsibility or obligation to rear their children in accordance with Christian ideals? What theological justification is offered for such a responsibility? What is the goal of upbringing? What are its substance and methods? These are the most important questions we shall put to our sources.

Jerome and John Chrysostom are the only patristic writers who devote explicit attention to this area, which is indeed the main subject in some of their writings. The most important text is Chrysostom's *De Inani Gloria*. I shall therefore refer to it very frequently. But although there are no texts earlier than the end of the fourth century concerned specifically with the upbringing of children, we do find summary statements about upbringing in a long line of documents covering a span of time from the late New Testament epistles to the fifth century, and this allows us to see a number of lines of development: we can follow the thinking of the literary representatives of the early church about parents' responsibility to bring up their children, about the fundamental or theological reasons for this responsibility, and about the goal, contents, and methods of upbringing.[1]

Although the terms "upbringing" and "education" are not completely synonymous, they are used interchangeably here. One might of course maintain that "upbringing" denotes the total interaction between parents (and perhaps other persons in the household) and children with the aim of socializing the children into particular ways of living, while "education" denotes only one part of this activity; understood on these lines, "upbringing" obviously encompasses more than "education." However, I prefer to follow the sources here. The basic term they employ for the activity that we shall discuss—*poideuô/paideia*—does not make this distinction. *Paideuô* can mean to "bring up," "rear," "train," "correct," and "educate."[2]

Accordingly, our main focus will lie on the upbringing and education that took place in the household. Since the school played an important role in intellectual and moral education, and indeed in cultural socialization as a whole, we touch briefly on Christian attitudes to the public schools at the end of this chapter. In the few families where the parents were so wealthy that they could afford to send their children to school, the position they took on this question had considerable significance for the daily lives of their children: to put it quite simply, this determined whether or not their children became pupils in school.

THE OBLIGATION TO MOLD CHILDREN ACCORDING TO THE CHRISTIAN IDEALS

The New Testament and the Apostolic Fathers

As early as the New Testament epistles, we find an awareness that it is the parents' responsibility to look after their children and bring them up. In the framework of a household code, the author of Ephesians addresses the children directly at 6:1 and exhorts them to be obedient to their parents.[3] He justifies this exhortation by referring to the commandment in the Decalogue to honor one's father and mother. But it is not only the subordinate partner in this relationship who has obligations: at 6:4, he addresses the fathers directly and urges them not to treat their children in such a way as to kindle anger in them, but to "bring them up in the discipline and instruction of the Lord." We find a similar household code at Colossians 3:20 and following. Here, too, the children are first exhorted to be obedient to their parents, and then the fathers are urged not to be too harsh in disciplining their children. This is not the place for a detailed discussion of the relationship between the household codes in these two letters. I agree with those scholars who hold that the author of Ephesians employs Colossians and Christianizes the exhortations in the earlier epistle to a certain extent, by linking them more closely to a life in keeping with the commandments of the Lord.[4] We note that in both cases, the authors directly address the children. This implies that they take it for granted that the children are part of the community and are members of the group that assembles when the letter is read during worship in the various domestic churches. It is reasonable to assume that the authors envisage children old enough to be aware of having a relationship to Christ and capable of making sense of exhortations based on such a relationship—perhaps children aged twelve to thirteen and older.[5]

In the framework of a household code that regulates the relationships between the various groups in the household, the author of the Letter to Titus exhorts young women at 2:4 "to love their children." His prescriptions reflect the hierarchical patriarchal structure in the Greco-Roman household; the woman is told, among other things, that she must be subordinate to her husband, show him love, and be a good housekeeper. It is in this context that the exhortation to love her children must be read.[6] The epistle does not spell out precisely what this commandment entails, but it is reasonable to suppose that the author envisages the daily care of children—and this implies that the mother gives them an appropriate upbringing. In other words, this text assumes that it is the mother who is most directly involved in the children's upbringing.

Another reference to children in the same letter is interesting. At 1:6-9, the author gives instructions about the qualities to be looked for in those who become elders in the community. In addition to various other qualities, the candidate for the ministry of elder must be in charge of his own household. His children must be "believers, not accused of debauchery and not rebellious." The idea is that one who is to be leader in a Christian community must first have demonstrated the ability to lead his own household. This is stated explicitly at 1 Timothy 3:4, where the author writes that good management of one's household implies that children show their parents obedience. It appears that the patriarchal structure in the household is emphasized here even more strongly than in Ephesians and Colossians.[7] Although catalogs of virtues in Greek paraenetic texts likewise require that an office-holder be capable of governing his household well,[8] the focus in the Pastoral Letters on children and their conduct is striking.[9] When we bear in mind the *patria potestas* that went with the father's position in the Greco-Roman household, it is not surprising that stress is laid on obedience and respect in the children's relationship to him; we are not however told what this actually implies, except that the author expects the children to have accepted the Christian faith and to live in accordance with it. As we shall see, both the Syriac *Didascalia* and the *Apostolic Constitutions* apply the same criterion to potential candidates for the episcopal ministry.

It is helpful here to remember that Mediterranean culture at this period was what cultural anthropologists call a "shame/honor culture."[10] One primary aspect of such a culture is that, unlike modern Western culture, the group and the collective are more significant than the individual, who receives his or her status from the group. People perceive themselves primarily in terms of their relation to other persons and groups. This does not mean that a person's own estimation of himself or herself is irrelevant to that individual's perception of his or her own value; but the degree of honor depends ultimately on the response and evaluation of others. Accordingly, although one may claim honor on the basis of one's own self-estimation, this becomes real honor only when the group recognizes and confirms the claim.[11] Thus, interaction between people was largely orientated toward securing the recognition and defense of one's own status and honor.

Basically, honor could be achieved in two ways. A person might claim honor because of his status, for example, because of inherited wealth or his noble family. In such cases, one need not do anything active in order to be honored, and this is called *ascribed honor. Acquired honor* is based on deeds that the group recognizes as virtuous.[12] In cases where a person's claim to honor is not recognized by the group with which he identifies, that is, the "significant others," he is put to shame. Such a culture might therefore be described as a culture of competition—competition to increase honor and avoid shame.[13]

In our context, it is important to note that "Honor indicates a person's social standing and rightful place in society." This depends on one's gender, among other things.[14] For example, the household codes entitle the father of the household to expect that his wife and children would obey him, and thereby treat him honorably. If, however, they behave otherwise than is considered consistent with the proper social codes, they bring shame upon him. This means that one who behaves otherwise than in the manner that is considered consistent with the proper order is acting dishonorably, and a man who is not treated in keeping with his place in society will suffer shame. As Bruce J. Malina writes,

> Honor is the value of a person in his or her own eyes (that is, one's claim to worth) *plus* that person's value in the eyes of his or her social group. Honor is a claim to worth along with the social acknowledgment of worth. Society shares the sets of meanings and feelings bound up in the symbols of power, sexual status, and religion. Whom you can control is bound up with male and female roles, which are also bound up with where you stand on the status ladder of your group. When you lay claim to a certain status as embodied by your power and in your sexual role, you

are claiming honor. For example, a father in the family (sexual role, status on the ladder of society) commands his children to do something, and they obey (power): they treat him honorably. Other people seeing this would acknowledge that he is an honorable father. But should this father command and his children disobey, they would dishonor him, and his peers would ridicule him, thereby acknowledging his lack of honor as a father. . . . Say a teacher . . . sets out a teaching which his disciples do not agree with; they do not acknowledge his teaching power. To bystanders, this would be an occasion of dishonoring him, since even his disciples do not believe him. Should his disciples believe him, see the truth of his teaching, accept what he says on his authority, then the bystanders of the community would acknowledge that he is in fact a teacher, hence worthy of honor.[15]

Shame and honor are "pivotal values" in the culture in which the Pastoral Letters were written, and I believe that this background helps us to understand their requirements that one who is to be leader in the community should himself have children who are believers, and that these children should show him obedience and respect. If the children were to break with their father's Christian faith and with the ideals for conduct inherent in that faith, this act of disobedience would bring disgrace both upon him and upon the rest of the family. Such children would not be responding to their father's instructions in the way that he could expect, given his social position in the family: in other words, they would be failing to show him the honor appropriate to one who is a father. Within the Christian group, such a man would lose face, and this would weaken his authority as a community leader. One who is to head the community must first have demonstrated in his own household that he possesses the authority that leads those lower than him in the hierarchical order to give him the honor demanded by contemporary social conventions. If a man fails to establish his authority in his family, it is unlikely that he is suited to lead a community.

It is also reasonable to believe that the pagan surroundings played a role. At this period, the Christians gathered in private houses, and this entailed geographical proximity to their pagan neighbors; people lived close to one another, since the residential area in the cities in classical antiquity was concentrated in a relatively small space.[16] This made life transparent. Any breach of social conventions would soon be known in the neighborhood, and this meant that a leader in the Christian communities who was not shown obedience and respect by his children would lose face, not only among the insiders in the group itself, but also among outsiders—his neighbors and other non-Christians. And this would weaken the plausibility of the Christian religion.[17] Outsiders will think that if the leader of the Christian community lacks authority over his own children, he deserves contempt; and if even his own children do not listen to him, this detracts from the plausibility of the religion and the worship of God for which he is supposed to be the leader. This missionary aspect helps, in my view, to explain why the Pastoral Letters differ from pagan texts, when they underscore that persons who are to have leadership ministries must have obedient children. Another element that explains this emphasis is the ideal that parents were responsible for introducing their children to the Christian faith and bringing them up in keeping with Christian ideals. As community leaders, presbyters and bishops had a particular function as models for the other members, and this entailed ensuring that their children received instruction in the Christian faith and that they lived in accordance with Christian ideals.[18]

I believe that the categories of shame and honor help explain why the Pastoral Letters underscore that community leaders must have children who obey them. Later in this chapter, I shall argue that this is not restricted to the children of leaders; the same perspective also helps explain why our sources continually emphasize that children in general must be obedient to their parents.[19]

Although the New Testament references to the instruction and upbringing of children are not extensive, the fact that they have their place in the paraenetic sections indicates an awareness that parents were obligated to bring up their children in the Christian religion. Broadly speaking, the same applies to the apostolic fathers too. In the *Didache* and the *Letter of Barnabas*, the exhortations about upbringing are part of the doctrine of the "two ways," and the formulation is identical in both texts: "Thou shalt not withhold thine hand from thy son or from thy daughter, but thou shalt teach them the fear of God from their youth up."[20] In the *Didache*, this exhortation comes in a section that has a number of points of similarity to the New Testament household codes; in *Barnabas*, it follows the prohibitions of abortion and infanticide, and functions as an exposition of the commandment to love one's neighbor. This last point is interesting, because it shows that the author understands the appropriate upbringing of children as a realization of the Christian commandment of love. We also find an exhortation to teach children the fear of God in a household code in Polycarp's *Letter to the Philippians*, where he urges the men to teach their wives "to educate their children in the fear of God."[21] Polycarp is probably drawing here on the household code in *1 Clement* 21:6, which exhorts the readers to "instruct the young in the fear of God." A little later in the same household code, Clement exhorts his readers to let "our children share in the instruction which is in Christ."[22]

Hermas does not explicitly exhort parents to bring up their children, but he does touch indirectly on this theme. The woman who reveals herself and speaks to Hermas on behalf of God accuses him of failing to take with sufficient seriousness the task of admonishing his children: he has made too little use of his authority over them, and the reason for this gentle attitude is that he loved his children too much.[23] As a result, they are now adults who sin against both God and their parents. It is not so important here to determine the precise nature of this sin.[24] The interesting point is that Hermas is accused of not taking seriously enough his task as *paterfamilias*, that is to say, the formation of his children in keeping with the Christian ideals, and he is admonished in the following words: "For this reason the Lord is angry with you."

The *Didascalia* and the *Apostolic Constitutions*

The *Didascalia* goes even further in emphasizing the obligation to raise one's children in accordance with Christian ideals. It was composed in Syria in the first half of the third century and combines a church order and pastoral exhortations. The fact that it devotes an entire chapter (though one that is relatively brief) to the upbringing of children makes it the most detailed discussion of the subject in the Christian tradition up to that date.[25] The author underscores that if parents neglect to correct their children, their children will imitate the evil actions of the pagans. Much is at stake here, and this is why the author admonishes parents not to be slow to "rebuke and correct and teach them; for you will not kill them by chastising them, but rather save them alive."[26] He writes that such a practice is in keeping with the doctrine of the Lord, and adduces as scriptural proof Proverbs 23:14 ("Chasten thy son, that there may be hope for him: for thou shalt strike him with a rod, and deliver his soul from Sheol") and 13:24 ("Whosoever spareth his rod, hateth his son"). The "rod" in these texts is not understood literally, but as a metaphor for the Word of God, Jesus Christ; the author draws the conclusion that anyone "who spares to speak a word of rebuke to his son, hates his son." He further emphasizes the responsibility incumbent on parents by holding them responsible for their children's salvation, and claims that they will be judged by God on account of their children's sins:

> Now, whether this [that is, the sons' falling into fornication] hap-
> pen to them without their parents, their parents themselves will
> be accountable before God for the judgment of their souls; or
> whether again by your license they are undisciplined and sin, you
> their parents will likewise be guilty on their account before God.

The context of these words shows that the author is primarily concerned
about sexual sins: parents must bring up their children in such a way that
they refuse to imitate pagan conduct in this sphere. More important is
to note how clearly he formulates the principle that parents will be held
responsible for the eternal fate of their children, and that they themselves
will be punished if it was their lack of discipline that caused their children
to sin.[27] It is scarcely possible to emphasize more strongly parents' responsibility and duty to bring up their children in keeping with Christian ideals. As we shall see, another Syrian theologian, John Chrysostom, employs
the same line of argumentation roughly one hundred years later.

Other passages in the *Didascalia* reflect the importance of giving children a proper Christian upbringing. When he instructs the bishop about
how he is to care for widows and look after them, the author urges him
to help the poor, even those who are not widows, in the rearing of their
children.[28] He also urges the bishop to display his concern for orphans
who have not been adopted: the episcopal function requires him to "take
pains over their upbringing, so that nothing may be wanting to them."[29]
These passages do not define more precisely the goal of upbringing, but
it seems that the word is employed in a broad sense here. In addition to
upbringing in the narrower sense of the word, it also involves ensuring
that the children receive the material goods they need for daily living. As I
have mentioned, the *Didascalia* lays down, as one of the criteria to be met
before a man can be appointed bishop, that he has given sufficient attention to the proper Christian upbringing of his children and that he has
been successful in this task. The author employs the formula we have seen
in several of the apostolic fathers, when he summarizes the essence of this
task as bringing up children "in the fear of God."[30] This implies teaching
children the contents of the Christian faith and admonishing them to live
in accordance with the ideals relevant to the Christian life.

The *Apostolic Constitutions*, from the close of the fourth century, take
over and frequently elaborate the statements of the *Didascalia* about the
education of children.[31] Fathers are adjured to "educate (*paideuô*) your
children in the Lord, bringing (*entrephô*) them up in the nurture (*paideiô*)
and admonition (*nouthesia*) of the Lord."[32] If this is not done, the children

will gradually come to do actions opposed to what is good. Unlike the *Didascalia*, the author of the *Apostolic Constitutions* states that the formation of children is to begin from a very tender age; but he agrees with the *Didascalia* in making parents responsible for their children's eternal destiny, and affirms that they will be punished for their children's sins. The approach of the *Apostolic Constitutions* is somewhat milder, however, since they specify that it is parents who have neglected the upbringing of the children who will be held responsible, if these children commit fornication and do not come to salvation:

> If this happen [that their children fall into fornication] by the carelessness of their parents, those that begat them will be guilty of their souls. For if the offending children get into the company of debauched persons by the fault of those that begat them, they will not be punished alone by themselves; but their parents also will be condemned on their account.[33]

In patristic literature, the Greek noun *ameleia* denotes a general "carelessness, indifference," but also expresses more specifically—as in this passage—"moral indifference, lack of watchfulness."[34] The author condemns those parents who failed to take with sufficient seriousness their task of teaching and ensuring that the children lived in accordance with Christian morality. It is this category of parents who will be punished by God, if their casual attitude with respect to the moral dimension of upbringing leads their children to commit fornication. Although the author does not say this directly, it is reasonable to assume that this applies even to parents who otherwise lead pious and God-fearing lives. Hence, although the *Apostolic Constitutions* represent a somewhat milder view than the *Didascalia*, they too emphasize very clearly the parents' obligation to bring up their children in keeping with the Christian moral code. Lack of commitment in this sphere may have the dramatic consequence of condemnation by God.

Jerome
Jerome's two letters about the upbringing of children are interesting, although we must remember that the advice and exhortations in these texts are not addressed to parents in general, but to parents who have consecrated their little girls to a life of virginity. One of these girls, Paula, was indeed "consecrated to Christ before her birth and vowed to His service before her conception."[35] This leads Jerome to compare her relationship

to her mother with the relationship between Samuel and Hanna, and John the Baptist and Elizabeth. She is a special child, and must receive a special upbringing. Jerome's advice is colored by the exceptionally high moral demands that are made of those who are to enter the life of consecrated virginity, and we may not simply assume that he would have given the same counsel to parents whose task it was to bring up "ordinary" children. Interestingly enough, he himself expresses his doubts about whether it is possible to carry out the program he prescribes in Rome; in this case, he advises Laeta to send her daughter Paula to a convent in Bethlehem, where her grandmother (Paula the Elder) and her aunt (Eustochium) would take care of her.[36] On the other hand, Jerome was a man ablaze with enthusiasm for the ascetic ideals that permeate his exhortations in these two letters, and it is certainly not improbable that these texts reflect his fundamental convictions about how parents in general ought to raise their children.

In one of these letters, Jerome emphasizes that parents are responsible for what their children do (*Ep.* 107.6). In this part of the letter, he seems to be discussing this issue on a more general basis, giving the impression that his words apply not only to a woman who is to bring up a girl for the state of consecrated virginity, but to all parents.

He refers to the priest Eli, who was condemned by God because of the sins his adult sons committed, and to the statement at 1 Timothy 2:15 that one who has rebellious sons is disqualified from becoming a bishop. Jerome argues from the lesser to the greater and asks the rhetorical question: if parents are responsible for children when these are "of ripe age and independent," how much more are they responsible for underage children who do not even have the ability to distinguish right from wrong? When he speaks here of children who are as yet "unweaned and weak," we see that he is thinking of small children under four or five years of age.[37]

Jerome goes on to refute a potential objection to the view that parents are responsible for their children's conduct. There is indeed a biblical text that points in the opposite direction—the affirmation at Ezekiel 18:20 that parents will not be punished for the wickedness of their sons. Jerome does not reject these words, nor call them into question, but he asserts that the prophet is not speaking here of children in every age group. One must distinguish between older and younger children; and without adducing any arguments in support of his interpretation, he claims that the words in Ezekiel 18:20 refer to "those who have discretion," that is, to children who have reached the age at which, according to the Gospel of John (though

in a different context: see John 9:21), one is able to "speak for himself."
Jerome concludes: "While the son is a child and thinks as a child and until
he comes to years of discretion to choose between the two roads to which
the letter of Pythagoras points,[38] his parents are responsible for his actions
whether these be good or bad." When children are old enough to be able
to make their own choices, the parents can no longer be held responsible
for what they do.

On the one hand, by citing biblical texts that imply that parents are
held responsible for their children's actions, Jerome emphasizes their obligation to take the duty of upbringing seriously. On the other hand, by
specifying that it is with regard to younger children that parents are responsible for their actions, and by refraining from saying that parents' salvation depends on how their children live, he does tone down this responsibility to some extent. In comparison to the *Didascalia* and the *Apostolic
Constitutions*, and to John Chrysostom (see the next section), Jerome does
reduce somewhat the grave consequences to parents of an upbringing that
goes wrong or of a lack of commitment in this sphere.

John Chrysostom

As I have mentioned, of all the patristic writers, it is John Chrysostom
who discusses in greatest detail the upbringing of children, and this makes
it natural for us to devote particular attention to this central figure of early
church history. After his return from living as hermit, Chrysostom became
a priest in Antioch and a spokesman for the ascetic ideals of the desert. He
did not go so far as the most radical voices, who rejected marriage, but
he insisted that sexual abstinence was preferable, in order to create a pure
heart and to be united to Christ. Marriage was no part of God's original
creation, but became necessary as a result of the fall, in order to ensure
the continued existence of the human race and as a framework for the
legitimate experience of sexual pleasure.[39] His view of family life changed
in his later writings, which reflect his experiences with well-off families
in Antioch. He realized that if Christianity was truly to transform society,
more was needed than a spiritual elite who practiced radical ascetic ideals.
Chrysostom recognized that only a minority of Christians could ever be
expected to shoulder the burden such ideals represented; if society was to
be Christianized, it was more important that the great majority of people
who live their ordinary lives in the cities should receive a formation in
keeping with the Christian faith.[40]

In classical times, Antioch had the reputation of a town offering much
entertainment, where morality was not taken too seriously and people

yielded to their lusts. Chrysostom believed that he saw symptoms of this hedonistic culture among well-off Christians: they longed for wealth, luxury, honor, and positions in this world, while all the time poor and suffering persons could be seen on the streets. This was the greatest sin, and a threat to the cohesion of the Christian community.[41] If his ambitious program of Christianization was to have any success, Chrysostom recognized that he had to begin with the basic unity in society—the family. In a homily on Ephesians 5:22-33, he compares the household with a church where the Christian virtues are to be put into practice.[42]

The "church-family" will function properly only if the parents take seriously their role in upbringing. Chrysostom never tires of emphasizing their obligation to rear their children in accordance with Christian ideals; this is often combined with criticism of their one-sided concentration on providing their children with what they need in order to achieve prosperity and success in this world. In a homily on Ephesians 6:1-4, Chrysostom writes:[43]

> Let everything take second place to our care for our children, our bringing them up in the discipline and instruction of the Lord. If from the beginning we teach them to love true wisdom, they will have greater wealth and glory than riches can provide. If a child learns a trade, or is highly educated for a lucrative profession, all this is nothing compared to the art of detachment from riches; if you want to make your child rich, teach him this. He is truly rich who does not desire great possessions, or to surround himself with wealth, but who requires nothing. This is how to discipline and teach your child; this is the greatest riches. Don't worry about giving him an influential reputation for worldly wisdom, but ponder deeply how you can teach him to think lightly of this life's passing glories; thus he will become truly renowned and glorious. . . . Don't strive to make him a clever orator, but teach him to love true wisdom. He will not suffer if he lacks clever words; but if he lacks wisdom, all the rhetoric in the world can't help him. A pattern of life is what is needed, not empty speeches; character, not cleverness; deeds, not words. These things will secure the Kingdom and bestow God's blessing. Don't sharpen his tongue, but purify his soul.[44]

As these words show, the definitive goal of upbringing is to equip the child for the kingdom of God.[45] The intention is to form children so that they will live in keeping with what Chrysostom defines as the ethical-moral ideals in Christianity. Children must be socialized into Christian virtues and the Christian pattern of religious life. He often speaks of bringing children up to be athletes (*athlêtês*) for Christ,[46] but he employs other expressions too; parents are to form their children to become philosophers, in the sense that they will practice the correct virtues,[47] and this is why Chrysostom urges them to bring up their children "in the discipline and instruction of the Lord." He can employ this phrase as a synthesis of the entire contents of upbringing: "Let everything take second place to our care for our children, our bringing them up in the discipline and instruction of the Lord."[48] He sees the primary aim of upbringing as the creation of the correct moral or ethical attitude in the child; this is reflected, not only in his favorite metaphor of children as statues in the artist's hand,[49] but also in his preference for the verb *huthomizo* as a description of the praxis of upbringing.[50] The general meaning of this word is "to order, arrange, compose," and here it means bringing someone's life into the order desired:[51] the goal and intention of upbringing is to order the child's life aright.[52] For John Chrysostom, this means an order in keeping with "the discipline and instruction of the Lord" or, as he also puts it, an order that uncovers the likeness of God in the child.[53]

An upbringing on these lines entails a change of priorities, especially for those who are rich: What is it important to seek or to attain, as long as one lives one's life here on earth? The vital point is not to bring up the child in view of success, honor, and wealth in this life, since all these things entice a person away from God and from a life of virtue. Nor are parents to ask how their son can "enjoy a long life here, but how he can enjoy an infinite and eternal life in the age to come. Give him the great things, not the little things."[54]

This should not lead us to believe that Chrysostom is interested only in eternity when he gives his advice on upbringing. On the contrary, he is convinced that his program will equip children to encounter the various difficulties life presents: "So, let us raise our children in such a way that they can face any trouble, and not be surprised when difficulties come." In this context, Chrysostom's main warning is against the effect prosperity and wealth have on the personality when we must tackle trials in life: "it leaves us unprepared for the hardships of life."[55] It must be underscored that Chrysostom argues that the ideal he proposes for the upbringing of children will prepare them to meet any and all difficulties, and give them the skills needed to master these. In other words, even if the primary goal is undoubtedly to equip children for the kingdom of God, Chrysostom

also sees upbringing in a wider perspective: its goal is also to form individuals who will be capable of tackling the difficulties and challenges
posed by life in general.

Parents have a weighty responsibility here, since something immense-
ly valuable—the eternal salvation of their child—is at stake. In negative
terms, Chrysostom says that "the greatest sin of all and the absolute height
of wickedness is to neglect one's children."[56] In order to lend emphasis
to his assertion that it is so serious a matter for parents to be concerned
only about their own affairs and hence to neglect their children, he claims
that such parents are worse than those who kill their own children: "To
sharpen a sword, take it in hand, and plunge it into the very throat of one's
child, is not so terrible as to destroy and corrupt the souls, for to us there
is nothing equal to this."[57]

Not content with using strong words about those parents who are so
absorbed in their own affairs that they fail to give the upbringing of their
children sufficient time and commitment, Chrysostom also attacks those
who sincerely attempt to bring up their children in keeping with Christian ideals, but fail—with fatal consequences for both parents and children. His starting point is the story of the priest Eli in the Old Testament.
Chrysostom does not call into question Eli's service of God and of Israel
in general: Eli did what was expected of him. However, he did not succeed
in the task of upbringing, as we see when he fails to call his two adult sons
to account for their sins of fornication and greed (1 Samuel 2:12-36):

> What, then, did God say to Samuel? *He knew that his sons cursed
> God, and he did not correct them.* However, this is not exactly true
> because Eli certainly did correct his sons, but God says that his
> was not a true correction. God condemned his warning because it
> was not sufficiently forceful. Therefore, even if we show concern
> for our children, if we fail to do what is necessary, it will not be
> true concern, just as Eli's correction was not a true one. After God
> had stated the charge against Eli, he added the punishment with
> great wrath: *For I have sworn,* he said, *to the house of Eli that the
> iniquity of Eli's house shall not be expiated by sacrifice or offering for
> ever.* Do you see God's intense anger and merciless punishment?
> Eli must perish utterly, he says, and not only him and his children,
> but his entire household with him, and there will be no remedy to
> heal his wound. Except for the man's negligence in regard to his
> children, however, God had no other charge to make against the
> elder at that time; in all other respects Eli was a marvelous man.[58]

The main point is that, even though Eli's service as priest was excellent in every way, he was punished by God because he did not succeed in calling his sons to account: he is criticized for being too mild a disciplinarian. In other words, Eli is made responsible for the sins of his children, and Chrysostom applies this to the parents of his own days, asking rhetorically what punishment *they* may expect, when this venerable man who served Israel irreproachably for more than twenty years "died a violent and miserable death because he did not care for his children with diligence; and if this sin of negligence, like a great, tidal wave, overcame all these actions and wiped out all his virtuous deeds."[59] The implied answer is, of course, that a harsh punishment awaits those parents who do not succeed in rearing their children in such a way that they lead virtuous Christian lives when they reach adulthood. The parents are held responsible for their children's sins, and this implies that their own salvation depends on bringing up their children to become Christians who live in accordance with the Christian moral code. This line of thought is formulated in greater detail and plays a more central role in Chrysostom's argumentation in his *Adversus Oppugnatores Vitae Monasticae,* probably written shortly before his ordination to the priesthood in 386, that is, at a period when he was a zealous adherent of strict ascetic ideals, but we also find it in a later writing, after he had recognized that not everyone was capable of living up to these ideals. At the close of his homily on Ephesians 6:1-4, Chrysostom exhorts his hearers first to bring up their children in "the discipline and instruction of the Lord." One argument he puts forward to show the necessity of this task is his question how a man with rebellious children can enter the kingdom of heaven, given that such a person is not even worthy to become a bishop.[60] He answers in the negative. A man will be held accountable for "unruly children" and for an "undisciplined wife," because "we can't be saved through individual righteousness alone . . . but the virtue of those for whom we are responsible is also required."[61] This shows that what we might call a principle of solidarity between children and parents in regard to their future salvation, or "the corporate nature of salvation," was a consistent element in his thinking. We should note, however, that this homily speaks in general terms of parents who have neglected the Christian education of their children; Chrysostom says nothing explicit about the fate of those parents who had attempted to provide a fit upbringing, but whose children later abandoned the norms of a respectable Christian life, and this may perhaps indicate that his attitude had softened as the years passed. At any rate, he takes a strict line with all parents, asserting that their salvation depends on whether their children live in the fear of God.

When Chrysostom makes the upbringing of children a question of salvation, he is emphasizing as strongly as possible the parents' responsibility. This can, of course, be explained in pragmatic terms. Given his ambitious goal of transforming the broad mass of the populace into persons leading virtuous Christian lives, it is a good strategy to ensure that children are socialized into the Christian way of life. The same thinking is found in church life today, where emphasis is laid on the role of the family as bearer of the Christian faith and values, so that new generations will have a firm rooting in Christianity. However, we would be doing Chrysostom an injustice if we interpreted his words exclusively on the pragmatic level. His argument that parents are obligated to bring up their children in keeping with Christian ideals is conducted on the level of fundamental theological principles.

First, Chrysostom anchors this obligation in New Testament exhortations to display love and concern for one's neighbor: "For the Judge demands of us with the same strictness both our own and our neighbor's salvation. That is why Paul everywhere urges everyone to seek not merely their own interest, but also the interest of their neighbor."[62] This attitude is not confined to a generalized goodwill; it also presupposes an active interest and commitment to the salvation of one's neighbor. Chrysostom points to Paul's Letter to the Romans among other things, where he admonishes the strong to refrain from conduct that could lead the weak to fall, and to Jesus' logion that it is better to be cast into the depths of the sea with a millstone around one's neck than to lead one of his little ones astray. In order to demonstrate that "the greatest sin of all and the absolute height of wickedness is to neglect one's children," he lists various relationships in which people neglect the needs of their neighbor. He begins with the affirmation in 1 Timothy that whoever fails to take care of his neighbor, and especially of his own family, has denied the faith, and argues that the lack of love becomes all the more serious, the closer one's relationship to one's neighbor is. Since the child is the parents' closest neighbor, the gravest sin they can commit is a lack of commitment to bringing it up in the Christian faith. Parents who fail in this sphere will "receive the most severe punishment," even if in other respects they conduct their "affairs properly." In other words, Chrysostom relates the obligation to give one's children an appropriate Christian upbringing to the norm of displaying love and concern for one's neighbor that is so central in the New Testament.

Second, Chrysostom points out that God has given parents an instinct to show care for their children, and interprets this as evidence that "God shows great concern for the education of children." On the level of creation, God prompts parents to look after their children. Chrysostom also cites scriptural passages in the Old Testament where God commands the Israelites to teach their children the substance and meaning of religious feasts: "All these commands were given to lead them to a knowledge of God."[63] Accordingly, parents who take their task of rearing their children with sufficient seriousness are making the proper response both to an instinct God has given them on the level of creation and to concrete commandments in the Bible.

Third, Chrysostom anchors the obligation to bring up one's children in the idea that parents who do this correctly uncover or reveal God's image in their child. In his homily on Ephesians 6:1-4, he writes:

> Let us bring them up in the discipline and instruction of the Lord. Great will be the reward in store for us, for if artists who make statues and paint portraits of kings are held in high esteem, will not God bless ten thousand times more those who reveal and beautify His royal image (for man is the image of God)? When we teach our children to be good, to be gentle, to be forgiving (all these are attributes of God), to be generous, to love their fellow men, to regard this present age as nothing, we instill virtue in their souls, and reveal the image of God within them. This, then, is our task: to educate both ourselves and our children in godliness; otherwise what answer will we have before Christ's judgment-seat?[64]

In my discussion of Chrysostom's view of children's nature and qualities in chapter 3 of this book, I noted that—as is typical of Eastern patristic thought—he does not hold that the fall entailed any essential diminution of the image of God in the human person.[65] However, the likeness to God and the potential for growing more like God were weakened. This defect in human existence was healed or restored through Christ's life and work. This means that a child is still born with a weaker measure of the likeness to God, but—thanks to Christ—has the potential to grow or develop into a greater likeness to God. This is where the parents' responsibility comes in: by rearing the child in virtues associated with God, they uncover the likeness to God, or help this to grow. This idea lies behind Chrysostom's favorite metaphor of the child as a work of art formed by the artist (that is, the parents): like an artist, they are to remove all superfluous material and add everything that is lacking:

> To each of you fathers and mothers I say, just as we see artists fashioning their paintings and statues with great precision, so we must care for these wondrous statues of ours. Painters when they have set the canvas on the easel paint on it day by day to accomplish their purpose. Sculptors, too, working in marble, proceed in a similar manner; they remove what is superfluous and add what is lacking. Even so must you proceed. Like the creators of statues do you give all your leisure to fashioning these wondrous statues of God. And, as you remove what is superfluous and add what is lacking, inspect them day by day, to see what good qualities nature has supplied so that you will increase them, and what faults so that you will eradicate them.[66]

Thus, parents are to hone, polish, and form their children so that they become virtuous Christians; by doing so, they uncover God's likeness in them. In other words, the upbringing by parents is a constant creation of the child, so that God's intention is realized in it, and it attains to its full participation in God.[67] In theological terms, therefore, Chrysostom roots upbringing both in creation theology and in soteriology.[68]

Earlier in this chapter, I have argued that the emphasis in the Pastoral Letters that those who are to be leaders in a community must have obedient children reflects the great role played by shame and honor in the contemporary cultural environment, and I believe that this perspective can help us to understand John Chrysostom too.[69] We have noted that he assigns to parents a grave responsibility to bring up their children in keeping with Christian ideals; for Chrysostom, this is directly linked to the ultimate goal of upbringing—the children's eternal salvation. Parents who fail on this point must expect dramatic consequences: God will punish them for their children's sins. Chrysostom backs these affirmations with biblical proof texts: God punished Eli when his adult sons sinned. As we have seen, he also refers to the statement at Titus 1:6 that those with unruly children are unsuited to the office of bishop and explains this by arguing that "the virtue of those for whom we are responsible is also required."[70] In other words, he argues for his own position on either biblical or theological grounds.

We can, however, go further. I believe that shame and honor also belong to the premises underlying Chrysostom's theological argumentation, and that this is indicated by the collective way of thought implicit in the idea that "the virtue of those for whom we are responsible" is a precondition of salvation. If children reject the ideals of their parents' Christian lifestyle, this means that they are disobedient to their parents. Chrysostom frequently defines the aim of upbringing as the formation of obedient children. If this is unsuccessful, and the children do not respond with obedience and respect to what their parents say, this brings shame on the rest of the family, especially the father. Although Chrysostom does not spell this out, it is reasonable to assume that he is alluding indirectly to the great significance of honor and shame in contemporary culture.

A further indication of this is the fact that although he is critical of members of the community who seek status and honor, it is indisputable that his own arguments appeal to the great value of honor, although redefining to some extent the object of this honor: he says that his contemporaries associate honor with wealth, high positions, eloquence, and "an influential reputation for worldly wisdom."[71] It is not by chance that he mentions "reputation," for it is vitally important in a "shame/honor" culture, where "significant others" function as mirrors for the individual, to have a good reputation and be well spoken of. Chrysostom calls such things "life's passing glories," and this is the main point in the first part (chapters 1–15) of De Inani Gloria. This, however, does not in the least mean that honor is irrelevant. Rather, he redefines it to mean leading a life in keeping with the Christian ideals. The following text from De Inani 15 sums up his thinking in this area:

> Place does not consist of a well-furnished house nor of costly tapestries nor a well-spread bed nor a decorated couch nor a crowd of servants. All these are externals and concern us not; but the things that concern us are fair dealing, disdain of money and fame, contempt for what the many think honor, disregard of human values, embracing poverty, and overcoming our nature by the virtue of our lives. It is these that constitute good place and reputation and honor.

If parents bring up their son in keeping with the ideals prescribed here, he will "become truly renowned and glorious."[72] In context, this refers primarily to one's relationship with God, but we may assume that Chrysostom also envisages the honor and fame a virtuous Christian life will win within Christian circles. Despite his endeavor to redefine what bestows honor and fame, he nevertheless concurs with his contemporaries in according these values fundamental significance, and it is to this that his argumentation refers (whether consciously or not). The fact that he redefines some aspects of the understanding of what bestows honor does not mean that he calls other traditional ideas into question. This is particularly true where the biblical tradition and general human culture are in agreement—as when we are told that the aim of upbringing is to form obedient children. My point is that elements in the shame/honor culture, in which Chrysostom himself is steeped, contribute to his theological arguments that parents must bring up their children in keeping with his ideals. Hence, there is a connection between the strong emphasis he places on parents' obligation to bring up their children to a virtuous Christian life—which implies that they obey their parents—and the fact that children who display the opposite attitude are a cause of shame.

This must not be taken to mean that I wish to downplay the importance of Chrysostom's fundamental theological arguments in favor of the obligation to bring up one's children. All I wish to do is to suggest that elements in the contemporary shame/honor culture can help explain why he makes the rearing of children such an important theological topic.

As I have indicated, Chrysostom's educational ideals also imply that the growing generation are socialized into a group with specific ideals and social patterns. Although he is speaking on the individual level, and defines the goal of upbringing as the salvation of the individual, his program certainly entails the socialization of this individual into a group, and his educational ideals are an attempt to construct particular social patterns within this group. Accordingly, the upbringing of children becomes a strategy to transform the Christian group in keeping with specific ideals of societal conduct. We have seen that this entails a break with and isolation from the pagan environment in many sectors of life. This means that upbringing is meant to create a sense of belonging to a specific group, in which one finds one's identity; the consequence is that a clear boundary is drawn in relation to outsiders.

Chrysostom also seems to presuppose a link between correct upbringing and the plausibility of Christian preaching. As I have just emphasized, one central element in his educational program is the requirement that children learn to despise that which bestows status and honor in this world. In his discussions of upbringing, Chrysostom himself makes no direct connection between this vital educational element and the plausibility of Christian preaching, but I believe that this too can help explain why he so strongly underscores parents' educational responsibility. In his tenth homily on 1 Timothy, he discusses the relationship between life and doctrine:

> For those who are taught, look to the virtue of their teachers: and when they see us manifesting the same desires, pursuing the same objects, power and honor, how can they admire Christianity? They see our lives open to reproach, our souls worldly. We admire wealth equally with them, and even more. We have the same horror of death, the same dread of poverty, the same impatience of disease; we are equally fond of glory and of rule. We harass ourselves to death from our love of money, and serve the time. How then can they believe? From miracles? But these are no longer wrought. From our conversation? It has become corrupt.[73]

Clearly, John Chrysostom holds that the Christians' "worldly" lifestyle prevents acceptance of the Christian message that the church is charged to proclaim. This suggests that we should see his program for the upbringing of children, which has the precise intention of forming them in accordance with qualities he looks for in vain among the Christians of his own age, in connection with the church's missionary role. We may exaggerate a little and say that, if pagan ears are to find the Christian testimony and preaching credible, parents must succeed in rearing their children in such a way that they will live as adults in accordance with the Christian ideals.

Ambrose and Augustine

We find scattered references in Ambrose to the upbringing of children. Although these do not provide a complete picture of his thinking on this subject, they show that he took it for granted that parents had a duty to bring up their children. The most interesting point is perhaps that Ambrose, too, takes it for granted that parents bear responsibility for the misdeeds of their son—in this case, that means the father. He quotes Sirach 11:28 ("Praise no man before death"), and explains why this is so: "For each man is known in his last end and is judged in his children, if he has trained his children well and has taught them with suitable teachings, since the dissoluteness of the children is ascribed to the negligence of the father."[74] The context indicates that Ambrose is speaking of condemnation by other people, but he does not develop this idea in any detail. His words certainly imply an admonition to fathers to take the upbringing of their children seriously, but this is not stated explicitly.

At the beginning of his *De Patriarchis*, Ambrose says that God has given parents the task of teaching their children respect, and writes: "The formation of the children is, then, the prerogative of the parents." Here too, he speaks only briefly of this obligation; he concentrates primarily on the blessing that will come to those children who honor their father. In both these texts, Ambrose is thinking mainly of adult children, but his brief summaries of the relationship between parents and children assume the parental right or obligation to rear their children from the time when they are still very small.[75]

Unlike John Chrysostom, Augustine does not make the upbringing of children the subject of a special treatise. Indeed, it is striking how little he has to say on this subject, especially with regard to parents' responsibility for bringing up their children; nevertheless, sporadic remarks in a number of his writings show that Augustine takes it for granted that parents are obligated to form their children in accordance with contemporary ideals for good conduct. I have noted above that he reproaches his parents, and especially his father, in the *Confessions* for a one-sided focus on ensuring that he received a good education that would equip him for a future career in the world; his father was not particularly interested in giving Augustine a moral formation in keeping with Christian ideals, and did nothing to check Augustine's sexual desire. Augustine writes that his father was "left fallow of your cultivation, O God, who are the only true and good owner of your field, my heart."[76] Augustine takes a gentler line with regard to his mother, who warned him with "intense earnestness" against committing fornication and especially against adultery with another woman; looking back, he saw her admonitions as an instrument of God's will. Nevertheless, Augustine criticizes Monica for failing to arrange a marriage for him that would have allowed him to live out his sexuality within the only legitimate framework. As he writes, she was afraid that a wife might hamper him in his quest for academic success.

In one of his sermons, Augustine exhorts parents to teach their children to show respect, but he does not spell out what this might entail.[77] In another sermon, he speaks of the use of physical force in upbringing. He assumes that it is the father's duty to inculcate obedience in his son, and if the son does not obey, it is right for the father to beat him and employ physical force, even when the son puts up resistance. Augustine asks why this should be so, and himself supplies the answer: "Because he is a father, because he is getting an inheritance ready, because he is bringing up an heir. This is how a father shows kindness by beating, by beating his son shows him mercy."[78] I return below to the question of the use of physical force in upbringing; let us note here that Augustine takes it for granted that fathers are responsible for rearing their children. He does not go into detail about the contents of the educational program, but he clearly assumes that his hearers know what is required of one who is to be a good heir—presumably, the son must learn to handle the money and property that will one day be his. This interpretation finds support in another passage in which Augustine argues explicitly that a father must employ physical force if necessary, in order to bring up his son to be a responsible heir.[79]

THE CONTENTS AND THE PROCESS OF UPBRINGING

The previous section of the present chapter has focused on parents' obligation to bring up and form their children in keeping with Christian ideals, and we have seen how Christian writings from the first century onward emphasize this responsibility. This is expressed most clearly in the *Didascalia*, the *Apostolic Constitutions*, and John Chrysostom: these three authors make upbringing a question of salvation, in the sense that parents will be held accountable to God for their children's sins.

It is obviously impossible to discuss the obligation to bring up one's children without touching on some aspects of the goal, contents, and method of education; our sources do not discuss this responsibility on some abstract level, but almost always link it to specific contents. I have touched on the contents of upbringing only where this is necessary, if we are to understand what the sources say about the responsibility for bringing up children and the reasons they give for this responsibility. In what follows, I shall discuss in greater detail the goal, contents, and method of upbringing. What is the aim of education, and how are parents to accomplish this? We shall also ask which of the parents is responsible for putting the educational program into effect, and what role other persons in the household have.

The New Testament and the Apostolic Fathers
We have seen that the household codes in Ephesians and Colossians exhort fathers to bring up their children.[80] The letters speak only in general terms about the contents of this upbringing; Colossians says nothing specific about it at all, while Ephesians says that children must be brought

up "in the discipline and instruction of the Lord" (Ephesians 6:4). This expression, too, is not specific—a generic reference to the Christian faith with special reference to Christian morality. We should note, however, that the exhortation to parents to bring up their children "in the discipline and instruction of the Lord" comes immediately after an exhortation to children to be obedient to their parents (Ephesians 6:2). In support, the author quotes the commandment in the Decalogue to honor one's parents (Ephesians 6:2), indirectly identifying one element in upbringing: parents are to teach their children to obey them. This is presupposed in Colossians too, where the author emphatically affirms that children's "acceptable duty in the Lord" is to show obedience to their parents "in everything." This phrase may seem to indicate that parents have a right to demand absolute obedience. However, Epictetus also speaks of obedience to one's father in all things, but without inferring from this principle that a father has an unlimited right to demand obedience.[81]

We find a corresponding emphasis on parents' duty to bring up their children to be obedient in Titus and 1 Timothy. As we have seen, one of the criteria to be met by candidates for the ministry of bishop or presbyter is that they have successfully brought up their children in the Christian faith and that these children have shown them obedience and respect.

When we recall the position of the father as *paterfamilias* in the Greco-Roman household, it is not surprising that the accent lies on the need to show him obedience and respect.[82] But the affirmations in Ephesians, Colossians, and 1 Timothy about upbringing, and their implications for the relationship between parents and children, must also be read in the light of Hellenistic Judaism, where we find corresponding ideas about parental status and authority.[83]

I mention only a few examples here. Philo draws an analogy between God and parents: "Parents, in my opinion, are to their children what God is to the world, since just as He achieved existence for the non-existent, so they in imitation of His power, as far as they are capable, immortalize the race. And a father and a mother deserve honor, not only on this account, but for many other reasons."[84] The holiness code in Leviticus prescribes the death penalty for one who curses his mother or father, and according to Deuteronomy, sons who rebel against their parents' will are to be put to death by stoning.[85] Philo agrees with this, and puts forward the view that parents are obliged to inflict the death penalty on their children when they refuse to obey, even after their father has spoken sternly to them and threatened them with physical punishment.[86] There is no doubt that such statements affirm parents' juridical right to expect obedience and respect from their children; but we should be cautious about assuming that they actually made use of such rights to any great extent. Philo gives the impression of a very strict regime in the home, but we have evidence pointing in the opposite direction too: for example, critical voices argued that fathers should refrain from excessive harshness when using their power with regard to their children.[87]

It is also interesting to note the strong emphasis in the Jewish tradition on the religious dimension of upbringing. The overall responsibility for this lay in the father's hands; even where he sent his children to school, the ideal saw the home as the primary place of instruction, and the heart of education was the introduction to the Torah.[88] The *Shemaʿ*, an important text in early Jewish liturgy, reminds the Jews of their obligation to worship the one God and to observe the commandments, which "shall be upon your heart; and you shall teach them diligently to your children, and shall talk of them when you sit in your house, and when you walk by the way, and when you lie down and when you rise up."[89] Josephus (to take one example) claims that the Jewish tradition shows its superiority to the surrounding culture through the weight it attaches to the instruction of children: "Above all we pride ourselves on the education of our children, and regard as the most essential task in life the observance of our laws and of the pious practices based thereon."[90] Many other texts, especially in the Jewish sapiential tradition, reflect a clear awareness of parents' right and duty to teach and form their children in keeping with the ideals of the law.[91] John M. G. Barclay concludes that "there is no good reason to doubt Philo when he claims that Jews have been trained 'from a very early age,' even 'from the cradle,' to honor the One God alone and to observe the Jewish law."[92] Hence, although it is true that the exhortations in Ephesians and Colossians must be read in the light of the hierarchical structure in classical households in general, it is reasonable to see the specific exhortation to bring up one's children in accordance with the commandments of the Lord as an analogy to, or a continuation of, the Jewish praxis that attached such importance to giving children instruction in the law.

Although the New Testament writers stress that parents are to bring up their children to be obedient, we should note that they also find it appropriate to urge fathers not to discipline them too harshly. It is striking that the only explicit charge to fathers by the author of Colossians is an exhortation to be moderate in the methods employed: "Fathers, do not provoke your children, or they may lose heart."[93] The author of Ephesians repeats the admonition not to "provoke your children to anger," and draws a contrast between a discipline that causes anger and the upbringing of children "in the discipline and instruction of the Lord."[94] This does not mean that corporal punishment was completely excluded; it is certainly possible that these two authors envisage situations where it would be correct to employ physical force against one's children, without this provoking the negative reactions they mention. All we can say with certainty is that they warn against excessive harshness in the treatment of one's children.

We have seen above that several of the apostolic fathers incorporate into their paraenesis admonitions to parents to bring up their children to fear God. It is possible that the formula "the fear of God" is partly influenced by motifs from Hellenistic morality,[95] but I find it more likely that Jewish usage—especially in the sapiential tradition—supplies the primary background against which we must understand the occurrences of this phrase in early Christian literature. In wisdom literature, the "fear of God" refers to a basic moral attitude whereby a person refrains from wickedness and hates sin.[96] In other words, to fear God means to possess a fundamental moral attitude that prizes highly a life in accordance with the commandments and regulations of the Lord. In other texts such as the Book of Psalms, the "fear of God" refers primarily to the correct religious attitude, which finds expression in thanksgiving, adoration, and trust in Yahweh.[97] Nevertheless, if we take the Old Testament as a whole, it is the ethical usage that predominates.[98] I have observed above that the doctrine of the "two ways" in the *Didache* and *Barnabas* is based on Jewish traditions, and that it includes exhortations in both these texts to bring up one's children to fear God; it is clear that this must be read against the background of the Jewish usage. Hence, when the apostolic fathers exhort parents to teach their children the fear of God, this entails a general admonition to give them a Christian education that focuses on the internalization of the Christian virtues.

In the first Letter of Clement, this interpretation is confirmed by another admonition. After exhorting parents to teach young people the fear of God, the household code continues with an exhortation to let "our children share in the instruction which is in Christ."[99] The text goes on to make this general exhortation specific: they are to teach them humility and love, and that fear of God that is expressed in a life marked by holiness and a pure mind.[100] These are important virtues in the author's eyes, and he repeatedly urges all the Christians in Corinth to practice them, in order to put an end to the conflict that has divided the community.[101] Thus, when Clement specifies the implications of instructions in Christ he does not distinguish between virtues appropriate to the education of children and virtues that adults are to practice.

How are parents to bring up their children to fear God? Here, all we have are summary statements. Both the *Didache* and *Barnabas* urge the reader: "Thou shalt not withhold thine hand from thy son or from thy daughter."[102] This is probably meant both literally and metaphorically. In the first instance, it refers to the use of physical force in teaching children to fear God; by metaphorical extension, it signifies that one accepts general responsibility for children and their *paideia* (upbringing/education).[103] The apostolic fathers usually say that parents are to form their children by means of exhorting or teaching them, without going into detail about how this is to be done.[104]

The fathers are a little more explicit about who is to bear responsibility for upbringing. The *Didache* and *Barnabas* urge fathers to teach their children the fear of God, while Polycarp assigns this task to his mothers in his *Letter to the Philippians*. The author of *1 Clement* does not specify who is to let "our children share in the instruction which is in Christ"; this is one element in the many exhortations addressed to the entire Corinthian community.

The *Didascalia* and the *Apostolic Constitutions*

The *Didascalia* gives more detailed instructions about upbringing, and is also more specific than Christian writings from the first two centuries about the contents of education. We have seen above that this author places a strong emphasis on parents' duty to bring up their children in keeping with the Christian ideals, and it is here that we find the earliest formulation of the idea that parents must bear responsibility for their children's sins. Since the parents' eternal salvation depends on the way in which they educate their children, it is unsurprising that the author underscores their duty to bring up their children to be obedient and to submit to their parents' will and to the instructions they receive about living a virtuous Christian life: "bring them into subjection from their youth by your word of religion. And give them no liberty to set themselves up against you their parents."[105]

What, specifically, are parents to do in order to succeed in forming their children in keeping with Christian ideals? The author of the *Didascalia* begins his chapter on upbringing by exhorting parents to train their children in a profession that is compatible with a pious life: "And teach your children crafts that are agreeable and befitting to religion."[106] This indicates that he is thinking primarily of older children, an impression confirmed by the rest of the chapter. Some professions were unacceptable to Christians because they entailed a conflict with their faith, and the author lists several of these in chapter 18. First of all, he mentions professions that may be linked to the worship of pagan gods—for example, artists, because they paint pictures and make sculptures used in pagan worship—and then professions associated with dishonesty and criminality, such as lawyers, tax-gatherers, those who buy and sell, soldiers, and positions linked to the administration of the Roman empire. The *Didascalia* was not alone in holding that certain professions were incompatible with Christian faith and morality; we find a similar list in Hippolytus's church order, where the author lists professions that must be abandoned by those who are receiving instruction for baptism; in some cases, they must commit themselves not to exercise specific parts of these jobs, if they wish to become members of the church. Here too, most of these are related directly or indirectly to pagan worship and belief: Hippolytus's list includes actors, sculptors and artists (who must promise not to make idols), magicians, astrologers, and those who make amulets. Another category of professions includes commanders and soldiers, for the obvious reason that such persons risk incurring guilt by killing; nevertheless, a soldier is allowed to retain his job, provided that he promises to refuse to obey the order to kill.[107] We note that the practice of these forbidden professions would lead to conflicts with the first and fifth commandments of the Decalogue, and this is not by chance: in early Christianity, the three sins reckoned as mortal were the breach with monotheism and infringements of the commandments not to take life and not to commit fornication.

Accordingly, one element in upbringing was to teach one's children a profession that did not run contrary to Christian faith and morals. We might have expected the *Didascalia* author to specify in chapter 22 which professions were not "befitting to religion" and to point out the consequences of adopting these, but he does not do so, possibly because (as we have just seen) he has already provided a list of problematic jobs in chapter 18. Instead, he justifies this exhortation to parents by recalling the danger idleness posed to the moral life of their children: if they are not trained in a profession, "through idleness they give themselves to wantonness."[108] Other passages in the *Didascalia* concur in portraying idleness as a great vice.[109] When he emphasizes in chapter 13 how necessary it is for Christians to assemble regularly for church meetings, he also prescribes how they are to employ their time when they are not in the church: "Do you the faithful therefore, all of you, daily and hourly, whenever you are not in the Church, devote yourselves to your work; so that in all the conduct of your life you may either be occupied in the things of the Lord or engaged upon your work, and may never be idle." He then cites a text from Proverbs that speaks positively of work as a virtue and of idleness as a vice,[110] and draws the conclusion that Christians should always be "working, for idleness is a blot for which there is no cure." Finally, he quotes Paul's words that one who is unwilling to work is not to receive any food,[111] and he justifies this attitude as follows: "for the Lord God also hates sluggards, for it is not possible for a sluggard to be a believer."[112] He does not emphasize the value inherent in the work itself, nor work in the perspective of our responsibility as stewards of God's creation: when he urges Christians to be diligent, his intention is to occupy their time, so that there will be little opportunity for them to have social contact with pagans or be present at their gatherings. In particular, he warns against what goes on in the theater. He holds that the young and the rich are especially exposed to the danger to Christian faith and morals inherent in idleness, since this opens the door to contact with their pagan surroundings.[113] It is in the context of such ideas that we must understand his admonition to teach one's children a profession. Obviously, such work must be compatible with Christian faith and morals, but that is not the main point: by being trained in a suitable profession, children's morals are protected from the insidious influence that is a consequence of idleness.

A little further on in the chapter dealing with upbringing, the *Didascalia* author explicitly urges parents to ensure that their children do not spend time with others of their own age, for this can expose them to bad influences. If their parents allow them to do whatever they want, the children will "go with those of their own age and meet together and carouse; for in this way they learn mischief." The continuation of the text shows that the author's main fear is that fornication can be the consequence, if the children of Christian parents spend time with those of their own age; but in view of what he has said about idleness as leading to "wantonness," it is reasonable to assume that he has other vices in mind too. Although he does not say specifically whether he is thinking only of pagans in the same age-group as the Christian youngsters, or includes other Christians in his warning, it is probable that his primary concern is young pagans: after warning that idleness leads to "wantonness," he claims that a lack of guidance by their parents leads children to "do those things that are evil, like the heathen." This suggests that he wishes children to be protected from the immoral behavior of pagans of their own age.[114] He does not demand that parents isolate their children totally from the heathen surroundings, but they must ensure that they give children no opportunity to spend their free time unsupervised with others of their own age. This is the earliest text that directly specifies the limitation of children's contact with the pagan environment as one element in their upbringing. As we shall see, Jerome emphasizes this even more strongly.

Another element first articulated in the *Didascalia* is the exhortation to parents to arrange marriages for their teenage sons. It appears that the author holds this to be the only possibility parents have of preventing their sons from illegitimate sexual relationships: "Therefore be careful to take wives for them, and have them married when their time is come, lest in their early age by the ardour of youth they commit fornication like the heathen."[115]

If parents are to initiate their child in the way of life that the *Didascalia* author believes to be right, they must attach importance to discipline; indeed, their zeal in this area appears to be essential, if a child is to be formed in a life of virtue. "Therefore spare not to rebuke and correct and teach them; for you will not kill them by chastising them, but rather save them alive." He offers scriptural testimony to the necessity of discipline, which does the child good, by adducing what "our Lord" says in Wisdom: "*Chasten your son, that there may be hope for him: for you shall strike him with a rod, and deliver his soul from Sheol. And he says again: Whoever spares his rod, hates his son.*"[116] The first words are a combination of Proverbs 19:18 and 23:14, while the second quotation is taken from Proverbs 13:24a; the second half of this last verse draws the positive conclusion that parents who love their children make sure that they discipline them, and this is an implicit premise in the argumentation in the *Didascalia*, when the author speaks of "delivering the soul" of the child. After quoting Proverbs, the author goes on: "Now our rod is the Word of God, Jesus Christ: even as Jeremiah also saw Him (as) an *almond rod*. Every man accordingly who spares to speak a word of rebuke to his son, hates his son. Therefore teach your sons the word of the Lord, and punish them with stripes, and bring them into subjection from their youth by your word of religion."[117] We are told that children must be obedient, but otherwise nothing is said in detail about instruction in the Word of God.

What methods are parents to use? The *Didascalia* speaks of rebuking, punishing children with "stripes," bringing them into subjection, and teaching them the Word of God. The author favors the use of physical force as a suitable educational instrument, and his quotations from Proverbs offer a theological argument that the use of force is necessary to save children's souls and is an expression of their parents' love for them.[118] It is, of course, significant that the text, as we have it, offers a symbolic exegesis of the "rod" as a metaphor for God's Word, and that this plays down the element of physical punishment. It is, however, likely that this is a later gloss, introduced into a text that originally interpreted Proverbs literally, in order to tone down this element in education.[119] However, even if this hypothesis is not correct, the text of the *Didascalia* invites parents to practice what modern readers would call an authoritarian upbringing that includes the use of physical force. Let me once again underscore that the author has older children in mind, and teenage sons in particular; this text says nothing about the rearing of small children. Nevertheless, the gravity of the responsibility incumbent upon parents to bring up their teenage sons to become virtuous Christians makes it reasonable to suppose that the *Didascalia* envisages a conscious formation of children from a very young age. Similarly, nothing suggests that the authoritarian approach, which urges parents to ensure that their teenage sons receive a strict discipline, including the use of physical force, would not also apply to younger children.

Who is responsible for carrying out the practical aspects of this upbringing? The first point we should note is that the parents are the only persons mentioned in this context in the *Didascalia*. It is they who are charged with Christian education; this task is not assigned to nurses, pedagogues, or other servants. Second, it appears that both mother and father bear this responsibility, since the author addresses them directly in the plural: "And give them no liberty to set themselves up against you their parents; and let them do nothing without your counsel." He writes that children must be "corrected by their parents," and it is the parents who must give an account to God of their children's sins. Naturally, the fact that he says that both parents are responsible does not entitle us to infer that he envisages an ideal situation in which both parents would be involved in equal measure in the practical work of upbringing. Established patterns of gender roles assigned the chief responsibility to the father as *paterfamilias*, but in day-to-day living he delegated much of the practical side to his "second in command," his wife. Nothing in the *Didascalia* suggests a departure from normal praxis in this sphere.

The *Apostolic Constitutions* draw on the *Didascalia* and broadly reproduce at 4.11 what the earlier text had said about the upbringing of children, though with some nuances that are worth noting. After citing the same passages from Proverbs that the *Didascalia* had offered as scriptural proof that harsh discipline is best for children, the *Apostolic Constitutions* add one more quotation—"Beat his sides whilst he is an infant, lest he be hardened and disobey thee" (Sirach 30:12)—as a further underscoring of this point. After exhorting parents to teach their children the Word of God, the author urges them to "bring them under with cutting stripes and make them submissive." In other words, they are to employ physical force in the disciplining of their children.[120] In keeping with his quotation from Sirach 30:12, but unlike the *Didascalia*, he also emphasizes that Christian formation should begin at a tender age. Both writings say that parents must teach their children "the Word of the Lord," but the *Apostolic Constitutions* go further. Parents must do more than just instruct the children about the contents of scripture: they are to give them "every sacred writing." In other words, once the children have learned to read, they are to read the scriptures on their own. The *Didascalia* also probably envisages that scripture will be read when parents teach their children the Word of the Lord, but this is emphasized more strongly in the *Apostolic Constitutions*. Instruction in God's Word, whether taught by the parents or read by the children themselves, is seen as a means of formation: children are to learn to show their parents obedience. In the present context, the primary implication is that they follow the instructions of their parents about what a life in accordance with sacred scriptures means.

We should also note that the *Apostolic Constitutions* do not offer any symbolic exegesis of the "rod" in Proverbs 13:24. Parents are exhorted to employ corporal punishment, so that their children will learn to submit to their will and to lead a virtuous life. Like the *Didascalia*, the author goes beyond general admonitions, and offers theological arguments in justification of his position.

Finally, the *Apostolic Constitutions* seem to assume that fathers have the primary responsibility for upbringing. The chapter devoted to this topic begins with a direct address to fathers, exhorting them to teach and instruct their children in a fitting manner. At the same time, the *Constitutions* affirm that "the parents" will be condemned for the sins their children commit. In context, this plural noun may refer to fathers as one group of parents, but it is more likely that the author has in mind the two parents of a child; if this is correct, mothers also are seen as responsible for their children's sins, and therefore as sharing responsibility for the upbringing they receive. Although fathers may have the primary responsibility, it seems that the author also includes mothers in this task.

Jerome

Let us recall the background to Jerome's two letters about the rearing of children. Two parents have consecrated their small daughters to a life of virginity, and have asked him for advice about how they should bring the girls up with this goal in view. This means that Jerome's observations about this topic in these letters envisage children destined for a life with extraordinary obligations and demands; accordingly, we cannot simply assume that Jerome thought that his words were applicable to children in general. Nevertheless, given that he was a zealous adherent of ascetic ideals, it is reasonable to think that he would consider the basic principles in the upbringing he prescribes here as relevant to all children.

Jerome begins *Epistle* 107.4 with an exhortation that Paula "must learn to hear nothing and to say nothing but what belongs to the fear of God," and this can be taken as a summary of how the girls are to be formed for a life in consecrated virginity. We have seen how the *Didascalia* and the *Apostolic Constitutions* admonished parents to limit their children's contact with pagan youngsters of their own age, in order to shield them from bad influences. This referred primarily to older children, that is, teenagers. Jerome emphasizes much more strongly the importance of isolation from the surrounding world, and affirms that the girls must be sheltered from negative input from their earliest years. This is because he is convinced that it is difficult in later life to shake off the vices one has learned as a little child: "Early impressions are hard to eradicate from the mind."[121] Accordingly, the girls must always be under the supervision of persons of high moral integrity, and all the influences to which they are exposed and everything they do must be rigorously invigilated in view of their formation for what Jerome defines as a life in the fear of God.

They must not learn impure words, and instead of worldly songs, they must learn to esteem "the sweetness of the psalms" while their tongues are "still tender." Jerome says that when Paula is a little older, she must be "deaf to the sound of the organ, and not know even the uses of the pipe, the lyre, and the cithern"[122]—instruments associated with secular music. When she practices putting letters together to form words, these should not be chosen at random, but should be words with a spiritual meaning, for example the names of the prophets and apostles.[123]

Even when she is small—four or five years old—she must be kept apart from "boys with their wanton thoughts." A girl should spend her time only with other girls; "she should know nothing of boys and should dread even playing with them."[124] When she is a little older, young men must not be allowed to "greet her with smiles," nor should any "dandy with curled hair pay compliments to her."[125] She must never show interest in younger men, nor "turn her eyes upon curled fops."[126] Nor must she ever be alone with a man, not even a Christian teacher with whom she might wish to discuss religious questions.[127] The girls must be protected from the opposite sex, and so they must not "appear in public too freely or too frequently attend crowded churches."[128] Indeed, Jerome makes a point of telling Paula's mother that she must always be present when her daughter appears in public, even when she goes to church and visits a martyr's grave.[129] Instead of letting themselves be seen in public, they are to take their pleasure in a withdrawn life where they study sacred scripture and pray in their own room.[130]

Clearly, the ideal is that the girls should frequent the public sphere as little as possible. When they go out of their homes, this should always be under the supervision of their mothers. "Leave her no power or capacity of living without you." It seems that Jerome expects that this close supervision, or rather control, that the mothers must exercise over their daughters will lead to a kind of dependency; at any rate, he encourages Laeta to let Paula "feel frightened when she is left to herself."[131]

Paula must refrain from wearing earrings, cosmetics, tinted hair, gold chains, pearls on her neck, and other jewelry.[132] Jerome recommends that one who is consecrated to a life in virginity should not use the linen garments that other women wear: her mother is to "wrap her up in a dark cloak." It is better to be strict with the girls from a tender age, for otherwise one will need to wean them away from bad habits when they are older.[133] When she is old enough to learn how to spin, the clothes she makes for herself are to keep the cold out, "not expose the body which it professes to cover."[134] As long as Paula is at a tender age, she is to be allowed to take a bath whenever she requests this, but when she is older and has passed through puberty, Jerome advises in emphatic language that she should never take a bath at all. A virgin at that age "should blush and feel overcome at the idea of seeing herself undressed.... Why, then, should she add fuel to a sleeping fire by taking baths?"[135] Instead of exposing herself to the sight of her own naked body—and to the risk that sexual desire might be kindled—Paula is to mortify her body with vigils and fasting, and bring it into submission.

This brings us to one important aspect in the formation program of girls destined for a life in harmony with the ideals appropriated to the state of virginity. From the age seven onward, they must practice a comprehensive and regulated devotional life.[136] Jerome prescribes the kind of food Paula is to eat. The menu consists of herbs, wheaten bread, and occasionally fish; more importantly, Jerome emphasizes that she is never to eat her fill at table, because she must be capable "on the moment to begin reading or chanting."[137] This reflects the idea that a full stomach has pernicious effects on the spiritual life. In his conflict with the monk Jovinian (died c. 405), who refused to accept many of Jerome's ascetic ideals,[138] he develops this point in considerable detail: "For nothing is so destructive to the mind as a full belly."[139] He advises against extreme fasting, especially in the case of small children, since this is harmful.[140] Accordingly, he urges that children should eat in moderation, since this will best equip Paula to consecrate herself to a life of devotion.

Paula's life is to be structured by the regular reading of scripture and by prayer, both by day and by night:

> She ought to rise at night to recite prayers and psalms; to sing hymns in the morning; at the third, sixth, and ninth hours to take her place in the line to do battle for Christ; and, lastly, to kindle her lamp and to offer her evening sacrifice. In these occupations let her pass the day, and when night comes let it find her still engaged in them. Let reading follow prayer with her, and prayer again succeed to reading.[141]

As we have seen in an earlier chapter, Jerome suggests the order in which the books of the Bible are to be read.[142] In addition to the canonical scriptures, the girls should read Cyprian, Athanasius, and Hilary, but they should avoid apocryphal writings. The reading of sacred scripture is a central element in the formation for a life in consecrated virginity. The treasures of these girls should not be silk or "gems," but "manuscripts of the holy scriptures."[143]

From a very early age, then, the girls' existence is to be structured around a comprehensive devotional life. The parents are to exercise strict control over them, and they must be isolated from contact with the surrounding world; it must be completely impossible for them to meet anyone on their own. Jerome says little about the methods the parents should employ to make their daughters obedient to the ideals they wish to implant in them. He gives only a little pedagogical counsel when he says that Paula must learn to read and write:[144] if she is slow to learn, she must not be "scolded," but rather encouraged. She is to be rewarded with gifts when she does her work well. Jerome also underscores that she must be allowed to be with other children, because this stimulates the learning process. He warns that the instruction must not be boring, since that could have the effect, for a long time to come, of killing her interest in the matters she must study.[145]

In his advice about how the girls are to be formed in view of a virginal life, Jerome shows little understanding of children and of their needs, but here he writes with striking gentleness, indeed with a surprising insight into children's psychology. This, however, is readily explained: most of what he says about the early instruction of children is borrowed from Quintilian's *Institutio Oratoria*.[146] This, however, does not make Jerome's remarks irrelevant to our present study, since the very fact that he chose to include this pedagogical material shows that Jerome found Quintilian's ideas reasonable. And yet, we cannot say that he has genuinely integrated them into his own thinking—virtually nothing indicates a comparably gentle or understanding attitude with regard to children's nature when Jerome gives advice about the spiritual formation of the girls when they are older. Jerome does not discuss the methods the parents should employ if the girls act in a manner that negates or opposes the upbringing he prescribes. He does indeed adopt from Quintilian a gentle attitude with regard to the initial instruction in the art of reading and writing, but this does not permit us to assume that he approaches the spiritual formation of the girls in the same spirit. It seems not to occur to him that girls who are consecrated to the virginal state could put up any resistance to the upbringing that seeks to form them in view of such a life; the closest he comes to a discussion of this problem is in his description of the position one should aim to have with regard to one's daughter: "She [the daughter] should love her [the mother] as her parent, obey her as her mistress, and reverence her as her teacher."[147] But he says nothing about what the mother must do to create such an attitude in her daughter, apart from exhorting her to exercise strict control over the girl.

Jerome emphasizes that adults who have dealings with the girls, whether in the initial instruction in reading and writing or in their spiritual formation, must be good models for them. Their master must be chosen with care. He must be "of approved years, life, and learning," so that it is certain that Paula will pronounce words correctly from the very start. Jerome warns against hiring an uneducated woman who lacks professional qualities and covers herself with gold and purple—the latter has a negative impact on spiritual formation. Paula's nurse must not be "intemperate," nor may she lose her self-control or indulge in gossip.[148] As the girl grows up, Laeta must see that she is given as role model a somewhat older virgin "of approved faith, character, and chastity, apt to instruct her by word and examples."[149] Jerome underscores how important it is that the parents are good examples of a virtuous life: he admonishes Laeta that she herself is to be her "mistress, a model on which she may form her childish conduct. Never either in you nor in her father let her see what she cannot imitate without sin. Remember both of you that you are the parents of a consecrated virgin, and that your example will teach her more than your precepts."[150] The interesting point is that these words so explicitly affirm that it is not enough to give the girls instructions about how they are meant to live: if Christian formation is to succeed, it is even more important that the parents demonstrate by means of their own lives what a Christian life of virtue means in practice.

The parents are the central persons in the upbringing of these girls. They are to exercise full control over them and never let them out of their sight. The fact that mothers are the fundamental educators does not mean that they carried out this task unaided. In keeping with normal praxis among those who were reasonably well-off, Jerome takes it for granted that the parents will hire teachers and a nurse to share in looking after and bringing up the child. However, there is no doubt that the parents bear primary responsibility for the spiritual formation, and the practical tasks this entails are in their hands.

John Chrysostom

As we have mentioned, the upbringing of children has a clear goal in Chrysostom's eyes: they are to be formed so that they will live in accordance with what he defines as the ethical-moral ideals in Christianity. The definitive goal is to equip children for the kingdom of God.

What specific moral-ethical patterns and virtues does Chrysostom see as central to children's upbringing? Or (to keep to the metaphor he himself uses) what is the statue to look like, once it has been formed and honed by the artist's hand? What does it actually mean to bring up children in a life consistent with "the discipline and instruction of the Lord"? The starting point for our discussion of these questions is Chrysostom's *De Inani Gloria*.

In this work, Chrysostom compares the child's soul to a city surrounded by a wall with four gates, which must be maintained in good working order. These four gates are metaphors for various senses: "The whole body shall be the wall, as it were, the gates are the eyes, the tongue, the sense of smell, and, if you will, the sense of touch."[151] After introducing this metaphor in chapter 27, he devotes most of the rest of the treatise to a description of how these senses are to be used, and how parents are to teach their children to use them correctly. The main point is the necessity to keep all the gates closed, so that the child's soul may not be influenced by the world outside the city, that is, the vices that Chrysostom associates with the pagan lifestyle and morality.

He begins with "the gate of the tongue," which he calls "the busiest of all."[152] This gate must be shut with doors and bolts of gold, not of wood or iron.[153] Indeed, he goes further than this: the whole city (the child's soul) is to be of gold, for it is God, the king over the whole universe, who is to dwell in it.[154] Chrysostom explicitly draws attention to the metaphorical meaning of the golden gate and bolts: they symbolize God's Word. He emphasizes very strongly that parents are to instruct their children in God's Word. They are to "teach the child so that the words revolve on his lips all the time, even on his walks abroad, not lightly nor incidentally nor at rare intervals, but without ceasing."[155] As we shall see, Chrysostom returns to the central importance of initiating children into the Word of God later in this writing when he speaks of "the sense of hearing."

After exhorting parents in general terms to teach their children the Word of God, Chrysostom goes into more detail when he discusses the kind of words they must try to stop their children from employing. They must expel all "words that are insolent and slanderous, foolish, shameful, common, and worldly."[156] Instead, they are to sing Christian hymns and speak all the time "about heavenly philosophy"; the term "philosophy" in this passage means the confidence that believers have in God.[157] The *De Inani Gloria* three times demands that children sing songs with Christian contents.[158] It is in his ninth homily on Colossians that Chrysostom gives the fullest commentary on the place the singing of the Psalms has in the upbringing of children.[159] He complains that the fathers in his congregation in Constantinople are neglecting their obligation to spend an adequate amount of time on instructing their wives and children in the Christian faith. Things have got so bad the children do not know one single psalm, although they sing the same satanic psalms as "cooks, and caterers, and musicians."[160] He emphasizes that children must learn the psalms from a very early age. As they grow older, they are to learn hymns. In Christian families, therefore, hymn singing is to take the place formerly held by secular songs. Like the reading of scripture, hymn singing is to be a regular activity in the home; hymns are to be sung especially before and after the family meals.[161]

Chrysostom's use of terminology is not completely consistent, but he does make a rough distinction in his writings between "psalms" and "hymns."[162] The former term denotes the psalms in the Old Testament, while the latter denotes other scriptural hymns, for example the Gloria and the Sanctus; sometimes, however, the biblical psalms too are hymns. This makes it not clear what hymns in *De Inani* 28 refers to. In chapter 34 of the same work, he says that children must learn to sing psalms to God. According to Chrysostom, this has a twofold usefulness. First of all, like the other scriptures, the psalms impart instruction.[163] Unlike other biblical texts, however, the psalms have the pedagogical advantage of being

set to music, and this allows us to remember their contents more easily. Hence, the singing of psalms contributes to the moral formation of
children. The second point is linked to the first: Chrysostom appears to
believe that singing psalms has the effect of subduing or calming the passions. At any rate, one of his many suggested ways to control sexual desire
is the singing of psalms.[164]

Chrysostom goes on to give specific advice about what parents must
do to achieve the conduct they desire. It is important to establish laws
and rules from a very early age. More specifically, chapter 30 of *De Inani
Gloria* states that parents are to make it a law that their boy is forbidden
to despise anyone, to speak ill of anyone, to swear, and to be quarrelsome.
The focus here is on vices that affect other people. Later in the *De Inani*,
he sums up the correct moral attitude as the virtue of *sophrosynê* (good
judgment), and affirms that the vices of *hubrizein* (reproach)and *homnu-
nai* (cursing) are the antonyms of this virtue.[165] A life in *sophrosynê* means
that one refrains from these two vices and leads a life of fasting and prayer.
Chrysostom also emphasizes that failure to comply with these laws and
rules must have consequences for the child; mostly, this means that the
child will be punished with a sharp look, a harsh rebuke, or reproaches. We note that Chrysostom has reservations about the use of physical
force—though not because this would be harmful to the child in some
way, but because excessive use of the whip will ultimately prove ineffective. One should indeed threaten the child with corporal punishment, but
one should be slow to carry it out (though without giving the child the
impression that is one merely speaking empty words). The following passage is typical of Chrysostom's thinking in this area:

> Have not recourse to blows constantly and accustom him not to
> be trained by the rod; for if he feel it constantly as he is being
> trained, he will learn to despise it. And when he has learnt to de-
> spise it, he has reduced your system to naught. Let him rather at
> all times fear blows but not receive them. Threaten him with the
> tawse, but do not lay it on and do not let your threats proceed to
> action. Do not let it appear that your words do not pass the stage
> of threats; for a threat is only of use when attended by the belief
> that it will be put into effect. If the offender learn your intention,
> he will despise it. So let him expect chastisement but not receive
> it, so that his fear may not be quenched but may endure, like a
> raging fire drawing thorny brushwood from every side or like a
> sharp and searching pick digging to the very depths.[166]

Chrysostom is slow to recommend the use of physical force, but threats and fear are fundamental elements in the upbringing he envisages. Nevertheless, the *De Inani* proposes a somewhat milder approach than we have seen in the *Didascalia* and the *Apostolic Constitutions*, and it seems that Chrysostom himself subsequently changed his views about the strictness parents ought to display toward their children. In the *Adversus Oppugnatores Vitae Monasticae*, he explains the sinful actions of Eli's sons, and their consequences for the priest himself, by saying that Eli was too lax a disciplinarian. He criticizes Eli's weakness on this point: "He should have threatened them, cast them from his sight, beaten them, and been much stricter and more severe."[167] It is indeed true that this passage does not explicitly urge parents to employ physical force as an instrument in upbringing; but the fact that Eli functions as a negative example, showing how parents ought not to treat their children, clearly implies that they ought to use force. This impression is confirmed when Chrysostom asserts that Eli was punished by God for not disciplining his sons with sufficient harshness.

Although verbal punishments and the threat of physical punishment play a dominant role in his educational program, John Chrysostom is certainly aware that treating a child with "gentleness and promises" can be an effective way of forming it in the direction one desires.[168] He speaks only briefly of the effect a promise of reward has on a child, and he gives no examples of appropriate rewards in this passage. In *Homily on Col.* 4, however, he assumes that everyone knows that parents buy their children pieces of cake and give them money as a reward for going to school.[169] He also counsels parents to appeal to the satisfaction a child experiences when it is praised by other people and when it sees that it has mastered something; one example is the joy a child will feel if it is in church and hears a story from scripture that it already knows well, while none of the other children is familiar with it.[170] He holds that the need for positive affirmation and acknowledgement by others is a fundamental trait of human nature, and is something that honors the human person.[171] Above all, children need to be affirmed and acknowledged by others. Chrysostom regards rewards in the form of positive comments on their behavior as more valuable than material rewards.[172] A positive response from people around them motivates children: when they see that their conduct is praised, they will intensify their efforts in that particular area.[173]

Chrysostom argues that parents should use both punishment and reward in bringing up their children. This dual approach is modeled on God's relationship to the world: "Even so God rules the world with the fear of Hell and the promise of His Kingdom. So must we too rule our children."[174] This provides a theological justification both for using punishment and for giving rewards.

After a brief discussion of punishment and reward, Chrysostom indicates the goal of upbringing. He has just said that boys must be taught not to despise anyone. Now he formulates this principle in positive terms: they must be taught to be "fair and courteous" (chapter 31). The first of these two virtues is the more important in Chrysostom's eyes. It entails that one is patient and does not claim one's own rights, even when one suffers injustice at the hands of persons of a lower social rank.[175] Chrysostom underscores that this applies even with regard to slaves: if a free-born boy treats a slave badly, the parents are not to tolerate this, but must punish him. This should not be read as meaning that Chrysostom has a higher esteem for slaves' position and rank than was general in classical antiquity. The point is that, if a boy learns that he is not to treat a slave in a humiliating manner, he will be all the less inclined to do so to one who is free and belongs to his own social class.[176]

Chrysostom urges parents to close "the gate of hearing"—an important gate, closely related to "the gate of the tongue," since nothing evil will come out of a child's mouth, if nothing evil enters it by means of its ears.[177] Consequently, it is vital that parents prevent the child from hearing anything that might have a bad moral influence upon it, and this means that they must be careful in their selection of nurses and slaves, so that the child will hear nothing morally degrading from their lips. If some slaves are in fact bad examples, whether in word or in deed, they must be kept away from the child. Chrysostom affirms in very clear terms that the influences to which a boy is exposed when he is small determine how he will turn out as a youth: the foundations are laid in his childhood.[178]

In this part of De Inani, Chrysostom's central point is the necessity of reading or telling stories from the Bible. Instead of telling tales that begin: "This youth kissed that maiden . . ." and focus on things that are morally reprehensible, those who are close to the child should speak of things related to scripture. His homily on Ephesians 6:1-4 further emphasizes the importance of reading the Bible. Here Chrysostom warns parents not to question whether it is necessary for children to listen to scripture. Everyone must know what scripture says, and this is "especially true for children. Even at their age they are exposed to all sorts of folly and bad examples from popular entertainments. Our children need remedies for all these things! . . . from their [children's] earliest years let us teach them to study the Bible."[179] He also argues against the idea that only monks need to study scripture. On the contrary: people who must live in a stormy world have a greater need of studying scripture than those who lead a withdrawn life behind monastery walls.[180]

This general exhortation to give children instruction in the Bible is followed by more concrete suggestions about what biblical material parents should teach their children, and by examples of what children can learn from these narratives. Clearly, Chrysostom is aware that the material must be adapted to the children's age and the level of maturity they have reached. One should begin with the story of Cain and Abel, which the father is to relate at the dinner table in the evening. Later, the mother is to tell the same story, and then ask the boy himself to relate it, so that it will lodge in his memory. As part of this instruction in sacred scripture, parents are to take their children with them to church. When they hear the same stories told here that they have learned at home, they will recognize them and be happy; this too will help them not to forget the narrative (chapters 39–42). This particular narrative will teach children what a terrible sin greed is,[181] what a terrible sin it is to be jealous (*phthonos*) of one's brother,[182] and what a terrible sin it is to believe that we can conceal something from the God who sees all things. If the parents succeed in implanting this in the child, it will fear God in its soul, and this lays a good foundation for right conduct (chapter 40).

Next, children are to hear another story about two brothers—Jacob and Esau (Genesis 25:27-34), which will teach them "to reverence and honor their fathers, when they see so keen a rivalry for the father's blessing." This attitude will lead them rather to "suffer a myriad stripes than to hear their parents curse them." The narrative also shows the grave consequences of giving in to the belly's greed: "Because of the greed of his belly he [Esau] betrayed the advantage of his birthright" (chapter 44). Chrysostom sees Esau as an exemplary figure who warns of the fatal consequences that await those who fail to practice self-control and moderation.[183] In other passages, Chrysostom speaks of people whose belly is their god—those who yield to their desires and are obsessed with the things of this world, so that all their energies are devoted to the struggle for honor, good positions, and material prosperity. Those whose belly is their god wallow in a life of pleasure in this world, and lack both self-control and moderation. Here, he is employing a *topos* (topic) that was widespread in the pagan moral traditions of antiquity and was taken over by the early Christian traditions.[184]

Chrysostom urges that children not be exposed to stories that might frighten them when they are still too young: "for thou shouldst not impose so great a burden on his understanding while he is still tender, lest you dismay him." A boy is to be told about hell only when he is fifteen years old, though he may hear narratives in which God's punishment is a central motif (for example, Noah's flood and the destruction of Sodom) when he is eight years old or even younger. When he is older, he is to be introduced to "the deeds of the New Testament—deeds of grace and deeds of hell" (chapter 52).

It is clear that instruction in scripture plays an important role in the upbringing that Chrysostom proposes, but it is striking that the Old Testament is emphasized more strongly, at any rate until the child has reached adolescence. One obvious explanation is that it has a larger supply of accessible narratives. The program put forward here for the study of scripture suggests that Chrysostom is aware that this is precisely the kind of material that children can most easily assimilate. Another factor influencing the emphasis on the Old Testament is that it contains much material suitable for teaching the morality and virtues that Chrysostom believes to be in accord with correct Christian behavior.

The next gate of which Chrysostom speaks is "the gate of smell." He has not so much to say about this, but he underscores that it must be "kept barred": nothing weakens the appropriate attitude in a soul more than "a pleasure in sweet odors." Accordingly, no one should give the boy perfume.

The next gate is that of "the eyes," which is the most difficult of all to keep watch over. Here, Chrysostom warns against certain things that the boy must not be permitted to see when he is out of doors. The parents must never permit him to go to the theater, since what he sees and hears there will corrupt him. They must also take care to shield his eyes from anything that would draw him away from true morality when he is out on the street. It is, however, not only external things that can corrupt the soul: his own appearance may lead him into temptations. In order to avoid this, his hair should be cut in a way that makes it unattractive. If the boy complains about this, his parents are to teach him that "the greatest charm is simplicity" (chapter 57). Above all, Chrysostom emphasizes that he must have little contact with women. He may certainly not bathe together with them, nor may he have any occasion to enter conversation with a large group of women (chapter 60). In the course of his remarks, Chrysostom becomes more and more restrictive, until he finally says that the boy is not to look on any woman other than his own mother (chapter 62). He proposes a remedy against the desire that (as he says) burns like a fire within the boy: one should teach the boy hymns and draw his attention more strongly to other things such as the clouds, the sun, flowers, and good books (chapters 59–60). His parents are to "speak to him of the beauty of the soul, instill into him a resolute spirit against womankind," and they must assure him that they will find a virtuous wife for him when the time is ripe—in other words, the boy himself "need" not be concerned about the other sex. Chrysostom also warns the parents not to give him money, probably because that would tempt him to visit persons and places with a negative influence. They must also teach him to renounce all forms of luxury (chapter 62).

Chrysostom then speaks briefly of the last gate, that of "touch" (chapter 63), urging that we must not let this gate "have any truck with soft raiment or bodies. Let us make it austere."

More is required, however, than a close vigilance over the gates that lead into the city of the soul. We must also pay due attention to the various parts or characteristics of the soul,[185] namely, *thymos, epithymia,* and *logistikon.* It is not easy to find one English word which adequately covers all the meanings of *thymos.* Michael Gärtner follows G. W. H. Lampe's definition of *thymos* as the "non-intellectual principle in the soul,"[186] and gives his own summary definition: "it is that which provides a strong impulse to action."[187] Chrysostom's employment of *epithymia* and *logistikon* makes it easier to find satisfactory translations of these terms: *epithymia* can be translated as "desire, lust" and *logistikon* as "rationality."[188] Chrysostom's tripartite division of the soul reflects a long tradition that goes back to Plato, and was adopted and further refined by the church fathers.[189] Each of these characteristics can be the origin of good or evil qualities, and it is the task of education to suppress what is evil and cultivate the good. Chrysostom writes: "Let us then have a care that the good qualities come to birth in these places and that they bear citizens of like character and not evil."[190] He discusses each of the three parts of the soul and gives advice on how this goal is to be achieved.

Chrysostom begins with *thymos,* to which he ascribes the good qualities of "sobriety and equability" and the bad qualities of "rashness and ill temper" (chapter 65). He maintains that it is important that this part of the soul be trained in patience and self-control, and that this should begin at an early stage: "Let us train boys from earliest childhood to be patient when they suffer wrongs themselves, but, if they see another being wronged, to sally forth courageously and aid the sufferer in fitting measure" (chapter 67). He offers practical advice about how such attitudes can be inculcated. Firstly, instead of punishing a slave for disobedience and bad conduct, boys are to be led to think through the errors they themselves have committed in relation to other persons.[191] Secondly, members of the household—the father, brothers, or slaves—are intentionally to treat the boy with contempt and to provoke him, thus training him to remain calm and not let himself be provoked. If the boy strikes a slave, he is to be punished immediately. He is to be trained to be neither "indulgent nor harsh," but always "equable" (chapter 69). If he sees that his servant has broken a brush, or that the strap around his writing tablets has been damaged, he is to be taught not to react with anger, but to be forgiving and conciliatory: "Believe me, the boy who is indifferent to such things and placable will endure every loss when he becomes a man" (chapter 73). Chrysostom also emphasizes that the boy is not to be served by the slaves: he is to do as much as possible for himself, for example, washing his feet, seeing to his own toilet needs, and bathing himself. "This will make him strong and simple and courteous" (chapter 70). Chrysostom admonishes parents to teach him friendliness, a quality manifested by his treatment of the slaves as if they were his own brothers.

Chrysostom then turns to that part of the soul where desire (*epithymia*) dwells, and asks how one can tame "this wild beast," which begins its savage attacks once the boy reaches his fifteenth year (chapter 76). The main point in this section is that the parents must protect him from surroundings that kindle desire; or, to express the same point in different terms, the boy must be trained in self-restraint. Chrysostom's practical advice about how this is to be done repeats part of what he has already said in this treatise: the boy must be taught to keep his distance from shameful theatrical plays and songs, and he must never visit the theater or have contact with young girls. In this context, Chrysostom emphasizes the importance of good examples. If the boy nevertheless wishes to visit the theater,[192] his parents are to tell him of other boys who are forbidden to go, so that he "may be held fast in the grip of emulation." He sees this as a very effective educational method: emulation "is a more potent instrument than fear or promises or aught else" (chapter 77). Not only contemporary examples have an educational effect, however; historical examples also are important. He exhorts the parents to praise both Christian and pagan persons who practiced self-restraint:[193] "Let us constantly flood his ears with talk of them" (chapter 79). For the same reason, the boy ought to fast in moderation.[194] He is to go to church and learn to pray "with great fervor and contrition," and he is to "keep vigils as much as he is able, and let the stamp of a saintly man be impressed on the boy in every way" (chapters

79–80). All these are instruments to dampen or overcome desire. He also emphasizes the importance of regular meetings with the bishop. If the boy is praised by the bishop, this will motivate him to continue his pursuit of a life of virtue. Chrysostom also encourages the father to show others who are present how proud he is that the bishop praises his son (chapter 83). All this is meant as positive affirmation of the boy, and in a culture where public recognition and honor were fundamental values, praise from important personages was even more strongly motivating than it would be in our modern Western culture. All of this is meant to tame sexual desire in the boy, or at least to prevent him from yielding to it. In order that sexuality may be lived out in the only legitimate framework, Chrysostom encourages parents to see that their boys marry while they are young. They are to convince them that no love is more beautiful than that between two young people who have lived in sexual abstinence until their wedding. Like the *Didascalia* and the *Apostolic Constitutions*, therefore, Chrysostom prescribes early marriages as an antidote to the illegitimate expression of sexual desire.

Chrysostom goes on to discuss the third part of the soul, the reason (*phronêsis*), which he describes as "the master principle which keeps everything under control" (chapter 85). He reflects the widespread view in the early church that good actions are a natural consequence of correct insight into what is good. This makes correct insight a presupposition of right conduct.[195] Hence, it is decisively important that children receive knowledge of what is right, and Chrysostom says that they must be trained in the true philosophy, which includes the basic truths about God and about "all the treasure laid up in Heaven, and Hell and the kingdom of the other world."[196] If one is to practice the right virtues, one must have knowledge of God and of divine things; for as he says, quoting Proverbs 1:7, "the fear of the Lord is the beginning of wisdom." One who is filled with this wisdom will despise what the world esteems highly, and this is why the boy must "be taught to think nothing of wealth or worldly reputation or power or death or the present life on earth."

In his discussion of the goal of upbringing, and his concrete advice about its contents and methods, Chrysostom has boys in mind. This is reflected throughout the whole treatise, but at the very close of *De Inani* he writes that what he has said about boys applies to girls too: "Let his mother learn to train her daughter by these precepts" (chapter 90). However, since—according to Chrysostom—women suffer from a number of gender-specific vices, he clearly finds it necessary to say something about these. Prostitutes in particular were associated with "extravagance and personal adornment," and mothers must teach their daughters to refrain from this. While "young men are troubled by desire," girls succumb to "love of finery and excitement." He emphasizes that the goal of upbringing is to suppress both of these errors.

Who is considered responsible for upbringing? I have noted earlier that it was the father, as *paterfamilias,* who had the overall responsibility for rearing children in the classical household, and Chrysostom simply takes this for granted. In his homily on Ephesians 6:1-4, he says explicitly that the father, "as the head and source of authority in the family," is responsible for teaching his children obedience.[197] However, mothers do not disappear from the picture: Chrysostom appeals to them directly and exhorts them to reflect on the laudable example of Hannah, who handed over her child Samuel to God.[198] More interesting is the fact that he includes mothers in the total responsibility for upbringing, when he introduces the metaphor of children as statues in the artist's hand (*De Inani* 22). Here he addresses "each of you fathers and mothers" and exhorts both parents to "give all your leisure to fashioning these wondrous statues for God." It is clear that mothers have a responsibility for upbringing, and share in the practical realization of this task. When the father narrates stories from scripture, the mother is to be present, so that she can "praise the story." After the father has introduced a story for the first time, it is the mother's task to repeat it and to see that the boy learns it.[199] It may be going too far to say that Chrysostom sees this as the standard pattern of upbringing in the home, but he certainly assigns an important role to mothers in the instruction of their children in scripture. He also says that men should exhort their wives to talk to their children and guide them in their daily dealings with them.[200] The mother's role is perhaps best characterized as that of the second in command, who acts on her husband's behalf; and this corresponds to Chrysostom's description of the relationship between the marriage partners and their children in his exposition of 1 Timothy 3:4. The epistle says that the one who is to become a bishop must govern his own house well, and this entails that his children are obedient and show him respect. This leads Chrysostom to draw an analogy between the church and the household: "For the Church is, as it were, a small household, and as in a house there are children and wife and domestics, and the man has rule over them all; just so in the Church there are women, children, servants. And if he that presides in the Church has partners in his power, so hath the man a partner, that is, his wife."[201] Let us recall that Chrysostom is thinking primarily of the upbringing of boys in his *De Inani Gloria.* However, as we have seen, he remarks at the close of this treatise that the upbringing he has prescribed for boys is applicable to girls as well. He writes that both parents have the main responsibility for training boys; but it is the mothers who are responsible for the upbringing of girls.

It is clear that he envisages parents who not only have the ultimate responsibility for upbringing, but are actively involved in the practical tasks. His ideals for Christian education imply that the parents are genuinely present in their children's lives. This does not mean that he thinks that they are to carry out the work of education on their own. He reflects customary practice, at least among the more prosperous section of the population, when he takes it for granted that nurses, pedagogues, and other slaves were involved in upbringing. As I have noted, he insists that parents must be very selective when they choose nurses and other servants for their child; such persons must have a vocabulary and a way of life that are in keeping with his ideals about the education of a child as an athlete for Christ. He writes: "the harm done to the free [children] is incalculable, when we place over them corrupt slaves."[202] The father must admonish the child's "tutor and his servant"—along with its mother—to take care to prevent the child from doing anything wrong.[203]

Chrysostom underscores the importance of good role models for children. The power of example is very great—not only in the case of slaves, servants, and friends, but just as much in the case of the child's parents. He is convinced that if "husband and wife order their lives according to God's law, their children will also submit willingly to the same law."[204] He points to the value of good examples when he goes on to exhort parents to present biblical personages as models of a virtuous life. His primary example is Abraham, but he also mentions Noah, Joseph, Moses, and Isaiah, because "all these great men looked at this present life as nothing; they did not thirst for riches or other earthly attachments."[205] Chrysostom also argues that parents should not give children their own names or those of relatives, but should call them after the righteous, that is martyrs, bishops, and apostles, so that its name will inspire the child to imitate the virtuous life of the holy person whose name it bears.[206] His repeated injunctions to present children with examples (both contemporary and historical) of right conduct and the good Christian life reflect once more the goal of upbringing, which is not primarily to make the child a skilled rhetorician or to lay the foundation for some other brilliant worldly career: "a pattern of life is what is needed, not empty speeches; character, not cleverness; deeds, not words."[207]

It makes sense to see the centrality Chrysostom attributes to examples in the task of upbringing in connection with the great role examples of the virtuous life played in the moral formation that was imparted in school,[208] and in the light of the great importance attached to the use of examples in the Greco-Roman rhetorical tradition. Rhetorical theory and practice in antiquity show that a speaker who wished to influence his hearers to change their behavior appealed to examples; this was considered the most effective form of argumentation. I have in mind here the so-called deliberative rhetoric.[209] My point is that when Chrysostom, who himself had been trained in rhetoric and was celebrated for his rhetorical skill, so frequently appeals to parents to employ examples, he is arguing on the basis of established conventions.

Augustine

According to the *Confessions,* pupils were beaten harshly at school. Augustine compares the treatment meted out to them with torture.[210] The employment of physical force was part of the general culture, and was taken for granted as an appropriate tool in an educational setting.[211] As I have mentioned, Augustine is unambiguously critical in his evaluation of both the extent and the brutality of the methods of corporal punishment.[212] He criticizes adults for operating with double standards: they punish children, but do the same things themselves.[213] Nevertheless, he believes that he deserved punishment, and this implies a fundamental acceptance of corporal punishment as a reaction to children's behavior.

This accords with what Augustine says about how fathers should bring up their sons: if they are disobedient, it is right for their fathers to beat them.[214] He explains why fathers in certain situations are obligated to beat their sons, out of love for them. Augustine's scriptural proof is Wisdom 3:11 ("Whoever casts away discipline is unhappy"), and he argues that one who does "not apply discipline is cruel." In positive terms, "a father shows kindness by beating, by beating his son shows him mercy." The underlying premise is that the father knows what is best for his son.[215] Augustine seems here to be trying to convince his hearers, first, that it is necessary to employ corporal punishment and, second, that this is an expression of love for one's sons.[216] We can of course speculate on why he finds this necessary. Is it because Augustine—despite his criticism of the harsh discipline he had endured at school—nevertheless represents a stricter approach than was customary among his hearers? At any rate, it is striking that he notes the fact that physical force is employed in upbringing and sees this as an appropriate educational tool while also finding it necessary to argue that those who beat their sons are giving expression to paternal love.

We should note that the sons to whom Augustine refers in these passages are no longer small children: disobedience to their fathers is associated with the use of money and property, and one aspect of the situation is the requirement that a son be a responsible heir.[217] Such questions would not be urgent before boys were in their teens. He says nothing explicit about smaller children, but he does give some hints in the *Confessiones*. We have seen in an earlier chapter that this work views children as largely responsible for their own actions. This means that as they get older and reason develops, they will encounter harsher reactions to breaches of the norms for correct conduct.[218] This suggests that Augustine believed that parents should treat smaller children more gently than older ones.

Let me repeat: Augustine sees no contradiction between disciplining children harshly and loving them. Many passages in his writings simply assume that parents love their children—this is part of the order of nature. "Nobody can help loving his children. . . . Nobody at all, by the law of nature itself, can hate the one he has begotten."[219] In *Sermon* 302.1, Augustine describes how fathers treat their small children with paternal "lovingkindness." They give them toys spontaneously—the children do not need to weep loudly in order to get them. And they give them sweets. "A kindly and fatherly indulgence shares things, allows things, which he wouldn't like his children to remain attached to as they grow bigger, as they grow up. . . . Fatherly lovingkindness gives in to children at play and enjoying themselves with toys." According to Augustine, such a way of treating small children is accompanied by an awareness that fathers will not demand too much of them. He describes the obvious joy fathers take in their children, and it is interesting to note the gentleness and the understanding of children's reactions that are implicit in his words about the interaction of fathers and children. On the question of discipline, this text and the *Confessiones* agree. We should likewise note that Augustine assumes that it is the father who has this kind of contact with small children. The traditional pattern of gender roles in antiquity made it more natural and customary for the mother to spend most time with small children.

A Brief Discussion of the Attitude of Christians toward Pagan Schools

We have seen that several Christian texts encourage parents to protect their children against negative input from the pagan environment in which they live. Adolescents in particular must be kept under close supervision, and they are to have as little contact as possible with pagans of their own age. One expression of this attitude was the prohibition of attending the theater, which was an important institution and meeting place in classical society. But an even more important institution in terms of handing on pagan religious ideas was the school.[220]

The word "institution" does not refer here to buildings or organizational units, but to the important position occupied by schooling over a long period in the Greco-Roman world, and not least to the substance of school education, which was strikingly consistent for almost a thousand years, despite geographical variations and changes introduced in the course of time. This is true above all of the literature that was employed to teach reading and writing—the Greek (and later also the Roman) "classics."[221] Homer was basic;[222] other important authors were Hesiod, Euripides, Menander, Isocrates, Demosthenes, Cicero, Virgil, and Horace.[223] Much of their works (especially in the case of Homer) deals with mythological figures and their sometimes immoral love lives, wars, and other exploits. In addition to helping pupils to learn to read and write, these texts were meant to give them a cultural education and not least a moral formation.[224] The problem was, however, that the gods in Homer and other poets behaved in a way that contradicted what was considered good morality, and that these works taught errors about the gods and about morality. This led to criticism of the contents of Homer, and Plato and others maintained that one must be selective: texts with a negative influence on moral formation should not be used in an educational context.[225] One way to cope with the offensive aspects was to interpret them allegorically.[226] Many authors in antiquity felt that the study of Homer and other classic texts posed a problem with regard to the pupils' moral formation; nevertheless, these texts remained "canonical" in education throughout the whole of the classical period, not least thanks to the interpretative skills that were employed to deal with their offensive aspects. This meant that the classic narratives which gave the culture its language, its identity, and its morality dealt to a large extent with pagan gods and their doings. The entire school year was structured around the pagan religion; school holidays coincided with religious festivals.[227]

Schools were seldom organized or financed by the governing authorities, and it was rare for a building to be specifically designated for use as a school. Pupils were taught in a variety of places: out of doors, often under a shady tree, in the *palaestra* or wrestling school, in the gymnasium, or in the teacher's own home.[228] There was no public body to organize the work of teaching, nor any association of teachers. Teaching was a private industry, so to speak; teachers had to find their own pupils, and they had to live off what the parents paid them.[229] Becoming a pupil and receiving a school education in classical antiquity did not entail what we associate with these concepts, that is to say, registering in an institution that provided instruction and then taking the examinations required. In the classical period, it meant receiving instruction from various teachers, until the pupil had finished the full program of "the encyclical studies." The term is not applied consistently, but it usually denotes the instruction that, taken as a whole, provides a full education. This program involved a number of subjects that were taken in a particular sequence: instruction in reading and writing, grammar, the study of literature, geometry, mathematics, music, astronomy, and rhetoric. The encyclical studies could also include other subjects in addition to this basic plan.[230] We should also note that philosophical critics such as Seneca and Plutarch thought that the encyclical education was necessary but insufficient. It was a necessary preparation for learning that virtue which only philosophical studies could impart.[231] They call the encyclical studies "propaedeutic." Our sources use this word frequently to indicate the preparatory and subordinate role of the encyclical education in relation to philosophical studies.[232]

Given the clear profile of Christian upbringing in the texts we have seen above, it would be reasonable to expect Christians to refuse to have anything to do with the classical schools, and perhaps to establish their own alternative schools where Christian texts replaced pagan writings. This, however, is not the case.

It is certainly true that a number of sources reflect the tension that Christians clearly felt between what was taught in the schools and their Christian faith. But a variety of answers were given to the question of how they were to deal with this tension. (1) Some held that Christians should not take part in the encyclical studies at all; (2) some held that attendance at school was necessary; and (3) some took a positive view of the classical school and saw it as a preparation for the study of Christian writings.

One of the few spokesmen for the first, restrictive attitude is Tatian. In his apology, the *Oratio ad Graecos,* he launches a sweeping attack on Hellenistic culture, claiming that the root of the folly of the Greeks is the teachers, who give instruction in literature (26.2.). He himself has abandoned the wisdom he learned in school (1.3) and has devoted himself to the Word of God, which is the true wisdom and *paideia* (12.5; 35.2). After observing that the teachers in the schools of grammar are the origin of what he calls the folly of the Greeks, he seems to reject all contact with the schools of antiquity when he writes "that we have abandoned you, and

no longer concern ourselves with your tenets" (26.3).[233] Christians should
be neither pupils nor teachers. After their conversion, they exchange the
stories of the Greeks for new stories (21.2) that represent the true *paideia*.
Tatian does not discuss how this is to be done, nor whether it was possible
in practice for young Christians to hold completely aloof from the classical schools.

The author of the *Didascalia* takes the same line, emphasizing (as we
have seen) parents' responsibility for giving their children a Christian instruction and upbringing. In negative terms, this means that they must have
nothing to do with the books of the "pagans," as he writes in chapter 3:

> But avoid all books of the heathen (*Gentiles libri*). For what hast
> thou to do with strange sayings or laws or lying prophecies, which
> also turn away from the faith them that are young? For what is
> wanting to thee in the word of God, that thou shouldst cast thyself
> upon these fables of the heathen (*fabulae*)? If thou wouldst read
> historical narratives, thou hast the Book of Kings; but if wise men
> and philosophers, thou hast the Prophets, wherein thou shalt find
> wisdom and understanding more than that of the wise men and
> philosophers; for they are the words of the God, the only wise.
> And if thou wish for songs, thou hast the Psalms of David; but if
> (thou wouldst read of) the beginning of the world, thou hast the
> Genesis of the great Moses; and if laws and commandments, thou
> hast the glorious Law of the Lord God. Therefore avoid all these
> strange and diabolic writings (*alienis et diabolicis scripturis*).[234]

Although the author does not mention school explicitly, the rejection of
pagan books in this passage strongly suggests that he also rejected the classical school. The books of the pagans, which belong to the devil, must be
replaced by the biblical writings. The author does not actually draw up
an alternative program of studies, but he clearly means that Christians
will find all they need here: Homer is to be replaced by the Bible. The pagans thought that one found all one needed in Homer, but the *Didascalia*
claims that Christians will find all they need in scripture, which is an encyclopedia of knowledge containing various genres such as history, wisdom,
songs, and laws. If we read this passage bearing in mind what the author
writes about parents' responsibility for teaching their child the Christian
faith, it seems that he expects that elementary instruction in reading and
writing will be given at home, with the Bible as textbook.

Tatian and the *Didascalia* are the only sources that appear to assert that Christians must make a clean break with the public schools, although we should note that Clement of Alexandria reports the views of persons who broadly share this viewpoint. They remain anonymous; in his polemic against them, Clement describes them only as "some" or even "most people."[235] They hold that Greek literature has its origin with the devil and his demons, and consequently refuse to have anything whatever to do with philosophy and the instruction given in school. Clement says that they demand the faith alone and naked.[236] Clement's opponents see this as a spiritual battle, and they fear that anyone who has contact with the literature in the encyclical studies will become impure, or will be led astray by the devil and his demons. The starting point for this attitude is perhaps fear, skepticism, or uncertainty among "ordinary Christians," for which a theological justification is then supplied.[237] We do not know how many people actually thought along these lines, but the fact that Clement refers to his adversaries as "most people" certainly suggests that they were a numerous group in the Alexandrian community—perhaps the large group of Christians who had little acquaintance with Greek literature.

Tertullian very largely shares the same fundamental attitude to Greek philosophy and culture in general as Tatian, the *Didascalia*, and Clement's opponents: he sees a deep and unbridgeable chasm between the Christian faith and philosophy. This finds eloquent expression in the well-known words in Tertullian's *De Praescriptione Haereticorum* 7.9–13:[238]

> What indeed has Athens to do with Jerusalem? What concord is there between the Academy and the Church? What between heretics and Christians? Our instruction comes from "the porch of Solomon," who had himself taught that "the Lord should be sought in simplicity of heart." Away with all attempts to produce a mottled Christianity of Stoic, Platonic, and dialectic composition! We want no curious disputation (*curiositas*) after possessing Christ Jesus, no inquisition (*inquisitii*) after enjoying the gospel! With our faith, we desire no further belief. For this is our palmary faith, that there is nothing which we ought to believe besides.

In faith, in Christ, and in the Gospel, Christians have all the knowledge they require. They need no further knowledge. Although this passage is speaking about the relationship between philosophy and the Christian faith, it implies a negative attitude to Greek classical literature in general, as other passages in Tertullian's writings confirm: "We will have nothing to do with pagan literature and teaching, which is perverted in its best results."[239]

In *De Idololatria* 10, where Tertullian discusses in greater detail the problems that confront Christian teachers and pupils in the public schools,[240] he begins by noting that the very act of teaching is closely linked to pagan religion: teachers are obliged to praise the heathen gods and to make their names known. They are required to commemorate the feast days of the gods with flowers and to take part in the pagan festivals. Unsurprisingly, he concludes that Christians who teach in school are participating in idolatry (*idololatria*). It follows that they cannot work as schoolmasters (10.1).

It is perhaps more surprising, therefore, when we read that this same Tertullian—who can be so rigid on other questions and is not at all inclined to make compromises with Greek philosophy or the pagan lifestyle—argues that it is legitimate for children of Christians to be pupils in the classical schools. He reports the views of those who say that it is impossible to live in this world without acquiring the knowledge that is taught in school; nor is one entitled to despise worldly studies (*saecularia studia*), which are a presupposition for the study of divine things (*divina studia*), that is, the reading and interpretation of sacred scripture. Tertullian agrees with these views: "Let us see, then, the necessity of literary erudition; let us reflect that partly it cannot be admitted, partly cannot be avoided. Learning literature is allowable for believers."

The reader senses that Tertullian himself is aware that all this may seem confusing or illogical—on the one hand, he says that Christians cannot be teachers, while on the other hand, he maintains that the children of Christian parents may and indeed should be pupils in the very same schools. In the following passage, he argues in some detail for the distinction he makes between teacher and pupil. A teacher's work confirms, recommends, and bears witness to the idols, but a pupil is more free, and can take a selective attitude to the instruction he receives; if he hears anything that contradicts what he has learnt at home about God and the faith, he is free to reject it. Tertullian displays a startling confidence in the pupils' ability to discern elements that are opposed to the Christian faith, and a certainty that they will reject these.[241] In other words, he takes a pragmatic attitude to the schools of his day. He is critical about their ideological basis in paganism, but since there are no alternatives, and especially since it is necessary to master the skills of reading and writing if one is to study sacred scripture, Christians have no other choice than to become pupils in the public schools.

In the *Apostolic Tradition,* Hippolytus takes a milder tone on this question. In his discussion of the criteria for membership in the church (chapter 16), he lists a number of professions that are incompatible with the catechumenate. Clearly, the teacher's job is problematic, and it is preferable that a man who is receiving instruction for baptism should give up this work; if, however, he has no other profession he can exercise, he is permitted to continue.[242] We find the same attitude in the Canons of Hippolytus, a Syriac church order that is a reworking of the *Apostolic Tradition* from c. 500: Christian teachers are allowed to continue in this work if they cannot earn their living in any other way. We see that pragmatic considerations are given priority over the moral and theological problems associated with the work of teaching. The Canons of Hippolytus, however, enjoin on those who do continue teaching that they must make it clear to their pupils that the pagan gods are demons. In positive terms, they must testify every day in the classroom that there is no other God than the Father, the Son, and the Holy Spirit.[243]

Most of the patristic theologians who take up this question display a more positive evaluation of the encyclical studies than Tatian, the *Didascalia,* the opponents of Clement of Alexandria, and Tertullian. This is evident in a whole series of Eastern theologians: Clement himself, Origen, Basil of Caesarea, Gregory of Nyssa, Gregory Nazianzen, and to some extent John Chrysostom. Space prevents the presentation of all of these theologians here; we shall therefore take Clement as a representative of the Alexandrian tradition and Basil as spokesman for the Cappadocians. Since John Chrysostom devotes so much attention to the upbringing of children, it is natural to hear his testimony here too.

Clement of Alexandria offers a thorough discussion of the relationship between the Christian faith and Greek philosophy and the entire cultural patrimony that was transmitted by the encyclical studies. In his *Paedagogus,* he examines culture as a whole from the perspective of God's *paideia,* with the Christian faith as the summit to which all education tends. Clement (like Origen after him) thus emphasizes the continuity with classical culture: the Christian tradition continues the Greek paideutic tradition.[244] The primary goal of instruction is to prepare the soul and to heal its desires—and this happens only through faith (*Paed.* 1.1.1.4). In the introduction to this treatise, he presupposes that the healing (faith) precedes knowledge, but he also argues in several passages that knowledge comes first and prepares the path for faith. His main intention is to affirm that knowledge reaches its goal only in the Christian faith.

In *Stromateis* 1.4–9, this idea is developed with great clarity. Here, Clement is discussing the relationship between Greek philosophy and the Christian faith, a vast theme that includes the encyclical studies. He does in fact refer to these several times, but in such a way that we cannot make any sharp distinction between this specific question and the overarching theme. One central premise for Clement's understanding of the relationship between faith and philosophy is the idea that all wisdom, both philosophical and divine, has its origin in God. He exemplifies this at the beginning of chapter 4 by means of quotations from Homer, Hesiod, the Old Testament prophets, biblical wisdom texts, and the epistles of Paul. Before the coming of Christ, philosophy was necessary, in order that the Greeks might attain righteousness. Now, its significance is lessened. It is useful as a means to achieve the fear of God, because it prepares the way for the most important thing of all, that which comes later—faith. Philosophy is merely a *propaideia* for those who have come to faith. In order to make this clearer, Clement compares the function and role of philosophy with the function and role of the Law in the old covenant. Just as the law was a *paidagôgos* or pedagogue for the Jews, so philosophy was a *paidagôgos* for the Greeks:

> Accordingly, before the advent of the Lord, philosophy was necessary to the Greeks for righteousness. And now it becomes conducive to piety; being a kind of preparatory training to those who attain to faith through demonstration. "For thy foot," it is said, "will not stumble, if you refer what is good, whether belonging to the Greeks or to us, to Providence." For God is the cause of all good things; but of some primarily, as of the Old and the New Testament; and of others by consequence, as philosophy. Perchance, too, philosophy was given to the Greeks directly and primarily, till the Lord should call the Greeks. For this was a schoolmaster to bring "the Hellenic mind," as the law, the Hebrews, "to Christ." Philosophy, therefore, was a preparation, paving the way for him who is perfected in Christ.[245]

Philosophy is now only useful; it is no longer necessary. This means that it is still viewed in a positive light, as something that prepares the way for faith. This is confirmed in the following passage, where Clement takes up Philo's allegorical exegesis of the story of Abraham, Sarah, and Hagar in

Genesis 16: Hagar symbolizes the preparatory function of the encyclical studies,[246] which are the handmaid of theology. Clement writes at *Strom.* 1.5:

> Wherefore also, when Sarah was jealous at Hagar being preferred to her, Abraham, as choosing only what was profitable in secular philosophy, said, "Behold, thy maid is in thine hands: deal with her as it pleases you," manifestly meaning, "I embrace secular culture as youthful, and a handmaid; but thy [God's] knowledge I honour and reverence as true wife."

The model Clement employs here to explain the relationship between faith and philosophy is clearly drawn from those classical philosophers who maintained that the encyclical studies were a preparation for philosophy. Clement's main point is that philosophy contains elements that are useful and good for faith. This is why Christians ought to study philosophy; and this in turn means that they must undertake the encyclical studies, which are a necessary preparation for philosophy. He does indeed write that it is possible to be a believer without knowing classical literature, but it is impossible to understand what the faith says, unless one has been taught in school (*Strom.* 1.6):

> But as we say that a man can be a believer without learning, so also we assert that it is impossible for a man without learning to comprehend the things which are declared in the faith. But to adopt what is well said, and not to adopt the reverse, is caused not simply by faith, but by faith combined with knowledge. . . . And we avow, that at once with more ease and speed will one attain to virtue through previous training. But it is not such as to be unattainable without it; but it is attainable only when they have learned, and have had their senses exercised.

We have already seen that John Chrysostom criticizes parents for a one-sided concern to ensure worldly success for their children. They are excessively concerned with providing an upbringing that lays the foundation for their sons, once they have reached adulthood, to enter professions and political positions associated with wealth and honor; they fail to see that the primary intention and goal of upbringing is to form children in accordance with Christian ideals. Here, however, we should underscore that this is no "either/or": the *De Inani Gloria* does not attack the encyclical studies as such. We might perhaps have expected some such polemic, given his unsparing criticism of a lifestyle dominated by the search for honor and riches: after all, it was precisely the encyclical studies that gave a man access to positions with wealth, honor, and social status.[247] But Chrysostom simply takes it for granted that the children of Christian parents are pupils in ordinary schools; his concern is to ensure a correct balance or relationship between their Christian formation and the encyclical studies: "First train his soul and then take thought for his reputation in the world."[248] The moral formation has the priority, but this certainly does not mean that parents would be forbidden to take their sons to the Greco-Roman schools, where the foundations of "their reputation in the world" are laid. Here we should also note that Chrysostom accepts that pagan heroes can function as models in the moral formation of children. He exhorts parents to "constantly flood his [the boy's] ears with talk of" both pagan and Christian "men of old" who practiced self-restraint.[249] This kind of selective use of persons from the pagan tradition as models probably implies that the parents may also employ suitable pagan literature alongside the Bible in the formation of their children.[250] The school was the primary context for instruction in such literature.[251]

The *Ad Adolescentes de Legendis Libris Gentilium* ("Address to young men on the right use of Greek literature") was written by Basil of Caesarea either in 363/364 or in the late 370s.[252] This interesting treatise focuses primarily on Greek literature rather than on the school as such, but the close link between the school and Homer, Hesiod, and other classical authors make it highly relevant to our investigation; the instruction given in school forms the framework and background for Basil's discussions. The treatise is addressed to a young nephew who had received a classical education, but it is likely that Basil assumed that it would be published and made available to a wider readership.[253]

The title shows that Basil assumes that Christians are pupils in the ordinary Greco-Roman schools, and he never poses the question whether the encyclical studies are legitimate for them; on the contrary, the title indicates a conviction that Greek pagan literature contains elements that are valuable from a Christian perspective too. The Christian student should neither reject nor make use of everything in Greek pagan literature. He must learn to distinguish between what is valuable and what is worthless, between what is useful and what is harmful.

The fundamental criterion of usefulness is that nothing can be good if it is exclusively concerned with life here on earth. Useful things must be concerned with the human person's highest good—the life to come:

We, my children, in no wise conceive this human life of ours to
be an object of value in any respect, nor do we consider anything
good at all, or so designate it, which makes a contribution to this
life of ours only. . . . Everything we do is by way of preparation for
the other life. Whatever, therefore, contributes to that life, we say
must be loved and pursued with all our strength; but what does
not conduce to that must be passed over as of no account.[254]

The main point in the first three chapters of Basil's *Ad Adolescentes* is that
Greek literature contains things useful to Christians, largely because the
knowledge thus acquired prepares one for the study of sacred scripture.
Just as soldiers in battle are grateful for the instruction they were given
earlier, and now draw profit from it, so too ought Christians to equip
themselves for the greatest of all battles by learning from the useful elements in Greek literature. The Greek philosophers had presented the encyclical studies as a preliminary stage or preparation for philosophy, and
Clement of Alexandria had seen them as a preparation for the study of
scripture. Basil, too, says that Greek literature has a propaedeutic function.
I quote a typical passage:

Now to that other life [the eternal life] the Holy Scriptures lead
the way, teaching us through mysteries. Yet so long as, by reason
of your age, it is impossible for you to understand the depth of
meaning of these, in the meantime, by means of other analogies
which are not entirely different, we give, as it were in shadows and
reflections, a preliminary training to the eye of the soul, imitating those who perform their drills in military tactics, who, after
they have gained experience by means of gymnastic exercises for
the arms and dance-steps for the feet, enjoy when it comes to
the combat the profit derived from what was done in sport. So
we must also consider that a contest, the greatest of all contests,
lies before us, for which we must do all things, and, in preparation for it, must drive to the best of our power, and must associate
with poets and writers of prose and orators and with all men from
whom there is any prospect of benefit with reference to the care of
our soul. . . . If the glory of the good is to abide with us indelible for
all time, [we must] be instructed by these outside means, and then
we shall understand the sacred and mystical teachings; and like
those who have become accustomed to seeing the reflection of the
sun in water, so we shall then direct our eyes to the light itself.[255]

Basil's positive evaluation of the usefulness of Greek literature is the result of his conviction that there is a kind of affinity between this body of writings and the scriptures (3.1). He finds justification for this view in the Bible itself: Moses, "whose name for wisdom is greatest among all mankind," was instructed in Egyptian wisdom before he saw in the thorn bush the One who truly is, and Daniel likewise learned from the wisdom of the Chaldeans before he began his instruction in divine things.

After discussing the basic relationship between the Christian faith and Greek literature, Basil focuses more specifically on what one can learn about the life to come in the Greek texts (chapters 4–7). Once again, he emphasizes that one must distinguish between the useful and the worthless. He argues that Christians should imitate the poetic writings when they tell of the deeds of good people, and that they should refrain from doing so when they tell of the deeds of the wicked: in other words, the usefulness of Greek literature is that it can teach us what virtue is. In chapter 5, he gives a number of relevant examples from Homer, Hesiod, Theognis, and Prodicus. Later, in his discussion in chapter 7 of the affinity between well-known persons and narratives from classical pagan literature and Christian literature, he mentions several examples of virtue that can be learned from the former category of texts.[256] On the other hand, when the poets write about vices and about the gods, Christians should not listen to them.[257]

The two other great Cappadocian fathers, Gregory of Nyssa and Gregory Nazianzen, take the same basic approach as Basil of Caesarea.[258] This means that the leading theologians in the Eastern tradition, from the beginning of the third century to the close of the fifth, all held that the Greek classics, which were the staple of the encyclical studies, contained elements valuable to Christians. The same is true of Western fathers such as Jerome and Augustine. It is true that we can sense a more ambivalent attitude in their works to the encyclical studies, but Jerome and Augustine also maintain that Christians will find elements in pagan literature that are useful for faith and for the correct understanding of the biblical texts.[259] All the fathers who discuss this question acknowledge the obvious fact that the encyclical studies contain pagan ideas and ideals that can pose a danger to Christian children, but (with the exception of Tatian and the *Didascalia*) none argues that Christians must avoid the school completely. On the contrary: they unanimously emphasize the usefulness of this education, which prepares the way for divine knowledge. They make the point that pagan literature should be read with a critical eye, and we may perhaps doubt whether this actually helped pupils much in their daily experience of school. It is important to remember that early Christian literature is the work of an elite, and reflects the attitudes of well-educated men. It is possible that the majority of Christians, who had not had the benefit of a school education and were not so skilled in theological reflection as the fathers, failed to share their confidence, and worried about the negative moral influence of the encyclical studies on children. It is not unlikely that the opponents of Clement of Alexandria—whom he himself calls "most people"—were voicing an anxiety that most Christians in fact felt in this area.

Nevertheless, despite the tension Christians certainly experienced with regard to the pagan culture that was transmitted in school, it seems that the church did not set up alternative schools. In this period, the church gradually developed a systematic and reasonably comprehensive program of instruction for catechumens, that is, for adults.[260] We have also seen the emphasis on parents' obligation to give their children a suitable Christian upbringing, in which social control of the children was a central element. But the church did not found any alternative schools, either on the primary or the more advanced level. The author of the *Didascalia* seems to assume that elementary instruction in reading and writing will take place at home, where pagan literature is replaced by the biblical writings, but we do not know to what extent this was actually practiced; and in any case, this would entail only the most elementary level of teaching. We should also mention the initiative taken by Apollinarius of Laodicea and his son (also called Apollinarius) as a reaction to the law of Julian the Apostate in 362, which forbade Christians to teach in school: they produced an edition of the biblical texts on the model of the classical literary genres, so that Christians could continue to receive elementary education in reading and writing, but now with the Bible as their textbook. Again, we do not know to what extent their book was actually used to teach children. Since Julian's legislation was revoked after only two years, in 364, this seems rather doubtful.[261] We might perhaps have expected that the church would have imitated the pattern of elementary instruction in reading and writing that was given in the synagogues, using the Jewish sacred writings as a textbook, with subsequent instruction in the interpretation of the Law; but this was not in fact the case.

William Barclay suggests three reasons why the church did not establish alternative schools. First, there was an intense expectation that Jesus would return soon. Since life in this world had such a short temporal perspective, there was no reason to establish schools providing a general education in view of future careers for Christians. Second, there were not many well-off people in the Christian communities in the earliest period; hence, there was no money to hire buildings and pay teachers. And third, before things changed under Constantine, the Christians were outside the law: the very fact of confessing the name of Christ exposed them to prosecution as criminals. Their legal situation made it unthinkable that they could succeed in establishing alternative schools of their own.

Apart from the second argument—where Barclay mistakenly assumes that pupils were taught in specifically designated school buildings and that it was very expensive to run a school—these explanations seem plausible, at least as far as the first three centuries are concerned. They lose their validity with regard to the fourth century, when the secular government looked with increasing favor on the church until finally, in 391, emperor Theodosius declared Christianity the only legally permitted religion in the Roman empire. The church had access to the necessary economic resources, and had attained a position in society that would probably have allowed it to set up a school with a distinctly Christian profile. I do not wish to speculate here about why this was not done, but I would suggest that an important factor may have been the presence of numerous Christian teachers at all levels in the schools:[262] this led to a measure of Christianization of the educational setting.[263] It is not hard to imagine that Christian teachers would have criticized the contents of pagan literature and spoken against it, at least to some extent. By the time the church was in a position to establish an alternative system of education, Christians pupils had been attending the ordinary schools for over three centuries. Despite the problematic aspects of the schools, they had found that the knowledge acquired by means of the encyclical studies made it possible for them not only to acquire jobs and positions in society, but also to study and assimilate the Christian holy writings.

The most important point here is the simple fact that the children of Christian parents were pupils in the ordinary schools, and that the literature used there exposed them to pagan religious ideas and morality, as well as to contact with pagan children, with the inherent risk of a negative moral influence. We should, however, remember that most children were accompanied by a *paidagôgos*, a slave who observed what the child did in the course of his day at school and reported this to the parents. This meant that social control over the child was maintained even while he was at school. The children of Christian parents attended the same schools as other pupils, and were in general subjected to a heavy-handed teaching method where corporal punishment (or the threat of it) was completely normal. Augustine's experiences at school bear eloquent testimony to what this meant in practice.[264]

The Formation of Children

We have seen that Christian texts emphasize to varying degrees parents' responsibility for bringing up their children in keeping with Christian ideals. In this context, "children" almost always means boys—a reflection of the patriarchal culture in which our sources were written. We should however note that John Chrysostom mentions briefly, at the end of *De Inani Gloria,* that the principles that he puts forward for the upbringing of children apply to girls too.

In the New Testament epistles and the apostolic fathers, little attention is paid to the responsibility for upbringing, but the very fact that early Christian paraenesis includes relevant exhortations shows a clear awareness that parents are obligated to form their children in accordance with the Christian religion. In the *Didascalia* and the *Apostolic Constitutions,* church orders from the first half of the third century and the close of the fourth, this subject is discussed in greater detail, and the parents' duty to bring up their children is emphasized by being made a question of their eternal salvation: if they neglect this task, or are unsuccessful in forming their children to a life in keeping with the Christian ideals, this has the grave consequence of damnation by God. John Chrysostom expresses the same idea, but (unlike the two church orders) he backs it up with a biblical proof—the story of Eli who failed to call his two sons to account when they sinned.[265] Chrysostom also presents fundamental theological arguments in support of the obligation to bring up one's children. First of all, he roots upbringing in the central biblical motif of love of one's neighbor: the child is the parents' closest "neighbor," and to neglect its upbringing is the most serious sin they can commit. Second, when they bring up their children to practice virtues associated with God—such as being "good," "gentle," and "forgiving"—parents "reveal and beautify" the image of God in them. This idea lies behind Chrysostom's favorite metaphor of the child as a work of art that must be honed, polished, and given form. Third, the Old Testament contains explicit injunctions to teach children the contents of the religious festivals and instruct them in God's law.

Jerome agrees with Chrysostom in emphasizing that parents are responsible for their children's actions, but he limits this responsibility to small children, and he does not assert that the parents' salvation depends on how their children live.

Naturally, we must be cautious about drawing black-and-white generalizations on the basis of the relatively few sources from early Christianity that (to varying degrees) discuss this subject. Nevertheless, I believe we can discern a number of tendencies. Although the emphasis and the arguments vary somewhat, it appears that the Christian material underscores more strongly than pagan texts the parents' obligation and responsibility to form their children to lead a life of virtue. There is a striking difference between Cicero's affirmation that fathers cannot be blamed for the errors of their sons, and the position taken by the *Didascalia*, the *Apostolic Constitutions*, and John Chrysostom—that parents' responsibility for their children's actions is so grave a matter that their own salvation depends on their taking on the duty of upbringing with sufficient seriousness. I believe that this difference is largely due to the Christian authors' conviction that the most important issue of all—eternal salvation—was at stake here. We find explicit statements in John Chrysostom that point in this direction; but it is surely reasonable to assume that this motif underlies all the Christian texts we have been studying, since all their various exhortations urge parents to bring up their children in that faith and lifestyle that are required for gaining eternal salvation.

The overarching goal was to form children in keeping with the Christian faith and with the ideals governing a virtuous Christian life. The New Testament epistles and the apostolic fathers write only briefly and in general terms of the contents of education: they speak of giving children an upbringing in accordance with the will of the Lord, bringing them up "in the discipline and instruction of the Lord," and teaching them the fear of God. All these expressions imply that one central element in Christian upbringing is to teach children Christian morality and socialize them into the Christian virtues.

The most concrete detail in our sources about the contents of upbringing is that parents are to ensure that they bring up their children to be obedient. This element recurs constantly in the later sources too, and is a fundamental aspect of the goal of upbringing, probably because of the simple fact that children who are disobedient to their parents are behaving in a manner that contradicts and rejects the very essence of a Christian upbringing. A life in accordance with the Christian faith and its ideals for correct conduct implies that children are obedient. This emphasis must also be seen against the background of ideas about the status and authority of parents in Hellenistic Judaism and in the Greco-Roman household.

I believe that it is also correct to see the shame/honor perspective as an underlying implicit premise for the repeated exhortations to parents to ensure that their children display obedience and respect: if children disobey their parents, they bring disgrace upon them.

The church orders we have studied have little to say about the specific contents of upbringing. Apart from general exhortations, for example that children must be brought up "in the nurture and admonition of the Lord," these sources focus concretely on sexual sins. Parents must ensure that their teenage sons practice a morality that manifests itself in sexual abstinence before marriage.

This is a central element in Jerome and John Chrysostom too: parents must shield their children from anything that might arouse sexual desire, and they must see to it that their children avoid any environment that might tempt them to commit sexual sins. Social control plays an important role here. Children must be under constant supervision when they are outside the home. They must not be allowed to hear shameful songs and stories, nor may they visit the theater. Girls must wear simple clothing, without using any kind of makeup and cosmetics; boys must have their hair cut in a way that makes them unattractive. Contact with the other sex must be reduced to a minimum. Everything must be done to avoid the arousal of desire, and boys must be brought up to show self-restraint. In addition to these measures, Chrysostom prescribes a relatively comprehensive life of devotion where worship in church, prayer, fasting, vigils, and the reading of scripture are important elements. He also tells parents to draw the attention of their sons to other things, for example, the clouds in the sky, the sun, flowers, and good books. Many sources agree in urging parents to find wives for their sons when the time is ripe. The intention is to ensure that sexual desire is lived out within the only legitimate framework of marriage.

These observations about sexual desire and instructions about taming it apply naturally to children who have reached puberty, but many of our sources underscore that Christian upbringing is to begin while the child is still small and easily formed. Chrysostom points out that one lays in childhood the foundations of subsequent conduct in adolescence. From a tender age, children must learn not to use shameful and worldly language, nor words that insult other persons. Children must learn not to despise anyone, nor to speak evil of others. This means that they must be taught to be fair, and this in turn entails that they must be patient with others when they are treated unjustly, even by persons whose social status is lower than their own. They are also to learn that greed and envy of others are grave sins. Chrysostom emphasizes that his ideals for the upbringing of children reverse the priorities of his contemporaries, as seen in their values and attitudes. Instead of trying to make sure that their children get positions that bestow wealth and honor in this world, parents' primary aim ought to be to bring them up in keeping with the Christian ideals for a life of virtue. As he writes, they must "teach him to think lightly of this world's passing glories" so that in this way "he will become truly renowned and glorious."

What methods are parents to employ in forming their children for a life as "athletes of Christ" (to use Chrysostom's favorite image)? I have already mentioned the central role played by social control, and this is not restricted to the area of sexuality. There is a clear tendency in our Christian sources to have parents limit their children's contact with the pagan environment to the minimum, since the authors fear that they would be exposed to negative influences and might even copy the pagans' lifestyle. They emphasize that parents are to socialize their children into the ideals for a Christian way of life by instructing them in scripture and initiating them into a comprehensive life of piety that includes reading the Bible, singing psalms, prayer, fasting, and vigils. The parents are to take their children along to the meetings of the church community. Our sources especially underscore how important it is that parents tell biblical stories and read aloud from the Bible, since this forms the children for a life of virtue. This is illustrated very clearly by Jerome and John Chrysostom, who propose that the books of the Bible be read in a specific sequence. Chrysostom insists that parents must begin to teach their children the Bible from their "earliest years"—this will provide "remedies" for "all sorts of folly and bad examples from popular entertainments" to which the children are otherwise exposed. His confidence that children will behave aright, if they are given the correct knowledge of God and of divine things, reflects what has been called ethical intellectualism—the position that good actions are a natural consequence of correct insight into what is good.

Our sources also emphasize how important good role models are for children: examples have great power, and this applies not least to the parents' role. Chrysostom is convinced that if "husband and wife order their lives according to God's law, their children will also submit willingly to the same law."[266] But it is also important that parents are careful in their choice of the slaves and household servants who have day-to-day dealings with the child; their vocabulary and conduct must also be in keeping with the ideals governing a Christian life.

How are parents to motivate their children to behave as they wish? How are they to ensure that the children observe the rules for acceptable Christian conduct that the parents have laid down? What means must parents employ to form obedient children? Here, it seems that corporal punishment (or the threat of it) is a valuable instrument. Many of the Christian sources that speak of upbringing take it for granted that parents will use physical force on their children; some actually urge them to do so. Some authors—the *Didascalia*, the *Apostolic Constitutions*, John Chrysostom, and Augustine—find it necessary to present theological arguments in favor of this position, and one has the impression that the Christian texts advocate a more intensive use of corporal punishment than the classical ideal of the *bonus paterfamilias* (good father) would suggest (whatever the actual practice in households may have been).

How can we explain this plausibly? One answer is that the Bible supports such attitudes: we have seen how texts from Proverbs and Sirach were used to legitimate corporal punishment, with the argument that this is an expression of love for one's child. We have also seen how the story of Eli and his sons functions as a scriptural proof for the necessity of disciplining one's children. This, however, does not really explain *why* the patristic writers had recourse to these texts, and I believe that the most obvious answer is that they believed that nothing less than eternal salvation was at stake here. Ultimately, the goal of upbringing was the salvation of the child (and of the parents), and it is clear that the patristic writers believed one must employ strict methods to ensure success. This would mean that Christians do not support the corporal punishment of children simply because the Bible does so: on the contrary, they used biblical texts to legitimate views and attitudes they already possessed.

Another aspect that must be discussed briefly here is the relationship between corporal punishment and social status. The ideal in classical antiquity that one should be reluctant to inflict corporal punishment reflects attitudes found in the higher social strata. It is reasonable to assume that people in the lower classes thought differently.

Is it therefore possible that the difference between the Christian texts and the pagan sources is due to the fact that the authors and their readers belonged to different social classes? One possible indication that this is correct is Jerome's silence about corporal punishment in his letters to persons who belonged to the higher social groups. Similarly, the *De Inani Gloria,* where Chrysostom takes a somewhat milder view of the use of corporal punishment than in his earlier writings (though without rejecting it completely), is addressed to well-off Christian parents. This *may* explain why he moderates his tone when he speaks of the use of corporal punishment; in that case, he would be reflecting conventionally correct views. On the other hand, he strongly emphasizes that parents should threaten to employ physical force, and we should note the pragmatic reasoning he employs when he says that this threat is not to be put into practice: the threat will become ineffective if one uses the rod too often.

It may also be relevant here to note that those sources that argue most strongly for the use of corporal punishment, the *Didascalia* and the *Apostolic Constitutions*, are church orders addressed to a readership drawn from various social strata, although nothing indicates that the primary group of addressees are persons of low social status or even slaves. On the contrary, much of the contents of these church orders is addressed to bishops and other church leaders, and we must assume that these were generally men who had achieved a certain level of education. It is therefore reasonable to assume that the passages in these texts dealing with the upbringing of children are addressed to various social classes, including church members who had a high social status.

Finally, we should note that an elite writer like Augustine makes no distinction concerning the social status of children when he argues in favor of using corporal punishment. Our sources for his views are sermons to his congregation, which included persons from various social strata.

Accordingly, I do not believe that the question of social status can offer a convincing explanation of why the Christian sources exhort parents to inflict a greater measure of corporal punishment on their children than was indicated by the classical ideal of the *bonus paterfamilias*. It is in fact striking to see how those Christian authors who had enjoyed the highest level of education, and hence definitely belonged to the higher social classes, argue in favor of the use of corporal punishment—this applies first of all to Augustine, but also to John Chrysostom, despite his somewhat milder attitude (which, as I have mentioned, is due to pragmatic considerations). We do not know who composed the *Didascalia* and the *Apostolic Constitutions*, but the simple fact that they were capable of writing such documents shows that they were well-educated men.

In the Greco-Roman household, the daily care, supervision, and instruction of children was largely entrusted to nurses, pedagogues, and other slaves and servants. This is certainly the case in prosperous households, but a number of inscriptions indicate that even in the lower social strata, persons other than the mother could look after the child and bring it up on a day-to-day basis.[267] As the child grew up, the mother became more directly involved in its upbringing; this was especially so in the case of daughters. Nevertheless, it was the father, as *paterfamilias,* who had the ultimate responsibility for his children's upbringing, even if he entrusted this task to others in daily life. Christian texts also presuppose that fathers have this ultimate responsibility, especially with regard to boys, but we should note that mothers are exhorted to take their share in bringing up their sons, and that they too (like their husbands) are held responsible for their children's conduct. At the close of *De Inani Gloria,* John Chrysostom urges mothers to bring up girls on the same principles he has laid down for boys. In Jerome's educational letters, it is the mothers who have the primary task of bringing up their daughters in such a way that they will be suited to a life of consecrated virginity.

In comparison with the pagan sources, nurses, pedagogues, and other slaves and servants in the household play a smaller role in the Christian sources. It is true that Chrysostom assumes that children are surrounded by nurses, pedagogues, and other servants, but their role is much less prominent than that of the parents. Like the other Christian sources, he, too, presupposes that it is the parents who carry out Christian upbringing in practice, and this implies an ideal whereby parents were more involved in upbringing than seems to have been the case in pagan families in antiquity. It is particularly striking to note that several sources assume that fathers are actively involved in the upbringing even of smaller children. In other words, the ideal reflected here is one of greater social contact between parents and children than seems to have been usual in pagan households. This does not permit us to infer that the Christian texts envisage a closer emotional relationship between parents and children than was customary at that time; all we can do is point out that the ideal presupposed in the Christian texts implies that parents and children spend more time together.

It is not by chance that I have spoken frequently here of an "ideal." This is because the Christian texts that speak of upbringing are not descriptive, but prescriptive texts. They offer advice and exhortations about the contents, methods, and goals of upbringing. They are composed by persons who had particular views about how things *ought* to be, and they express specific ideals for upbringing. The available sources do not allow us to say anything concrete about the extent to which ideals and praxis coincided; let me emphasize, therefore, that everything I have written in this chapter about the upbringing of children refers to the ideals we find in the texts.

One final point: we might perhaps have expected that sources that propose this kind of ideal, where social control and the tendency to isolate children from their pagan surroundings are key elements, would have led to a breach with the Greco-Roman school. Our sources do indeed reflect the tension that Christians experienced between their faith and the pagan environment in the classical schools, but there are few indications that they thought of establishing alternative schools in which the Bible would replace pagan literature, and there are no sources that state that Christians actually established such schools (or even only attempted to do so). It may have been customary in some circles for parents to teach their children to read and write at home. Few sources discuss how Christian pupils are to react to the pagan religion that was taught at school; most of our authors argue that the encyclical studies are a presupposition for subsequent academic study, and enable one to understand the contents of sacred scripture. Indeed, the encyclical studies are themselves a preparation for the study of scripture. When they are in school, Christian pupils must reject everything that contradicts their faith, while making use of everything that is good and useful. This approach clearly presupposes that they have received a good initiation into the Christian faith in their own homes. The children of Christian parents had the same schooling as those of pagan parents.

6
CHILDREN'S PARTICIPATION IN WORSHIP

We have seen that John Chrysostom assumes that parents will take their children with them to church at an age at which it is natural to hold their children by the hand. This means that children were present during Christian worship, a fact we shall see attested in many other texts from the mid-third century to the end of the sixth.[1] Our sources say nothing about the earliest period, but New Testament exhortations dealing with the relationship between parents and children indicate that the latter were considered part of the congregation and that they took part in worship; the fact that the communities assembled in private houses also makes it reasonable to suppose that at least the host's own children were present.

Children were present during the services, then. But did they receive the sacraments, and to what extent were they involved in what happened? Were children baptized, and did they receive the Eucharist? Did they have special roles and functions in the liturgy? In the present chapter, I shall attempt to answer these questions, beginning with the reception of the sacraments. In view of the extent and character of our sources, as well as the considerable attention that scholars have paid to this question, most of this chapter will be devoted to the question of infant baptism.

BAPTISM

Scholars have debated since the sixteenth century whether babies or children were baptized in the earliest period of Christianity. At the beginning of the twentieth century, the prevalent view in historical-critical research was that the primitive church did not practice infant baptism, but this position was challenged from the 1920s onward by scholars such as A. Oepke,[2] J. Leipold,[3] Joachim Jeremias,[4] and Oscar Cullmann.[5] It was above all Joachim Jeremias who presented a wide-reaching defense of the hypothesis that the practice of infant baptism can be traced back to the apostolic age; he claimed that children who had been born before their parents converted to Christianity were baptized along with them. These new positions did not go unchallenged. Kurt Aland presented a critical analysis of Jeremias's arguments and concluded that these were untenable: the earliest church did not practice infant baptism, and children (not babies) began to be baptized only c. 200.[6] Jeremias replied with a new monograph in which he sought to refute Aland's criticisms, while at the same time discussing all the relevant questions in greater depth.[7] The work of these two scholars represents the weightiest contribution to the question of the historical origin of infant baptism, and most subsequent discussion has referred to their monographs and argued for or against the positions these authors took.[8] For this reason, they form the starting-point of my own discussion here.

It is not possible to offer an exhaustive examination of this question; I limit myself to those aspects that have played a central role in recent scholarship. Particular importance attaches to the earliest texts that explicitly attest the practice of infant baptism. These come from the close of the second century and the first half of the third. We shall then look at the further development in the fourth and fifth centuries. We begin with a brief discussion of those New Testament passages that scholars have found most relevant to this question.

The New Testament
The central issue in scholarly debate has been how the word "house" (*oikos*) is to be understood in the New Testament, especially in the phrase "NN and all his house." We read in the New Testament about "houses" or "households" who convert and are baptized. Paul writes that he baptized the house of Stephanas (1 Corinthians 1:16). Luke relates that Lydia received baptism together with all her house (Acts 16:15) and that the prison warder in Philippi was baptized with all his house (Acts 16:33). Other passages do not specifically state that a whole household received baptism but refer to the conversion of a person together with all his house. Crispus, the ruler of the synagogue in Corinth, "became a believer in the Lord, together with all his household; and many of the Corinthians who heard Paul became believers and were baptized" (Acts 18:8); and the centurion Cornelius is told at Acts 11:14 that he will hear "a message by which you and your entire household will be saved." The obvious question is

whether children are included when these texts speak of *holos pas* or *hapantes*, or whether such expressions refer exclusively to adult members of the household.

Kurt Aland and other scholars take the latter view. Aland holds it to be "virtually certain" that the households mentioned in the New Testament included slaves, and that the Greek terms *holos pas,* and *hapantes* refer to such persons.[9] This seems reasonable, when we recall how extensive slavery was in classical antiquity; but it is far from certain, since the sources are not explicit on this point. Aland also takes it for granted that when a "household" converts, this means that the whole group of servants and slaves follow the master and mistress of the house and receive baptism along with them, and this too sounds plausible. We have, however, sources that show that there was nothing automatic about the baptism of slaves and servants along with the master of the house. Onesimus, the slave of the Christian, Philemon, was converted by Paul only after he had fled from his master; and Aristides writes that Christians exhort their slaves to convert and call them "brethren without distinction" once they have done so.[10] One final objection to Aland's interpretation is the possibility that the slaves and servants themselves had children, as he himself concedes: "On the other hand these slaves might have been married and had newly-born children."[11]

This implies that Aland must find other arguments to support his hypothesis that the "households" mentioned in the New Testament did not include children. As Jeremias writes, he must "prove that in actual individual cases there could have been no intention of including them. Here it must be shown that the household in question contained no children or that what is said in the statement about the household can refer only to its adult members."[12] In my view, Aland does not succeed in making his case, with the possible exception of his comment on Acts 16:15, which speaks of the baptism of Lydia and all her house. Aland observes that since her *oikos* (house) was "that of an unmarried woman or of a widow," it did not include infants or small children: "Children or the very young or infants could be brought into this household only by the way of appeal to the slaves who belonged to it."[13] We cannot, however, exclude the possibility that Lydia's household included children of hers who had grown up and married, and their children in turn.[14] It would take up too much space here to set out Aland's arguments about the other New Testament texts that say that whole households were baptized; it suffices to refer to the detailed discussion of these same passages by Jeremias, in which he offers counterarguments in every case. I believe that he makes a generally convincing case for the position that "in no single case does the New Testament—alas!—tell us more precisely of whom the 'houses' embracing the Christian faith were composed; nor in any single case can children be excluded from belonging to the house."[15]

The texts, taken on their own, do not permit unambiguous conclusions about whether or not children were included in the "households" that received baptism. Nevertheless, a number of external factors indicate, or indeed make it probable, that children were baptized along with their parents, when the latter embraced the Christian religion. First, we must bear in mind the hierarchical structure in the classical household, where the father as *paterfamilias* was the definitive authority, to whom the other family members were obliged to show obedience and respect. In this kind of family structure, solidarity and the collective dimension played a much more central role than in the modern Western version of the family. The various members were mutually linked through particular codes of conduct, which aimed at maintaining the family honor.[16] This made the family a unit with a much stronger collective aspect than today's Western families, where an individualistic way of thinking dominates.

This collective quality applied also to the sphere of faith and religion. If the father converted to a new religion or religious fellowship, it was normal for the rest of the household, or at least the closest family members, to do the same.[17] One eloquent example of the decisive role played by the father of the house in such a situation is the story of the prison warder in Acts 16:30-34, who asks Paul and Silas:

> "What must I do to be saved?" They replied, "Believe in the Lord Jesus, and you will be saved, you *and your household*." They spoke the word of the Lord to him and to all who were in his house. At the same hour of the night he took them and washed their wounds; then he and his entire family were baptized without delay. He brought them up into the house and set food before them; and he [*singular*] and his entire household rejoiced that he had [*singular*] become a believer in God.

According to Luke's account, Paul and Silas take it for granted that when the warder comes to faith in Jesus, this entails that not only he himself, but his household too will be saved; it seems to be simply assumed that the others follow his example and embrace his new faith.[18]

Given this collective aspect in the family, this "family solidarity" in classical antiquity, as well as the father's authority as *paterfamilias*, I find it almost unimaginable that children should not have been baptized when the head of the household received baptism. A regulation in some Jewish-Christian circles says that all non-baptized family members must be excluded from the table-fellowship of the family, and this reflects a situation where it was taken for granted that children were baptized. It seems not to occur to those who formulated this regulation that the children of parents who converted to Christianity would not also be baptized.[19]

This collective character of the family is an important indicator that children were usually baptized along with their parents. Indeed, I would claim that even if no other indicators existed, this factor is itself so weighty that it makes it highly probable that if there were children in the households mentioned in the New Testament, these were baptized.[20]

Another factor that seems to support the idea that it was natural for the first Christians—who were Jews—to baptize their children is the analogy between circumcision and baptism. We cannot discuss here all the implicit or explicit analogies presented in the New Testament between the sign of the old covenant and baptism, but I believe that it has been convincingly argued that it is appropriate to speak of a functional and substantial analogy between the two.[21] Boys were circumcised on the eighth day and received thereby the sign of the old covenant; by analogy, the children of Jewish Christians received a share in "the circumcision of Christ," that is, baptism.

One can, of course, object that the oldest texts that explicitly discuss infant baptism do not refer to any such analogy as an argument in favor of the baptism of children.[22] The first to do so was Bishop Fidus in northern Africa, who consulted Cyprian about delaying baptism until the child was eight days old—most probably because he saw an analogy between circumcision and infant baptism.[23] This leads J. P. T. Hunt to conclude: "Had the analogy between circumcision and baptism been used from the first as an argument for infant baptism, the issue would surely have been raised, and settled, earlier. The fact that it had only now been raised is an indication that the application of the analogy between circumcision and baptism to infant baptism was a fairly recent one, and that the possible implications of this analogy for the administration of infant baptism were only now being realized."[24] Hunt is surely too categorical here; we must not forget that Fidus is the only spokesman of this idea, and this is too slender a basis for Hunt's far-reaching conclusions. For all we know, Fidus may have been an outsider; nothing in the answer he received from the northern African bishops indicates that any of them shared his views or put forward similar ideas about this question. At any rate, given that Fidus is an isolated voice in the third century, it is methodologically problematic to use him as testimony that "the application of the analogy between circumcision and baptism to infant baptism was a fairly recent one." Nor is the fact that this analogy was not applied to infant baptism in the earliest texts that discuss this practice a decisive argument: there are, after all, only very few relevant texts, three or four in Origen and one in Tertullian.

Another fairly prominent element in the debate about the historical origin of infant baptism is the relationship between Jewish proselyte baptism and early Christian baptism. Joachim Jeremias has compared these two forms of baptism in detail and has demonstrated a number of affinities between them. He maintains that the Christian theology of baptism adopts the entire terminology, catechetical praxis, and metaphors relevant to the theology of conversion that developed around proselyte baptism.[25] Proselyte baptism began when Gentile women, who by definition could not be circumcised, required a bath of purification. This need, of course, was generated by the idea that Gentiles were impure, and the decisive question here is how early this emerged within Judaism. Jeremias points to a number of texts that seem to show that it was established in the pre-Christian period, and to many sources that show that girls were baptized along with adults, when the latter converted to Judaism. After examining a wide spectrum of sources, he concludes: "In view of the close connections between primitive Christian baptism and proselyte baptism . . . it must be assumed that in the question of infant baptism also the Christian baptismal ritual corresponded to that of the proselyte baptism, i.e. that with the admission of Gentiles to Christianity children of every age, including infants, were baptized also."[26]

The main objection to this position is the fact that no pre-Christian sources mention proselyte baptism. Our earliest source is a rabbinic text that relates a discussion between the schools of Shammai and Hillel about whether one may take the bath of proselytes immediately after circumcision, or must wait for ten days. This discussion, which can be dated to c. 70 in the Common Era, presupposes the existence of proselyte baptism as a universally accepted rite at that period. The oldest references to proselyte baptism in non-rabbinic sources can be dated to between c. 80 and 95,[27] and this has led several scholars to question whether proselyte baptism really was a widespread practice in the period when the earliest Christian communities were being formed; some hold that we simply do not know enough to answer this question.[28] I myself believe that the existence of proselyte baptism as an established rite as early as 70 makes it reasonable to assume that this kind of baptism was probably practiced several decades earlier.[29]

If early Christian baptism does not in fact have its roots in Jewish proselyte baptism, the most obvious explanation of the affinities between the two rites would be that the influence went the other way, that is, that Christian baptism provided the model for proselyte baptism. When we consider the tensions that arose at an early date between Jews and Christians, however, this seems unlikely.[30] Other scholars emphasize the differences between proselyte baptism and Christian baptism, arguing that the former played no role in the formation of the early church's understanding and practice of baptism.[31] I believe that this view takes too little account of the many affinities that Jeremias has demonstrated between the two forms of baptism.

In view of the nature of our sources, it is impossible to say with certainty whether children were baptized along with their parents; a case can be made for this view only by building up a chain of indications such as the analogy between circumcision and baptism, and the affinities between proselyte baptism and the early church's baptism. In my view, the strongest indicator for the baptism of children is the collective dimension in the family in classical antiquity. If children formed part of the "entire households" who (according to the New Testament) received baptism, there is no reason why they too should not have been baptized.

What I have said here—with the exception of the analogy between circumcision and baptism—applies to conversions, that is, situations in which Jews or Gentiles who have children convert to the Christian religion. What about children who were born into Christian families? Were they baptized? Here, the situation with regard to our sources is even more difficult, since all the baptisms mentioned in the New Testament occur in the context of conversions where Jews or Gentiles accept the Christian faith.

It has been claimed that the early church used the pericope about Jesus' blessing of children (Mark 10:13-16; parallels Matthew 19:13-15; Luke 18:15-17) as a baptismal text, largely because of the occurrence of the verb *koluein* (to hinder), which is found in the New Testament and other early Christian literature in baptismal contexts when the question is posed whether anything "hindered" particular persons from receiving baptism. According to Cullmann, the occurrence of this verb in Mark 10:13-16 is to be understood in the technical sense and shows "that those who transmitted this story of the blessing of children wished to recall to the remembrance of Christians of their time an occurrence by which they might be led to a solution of the question of infant Baptism."[32] It has been objected that it is improbable that this verb is really a technical liturgical term, since it governs such a wide range of grammatical objects in the texts where it occurs;[33] but even if we accept the view that it is employed as a technical term in baptismal texts, it remains uncertain whether it has this specific sense in Mark 10:13-16. This verb is employed twenty-three times in the New Testament, and few of these passages have anything to do with baptism. It seems a perfectly natural word to use in the original historical situation, where the disciples are trying to hold the women with their children back from Jesus.[34]

The available source material does not allow us to draw any conclusions about whether the children of Gentile Christians were baptized in the period up to c. 150, but I have argued that the analogy between circumcision and baptism would have made it natural for Jewish Christian parents to baptize their children. Do sources from the period of 150–250 shed any light on whether children of Gentile Christians were baptized?

The First Direct References to Infant Baptism: Tertullian, the *Apostolic Tradition*, and Origen

The first sources to speak explicitly of the baptism of children are Tertullian, the *Apostolic Tradition*, and Origen. This makes it certain that infant baptism was practiced in northern Africa at the beginning of the third century (Tertullian), in Rome c. 215 (*Apostolic Tradition*), and in Palestine between 230 and 250 (Origen). On this point, all scholars agree, but there is no consensus on how widespread infant baptism was, nor on when this practice began. There are two main positions. (1) Some hold that it was a new practice, gradually emerging in this period. Supporters of this view argue that our sources reflect discussions and disagreements about infant baptism, because the first half of the third century was a transitional period in which this question had not been definitively settled. (2) Others hold that infant baptism was a well-established practice at this period. Unsurprisingly, there is a clear connection between the way scholars interpret these three sources and the view they take on the question of infant baptism in the New Testament.

Irrespective of what we think of the New Testament evidence, I believe that the third-century sources assume that infant baptism was a well-established practice in the church of that period, and I shall attempt to show that this is the most plausible interpretation of our sources.

We begin with our earliest source, Tertullian, who argues in *De Baptismo* 18 that children ought not to be baptized. After quoting Jesus' words to the disciples that they must not prevent children from coming to him, Tertullian continues:[35] "So let them come, when they are growing up, when they are learning, when they are being taught what they are coming to: let them be made Christians when they have become competent to know Christ. Why should innocent infancy (*innocens aetas*) come with haste to the remission of sins (*ad remissionem peccatorum*)?" This text shows us clearly what Tertullian thought about infant baptism, but it must be read in context if we are to uncover the underlying line of argument. The main question discussed in chapter 18 of *De Baptismo* is whether certain groups of people are in a situation or a phase of life that makes it unprofitable for them to receive baptism. Tertullian writes that "deferment of baptism is more profitable (*utilior est*), in accordance with each person's character and attitude, and even age: and especially so as regards children (*praecipue tamen circa parvulos*)."[36] But even if it is particularly relevant to postpone baptism in the case of small children, nothing in this passage suggests that Tertullian would have regarded infant baptism as invalid, so that those who were baptized in infancy would need to be baptized a second time when they were older.[37] The point is simply that it is more profitable for small children to put off baptism until later on. It is not only infants who should wait; the existential situation of others makes this advisable in their cases too:[38] "With no less reason ought the unmarried also to be delayed until they either marry or are firmly established in continence: until then, temptation lies in wait for them, for virgins because they are ripe for it, and for widows because of their wandering about." Tertullian concludes his discussion in this chapter of the postponement of baptism for certain candidates in a way that makes his primary concern clear: "All who understand what a burden (*pondus*) baptism is will have more fear of obtaining it than of its postponement."[39] Baptism is a *pondus* because of the high demands it makes of the life to be led afterward; in keeping with the ascetic movement that was growing in importance in Tertullian's lifetime, it is sexual sins that most worry him. This is why those who are not married should wait before being baptized—the risk of their committing sexual sins is too great. His rejection of infant baptism is largely governed by the same thinking: it is dangerous to receive the sacrament too early, that is, before the candidate is adequately rooted in the Christian faith and ideals, because this entails a high risk that he or she will commit serious sins after baptism.

David F. Wright summarizes Tertullian's thinking on this point with great precision:[40]

> The baptizing of babies and infants was bound to appear fraught with the greatest peril so long as such profound anxiety contemplated the possibility of moral lapses after baptism. At the very least, baptism should be given only to the person who asks for it, which in the context of Tertullian's baptismal treatise, must mean the person who receives baptism in the full knowledge of, even in spite of, its forbidding *pondus*. It makes no sense to entrust *substantia divina* to one too young to be trusted with *substantia terrena*. What emerges most clearly from the battery of arguments Tertullian discharges is that baptism is most wisely received by the person whose preparation for it has been so thorough that his or her maintenance of baptismal purity thereafter is as fully guaranteed as possible.

Baptism is a great obligation or burden (*pondus*) not only for the one who receives it, but also for the godparents (*sponsores*). In the early church, it was the parents who undertook this task;[41] it was only in the ninth century that other persons began to have this function. Naturally enough, the baptismal rite was elaborated with adults in view, and was only slightly modified when children were baptized. The most important task of the *sponsores* was to profess the faith on behalf of the child. They play no small role in Tertullian's critical attitude to infant baptism; he emphasizes that they are in danger of failing to fulfill the promises (*promissiones*) they have made at baptism, either because they themselves die or because they can "be deceived by the subsequent development of an evil disposition" in the child whose godparents they are.[42] It seems that the *sponsores* at baptism made binding guarantees about the future life the child would lead.[43] Tertullian's point is that they should be spared the grave obligation that is incumbent on godparents.

This *pondus*, the obligation or burden incumbent both on the one who is baptized and on the godparents, is the weightiest single argument Tertullian brings against infant baptism. He employs other arguments too: as already indicated, he believes that small children do not need to be baptized, since they are innocent (*innocens*). Since baptism imparts the forgiveness of sins, those who are at the age of innocence (*innocens aetas*) have little or nothing to gain by being baptized. Tertullian writes briefly here and does not explain how he understood the expression *innocens*, but it is reasonable to assume that it refers primarily to the fact that small children or babies have not themselves committed any sinful actions, and consequently have no personal guilt.[44] This brief reference to the *innocens aetas,* which plays a subordinate role in Tertullian's argumentation, does not however allow us to infer that he excludes any idea of original sin. Many statements in his treatise *De Anima* indicate that all human beings are affected by Adam's sin: every soul (*omnis anima*) is impure (*immunda*) until it is reborn in Christ,[45] and all share in the "evil in the soul" (*malum animae*), which "because of the original fault" (*ex originis uitio*) is antecedent to every sinful act.[46] It is not entirely easy to know how we should understand these and similar expressions in this treatise. It appears that impurity "encompasses a transmitted natural infection by sin,"[47] but Tertullian does not draw the conclusion that this state entails sin. Had he done so, he would surely have taken a different position on the baptism of small children.[48] Is it possible that he chose here not to draw the obvious implications of Adam's sin for human nature because these conflicted with other, more important concerns, that is, his desire to ensure as far as possible that candidates for baptism did not yield to grave sin after they had received the sacrament? His acceptance of emergency baptism for small children can certainly be seen as a reflection of such an attitude. If baptism's primary function is to purify from sin, and small children are genuinely innocent, then it would be illogical to baptize them. Do we then see him drawing the logical conclusion of his remarks about original sin in the case of the baptism of a dying child, where in the nature of the case there is no danger that sins will be committed after reception of the sacrament?

What conclusions can we draw on the basis of Tertullian's arguments against the baptism of small children? Is he opposing the established practice of baptizing them, or is he defending what had been the church's traditional view? First, his reference to *sponsores* (godparents) and to the promise they make shows that the church in northern Africa at that period practiced a baptismal rite for small children (*parvuli*), a rite that had been in use for such a long time that he does not find it necessary to speak in greater detail about the godparents' role and function: he takes it for granted that his readers are familiar with this. This indicates that the baptism of small children was well-established practice by the time he wrote against it in his treatise *De Baptismo.* Second, we do not find in earlier sources the idea that one should postpone baptism because of the risk that the candidate might commit grave sins after receiving the sacrament. It appears that this view emerged toward the close of the second century, and won wide acceptance in the following centuries. This means that Tertullian's main objection to the baptism of unmarried women and small children is probably based on a viewpoint or premise that is relatively recent. Third, Tertullian's fleeting reference to the innocence of small children has the appearance of an ad hoc argument; it is unlikely that he is drawing here on standard criticism of infant baptism. On the contrary, it seems that the question of children's nature had not yet played any significant role in the debate about infant baptism. We see this in Tertullian himself, who (though not formulating any explicit doctrine of original sin) tends strongly to consider the human person as born impure or with original sin—but without making any direct connection between this and the question of baptism. Fourth, it is impossible to shake off the impression that the great anxiety Tertullian expresses on behalf of the godparents is a somewhat far-fetched argument against infant baptism; Kurt Aland agrees.[49] It is striking that Tertullian uses this kind of argument without playing what would have been his best card, that is, reminding his readers that his position can be traced back to the apostles. The most obvious explanation of Tertullian's silence on this point is that he had no such card to play.[50] Had he in fact argued that his position represented continuity with the church's ancient practice, his contemporaries would have seen through him.

The fact that the sixty-eight bishops who took part in a synod in Carthage roughly fifty years later (in 251 or 253) unanimously declared that baptism was to be conferred when children were two or three days old seems to confirm my reading of Tertullian. As I have mentioned, this synod gathered because Bishop Fidus had addressed a letter to Cyprian in which he refused to baptize children before they were eight days old.[51] One reason for this was that Fidus found it disgusting to give the kiss of peace to children who were only two or three days old; another reason was that he considered infant baptism analogous to the Jewish practice of circumcising boys. The synod completely rejected Fidus's views and laid down that children were to be baptized when they were two or three days old. They envisage no possibility of postponing baptism even for a few days only, nor any reasons that might justify this. This synodal decision can only mean that the baptism of babies was a well-established practice in the northern African church in the mid-third century. If this had begun only fifty years earlier—a short period, when changes in the church's theology and practice are involved—it would surely not have been so deeply rooted as it seems to have been.

Only small fragments of the original Greek text of the *Apostolic Tradition* have survived; it formed the basis of a number of early church orders whose texts survive, but since these display extensive mutual divergences, it is often difficult to reconstruct the original. In the section that discusses infant baptism, however (21.3f.), the various textual witnesses (Coptic/ Sahidic, Arabic, and Ethiopic) basically agree,[52] making it highly probable that this section was part of the original version of Hippolytus's *Apostolic Tradition*, which he wrote c. 215.[53] After laying down regulations about the date at which baptism is to be administered and about the baptismal water, and stating that the candidates are to take off all their clothes, the author prescribes the order in which the various groups are to be baptized: first children, then men, and finally women. The mention of adult men and women obviously reflects a missionary situation in which those who converted to Christianity were baptized after receiving a thorough instruction in the Christian faith as catechumens. This is not the case with children: they were baptized along with their family, as seems to have been the practice in the New Testament period.[54] The relevant section reads as follows in the Coptic version:[55] "And first baptize the small children (*parvulos*). And each one who is able to speak for themselves, let them speak. But those not able to speak for themselves, let their parents or another one belonging to their family speak for them." It is taken for granted here that children receive baptism; no discussion is required. We should note that "those not able to speak for themselves" need not necessarily denote children so small that they have not yet learned to speak; this phrase can include children up to the age of seven, since the term *infantes* could be used in classical Rome to cover the first seven years of a child's life.[56] Nothing in the text itself, however, suggests that very small children were excluded, and we may therefore conclude that infant baptism was practiced in Rome around the year 215.

Kurt Aland claims that Hippolytus's *Apostolic Tradition* is attempting to introduce an innovation—for why else would it have been necessary to write a church order? It follows that infant baptism is "relatively new" as "a general Church custom."[57] Against this, we may point out that the title of Hippolytus's work defines its program: the author intends to preserve the doctrine and practice that are in accord with tradition. In his prologue, Hippolytus writes that he intends to set up a bulwark against heretical innovations by codifying the ancient traditions of the church.[58] However, the fact that he employs the adjective "apostolic" as a theological value judgment rather than as an historical category ought to warn us to be cautious about supposing that every phenomenon he calls "apostolic" actually goes back to the apostles themselves. Nevertheless, there is no doubt that Hippolytus does intend to codify what he perceives to be the ecclesiastical tradition, and it is difficult to see how he could have formulated his prologue in this way if infant baptism had not been a well-established practice in Rome in his day. If, in fact, some of his contemporaries who belonged to families that converted to the Christian religion had *not* been baptized along with their families (or knew that this had been the case with their parents or grandparents), then Hippolytus would have laid himself open to the charge that it was he who was introducing something new to the church's life. This makes it highly probable that infant baptism was practiced at Rome at least by the 150s. This seems to be confirmed by other arguments: it has been proposed that "In the light of parallels with the *Didache* and Justin Martyr's *1 Apology,* the core material [which includes the reference to infant baptism] may well go back to the mid-second century."[59]

Let us now turn to Cyprian's older contemporary, Origen of Alexandria, who refers to the practice of infant baptism in three writings from between c. 230 and c. 250, the latter part of the time he lived in Caesarea in Palestine: *Homiliae in Luc.* 14 (on Luke 2:22), *Homiliae in Lev.* 8.3.5 (on Leviticus 12:2), and *Commentarii in Rom.* 5.9.11. All these texts reflect his awareness of the problem posed by infant baptism: how could this be justified, if the child had not sinned? Kurt Aland argues that a close examination of these texts shows that[60]

> they all stand on the defensive against the belief that infants do not need baptism, on the ground that as infants have not actually committed any sins, they do not require forgiveness of sins. . . . There must have been circles, and not that small and uninfluential, whose members held a different opinion as to the necessity of infant baptism and who correspondingly maintained a different practice, in that they abstained from baptizing infants. Hence arises Origen's appeal to the "tradition of the Church received from the Apostles" (*traditio ecclesiae ab apostolis*), which was the strongest argument that he possessed.

According to Aland, this alleged opposition to infant baptism shows that wide sections of the church in Palestine did not accept it as late as c. 250; but I find this interpretation of Origen unconvincing. The situation seems in fact to be the reverse. The problem facing Origen and others is to give a theological account of *why* children are baptized, given that they have no sins that need forgiveness. In other words, the challenge is to offer a theological legitimation of the already-established practice of baptizing babies.[61] We cannot discuss this question in great detail here, but I shall try to present a plausible understanding of the relevant texts.[62]

In his *Homiliae in Luc.* 14, Origen tries to come to terms with the statement at Luke 2:22 that "When the days of their purification were fulfilled, according to the law of Moses, they brought him into Jerusalem."[63] The problem is not that Mary needed to be purified, but that the plural form "their" implies that she was not alone. Someone else needed purification—namely, Jesus. Origen finds this idea offensive; but the words of scripture here, as well as the affirmation at Job 14:4-5 that "no man is clean of stain, not even if his life had lasted but a single day,"[64] force him to this conclusion. In order to reduce the offensiveness at least a little, he emphasizes that Job is not talking about sin (*hamartia*), but about "stain" (*rupos*). Jesus was not sinful. But Origen maintains that "every soul [that is, including Jesus'] that has been clothed with a human body has its own 'stain.'"[65] Accordingly, the prescription in the law of Moses that a sacrifice had to be offered for purification must apply to Jesus too. His discussion of Luke 2:22 leads him to take up a question that has been the subject of some debate:[66]

> Christian brethren often ask a question. The passage from Scripture read today encourages me to treat it again. Little children (*paidia*) are baptized "for the remission of sins." Whose sins are they? When did they sin? Or how can this explanation of the baptismal washing be maintained in the case of small children, except according to the interpretation we spoke of a little earlier? "No man is clean of stain, not even if his life upon the earth had lasted but a single day." Through the mystery of Baptism, the stains of birth are put aside. For this reason, even small children are baptized.

Three points are important here. First, the problem often posed by the "brethren" is not whether children ought to be baptized, but what the meaning of their baptism is. Second, nothing indicates that these "brethren" refrained from baptizing their children. In other words, infant baptism is standard practice; what seems to be missing is a theological justification for doing so. Third and significantly, Origen appeals to the church's practice of infant baptism to confirm the correctness of his interpretation of Luke 2:22. If this argument was to convince others, it was necessary both that the practice of infant baptism was well established and that there existed a broad consensus that small children ought to be baptized.

In his *Hom. in Lev.* 8, Origen takes up the challenge posed by the prescription at Leviticus 12:2-8 that a woman who has given birth to a son is impure for seven days after the birth, and that she must be purified by offering a sacrifice for sin.[67] He cannot explain why "'the woman' who conceives by the seed and gives birth is called 'unclean,' just as the one guilty of sin is commanded to offer a sacrifice 'for sin' and thus to be purified." There remain "some hidden mysteries contained in these things."[68] He then says that, according to scripture, it is not only the woman who has given birth that is unclean, but also her child too, as is shown by a number of passages in scripture. One text he quotes is the psalmist's words: "In iniquity I was conceived and in sins my mother brought me forth"; he also quotes the words from Job to which he refers in his *Hom. in Luc.* 14: "No one is pure from uncleanness even if his life is only one day long," and observes that this shows "that every soul which is born in flesh is polluted by the filth 'of iniquity and sin.'"[69] We may note that he seems to go one step further in this homily on Leviticus, when he says that child's soul is not only impure, but also stained by sin; this emphasis must be seen in connection with Origen's doctrine of the soul's fall in the pre-cosmic world, which presupposes "that the sinfulness attested by Job and the Psalmist was the legacy, not of solidarity with Adam's sin, but of each soul's previous transgression."[70] It is at this point that he briefly discusses the question of infant baptism:[71]

> To these things can be added the reason why it is required, since the baptism of the Church is given for the forgiveness of sins (*pro remissione peccatorum*), that, according to the observance of the Church, that baptism also be given to infants (*parvulus*); since, certainly, if there were nothing in infants that ought to pertain to forgiveness and indulgence (*si nihil esset in parvulis, quod ad remissionem deberet et indulgentiam pertinere*), then the grace of baptism (*gratia baptismi*) would appear superfluous.

Here too, Origen refers to the baptism of small children as standard practice, and nothing in this passage indicates that the validity of this practice was the object of any debate in the church.[72] Even more clearly than in the homily on Luke, Origen's reference to the baptism of small children functions here as a supporting argument for his view that children are "polluted by the filth 'of iniquity and sin.'" Origen holds that ecclesiastical practice confirms his theology. Let me repeat that such an argument would have been pointless if infant baptism had in fact been a new practice, about which his hearers had held conflicting views.[73]

We find much the same approach in Origen's commentary on Romans, when he expounds the expression "the body of sin" at Romans 6:6.[74] Once again, he quotes the psalmist's words, "I was conceived in iniquities, and in sins my mother conceived me,"[75] and refers or alludes to a number of New Testament texts that speak of "the body of lowliness" and "the body of death."[76] Origen then concludes: "Therefore our body is the body of sin (*Corpus ergo peccati est corpus nostrum*)."[77] Not content with this, he cites the prescription in Leviticus 12:6-8, mentioned above, that one must offer a sacrifice on behalf of the newborn child. This consisted of two doves, "one of which was offered for sin and the other as a burnt offering." Although the child has not personally committed sin, this text shows that it has "a sin for which sacrifices are commanded to be offered, and from which it is denied that anyone is pure, even if his life should be one day long."[78] In confirmation that this is the correct exegesis of the texts, Origen refers once again to Psalm 51:5. Then comes an affirmation that is very interesting in the context of our investigation:[79]

> It is on this account as well that the Church has received the tradition from the apostles to give baptism even to little children. For they to whom the secrets of the divine mysteries were committed were aware that in everyone was sin's innate defilement (*in omnibus genuinae sordes peccati*), which needed to be washed away through water and Spirit.

The practice of infant baptism functions here as an argument or confirmation that his interpretation of the texts is correct; besides this, he claims that infant baptism has an apostolic origin. Kurt Aland maintains that we cannot put any trust in this claim about history, since it reflects "the mentality and methods of Church Fathers engaged in controversy."[80] He is right that we should in general be suspicious of the way the fathers employ the argument from tradition; but this does not mean that they have nothing to tell us about how far back in history one particular ecclesiastical phenomenon goes. In the present case, Origen's appeal to the apostolic origin of infant baptism presupposes at least that the oldest Christians still alive at that time—and probably their own parents too—had been born into Christian families and had been baptized as children. It is a reasonable assumption that the oldest generation among contemporary Christians would have known whether their own parents had been baptized in infancy. If this had not been the case, Origen would have been revealed as a purveyor of inaccuracies—and why should such an intelligent and learned theologian take that risk? We need not accept as literal historical truth Origen's words about the apostolic origin of infant baptism; but I find it highly likely that the argument he employs in this passage allows us to conclude that it was well-established practice in Palestine by the mid-second century.

Let us sum up. The oldest Christian literary sources that refer to infant baptism make it certain that small children were baptized in northern Africa c. 200, in Rome c. 215, and in Palestine between c. 230 and 250. We should note the wide geographical spread of these witnesses. As I read them, the sources do not reflect the view that this was a relatively new phenomenon that was only beginning to win acceptance in the churches in these various areas. On the contrary, we may reasonably interpret Tertullian, Hippolytus, and Origen as witnesses to a well-established practice of infant baptism in the churches they knew. And this allows us to argue its existence backward to c. 150.

In the debates about the historical origin of infant baptism, a number of second-century texts that do not explicitly mention this practice have been studied by scholars.[81] We need not examine these in detail here; it suffices to say that they are ambiguous and shed little light on our question. The only exception is Irenaeus, bishop of Lyons, who includes infants (*infantes*), small children (*parvulos*), and boys (*pueros*) among those who are reborn in God (*renascuntur in Deum*).[82] The expression "reborn" in this text is most probably a technical term for baptism.[83] If this is the case, it is one further indication that infant baptism was established practice in the second half of the second century.

Several sources over a wide geographical spectrum indicate that infants were baptized at least from this period onward. This brings us down to a date roughly seventy years after the Acts of the Apostles was written. This, of course, does not *prove* anything with respect to the question of infant baptism in the apostolic age, but the proximity in time is nevertheless an *indicator* that the practice of baptizing small children began in the New Testament period.

What was the theological basis for the baptism of children in the first two centuries? This question is, if anything, even harder to answer than the question of the historical origins of the practice. Tertullian makes no clear link between the doctrine of original sin and baptism, although we must suppose that this link is the implicit premise of his view that small children in danger of death must be baptized. He cites Jesus' logion about children, but otherwise tells us nothing about how his opponents offered a theological justification of infant baptism. In the *Apostolic Tradition,* Hippolytus, too, is silent on this question. All his other remarks about the preparation and ritual celebration of baptism presuppose that those who receive it are conscious believers, and this would make it reasonable to suppose that he believes babies need to receive a share in the same saving gifts that conscious adult believers receive through baptism. How are we to combine the idea that the primary gift bestowed in baptism is the forgiveness of sins with the widespread idea in early Christian literature that a child is without sin (*innocens*)? It was this problem that caused difficulties to the "brethren" to whom Origen refers: they could not understand why the church practiced infant baptism. Origen's own contribution to this debate is his doctrine that the soul is stained by impurity and/or sin, and that this is why children must be washed clean in baptism.

Our sources presuppose the practice of infant baptism, but they are strikingly silent and reflect uncertainty about why babies were baptized. It is only in the fourth century and the early years of the fifth, especially in the Western church with Augustine, that the doctrine of original sin provided a theological justification for infant baptism.[84] In other words, it was only long after the practice of infant baptism was well established that it found a theological justification.[85] This is a good example of how a particular liturgical practice can supply support for a particular doctrine, illustrating the principle *lex orandi lex credendi*—the norm of prayer is the norm of belief—in the church's life. The practice of infant baptism was a catalyst in the emergence of the doctrine of original sin. I agree here with the observations of David F. Wright:[86]

> There is no doubt that the custom of infant baptism was the single most powerful catalyst of the formulation of doctrines of original sin, and that the direction of argument moved from the accepted practice of infant baptism to the truth of the doctrine, and not vice-versa. We have here an unmistakable illustration of the axiom *lex orandi lex credendi*. The church baptizes babies who, it is agreed, have not sinned *in propria persona*; therefore, we must believe that they are baptized for the cleansing or remission of original sin. Original sin must be part of the faith of the church; why else does the church baptize babies?

Attitudes to Infant Baptism from circa 250 to the Time of Augustine
Although the baptism of infants was well-established practice in a wide
geographical spectrum of the church in the first half of the third century,
this does not mean that it was continuously practiced everywhere in the
church until Augustine developed what was to become the classic theological defense of infant baptism. On the contrary, it is a well-known fact
that many of the foremost theologians and bishops in the fourth century
were not baptized as children, even though one or both of their parents
were Christians. The available biographical data from this period are very
limited, but this makes it all the more striking that all the sources which
tell us when someone received baptism refer to adults:[87]

Name	Year and Place of Birth	Year of Baptism
Basil of Caesarea	330/331, Caesarea in Cappadocia	358
Ambrose	333/334, Trier	374[88]
John Chrysostom	344/354, Antioch	368/372
Jerome	340–350, Strido in Dalmatia	366 (Rome)
Rufinus	345, Concordia	c. 370
Paulinus of Nola	c. 353, Bordeaux	c. 390
Augustine	354, Thagaste	387
Gregory Nazianzen	329/330, in Cappadocia	c. 360

None of these celebrated figures of the patristic age, all of whom were
born between 329 and 354, was baptized as a child, though one or both
parents were Christians. The geographical spectrum shows that the practice of postponing baptism was not limited to particular areas; it seems
to have occurred throughout the Mediterranean lands. Epitaphs from the
same period (from Rome, Capua, Bologna, and Milan) seem to confirm
the literary sources, but we must note that we do not know whether the
children of whom these inscriptions speak had Christian parents.[89]

The earliest attested postponement of infant baptism is the case of
Gregory Nazianzen, born in 329/330. We do not know for certain how
long this custom lasted, but we have some indications. At the close of the
370s and the beginning of the 380s, the Cappadocians Basil of Caesarea
and Gregory of Nyssa exhorted those of their hearers who had received
a Christian upbringing and education since their childhood to receive
baptism; everything suggests that they were addressing adults. In his discourse on baptism, the last of the great Cappadocians, Gregory Nazianzen, tries to persuade parents to baptize their children; he would not have
found this necessary had infant baptism been the normal practice.[90] He
is the only one of the Cappadocians to speak explicitly of infant baptism,
and he says unambiguously that babies who are in danger of death must
be baptized at once, "for it is better that they should be unconsciously

sanctified than depart this life unsealed and uninitiated." In other cases (that is, in the majority of instances), he recommends that one wait until the child is about three years old and has an incipient understanding of the sacrament.[91] It appears that the 380s were a period of transition with regard to the practice of infant baptism in the Eastern church. At any rate, John Chrysostom writes at the close of this decade, or the beginning of the 390s: "We baptize little children, even though they have no sins," in order that they may receive the gift of righteousness and become members of Christ's body.[92] If Chrysostom's words reflect normal practice, this means that at least part of the Eastern church practiced infant baptism circa 390. Bishop Siricius of Rome confirms that the church in Rome had reverted to the older customs of baptizing babies in 385. In that year, he issued a decree that parents must bring to baptism their small children who cannot speak for themselves (*infantibus qui necdum loqui potuerunt*); children who die unbaptized will not receive a share in eternal life and the kingdom of heaven.[93] Here, he anticipates Augustine's view on this question, which was to play a very central role in the Pelagian controversy.

As early as circa 365, Optatus of Milevis in northern Africa appears to take it for granted that infant baptism was the universally accepted practice of his church at that time. When he speaks of Christ as the garment with which the Christian clothes himself in baptism, he writes: "It shows no crease when infants put it on."[94] This may mean that the Western church, at least in northern Africa and Rome, had begun to revert to the older practice of baptizing babies a good decade before the first evidence of infant baptism in the church of Antioch; but this does not substantially change the general picture. During a period of five or six decades in the fourth century, the normal situation was that children did not receive baptism, and perhaps some area of the Eastern church did not practice infant baptism at all before the last two decades of the fourth century.[95]

We shall not discuss in detail here the reasons for this development; I limit myself to a few observations, since I believe that Augustine's *Confessions* tell us the main reason why infant baptism was not the normal practice in this period. His pious mother Monica did not bring him to baptism immediately after his birth, but she sought to have him baptized in the 360s, when he became gravely ill. However, she abandoned this plan when Augustine quickly recovered his health, "for it was held that the guilt of sinful defilement incurred after the laver of baptism was graver and more perilous." Augustine adds that one can still hear people say about other persons: "Let him be, let him do as he likes, he is not baptized yet."[96] There existed, in other words, a widespread idea that it did not matter so much how one lived, if one was not yet baptized—the underlying premise is, of course, that baptism conferred the forgiveness of whatever sins such a person might commit. This idea prompted the postponement of baptism until adulthood, especially in combination with the strict obligation, ensuing upon baptism, to lead a life in accordance with the Christian ideals, and not least with the idea that there was no post-baptismal forgiveness for the three mortal sins of apostasy, homicide, and fornication. As we have seen, Tertullian's warning that unmarried women ought not to be baptized seems linked to the gravity of the obligations incumbent upon those who received the sacrament. It is reasonable to see Monica's refusal to have Augustine baptized in this perspective. In view of the obligations ensuing upon baptism, she presumably thought it best to wait until her son had put the stormy years of adolescence behind him; when Augustine himself looks back on his youth in the *Confessions,* a central theme is the emergence of sexual desire and the sins to which this led. It is difficult to say what inspired the idea that it was not so serious to act in a manner contrary to the church's ethical ideals before one was baptized. Perhaps we should see this in connection with the increasing privileges accorded to the church in society at precisely this period, which led large numbers of the population to join the church. This, in turn, led to a watering down of general perceptions of what Christian baptism meant.

More important than the question why infant baptism, which was a common custom in a wide geographical area of the church, ceased to be the normal praxis throughout a large part of the fourth century is the question what was done with or for all those children of Christian parents who did not receive baptism. Did they receive a Christian upbringing, or was this neglected? The simple fact that many of the church's most prominent theologians, bishops, and monastic leaders came from this group of persons who were not baptized as children indicates that they did receive a Christian upbringing that laid the foundations for their subsequent ecclesiastical "careers."[97] This is confirmed by biographical and autobiographical texts: "The biographical and autobiographical evidence gives the lie to any implication that the non-baptizing of such children . . . betokened parental dereliction of duty or indifference."[98] The best known example here is Augustine's account of his early years in the *Confessions:*[99] "While still a boy I had heard about the eternal life promised to us through the humility of our Lord and God, who stooped even to our pride; and I was regularly signed (*signabar*) with the cross and given (*condiebar*) his salt even from the womb of my mother, who firmly trusted in you." As David F. Wright notes, the imperfect tenses of these two Latin verbs imply that this was not done only once, but was a frequently repeated ritual.[100] Nevertheless, it is reasonable to think that the first time this happened was a kind of dedication of the little child to Christ and the church. In another passage in the *Confessions,* Augustine writes that "the name of Christ was bestowed on me as an infant" in the church. If this refers to one single action, it can be interpreted as referring to the first occurrence.[101] At any rate, it shows that Augustine was brought to church as a baby and was there entrusted to Christ. We also read that his parents had him enrolled in the catechumenate, probably while he was a baby.[102] Wright holds that these texts indicate that "the commencement of his catechumenate was equivalent to his infant dedication to the church, and implicitly also to a pledge of intent by his parents . . . to his Christian upbringing."[103]

We know of at least two other celebrated fourth-century Christian authors who were dedicated to Christ as babies without being baptized. Jerome writes that he is "a Christian, born of Christian parents, and who carry the standard of the cross on my brow." Although he was not baptized until reaching adolescence, he had from the "very cradle " been "reared on Catholic milk."[104] Gregory Nazianzen lavishes praise on his mother, who even before his birth had promised to hand him over to God, and did so as soon as he was born.[105] When God answered her prayers that she might have a son, she responded by giving him to God, just as Hannah had consecrated Samuel to the Lord.[106] Gregory also compares Basil of Caesarea to Samuel, who was dedicated to God before his birth and consecrated to the Lord immediately after he was born: "Was not Basil from infancy and from the very womb consecrated to God, and presented with a mantle at the altar?"[107] In the light of this and other texts, David F. Wright has claimed that it was customary to consecrate children to Christ and the church by means of a ceremony in which the bishop or a priest traced the sign of the cross on the child's forehead, and that this rite marked its inclusion among the catechumens.[108] One may find this last element in Wright's thesis problematic,[109] but I find it reasonable to hold that a large number of children were enrolled in the catechumenate as babies.[110] Naturally, this meant that the parents intended to give their children Christian instruction and upbringing, though our sources say little about whether and how the majority of parents put this intention into practice. In positive terms, we know that church leaders and theologians such as Jerome, Gregory Nazianzen, and Augustine had parents who brought them up as Christians. Gregory, for example, says: "From earliest infancy I was nurtured in all

virtue, having as I had the best example in my home."[111] It is probable that
there were considerable variations; and although some prominent church
leaders and theologians say that they were given a thorough Christian upbringing, we have no real evidence that parents in general gave their children an education "not too different in essence from John Chrysostom's
counsel on the Christian nurture of children."[112] In the same way, we cannot assert that the church gave children (of whatever age) any form of instruction which was specifically aimed at them. It seems that parents usually took their children along to the worship of their congregation (and
perhaps to catechumenal instruction), and as they gradually grew older,
they will have understood something of what was said. Their presence in
these situations thus entailed a certain amount of instruction, but nothing
in our sources reflects what we might call a catechumenate for children.[113]
The family was the primary context in which children—whether baptized
or not—received Christian teaching.[114]

Holy Communion

Cyprian tells us that children took part in the Eucharist in northern Africa
in the mid-third century, but there are no sources from the first two centuries that speak of their participation in the Eucharist. As with baptism,
all we have to go on are indications—though the sources for holy communion are far fewer. The same applies to children's communion in the
period after Cyprian. Apart from Augustine, the first to offer a relatively
thorough theological treatment of this question, the only reference to
children's communion is in the *Apostolic Constitutions*. In addition to the
scantiness of the source material, the fact that the few explicit references
do not reflect any disagreement or debate comparable to the question of
infant baptism has meant that there is very little secondary literature on
this subject.[115] This is why our discussion will be shorter than that in the
case of infant baptism.

There are no direct references to children's communion in the New
Testament, but we have noted that children were present at worship. Let
us recall that the churches in the first two centuries were a network of
domestic communities, and this means that the Eucharist was celebrated
in Christian homes (Acts 2:42-46). It is reasonable to suppose that children who belonged to the household where the Christians assembled were
also present during the Eucharist. It is true that Acts 2 does not use for-

mulae such as "the whole household" (so typical when we are told that a household received baptism), but this is not a weighty argument against children's presence. It is of course possible that they were present without actually participating in the breaking of the bread; but if the first Christians too saw the similarities we discern in the biblical texts between the Eucharistic and the Jewish Passover Feast, which was celebrated in memory of the exodus from Egypt, then it is likely that children took part in the Eucharistic celebration.[116] The Jewish Passover was celebrated within the structure of the household, and all who were old enough to be physically capable of eating the food took part in it; our sources offer no basic objections to the participation of children who had not yet reached a particular stage of intellectual and religious maturity. The only limitation is physical: the child must be old enough to be able to consume the Passover food. For Christians with a Jewish background, therefore, it would have been natural to let small children take part in the Eucharist—always assuming, of course, that they did interpret it in the light of the Passover meal. This argument resembles the claim that the analogy between circumcision and baptism would probably have led Christians with a Jewish background to baptize their children;[117] in both cases, we have nothing more than indications to go on. The New Testament writings supply no certain evidence relevant to this question. We should however note that there is nothing in these texts, nor in Jewish tradition, which would suggest that children did not participate in the Eucharist.

In the subsequent period, there is interesting material in Justin Martyr and Hippolytus, who both speak of the Eucharist in connection with baptism. They take it for granted that all candidates for baptism receive their first communion immediately after they have been baptized.[118] Baptism and the Eucharist virtually form one single ritual, by means of which the individual is incorporated into the body of Christ. The entire context shows that these authors are thinking of adults, or of children who are so old that they themselves can make the appropriate liturgical responses. If it is correct (as I have argued above) that infant baptism was practiced from the mid-second century onward, does not the unity between baptism and Eucharist in the rite of initiation into the church make it reasonable to believe that children also received communion? It is more probable that children in the second half of the second century and the beginning of the third took part in the Eucharist as soon as they were old enough to be physically capable of eating the bread and drinking the wine, than that they did not do so.

As I have mentioned, the earliest witness to children's communion is Cyprian, who attests this as established practice in the North African church of his days. We have two examples of this in his treatise *De Lapsis*. He tells the story of a little girl whose nurse took her along to pagan worship without the knowledge of her parents.[119] She is given sacrificial food to eat: "bread mingled with wine." She was not given meat, for the interesting reason that she "was not yet able to eat flesh on account of her years." Cyprian writes in a later passage that she "was not yet of an age to speak of the crime committed by others in respect of herself."[120] This indicates that she was not more than two or three years old. The parents had no idea what had happened, until her mother took her to church. The first sign that something was wrong was her restlessness and unruly behavior during the service. When the Eucharistic chalice was presented to her, she turned her face away, bit her lips together, and refused to drink. However, "the deacon persisted, and, although against her efforts, forced on her some of the sacrament of the cup." The girl vomited at once, for, as Cyprian explains, "in a profane body and mouth the Eucharist could not remain." Thus was the secret deed of darkness unmasked in the light of the Lord. Irrespective of what we make of the details in this story and of Cyprian's interpretation of it, it is an unambiguous testimony to children's communion as established practice in the church of his period. He poses no questions with regard to this practice; on the contrary, he takes it for granted as something perfectly natural.

In another passage in the same treatise, he speaks of the future fate awaiting those who yield during persecutions and offer sacrifice to the gods of the pagans. Without any guilt of their own, small children were also involved in this activity, but this has negative consequences for their spiritual status, as Cyprian writes:[121]

> And that nothing might be wanting to aggravate the crime, infants also, in the arms of their parents, either carried or conducted, lost, while yet little ones, what in the very first beginning of their nativity they had gained. Will not they, when the day of judgment comes, say, "We have done nothing; nor have we forsaken the Lord's bread and cup to hasten freely to a profane contact; the faithlessness of others has ruined us"?

The words Cyprian imagines these children speaking in the scene of judgment are striking. They do not say in general terms that they have denied God, but that they have not denied "the Lord's bread and cup" of their own volition. When he speaks of their membership of the Christian community, he does so by speaking of their participation in the Eucharist, something he would not have done, had children's communion not been well-established ecclesial practice. It is also clear that he is speaking here of small children.

Cyprian does not offer any theological justification in these passages for children's communion, but he expresses views elsewhere that not only open the door to this practice, but make it necessary. As we have seen, he underscores that small children must be baptized; there is no difference between infants and adults in terms of the spiritual gifts bestowed on them from creation, and they receive the same grace in baptism.[122] A little child should be both "baptized and sanctified."[123] Cyprian is the first to link the words of Jesus at John 3:5 ("Unless one is born of water and the Spirit, one cannot enter the kingdom of God") with John 6:53 ("Unless you eat the flesh of the Son of Man and drink his blood, you have no life in you").[124] The combination of these logia implies that both baptism and the Eucharist are necessary if one is to become a member of Christ's body, which is the church. And this applies equally to children, since they have the capacity to receive the same spiritual gifts as adults.[125]

Apostolic Constitutions 8.13.14 is a similarly clear testimony to the practice of children's communion in Syria at the close of the fourth century. Just as the *Apostolic Tradition* of Hippolytus gives instructions about the sequence in which the various groups are to be baptized, the *Apostolic Constitutions* regulate the sequence in which the various groups in the congregation are to receive the bread and wine:[126] "And after that, let the bishop partake, then the presbyters, and deacons, and subdeacons, and the readers, and the singers, and the ascetics; and then of the women, the deaconesses, and the virgins, and the widows; then the children (*paidia*); and then all the people in order, with reverence and godly fear, without tumult." Children are the first group among the lay members of the congregation to receive the sacrament. The *Apostolic Constitutions*, drawn up at the close of the fourth century, are a collection of older material, and hence reflect the practice of earlier periods. The main source of 8.3–45, from which we have quoted this extract, is Hippolytus's *Apostolic Tradition*, but this does not contain any instructions about the sequence in which people are to receive the Eucharist. This means that we do not know how far back in time these regulations go.

An epitaph from the first half of the fourth century in Catania in Sicily attests that children received the Eucharist.[127] This inscription commemorates a little girl, Julia Florentina, who was eighteen months and twenty-two days old when she died. After becoming seriously ill, she received emergency baptism at 2 A.M. Just before her death, four hours later, she was given the Eucharist.[128] The obvious question is the link between the normal celebration of the Eucharist in church and the administration of communion to a dying child. In the case of baptism, we have seen that Tertullian was opposed to this as normal practice, but accepted the emergency baptism of small children who were dying; it is possible that similar views about children's communion existed. However, when we bear in mind the fact that Cyprian takes it for granted that children in northern Africa receive communion in the mid-third century, it seems more reasonable to assume that the practice of giving the sacrament to children who were dying reflects their participation in the normal celebration of the Eucharist in church.

Although the views put forward by Cyprian have an inherent dynamic that makes it logical that children should receive communion, he does not in fact discuss the implications of his own theology for this question. The first to discuss explicitly whether children should receive the sacrament, and to offer a theological justification for this practice, is Augustine. In his thinking and argumentation on this point, John 6:53 plays a particularly important role. He argues that the words of Jesus apply to every group, even small children: "Truly, truly I say to you, unless you eat the flesh of the Son of Man and drink his blood, you have no life in you."[129]

Let us look more closely at how Augustine develops this teaching in one of his anti-Pelagian treatises, the *De Peccatorum Meritis et Remissione*. Here, Augustine employs John 6:53 to refute his opponents, who claim that, because of children's innocence, unbaptized babies are not damned. They underscore that Jesus says that one who is not baptized cannot enter the kingdom of God; but he does not say that one who is not baptized is excluded from eternal life. They then apply this distinction between the kingdom of God and eternal life to baptism, claiming that it gives children a share in the former. Augustine replies that this distinction is artificial, and adduces the biblical proof John 6:53. After disposing of the possible objection that these words applied only to those who heard them for the first time in Capernaum, he continues: Christ's "flesh, which was given for the life of the world, was also given for the life of the little ones, and if they have not eaten the flesh of the Son of Man, they will not have life either."[130] Augustine's main point here is that since little children must take part in the Eucharist in order to receive eternal life, they must also be baptized, since the Eucharist presupposes baptism. This, in turn, functions as confirmation of his doctrine that children are born with original sin. In our

context, the most important thing is that he offers a theological justification of children's communion.

His theological defense of children's baptism and communion won
wide acceptance, as we see in synodal decrees and in a letter of Pope Innocent I.[131] We cannot discuss here the further historical development of
children's communion; I mention only that this was normal practice in
the West until the twelfth century, but disappeared in the course of the
following century. In the Eastern church, children's communion has continued until the present day.

Other Forms of Participation in Worship

Were children actively involved in services other than baptism and the Eucharist? Did they have specific liturgical functions and roles? As we would
expect, our sources show no trace of any discussion of the appropriateness
of including children in worship on their own terms by giving them specific things to do during the service; this is a typically modern approach,
and no one in the early centuries was aware of any problem in this regard.
The closest we come to such an awareness is John Chrysostom's admonition to parents in the *De Inani Gloria* to take their children with them to
church. However, even if there is no trace of our modern endeavors to
integrate children into worship, and no discussion of children's role in
liturgy, children did in fact play an active part and had specific liturgical
roles. Our sources speak of this only seldom and in passing, but they tell
us that children in general were active singers. It was their task to sing
particular responses in the liturgy and to sing in the choir, and they could
also function as lectors.

The reading of sacred scripture was a central element in synagogue
worship (cf. Luke 4:16f.; Acts 13:15) and maintained its centrality in early
Christian worship (cf. 1 Timothy 4:13; Revelation 1:3; Justin Martyr, 1
Apol. 67; Tertullian, *Apol.* 39). Tertullian is the first to employ the noun
lector for the one who reads the scriptures aloud (*Praescr.* 41). Hippolytus
states that it is the bishop who is to appoint the reader and hand him the
book; this procedure is followed because the lector is not ordained (*Apost.
Trad.* 12). In the gradual development of ecclesiastical organization and
of the liturgy, things took on a more settled pattern that included the ordination of lectors. From the mid-third century onward, they formed a
specific "order" among the clergy,[132] but this "could be regarded as merely
an initial clerical station" en route to a higher clerical order.[133] Cyprian

envisages that the lectors are to read the Gospel text from the pulpit, but this honorable task was assigned to deacons or presbyters from the close of the third century onward. The lectors retained the task of reading other scriptural texts.[134] From the fourth century, the lectors took on the task, usually assigned up to that time to the deacons, of washing the hands of the presbyters and the bishop in the course of the Eucharistic celebration.[135]

Cyprian is the earliest patristic author to tell us that a boy was appointed lector.[136] With his fellow bishops, he appointed the confessor Aurelius from Carthage as lector. In this case, they did not follow the customary procedure of consulting the laity (*plebs*) when someone was to be appointed to a clerical office, because God had already "cast His vote."[137] Cyprian refers here to Aurelius's character and his faith, which he had demonstrated by refusing to deny Christianity under persecution: "Tender in years he may be, but he is far advanced in glory for his faith and courage; though junior in terms of natural age, he is senior in honor" (*Ep.* 38.1.2).

The epitaph for Pope Liberius (352–366) records that he was *scripturarum lector* as a boy (*parvulus*).[138] A decree of Pope Siricius (died 298) lays down that one who devotes himself to the service of the church from his childhood must begin as lector.[139]

In a sermon, Augustine refers to the Gospel text that had just been read by the lector with his "boyish heart" (*corde puerili*).[140] When Victor of Vita tells the story of the persecution of the Catholic Christians in northern Africa by the Arian Vandals, he writes: "Amongst those who were exiled were many *lectores* who were little children." He also tells of a child lector whose throat was pierced by an arrow and who died, just as he was about to sing the Easter alleluia verse.[141] We are told that Popes Zosimus (417–418) and Simplicius (468–483) had to remain lectors until they were twenty or thirty years old; only then were they admitted to a higher order.[142] Inscriptions from the fifth and sixth centuries tell of lectors who were in their twenties when they died; but we also read that "Severus, an innocent lector, died aged thirteen." Others died at twelve or fourteen.[143]

Do our sources tell us anything about a minimum age for children who began as lectors? Ennodius's remark that Epiphanius became a lector at the age of eight is, of course, highly interesting,[144] as are epitaphs from the fifth and sixth centuries that speak of lectors who were no more than five years old when they died.[145] According to these sources, boys could be very young when they were ordained as lectors—indeed, so young that it is hard to believe they were sufficiently skilled at reading to be able to perform their tasks satisfactorily.

This brings us to a phenomenon that (unsurprisingly) has attracted the attention of scholars, namely the references in our sources to child lectors who do "not know letters." We hear of Aurelius Ammonios, a Christian lector in an Egyptian village in 304 who "not does know letters."[146] The same is said of Aurelius, the Carthaginian lector mentioned above: according to Cyprian, Lucianus (one of his opponents on the question of how the church should deal with those who had apostatized during the persecutions) wrote and distributed a number of certificates of forgiveness in the name of this confessor "on the grounds that Aurelius is illiterate (*quod litteras ille non nosset*)."[147] Only a few months later, Cyprian announced to his clergy and the people that "On Sunday, therefore, without waiting any longer, he read for us, that is to say he has given us an omen of peace to come by inaugurating his duties as reader."[148]

It is unlikely that Aurelius had undergone an intensive instruction in reading in the intervening months. But how are we to understand the affirmation that he was illiterate? Does this mean that Aurelius functioned as lector without being able to read? G. W. Clarke refers here to the roughly contemporary, anonymous treatise *Adversus Judaeos* 10.2f., which says that if a Jew asks any Christian child, or an old woman, a widow, or a peasant in the countryside, about the truth, the child will proclaim the scriptures elegantly, even if it cannot read (*sine litteris*), and will go on to teach the old man. Clarke concludes: "Equally the youthful Aurelius, inspirited after his glorious and defiant confession before magistrates and proconsul, could be relied upon to proclaim the gospel as lector even if he were 'without letters.'"[149] I prefer another interpretation, which Clarke herself supports elsewhere, when she points out the importance of the conjunctive mood in the clause *quod litteras ille non nosset*. This can be understood to mean that Cyprian "is reporting not so much established fact as the reason alleged for Lucianus' writing out certificates in Aurelius' name." She continues: "The clause is, therefore, not necessarily an obstacle to the identification of this 'illiterate' Aurelius with the Aurelius who is soon to be appointed reader in *Ep.* 38.2."[150] When we are told that the Egyptian Aurelius Ammonios "not does know letters," the implication is that he does not know the Greek alphabet. He may have been able to read other languages, such as Coptic.[151]

From the fourth and fifth centuries, those who took on the office of lector were given instruction in reading and singing.[152] As the influence and prestige of the clergy increased, it is not difficult to imagine that parents would try to secure a career in the church for their sons from a very tender age, and one way to do this was to "hand them over" to the church and let them begin to receive instruction as lectors. This may explain why funeral inscriptions call children as young as five years "lectors." Since they did in fact receive instruction, it is certainly possible that they really were able to read at that age; it is however also possible that they were still being trained, and had not yet begun to read the scriptures in church worship before they died. It is, in other words, possible to make sense of all the available data—both the tender age of the "lectors" and the information that some were unable to read. This latter fact does not oblige us to imagine a situation where illiterate boys served as lectors in the liturgy!

It is in any case indisputable that boys served as lectors from a very early age. This is confirmed by a decree promulgated by Justinian in 546, which laid down the minimum age of eight for those who were to assume the office of lector.[153] The need to establish a minimum age may be related to the desire of ambitious parents—or (perhaps more likely) poor parents—to ensure a future career in the clergy for their sons.

Children took an active part in worship in other ways too. Our sources relate that children (primarily boys) participated in the singing and had various liturgical functions. The *Pseudo-Clementine Recognitions*, composed in Syria in the fourth century, relate that children joined in crying out in prayer to God to show mercy and send rain after a lengthy drought.[154] Ephrem the Syrian (died 373) formed choirs of "daughters of the covenant . . . taught them *madrashê* . . . and they assembled in the church on the feasts of the Lord, on Sundays, and on feasts of martyrs."[155] As Johannes Quasten writes, Ephrem also writes that boys sang psalms in the liturgy:

> He speaks of the splendor of Nisan, the month of Easter, which adorns the Church with its array of flowers, and he compares the magnificently colored image of the spring month with the liturgical celebration: the flowers are the scriptures, which the voices of the boys and the virgins seem to strew over the congregation, as if the sun were shining on it. These flowers will be mingled with those that bloom on earth. The bishop will offer his homilies, the priests their encomia, the deacons their readings, the youths their shouts of joy, the boys their psalms and the virgins their songs.[156]

Here we see a choir of boys with clearly defined liturgical functions. The Gallican pilgrim Egeria probably envisages a choir of boys when she describes the liturgy she experienced in the church of the Anastasis in Jerusalem. After the deacon had mentioned the names of the persons for whom the congregation was to pray, the boys (*pisinni*) sang *Kyrie eleison*.[157] The *Testamentum Domini* speaks of a boys' choir with an even larger liturgical role, as Quasten writes:[158]

> The so-called *Testament of Our Lord* shows a significant development here. The boys still responded to the cantor together with the virgins and sang the psalms in the Office alternately with the virgins, yet for that very reason the choir of boys stood out ever more in opposition to the singing of the people at large. Thus the four canticles were sung by the boys, two virgins, three deacons and three priests. The canticles at vespers were sung by the boys alone, while the people replied in common with the Alleluia. So we see that the boy choir eventually relieved the cantor of his position; the word *respondeat* already points to this.

When the *Apostolic Constitutions* regulate the intercessory prayer for catechumens, we are told that when the deacons mention the individuals by name, the congregation is to reply with the *Kyrie eleison*. The text continues: "Let the children say it first (*et ante cunctos pueri*)."[159] John Chrysostom also makes a special link between children and the prayer imploring God's mercy. When he discusses the various kinds of prayers in the liturgy in his commentary on Matthew's Gospel, he writes:

> the third [prayer] also for ourselves, and this put forward the innocent children of the people entreating God for mercy. For since we condemn ourselves for sins, for them that have sinned much and deserve to be blamed we ourselves cry; but for ourselves the children; for the imitators of whose simplicity the kingdom of heaven is reserved.[160]

Not only does this passage confirm the special role children had in prayer during worship; Chrysostom also indicates why this was appropriate. Children function as intercessors because of their innocence. He seems to hold that this makes them particularly suitable to pray that God may have mercy on others, perhaps because of the idea that the children's innocence means that they are closer to God than other persons, so that their prayer is more effective. I shall return to the question of why children had particular roles and functions in worship.

Basil of Caesarea (died 379) paints a contrast between the indifference shown by many adult men and women to the hymns sung in the liturgy and the children's eager participation in the singing.[161] Gregory Nazianzen likewise underscores the eagerness with which children took their part in singing in church.[162] In connection with the celebration of All Saints Day in 396, the Syriac writer Cyrillonas exclaims: "See how the hymns resound in children's mouths, and women sing their psalms! See, on your glorious feast day, the creation with its children seeks you, to find mercy!"[163]

Our sources, most of which date from between the end of the fourth and the sixth centuries, reflect that children were active participants in worship in various ways, and several writers emphasize the eagerness with which they joined in singing. We are also told that children had a role in intercessory prayer, especially in the *Kyrie eleison,* and that they participated in specific parts of the liturgy. Not least, children were given the role of reader; our sources show that they could become lectors from the age of five, although (as I have argued) it is not reasonable to suppose that they carried out this role before they could read. As we have seen, Justinian laid down eight years old as the minimum age for lectors in a decree in 546. Since the lectorate was, in many cases, the first stage in a clerical career, it is obvious that only a small minority of children were lectors.

Nevertheless, bearing in mind the general status and position of children in society at that period, their relatively visible role in worship may surprise us, at least at first glance. How is this phenomenon to be understood or interpreted? Several factors are involved here.

First, children's participation may be connected with the idea that they were innocent. We have seen how John Chrysostom directly links their innocence to their qualification or suitability to ask God's grace for other persons. This presupposes that they are closer to God because of their innocence, and can therefore function as a channel or instrument between God and the adult world.[164] We have seen in an earlier chapter that innocence was the quality most usually associated with children in Christian texts prior to Augustine's controversy with the Pelagians.

Second, children's role as singers or cantors may have had an aesthetic element: their voices may have been perceived as more beautiful and pure than the voices of adults. We find this viewpoint in Lucian of Samosata,[165] and it is possible that this was a contributory factor in the assignment of liturgical functions to children in Christian worship.[166]

Third, as noted above, children had a prominent role in pagan worship in the Greco-Roman world, and this makes it a reasonable assumption that Christians would have found it perfectly natural that children would carry out functions in their liturgy.

Fourth, there is an educational dimension to children's participation in worship. We have seen that Christian authors strongly urge parents to give their children a Christian upbringing, so that they will live as adults in accordance with the Christian ideals. The reading of scripture, the singing of hymns, and prayers were important elements in this education, and the liturgy included all of these. When he is exhorting parents to teach their children the great biblical stories, Chrysostom refers to the joy they experience when they hear these stories read in the liturgy and recognize them. This educational aspect does not explain why children were employed as lectors and had particular liturgical functions, but it may help explain why they were present in church in the first place.

Fifth, the fact that children were baptized and received the Eucharist—at any rate from the mid-third century onward—implies that they were seen as subjects with needs of their own and with the capacity to receive the same spiritual gifts as adults. Christianity seems not to have altered children's position in the hierarchical structures of family and society; nevertheless, they were perceived as adults' equals in their relationship to God. This logically led to their presence during worship.

Thus, a number of factors seem to have combined to promote the participation of children in the liturgy and to assign them specific functions. Their roles as lectors and as intercessors who pleaded for God's mercy must be seen primarily in the light of the idea that children are innocent. Finally, I believe that the pagan practice of employing children in liturgical functions was a significant reason why Christians did the same.

The Presence of Children

To what extent were children involved in what went on in worship? Did they receive the sacraments? Were they assigned particular roles and functions in the liturgy? The discussion in the present chapter allows us to conclude that they were not only involved in worship, but also gave the liturgy a particular character through their responsibility for specific parts of the service.

From c. 250 onward, our sources agree that the church, in a wide geographical spectrum, practiced infant baptism (with the exception of a period of seventy years in the fourth century); with reference to the period before that date, the sources can be read in various ways. I have attempted to show that the most satisfactory interpretation of the earliest literary sources that explicitly refer to infant baptism—Tertullian, the *Apostolic Tradition*, and Origen—attest that it was well-established practice in northern Africa at the beginning of the third century, in Rome c. 215, and in Palestine between 230 and 250. I have also argued that when the New Testament says that whole households received baptism, the analogy it draws between circumcision and baptism and the affinities between Jewish proselyte baptism and early Christian baptism make it reasonable to assume that from the very beginnings of the church, children were baptized along with their families, when their parents converted to the Christian faith. Another important indicator pointing in this direction is the collective character of the family in classical antiquity. The analogy between circumcision and baptism strongly suggests that children born into Jewish-Christian families were baptized as infants; it is more difficult to say anything certain about the children of Gentile Christians before the mid-second century. Nevertheless, the fact that infant baptism appears to be the normal order by about 200 indicates that this practice can be dated back to the second century.

What of the Eucharist? Cyprian tells us that the church in northern Africa in the mid-third century gave children communion; according to the *Apostolic Constitutions*, the church in Syria did the same about one hundred years later. In the period between Cyprian and Augustine, nothing in our sources suggests that anyone found the practice of children's communion problematic. Augustine is the first to discuss this question explicitly, and he provides the same kind of theological justification as he does for baptism. Here, John 6:53 plays an important role. Jesus' words—"Unless you eat the flesh of the Son of Man and drink his blood, you have no life in you"—apply to absolutely all classes of human persons, including small children. This theological justification for children's communion won general acceptance. It is indisputable that the Western church practiced children's communion from the time of Cyprian onward, and this was the normal practice, at least from Augustine's time, until the twelfth century; it was abandoned in the following century. The tradition of children's communion has remained in force in the Eastern church until the present day. It is difficult to say anything more precise about the period between the New Testament and the mid-third century, but if the earliest Christians saw the same similarities that we discern between the Jewish Passover meal and the Lord's Supper, this would indicate that small children took part in the Eucharist. There is nothing in the New Testament or in the second-century Christian sources to indicate that they did not so.

From the mid-third century, and perhaps from the New Testament period onward, children received the sacraments: in a wide geographical area, they were baptized and took part in the Eucharist. This implies that they were regarded as subjects with needs of their own and with the capacity to receive the same spiritual gifts as adults. The fact that they received baptism and communion also shows that they were perceived as full members of the community.

Children's active participation went further, however. The sources tell us that they played an active part in hymn-singing, that they were cantors, and that they had a special responsibility in praying the *Kyrie eleison*. They also read scriptural texts in the liturgy. In other words, they were visibly present and made their own contribution to worship.

This highly visible presence had nothing to do with modern ideas that children should be included in worship on their own terms. Rather, the main reason seems to be the underlying idea that children were innocent. This may have generated the assumption that children were particularly suited to serve as God's instruments, or that their prayers for mercy and pardon were especially effective. It is also reasonable to hold that the church adopted the practice of contemporary pagan worship and public ceremonies in the Greco-Roman world, where children had liturgical tasks and functions; this made it natural for Christians to do the same. Other elements that may have prompted children's participation in the liturgy were their pure and clear voices, the educational dimension of Christian worship, and the fact that children were considered full members of the community, as subjects with needs of their own and the capacity to receive the good things of salvation.

7
CHILDREN AND A LIFE
OF RELIGIOUS PERFECTION

We have seen in the previous chapters that Christians in the first centuries had attitudes toward abortion, the exposure of children, and (to some extent) to infanticide that differed from prevalent views in the Greco-Roman world. The Christian sources that speak of these matters are consistently critical and condemnatory. Their critique is largely, though not exclusively, based on the commandment not to kill, and on the idea that God is the creator of all life. Children are the product of God's creative activity, and have, in principle, the same value as other human beings. In keeping with this attitude, we also find a generally positive attitude to procreation. Christian theology and ethics protected children's life in a way not found in the Greco-Roman world, and in this sense we can speak of Christianity as a "child-friendly" religion.

At the same time, however, some groups saw an incompatibility between caring for one's children and leading a life of religious perfection. We find as early as the New Testament a tension between family life and its obligations on the one hand and the radical following of Jesus on the other, and this tension was intensified and given clearer emphasis by the adherents of the ascetic movement. Some argued that one should not have children at all; others abandoned their children for lengthy periods; and even mothers could "abandon" their children in a yet more radical way by voluntarily accepting martyrdom. Others again encouraged their own children to become martyrs. Although our sources do not have many examples of such attitudes, we must look at them here in some detail, in order to complete our picture of attitudes toward children in the early church.

CARE FOR CHILDREN CANNOT BE COMBINED
WITH A LIFE OF RELIGIOUS PERFECTION

In the two short books addressed to his wife, Tertullian advises her against remarrying after his death.[1] He affirms in both books that marriage is legitimate, but celibacy is much preferable: marriage is a concession to persons who cannot overcome sexual desire. For the same reason, it is more valuable to live as a widow than to remarry. In chapters 6 and 7 of the first book, he lists a number of reasons why people remarry, including the wish to have children: "Further reasons for marriage which men allege for themselves arise from anxiety for posterity, and the bitter, bitter pleasure of children."[2] Tertullian insists that such motivations cannot inspire the conduct of Christians, since they long to be set free from this evil world and to come to the Lord; parents desire this for their children too. His point is that it does not make sense to bring children into the world, only to wish that the Lord might take them home to himself, either before their parents or together with them.

He makes considerable use of irony in his next argument against having children: "To the servant of God, forsooth, offspring is necessary! For of our own salvation we are secure enough, so that we have leisure for children! Burdens must be sought by us for ourselves which are avoided even by the majority of the Gentiles."[3] Clearly, the underlying idea is that looking after children is a time-consuming activity. Tertullian is concerned that the obligations incumbent on those who have children will take up time that otherwise could have spent working for one's eternal salvation—and that is something no one should neglect! Those who wish to have children make the mistake of thinking their own salvation is sure. He also refers to Jesus' logion about the difficulties in store for those who are pregnant and for those with babies at the breast on "the day of disencumbrance." Tertullian is thinking here of the extraordinary challenges that will face parents under persecution: he is afraid that they will deny the faith for the sake of their children, unlike single persons who "at the first trump of the angel will spring forth disencumbered—will freely bear to the end whatsoever pressure and persecution, with no burdensome fruit of marriage heaving in the womb, none in the bosom."[4]

We find much of the same subject matter and argumentation in the treatise *De Exhortatione Castitatis,* which Tertullian composed after joining the Montanists.[5] Here, he is attempting to persuade a friend not to remarry. As in *Ad Uxorem,* Tertullian mentions various reasons why most people get married a second time: these include the wish to have children, and to have a longer life thanks to these children. A Christian, however, is not allowed to reason in this way, since such a wish flatly contradicts Paul's desire to leave this world in order to be with the Lord. With biting irony, Tertullian underscores the exceptional difficulties that those with children will meet in times of persecution: "Assuredly, most free will he be from encumbrance in persecutions, most constant in martyrdoms, most prompt in distributions of his goods, most temperate in acquisitions; lastly, undistracted by cares will he die, when he has left children behind him—perhaps to perform the last rites over his grave!"[6] In addition to the fact that children make it more difficult to hold out under persecution and to accept a martyr's death, the costs involved in feeding and clothing them mean that their parents are absolutely required to possess a certain amount of material goods—and this makes it harder for them to give alms.[7] His final argument against having children is that parents will be anxious in the face of death, because they worry about the future of their children.

Although Tertullian calls children a "burden," this does not mean that he is generally hostile to them. It is important to bear in mind the context for his negative statements about children. He warns against having children because a situation of persecution may arise, where parents would have to choose between martyrdom (which means abandoning their children, or perhaps entrusting them to others) and denying their faith. Their very love for their children and the care parents show them may lead parents to deny the Christian faith, which in Tertullian's eyes is the worst thing that can happen to anyone. An equally important factor is that he speaks of children as a "burden" in the context of a broader argument in favor of sexual abstinence. In both of these treatises, Tertullian concedes the legitimacy of marriage, but he urges that celibacy and a life of abstinence are to be preferred. To sum up: Tertullian's negative affirmations about children must be read against the background of a real danger of persecution, and not least as part of a wider argumentation in favor of sexual abstinence.[8] Parents' wish for children, and the value or importance children had, are less important than his Encratite ideals. The necessary precondition for having children—sexual intercourse between a man and a woman—conflicts with Tertullian's ideals regarding a life of religious perfection. Similarly, the ties binding parents to their children, and the necessary daily care and nurture of their children, could prevent parents from putting these ideals into practice. In Tertullian's worldview, children posed a problem or indeed a hindrance to those who sought to live the perfect Christian life.

Parents Leave Their Children

Tertullian worried that the ties binding parents to their children might prevent parents from displaying the necessary fortitude under persecution: in other words, they might shrink from martyrdom. If we accept the premises of his argumentation, we can certainly grasp why he felt this worry. Love and concern for their children could indeed lead Christian parents to hesitate about holding out to the very end under persecution; accordingly, they might choose to deny their faith. However, although it is certainly reasonable to suppose that among those who sacrificed to the Greco-Roman gods and worshiped them under persecution were parents, motivated by concern for their children, there are in fact no sources that explicitly confirm such a hypothesis. As we shall see, there are sources that tell how mothers who were willing to give their lives for Christ are exhorted to think of their children. Such narratives may be historically accurate; they may also be a fictitious element employed by the authors of these texts to intensify the honor involved in accepting death for the sake of one's faith. In either case, they reflect the view that concern for one's children could prevent parents from embracing a martyr's death. But all these texts show that the potential martyrs gave priority to the ideal of a religious life—not to concern for their children.

The best known example is the *Martyrdom of Perpetua and Felicity*.[9] Vibia Perpetua, a twenty-two-year-old mother from a well-off family in Thuburbo in North Africa, was taken prisoner during the persecutions, along with some other catechumens: Revocatus and his fellow slave (*conserua*) Felicity, Saturninus, and Secundulus. Felicity was pregnant when she was arrested, and gave birth in prison; Perpetua already had a baby at the time of her arrest. The anonymous author of this account or *passio* reports in chapters 3–10 what happened to Perpetua during her time in prison. This takes the form of a first-person narrative. The author also lets Saturninus speak in the first person singular, and claims that it was he who wrote these things down (chapters 11–13). We need not accept the historicity of everything in the narrative, nor the authenticity of every word of Perpetua and the other martyrs; but most scholars evaluate this *passio* as an "authentic reflection of the period of the persecution in Africa about 200."[10]

The introduction (chapters 1–2) and the long conclusion (chapters 14–21) form a framework around the story of these martyrs. It is fairly obvious that the author wishes to support the concerns of the Montanists. In the introduction, for example, he challenges those who "restrict the power of the one Spirit to times and seasons" by writing: "the more recent events should be considered the greater, being later than those of old, and this is a consequence of the extraordinary graces promised for the last stage of time." Joel 2:28 is cited as scriptural proof, and the author concludes: "we hold in honor and acknowledge not only new prophecies but new visions as well."[11] If the first-person-singular descriptions in the *passio* of the visions and religious experiences of Perpetua and Saturninus genuinely corresponds to what these persons themselves believed they were experiencing, the author is certainly justified in employing this story in the way he does; the visions of Perpetua and the other persons in the narrative seem to be influenced by the Montanist movement, which was growing in strength at that period.[12] H. Musurillo describes this *passio* as "a proto-Montanist document, originating perhaps in the first decade of the third century from the Montanist circle of Tertullian himself."[13]

Perpetua had a child when she was arrested, a boy so young that she was still breast-feeding him. Her relationship to her child is a relatively prominent theme in the narrative, and it is clear that she is worried about him. Perpetua was resolved to die for her faith, if need be. A few days after her father had tried for the first time to persuade her to change her mind, she received baptism—probably in full awareness of how the Romans would perceive this step. Shortly afterward, she was thrown into prison, where her circumstances were very difficult and she became afraid: it was dark and crowded, the heat was extreme, and the soldiers treated her badly. She adds: "To crown all, I was tortured with worry for my baby there." During her first days in captivity, she was not allowed to have the boy with her. We are not told where he was; it is probable that other persons in the prison were looking after him. She was very worried about how he was while she was in captivity, but things soon changed for the better. Two deacons bribed the soldiers to transfer Perpetua and those who had been arrested with her to a better part of the prison. Her baby was brought to her, and she was able to feed the boy who "was faint from hunger." In her worry, she spoke to her mother about the boy, and they obviously agreed that her mother and her brother should assume responsibility for him. Perpetua says that it was very painful to her to see how her mother and brother suffered, since they felt sorry for her. After several days, something happened to alter Perpetua's imprisonment radically: she was allowed to have her son with her in prison on a permanent basis. This was a great relief, and she felt better immediately: "At once I recovered my health, relieved as I was of my worry and anxiety over the child. My prison had suddenly become a palace, so that I wanted to be there rather than anywhere else."[14] It is touching to read this description of the ties binding Perpetua to her little child, and to see how important his presence was for the way she experienced her situation, with all its tension.

A short time after this great change, her brother exhorted her to ask the Lord for a vision that would tell them whether Perpetua would be condemned or acquitted. Her prayers were heard, and this vision revealed to them that they would have to suffer. They had no longer any hope in this earthly life.[15] A few days later, her father came a second time from the city and attempted to persuade his daughter to change her attitude to martyrdom. He appeals to her to show compassion: "'Daughter,' he said, 'have pity on my grey head—have pity on me your father, if I deserve to be called your father, if I have favored you above all your brothers, if I have raised you to reach this prime of your life. Do not abandon me to be the reproach of men.'" Her persistence challenges her father's position of power in the Roman family: her refusal to accept her position *in patria potestate* brings disgrace upon her father.[16] He does not limit himself to a request to show compassion on him, and to point out the consequences for his reputation if she defies his will. He urges her to think of her brothers, her mother, and her aunt. And—most interesting of all in the present context—he appeals to her to think of her child: "Think of your child, who will not be able to live once you are gone." The description of how much her son meant to Perpetua certainly suggests that her father's appeal must have made a deep impression on her, although the text does not mention this. She interpreted his intervention as an expression of his love for her, and tried in vain to console him by saying that events would turn out as God willed.

One hour later, when Perpetua was to be taken off for trial, her desperate father took a new initiative. With his grandchild in his arms, he once again exhorted Perpetua to show compassion on her son: "Perform the sacrifice—have pity on your baby (*Supplica. Miserere infanti*)."[17] In his desperate situation, he tried to appeal to her maternal feelings and her responsibility for her child. The governor Hilarianus, who was to interrogate her and who had seen what had happened, tried at first to take the same line: "Have pity on your father's grey head; have pity on your infant son. Offer the sacrifice for the welfare of the emperors."[18] But neither her father nor the governor's appeal had any effect on Perpetua: she refused to sacrifice. In his desperation, her father interrupted the trial and begged her to change her mind. Hilarianus then ordered her to be laid on the ground and beaten. Perpetua felt sorry for her father, but she did not relent on the question of sacrifice.

After this, Hilarianus proclaimed that the whole group was to be condemned to death by being thrown to the wild beasts in the arena. According to the narrative, all returned to prison, glowing with zeal, after this sentence had been pronounced. But Perpetua was still thinking of her baby. Since the boy had become accustomed to being with her in prison and to being fed at her breast, she sent word to her father by means of a deacon and asked him to come with the baby; but he refused. Then something happened that gave Perpetua a greater measure of calm. In the narrative, this functions as yet another sign from God that she was on the right path: "But as God willed, the baby had no further design for the breast, nor did I suffer any inflammation, and so I was relieved of any anxiety for my child and of any discomfort in my breasts."[19] We are not told how she learned that the child no longer desired to be fed at her breast, but there is no doubt that this, as well as the disappearance of the pain in her breasts, was interpreted as a divine intervention. Perpetua's reaction is very interesting: from that point on, she no longer felt any worry about her child, and he is not mentioned again in the narrative. After this she made this decision, it seems that she was no longer troubled by the thought of her child, or by worry about him. She was ready to leave him forever. This seems to indicate that her main anxiety about him was that he should get the food or nourishment that he needed in order to survive; perhaps it was the boy's need of his mother's milk that lay behind his grandfather's concern that he would not survive, if Perpetua died (although this ought not to have posed any particular problem, given the widespread use of wet nurses in society at that time). We are not told that Perpetua worried about what it would be like for the boy to grow up without a mother; this may well be because she knew that he would be cared for by his grandparents or his uncle. And whatever she may have thought about all this, she chose to die for her faith, thus leaving her child for good.

What about the slave woman, Felicity? We are told that she was in the ninth month of pregnancy when she was arrested, and when she realized that the day when they were to be thrown to the beasts was drawing near, she was afraid that her martyrdom would be postponed on account of her pregnancy, "for it is against the law for women with child to be executed."[20] That might mean that she would have to "shed her holy, innocent blood afterwards along with others who were common criminals."

This prospect, as well as their desire not to leave her alone, led the others to pray together for her. Immediately after this prayer, the pain of birth came on Felicity. These pains were more violent than usual, because the birth started too early. She gave birth to a daughter. While she cried out in pain, one of the prison warders mocked her:[21]

> "You suffer so much now—what will you do when you are tossed to the beasts? Little did you think of them when you refused to sacrifice." "What I am suffering now," she replied, "I suffer by myself. But then another will be inside me who will suffer for me, just as I shall be suffering for him."

The narrative goes on to underscore Felicity's readiness to suffer martyrdom. When she is led out to the arena with the others, we are told that Felicity rejoiced "that she had safely given birth so that now she could fight the beasts, going from one blood bath to another, from the midwife to the gladiator, ready to wash after childbirth in a second baptism."[22] Even the pagan onlookers were horrified when they saw that one of those condemned to death was a "woman fresh from childbirth with the milk still dripping from her breasts."[23] The only thing we are told about the baby is that "one of the sisters brought her up as her own daughter." This commentary signals that Felicity was not indifferent to the fate of her baby; and yet she was not anxious, for she knew that her daughter was in safe hands. She is not portrayed as an irresponsible mother, even although she chose to abandon her child in order to realize the life of Christian perfection. The text indicates that Felicity felt even less conflict than Perpetua between being a mother and suffering martyrdom. On the contrary, these two young mothers' faith and constancy under persecutions, including their readiness to lay down their lives, is a model to others and bears testimony that they were filled with the Spirit. The author sums up his narrative as follows: "any man who exalts, honors, and worships his [Christ's] glory should read for the consolation of the Church these new deeds of heroism which are no less significant than the tales of old."[24] We are not surprised to see that Tertullian, the only contemporary source apart from the *passio* to mention Perpetua, marvels at her and calls her "the most heroic martyr."[25]

In the *Martyrdom of Saints Carpus, Papylus, and Agathonicê*, transmitted in Greek and Latin versions that sometimes diverge strongly, we hear of yet another heroic mother of children.[26] This narrative concerns a trial in Pergamum, which, according to Eusebius, took place during the persecutions under Marcus Aurelius.[27] While some scholars accept this dating as probable, others hold that we should follow the Latin version in dating the martyrdom of Carpus, Papylus, and Agathonicê to the persecutions under Emperor Decius. I myself agree with Herbert Musurillo's arguments in favor of the Greek as the original version. He sees the Latin text as "merely an abridgement" of this, "with some editorial additions."[28] One significant difference between the two versions is the use of the titles "bishop" and "deacon" in the Latin text, where Carpus is called the bishop of Gordos and Pamphilus (a Latinization of the Greek name) is described as a deacon. The interesting question in our present context is not the date of this text, but the picture it draws of Agathonicê.

In the Greek version, she is one of the onlookers. Nailed to a stake and about to be burnt alive, Carpus declares that he has seen the glory of the Lord and that he now rejoices. Immediately after his death, we are introduced to Agathonicê: the narrator says that after she, like Carpus, has seen the glory of the Lord, she experiences this as a vocation from God. She comes forward and says: "Here is a meal that has been prepared for me. I must partake and eat of this glorious repast!"[29] The mob seems horrified by her wish, and—like Perpetua's father—they appeal to her to think of her child: "The mob shouted out: 'Have pity on your son!'" As with Perpetua, this exhortation has no effect. She replies: "'He has God who can take pity on him; for he has providence over all. Let me do what I've come for!' And taking off her cloak, she threw herself joyfully upon the stake."[30] The flames immediately reach her body, and she cries out three times: "Lord, Lord, Lord, assist me! For you are my refuge."[31] The Greek version portrays Agathonicê as one who freely chose death. Unlike Papylus and Carpus, she was not threatened with martyrdom if she refused to sacrifice to the idols; she was not confronted with the choice between denying her faith and suffering death. She herself chose death in order to realize what she experienced as a vocation from God,[32] and this entailed freely leaving her child. The mob's cry that she must think of her son implies a criticism of her lack of maternal responsibility—a mother must take care of her child. Agathonicê's reply that God will look after him, at first, appears irresponsible, a kind of "spiritualization" of the situation, but she (or the author) may have in mind the church's well-organized system for caring for the poor and needy. According to Eusebius, there were "over fifteen hundred widows and persons in distress" in the church in Rome c. 250, "all of whom the grace and kindness of the Master nourish."[33] As with Perpetua and Felicity, this narrative signals that Agathonicê was sure someone would look after her child.

In the Latin version, Agathonicê is one of the martyrs: here, she is condemned to death for refusing to sacrifice to the idols. This redactional change from the Greek version may hint at shock over Agathonicê's apparently free embrace of death. When she is portrayed as a martyr, her action becomes noble and she joins the group of other Christian heroes who show what correct behavior is in times of persecution. In the Latin version, too, she is urged to think of her children (unlike the Greek version, where she has only one child); this is one element in the attempt to persuade her to sacrifice to the idols:[34]

> While the crowd cried out to her: "Have pity on yourself and on your children (*Miserere tibi et filiis tuis*)," the proconsul said: "Look to yourself; have pity on yourself and on your children, as the crowd cries." Agathonicê answered: "My children have God, who watches over them. But I will not obey your commands, nor will I sacrifice to demons."

We also find examples of parents who urge their children not to deny the faith, but instead to suffer martyrdom along with them. In the narrative of the passion of Sophia and her daughters, she exhorts them, since they will soon stand face to face with the persecutor, not to "look . . . at the childishness of your years," but rather to clothe themselves with "heavenly armour" and "place a crown upon your mother by your endurance."[35] When she sees one of her daughters roasted in a frying pan with her breasts cut off, the mother continues to encourage her to show strength in bearing witness to the One who sets them free.[36] Sophia admonishes her daughters to hold out until the end, and becomes joyful when they have attained the crown of martyrdom. After the first one had been killed, her mother "came joyfully, and embraced the body of the noble woman, and kissed her, and she praised God with a joyful heart."[37] This *passio* undoubtedly includes legendary elements, as we see in the daughters' names: Pistis (faith), Elpis (hope), and Agape (love); but this does not make it irrelevant to our present theme.[38] The decisive point is that it was Christians who presented Sophia as an ideal, as a woman to be admired and looked up to. The degree to which the narrative is a literary construction is less important.

In book 10 of his *Peristephanon* ("On the crown of martyrdom"), the Christian poet Prudentius (c. 348–c. 405) writes in a mixture of poetry and prose about the martyrdom of the holy deacon Romanus, which took place in Antioch in 303.[39] In the course of his trial, a little boy, "not long weaned," and his mother were brought forward.[40] Romanus is given permission to ask the little child, who still has "the natural understanding," what is more reasonable: to adore the one Christ, and through him the one God, or else to adore an endless number of gods as the pagans do. The boy answers, without a trace of doubt in his voice, that Christ is the one true God, and he adds that not even a child supposes that many gods exist. After the boy says that it was his mother who had taught him to speak in this way, the prefect Asclepiades decides to punish the mother by forcing her to see her child tortured and killed: she would find this a greater punishment than if she herself were tortured to death.[41]

The prefect's assistants immediately begin to torture the boy, whipping him until he is drenched in blood. All who see him are deeply moved—even the torturers—and no eye remains dry. The only one to show no sign of sorrow is the boy's mother: on the contrary, her face is radiant with joy for, as Prudentius asserts, "in the heart of the pious piety is the stronger force and from the love of Christ stands firm and unyielding in the face of pain, fortifying the emotion of tender fondness."[42] The explanation of her reaction is that she is a woman of God, filled with the love of Christ.

The mother exhorts her son to hold firm and not to show any weakness. When he cries out in pain and asks for a little water, she sees this as a sign that he is yielding, and cries out: "I suppose, my son, you are upset by a weak fear and the dread of the pain casts you down and overcomes you. This is not what I promised God the child of my body would be, this is not the hope of glory for which I bore you, that you should be able to retreat before death!"[43] Instead of water, she encourages him to drink from the spring of life, and tells him plainly that he will soon reach this spring of water, if he longs from the depths of his heart to see Christ: "This, my son, is the cup you now must drink."[44] Thousands of babies in Bethlehem cared nothing for milk; their bitter drink, that is, their bloody death, became life for them. In the same way, she now urges the boy to do the same: "Strive after this example, my brave boy, my noble child, your mother's greatness. The Father has ordained that all ages should be capable of courageous deeds, no time excepted, for He grants triumphs even to infancy."[45] She also reminds him of all the times she has told the story of Abraham and Isaac, emphasizing that when Isaac saw the sword and the altar where he was to be offered in sacrifice, "of his own will he stretched out his neck" to his father.[46] She also recalls the Maccabean martyrs, and the steadfastness of the seven sons, underscoring that their mother supported them and encouraged them to die for their faith. Just as those seven sons became a blessing for their mother, now she is to be blessed through her own son:

"That one birth shall make me fruitful in glory, it lies in your hands, my life, to secure."[47] Finally, she exhorts him to be "steadfast and maintain the cause of Him" who is the source of the boy's life and of the blessings in which he has come to share through his mother's care for him. "You will do well if you restore to the giver that which He gave."[48]

Her exhortations have the desired effect: the boy begins to laugh when they strike him. This provokes the judge, and the boy is taken away to the place where he is to be beheaded. When he leaves his mother to go to the executioner, she does not weep, but kisses him and says: "Farewell, my sweetest, and when in blessedness you enter Christ's kingdom, remember your mother, changing from son to patron." While he is being beheaded, she sings from the Book of Psalms: "Precious is the death of a holy one in the sight of God; he is thy servant, the son of thine handmaid."[49] When the boy's head falls from his body, she takes it and holds it to her tender breast.[50] This is the close of the narrative; the final remark is clearly intended to show that the mother loved her son.

She loved him—and yet there can be no doubt that Prudentius portrays the mother as a model of faith and obedience. Despite her love for her son, she exhorts him to be strong and steadfast, since there was something he would reach after death that was more valuable than life here on earth—to be united with Christ. Besides this, by becoming a martyr, her son could help ensure her eternal salvation: he is no longer her son, but her patron.

We find an example of the opposite attitude in Origen's mother.[51] Eusebius of Caesarea tells us that the young Origen, inspired by a large number of Christians who had won "the crown of martyrdom," was eager to die a martyr's death, and consciously sought out conflicts and dangerous situations. His mother initially sought to change his mind by appealing to her own maternal feelings; but when Origen heard that his father had been arrested and put in prison, he was all the more eager to follow in the martyrs' footsteps. According to Eusebius, the only strategy available to his mother was to hide her son's clothes, thus compelling him to stay at home. The boy wrote a letter to his father, encouraging him in strong terms to accept martyrdom: "Take heed not to change your mind on our account." Nothing suggests that Origen's mother was opposed to martyrdom as such; she simply did not want her young son to join the ranks of the martyrs. Eusebius sees her intervention to prevent Origen from becoming a martyr as an expression of "heavenly Providence." Nevertheless, it is interesting to note that he presents the boy's wish for martyrdom as an example of his "youthful wisdom and of his genuine love for piety."

We have other evidence of parents who left their children in order to realize the ideal religious life.[52] Let us begin with the most extreme example, where a man is willing to kill his only son in order to become a monk:[53]

> A Theban once came to abba Sisoes, wanting to become a monk. The old man asked him whether he had anyone in the world. He said, "I have a son." The old man said to him, "Go, throw him into the river, and then you shall be a monk." When he went off to throw him in, the old man sent a brother to stop him. The brother said, "Stop: what are you doing?" He said, "The abba told me to throw him in." So the brother said, "But now he has told you not to." He left him and went to the old man, and he became a proven monk because of his obedience.

Abba Sisoes certainly did not mean the father to drown his child; Gillian Clark suggests that he may have meant to make it clear that one who has family obligations cannot combine this life with that of a monk, since the two are mutually exclusive. However, if this is what Sisoes meant, the man misunderstood him. He went off to drown his son, clearly believing that he ought to obey the orders of a man of God like Sisoes, even if that meant taking the life of his own child. We should note that this man is not reproached in any way for having misunderstood Sisoes, or for his willingness to kill the boy. On the contrary, his obedience led to his acceptance as a monk.[54] In other words, this nameless man was willing to kill his son in order to lead the perfect divine life, and we are told that he was rewarded for this attitude.

We are told that Simeon the Mountaineer, in the course of the evangelization and instruction of a village, took a third of the children and founded two monastic communities in which they were the core members. When they were taken from their parents, some of the children wept, while others were silent. Only two families refused to contribute children to Simeon's monasteries—but, we are told, the children in these families died soon afterward.[55] This can only mean that they died as a consequence of their parents' disobedience. Perhaps the majority of families were so terribly poor that they had no real choice; they may have thought that their children would, at any rate, be better off in the church's monasteries than if they remained at home.[56]

Poverty was certainly not the reason why women in the Roman aristocracy abandoned their children for long periods. In the second half of the fourth century, a number of aristocratic women in Rome found inspiration in the ascetic ideals of the monks and hermits in the desert. Marcella and her kinswoman Paula were central figures in this circle of well-off women, which was based originally in the great villas on the Aventine Hill. One group met regularly in Marcella's house, another in Paula's, but they kept in contact: "Paula and her group spent each day in Marcella's house praying, studying, reciting the psalms and learning from Marcella the principles of the ascetic life."[57] These women tried, as it were, to transform their prosperous homes into a "desert" where the ascetic ideals of the monks and hermits might be realized: the ascetic life of the wilderness was adopted in Rome's finest residential district. One result was that they refused to marry, or to remarry when widowed. Jerome was invited to Marcella's home to give instruction in sacred scripture, and a close friendship developed between him and the women in this circle, especially Paula. He writes: "Our studies brought about constant intercourse, this soon ripened into intimacy, and this, in turn, produced mutual confidence."[58] He became an important guide and source of inspiration for these circles, but one should note that it was not Jerome who took the initiative in introducing asceticism to women in the aristocracy. This was Marcella's work.[59]

Some members of this network of wealthy aristocratic women traveled, for one reason or another, to the Holy Land. Melania the Elder was widowed at the age of twenty-two. She had had several abortions or miscarriages, and two of her sons died shortly after their father. Early in the 370s, she resolved to leave behind her only surviving son in Rome and to go on pilgrimage to Egypt and Palestine, where she founded a double monastery (for men and women) on the Mount of Olives. She returned to Italy c. 400; this means that she was absent at least twenty-five years. We do not know how old her son, Valerius Publicola, was when his mother departed from Rome. Paulinus of Nola, a relative with ascetic ideals whom Melania visited on her way back from Palestine, says that the boy was a baby when she left him. Jerome expresses his admiration and praises her decision to go away from her child: "She loved her child by neglecting him and kept him by relinquishing him. By commending him to the Lord she was to possess him in absence more firmly than she would have embraced him in person if she had entrusted him to herself."[60] He compares her attitude with that shown by Abraham when he was ready to offer Isaac in sacrifice. This indicates that Melania loved her son and that it was a sacrifice to leave him behind in Rome; nevertheless, bearing in mind the intention behind her travels, she did what was right.

The traditions concerning Valerius Publicola do not agree on his age. Other sources say that she did not leave him until he had set his foot on the first rungs of his public career.[61] But no matter what is historically correct, it is interesting in our present context that Paulinus of Nola assumes that the boy was still a baby and that Melanias's decision to set out on her journey was noble.

In the mid-380s, it was Paula's turn to set out for the Holy Land. A number of reasons seem to have motivated her. First, she had done her duty and at last had given her family a son, after first bearing four daughters. Second, she had just become a widow, and there was now no husband who could refuse her permission to travel. Last but not least, her close friend and spiritual director, Jerome, had been forced to leave Rome after coming into conflict with the clergy of the capital, and had traveled to Jerusalem a short time before. When Paula's daughter Blesilla was widowed only seven months after her marriage, Jerome had been in touch with her and had successfully persuaded her to begin to lead an ascetic life under his direction. However, her asceticism went beyond all bounds, and she died only three months after coming under Jerome's "direction." Understandably enough, his methods were criticized, and he did not make things any easier for himself when he wrote a letter to console Paula after her daughter's funeral.[62] There is no reason to doubt his affirmation that he is filled with grief and that he wept while writing his letter. Nevertheless, he says that there is no reason to grieve, since Blesilla is now with Christ; it is the devil who prompts Paula's tears, seeking thereby to draw her away from God. "Too great affection towards one's children is disaffection towards God," he says, and recalls that "Abraham gladly prepares to slay his only son." He accuses Paula of shedding "detestable tears, sacrilegious tears, unbelieving tears."[63] The clergy criticized Jerome so vehemently that he left the city.[64] Paula, however, clearly retained confidence in her friend and spiritual guide, and perhaps she even found a kind of consolation and encouragement in his letter. At any rate, she left her children and her friends in Rome, and was reunited with Jerome in Jerusalem. With the help of Paula's money, they jointly founded a number of monasteries in Bethlehem, which Paula governed until she died in 404.

Paula left her children behind when she set out on her journey. Jerome describes the farewell on the quay at Ostia in terms that say much about his understanding of the ascetic life and about the priorities that could guide a mother's actions in relation to her children, in order to lead this life:[65]

Not to prolong the story, she went down to Portus accompanied by her brother, her kinsfolk and above all her own children eager by their demonstrations of affection to overcome their loving mother. At last the sails were set and the strokes of the rowers carried the vessel into the deep. On the shore little Toxotius [Paula's youngest child] stretched forth his hands in entreaty, while Rufina, now grown up, with silent sobs besought her mother to wait till she should be married. But still Paula's eyes were dry as she turned them heavenwards; and she overcame her love for her children by her love for God. She knew herself no more as a mother, that she might approve herself a handmaid of Christ. Yet her heart was rent within her, and she wrestled with her grief, as though she were being forcibly separated from parts of her self. The greatness of the affection she had to overcome made all admire her victory the more. Among the cruel hardships which attend prisoners of war in the hands of their enemies, there is none severer than the separation of parents from their children. Though it is against the law of nature, she endured this trial with unabated faith; nay more she sought it with a joyful heart: and overcoming her love for children by her greater love for God. . . . No mother, it must be confessed, ever loved her children so dearly.

Jerome himself was not present in Ostia, and it is not easy to assess the accuracy of the details in this narrative. It is however reasonable to suppose that Paula told Jerome about how she had taken leave of her children, when they were reunited in Jerusalem, so it is certainly possible that the scene described in this letter has a historical core. It is not difficult to imagine that the children would have reacted as Jerome writes, nor that it was hard for Paula to leave her children. And yet the fact remains: Paula left a little child behind in Rome, in order to lead what she believed to be the correct Christian life.

Jerome has doubtless colored the story in order to emphasize the heroic dimension of Paula's choice. The tension between Paula's love for her children and her love of God runs right through this departure scene. By underscoring her love of her children, he signals that she was a good mother who took care of them; at the same time, this functions in Jerome's rhetoric to increase her heroism. Paula's love for her children was great, but she loved God even more. Jerome is aware that Paula faced a conflict between her role as mother and her call to lead a life of perfect religious devotion.

She chose the latter, and Jerome believed that this made her admirable. We do not know whether, in fact, many people shared his view; at any rate, Jerome expects or assumes that Paula's daughter Eustochium, who took over the government of the monasteries after her mother's death, will do so.[66]

Loving Children and God

We have seen that in some early Christian circles, the ideals about how a life of perfect devotion should be led came into conflict with parents' duty to care for their children. In view of the persecutions that were a genuine risk until the time of Constantine, Tertullian advised against having children at all. He was afraid that the ties linking parents to their children might lead them to deny the faith. At the same time, we must emphasize that these warnings must been seen in connection with his ideals with regard to celibacy and sexual abstinence.

The martyrdoms of Perpetua, Felicity, and Agathonicê (in the Greek version of the *Martyrdom of Saints Carpus, Papylus, and Agathonicê*) are examples of the opposite attitude: these mothers did not give way under persecution (as Tertullian feared). Although they had small children, they held fast to their confession of faith in Jesus Christ, and died for this faith. They chose to leave this life—and thereby, to leave their children—in order to reach the divine life. However, the texts reflect a tension between responsibility for one's children and accepting martyrdom for one's faith, as we see when other characters in the narratives urge Perpetua and Agathonicê to bear in mind the needs of their children. Many passages in the story of Perpetua indicate her strong feelings for her child. These women are not portrayed as irresponsible mothers, indifferent to the future that awaits their children; the texts signal their certainty that others will look after the children when they themselves are dead. Although there is a clear tension between maternal love and martyrdom, the sources tell us even more clearly that those mothers who remain steadfast and accept death for the sake of their faith have made the right choice. Like all the martyrs, they are presented as persons filled with the Holy Spirit, heroes of the faith, and examples whom other Christians ought to admire and look up to.

In the Greek version of the *Martyrdom of Saints Carpus, Papylus, and Agathonicê*, we encounter something striking: here, Agathonicê is not one of those who were taken captive because of their faith, but is one of the onlookers. Apparently, she goes voluntarily to her death after receiving a vision. Like the other martyrs, she also is driven by an intense desire to be united with Christ; but the fact that the Latin version includes her among the martyrs may indicate that this kind of voluntary death was seen as unacceptable behavior.

The *passio* of Sophia and her daughters shows us a mother exhorting her daughters to be steadfast in persecution, in order that they may share her martyrdom. Prudentius gives an example of a mother who encourages her son not to display any form of weakness under persecution. She does not ask the torturers to spare the boy, nor does she ask for anything that might lessen his sufferings. On the contrary, Prudentius writes that this nameless woman experiences a kind of joy as she sees the ill-treatment of her son, and she pleads with him, successfully urging him to remain steadfast. Her attitude too is clearly meant to function as an example of strong faith and deep devotion to Christ.

Not everyone left their children behind in such a radical fashion as these mothers who laid down their lives for their faith; but Roman mothers like Melania and Paula found it impossible to combine the role of mother with the realization of their ideals for the Christian life. First, Melania went on pilgrimage to the Holy Land, and at least twenty-five years passed before she returned to Rome. The traditions do not agree on the age of her son when she left him, but one source says he was only a baby. Somewhat later, in the mid-380s, Paula also went to Palestine and never returned to Rome. Her youngest son was very small when she left him, and Jerome describes, in one of his letters, the moving farewell at the harbor in Ostia, where the boy stretched out his arms toward the boat as it left the quay. Paula does indeed struggle against her feelings, but she succeeds in following her perceived vocation without any great emotional distress. She loved her child, but her love of God was greater—as Jerome writes, she overcame "her love for her children by her greater love for God." The strong emphasis on her maternal love has the rhetorical function of underscoring the nobility of her decision to follow God's call: she did so, even though the cost was so great.

We may therefore conclude that conflicts could arise in some circles between being a parent and leading a life of Christian perfection. Parents abandoned their children, either through martyrdom or through setting out on journeys; in a sense, the woman who exhorted her little boy to be steadfast under persecution likewise abandoned him. These women saw the obligation to care for their children daily as a hindrance to the realization of what they perceived as the correct Christian lifestyle. And they are all portrayed as heroines of the faith, as persons filled with the Holy Spirit, who follow God's will.

In our context, it is less important whether the details in these narratives are historically accurate. They may to a greater or lesser degree be literary constructions, but the point remains these texts were written by Christians who believed that the conduct they describe was noble.

A modern reader will find that the ideal reflected in these texts seems strange and almost incomprehensible. How is it possible to understand or explain such behavior?[67] Let me suggest a few pointers. First, we must never underestimate the significance of the fact that the early Christians lived long before the Enlightenment and the subsequent process of secularization in the West. God was the ultimate reality, and the world was a battlefield where human beings were influenced and ruled by God or by his adversary, the devil. When reality was understood in this way, it was supremely important to obey God's will, thereby ensuring that one attained eternal salvation; it is in this context we must read the texts about the martyrs. Martyrdom was not to be sought, but a person who was persecuted because of his faith and was confronted with the choice between denying the faith and dying was seen as one specially chosen by God. Such persons were filled with the Holy Spirit, who gave them the strength to endure—although the cost was high. The one who remained firm to the end received an eternal reward and was united with Christ forever, but apostasy entailed eternal punishment. The struggle to remain steadfast was a struggle against the devil and the demons.[68] This understanding of reality and this theology provide the framework within which we must attempt to understand the decisions taken by Perpetua, Felicity, and Agathonicê to abandon their children and die as martyrs. The *passio* of Perpetua emphasizes the strong ties that bound her to her child, who meant a great deal to her. But there was one thing even more important—obedience to the God who had chosen her to suffer for her faith. Perpetua's obedience would be rewarded with eternal salvation.

I believe that it is in the same context that we must interpret the story of the woman who displays a kind of joy or satisfaction when her little boy is tortured and joins the ranks of the martyrs, since she sees this as confirmation that he has been chosen by God, and she is certain that he will be united with Christ forever. The text also indicates her belief that he will now be able to function as her patron, helping her to attain eternal bliss.

These women were persecuted for their faith, and were forced to choose between offering sacrifice to the gods or being killed, but what of Melania and Paula? They were not faced with such a choice. They could have continued to practice their ascetically inspired Christianity while at the same time taking care of their children. I believe that their priorities must be understood within the framework of a theology and a perception of reality in which the all-important goal was eternal salvation, and everything else was subordinate to this. This theology made it imperative to realize that what one believed was God's call for one's life. Should there be any conflict, love for God had priority over love for one's children.

The primary explanation of the conduct of parents who abandoned their children is therefore theological: it is a question of how the implicit ideals for a life of Christian devotion are to be put into practice. Other factors, more sociological and societal, can also play a role. When Melania and Paula traveled to the Holy Land, they were liberated from all family obligations.[69] They lived more freely, and could use all their time to "realize themselves." In the case of Paula, we may speculate whether her close friendship with Jerome played a decisive role in her decision.

Finally, we must emphasize that our sources do not present many examples of parents who abandoned their children in order to live out their ideals for a Christian life. Perpetua and Felicity probably belonged to Montanist circles, while Melania and Paula were members of a relatively small milieu of aristocratic women in Rome. We know nothing about the social class or Christian circles to which the others belonged. This may have been a marginal phenomenon found primarily in radical ascetic groups.

8

EARLY CHRISTIANS AND THE HUMANITY
OF CHILDREN

What did Christians in the first five centuries of the church's history think about children's nature and qualities? How did they treat children, and what did they say about the way children ought to be treated? These are the two principal questions I have investigated in this book; an underlying question on which we have frequently touched is whether Christianity made any changes to the way adults in the Greco-Roman world customarily thought about children and treated them. In the introduction, I wrote that a broad approach is necessary, if we are to get the fullest possible picture of children, with all the nuances our sources indicate. What is the outcome of this investigation?

Since each chapter contains relatively detailed summaries, I limit myself here to a brief presentation of some of the most significant results. Although very few sources focus primarily on aspects related to children, I hope that our investigation has shown that early Christian literature offers more information about children than might have been expected. Naturally, the fact that virtually all of our informants are men who belonged to a spiritual elite raises the question whether their viewpoints and attitudes are representative of the majority of Christians. Besides this, many affirmations about children occur in what we might call argumentative texts, that is, in situations where the author is attempting to persuade his readers to accept particular ideals and behavioral patterns. Since much of the source material is prescriptive rather than descriptive, we must be cautious about making direct inferences from the ideals communicated in the texts to actual societal life. This is why I have often limited myself to a discussion of the ideals that are reflected in the texts. However, even if this approach makes the question of the historicity in the authors' words less vital, it remains true that there must have been at least some points of contact between the ideals in the text and the ideals of the readers, if the authors were to have any chance of persuading the readers to adopt specific ideals and behavioral patterns. And even if it is difficult to estimate how representative our sources are, it is nevertheless worthwhile to investigate the view of children and childhood put forward by the church's leaders and theologians.

Although the sources give more information about our subject than we might have expected, we may still wish that a greater number of the church fathers had written specifically about childhood. The nature of our sources makes it impossible to present a complete picture of the ideas early Christians had about children, of their ideals with regard to the treatment of children, or of how they actually did treat them. Our investigation has shown that we can reconstruct fragments of such a picture. If we put these pieces together, we can certainly say something about how the whole picture must have looked.

With regard to the nature and typical characteristics of children, all the Eastern sources that touch on this question emphasize that small children are innocent, or at least in a morally neutral state, as we can see in their lack of sexual desire, their obedience to their parents, and their lack of interest in wealth or in positions associated with honor and status in this world. We are told that it was these qualities in children that led Jesus to propose them as examples for adult conduct. In the West, a striking discontinuity occurred at the beginning of the fifth century with regard to the idea of children's innocence. In the course of the Pelagian controversy, where anthropology was a central battlefield, Augustine developed a theological defense of the doctrine of original sin. He emphasized that children enter a world marked by original sin, and that they are not innocent. This emphasis is linked to the fact that the doctrine of original sin was necessary, if the idea of God's justice was to be maintained: for if children do not share in original sin and hence are innocent, God is unjust when he punishes them with suffering and death.

The Eastern tradition also holds that passion or desire emerges in children while they are still very small. This makes it essential to form children from a tender age, so that they will live in accordance with Christian ideals. Children are moral individuals who become more responsible for their actions as the *logos* (word, speech, reason) grows within them. They are also portrayed as religious subjects who must build up their own relationship to God; it is taken for granted that they have the presuppositions necessary for practicing a comprehensive life of religious devotion. This, however, does not mean that children's religious and moral individuality is valuable per se. They are regarded as a kind of raw material that the parents must grind, clean, and polish so that their children will one day live in accordance with Christian ideals. We find the clearest expression of this view in Jerome, who concurs with Cicero's words that a child deserves praise, not so much for what it is now, but for what it will become in the future.

This apparently negative view of children is balanced, however, by some other aspects, above all by the idea that it was God who created children and that he saves them just as he saves adults. One reflection of this conviction is the fact that children usually received baptism in a wide geographical area, at least from the first half of the third century onward (and probably much earlier), with the exception of some decades in the fourth century; another reflection is the practice of children's communion in the same period. Children need the same salvific gifts God gives adults, and they have the same capacity to receive them. There is no difference between children and adults, as far as their relationship to God is concerned. While the society in which children lived tended not to see a newborn baby as a complete human being, the church fathers' thinking implies that newborn children were complete human beings from birth onward. Cyprian says that one who has been formed by God in his mother's womb lacks nothing. Augustine sees no contradiction between maintaining the reality of original sin on the one hand, and speaking positively of children's value and qualities on the basis of creation theology on the other. Creation theology was also used as an argument against abortion and the exposure of children.

Parents are admonished in the New Testament to give their children a Christian upbringing, and such exhortations were intensified from the third century onward. Indeed, our sources state that parents' salvation depends on their showing sufficient commitment to this task, or—even more radically—on their success in bring up their children in the Christian faith, so that they live as adults in keeping with the moral ideals inherent in this faith. This means that parents are held responsible for their children's sins. John Chrysostom elaborates a number of theological arguments in support of parents' obligation to form or socialize their children into the patterns appropriate to a Christian life. For example, he points to the central idea in biblical ethics that one must love one's neighbor—and children are their parents' closest "neighbor." The idea underlying such arguments is that nothing is more important than the salvation of one's soul; everything else is subordinate to this. The basic contents in upbringing are the reading of scripture, hymn singing, prayer, and exhortations to live in keeping with Christian ideals. When the children are a little older, fasting and vigils are added to this. A constant element in upbringing is the need for social control: children, especially once they reach puberty, are to be isolated as far as possible from the pagan environment, so that they may not be exposed to negative influence from their non-Christian friends or from public gatherings (such as the theater), which promote paganism and immorality. Another important aspect of upbringing is the need to isolate young people by gender, or hold them back from situations where sexual desire might be kindled. Several sources encourage parents to employ corporal punishment to obtain the desired conduct. Another prominent aspect is the importance of providing good role models for children. This applies to all who spend time with them—servants, *paidagôgoi* (teachers), and friends. Last but not least: parents must live in such a way that their children see how a Christian life is meant to be led. Thus parents will be good models for them.

We have, however, also seen that some circles held that it was impossible to combine the practice of a perfect life of religious devotion with parental responsibility with regard to raising one's children. This view can find expression in a generally negative attitude to procreation, as in Tertullian, who worried that the ties linking parents to their children would prevent them from holding fast to the faith under persecution and from suffering martyrdom, if that should be required. Perpetua and Felicity, women from Montanist circles, are examples of mothers of small children who held fast to their confession of faith in Christ and died as martyrs. The same is true of Agathonicê in the Latin version of the *Martyrdom of Saints Carpus, Papylus, and Agathonicê*. Other mothers exhorted their children to show endurance under persecution and to suffer martyrdom. Melania and Paula abandoned their underage children to travel on pilgrimage to the Holy Land, where both women founded monasteries. At least twenty-five years passed before Melania returned home to Italy, while Paula governed the monasteries until her death. Although this detail is not given equal prominence in all these stories of women who, in various ways, left their children behind in order to realize a life of Christian perfection, it is striking to note that several texts either imply or state explicitly that these mothers loved their children—but their love for Christ was greater. Their readiness to follow what they perceived as God's will, even when this entailed abandoning their children so that they might suffer martyrdom or go on pilgrimage, is portrayed as noble and exemplary.

The authors take it for granted that their readers will admire this kind of conduct. Although we must emphasize that these ideals seem to be restricted to radical ascetic groups, the fact remains that women in some of these elite Christian circles did in fact abandon their children, either by martyrdom or by pilgrimage, and that their actions are presented as noble and admirable.

Did the Christian religion introduce attitudes toward children that differed from those prevalent in the Greco-Roman environment? In many ways, I would say that Christianity continued conventional ideas in the contemporary cultural milieu, not least with regard to children's place in the social structure of the family, where obedience to one's parents was a central point. Another important factor is the fact that Christian parents continued to send their children to the classical schools, where they received the traditional education. Christian sources do not present children's characteristics and qualities as something valuable per se, nor do they in any way accept children and their qualities on their own terms, with the one exception of texts that present children as models for adults in the sense mentioned above. Although children took part in worship and received the sacraments, and hence had the same basic relationship to God as adults, they were marginal actors in the life of the Christian fellowship—just as in Greco-Roman society in general.

Nevertheless, it seems that some differences did exist, with fundamental consequences for children's lives. I have mentioned that one consequence of the idea of God as Creator was that early Christians, unlike the Greco-Roman tradition, saw children as complete human beings from the time of their birth. Even more importantly, belief in the Creator, which entailed obedience to the commandment not to kill, was used as an argument in support of the unambiguous condemnation of abortion and *expositio* that we find in the Christian texts. Children who were exposed either died or were taken care of by others, usually with the intention of using them as slaves later on. Although this cannot be verified in our sources, it is reasonable to assume that this condemnatory attitude meant that abortion, and especially *expositio,* occurred less frequently among Christians than among others. In other words, a child born into a Christian household had a greater chance of actually growing up in that household than a child born into a pagan household.

Another change that came in the wake of Christianity was a great reduction in the number of children (especially boys) who were involved in sexual acts with adult men. A long tradition of pederasty, that is, intercourse between boys and men, existed in Greco-Roman antiquity, where this was seen as normal or natural sex, since the fundamental dichotomy in people's understanding of human sexuality was not heterosexual/homosexual, but active/passive. It was also relatively common for boys and girls to be put to work as prostitutes. As ascetic ideals gradually gained ground in the church, a very restrictive view of the proper framework for living out sexual desire emerged. The ideal was to abstain from sex; marriage was a second-best solution for those who could not live up to this ideal, but even within marriage, the only legitimate way to live out sexual desire was linked to procreation. One consequence of this was the condemnation of all other forms of sexual relationships. Although the starting point was not a consideration of what was best for children, Christian sexual ethics meant that children were much less exposed to what we today would call sexual abuse than was generally the case in the Greco-Roman world.

I have already noted that many of our sources strongly exhort parents to take seriously their obligation to bring up their children to lead a Christian life; one method they recommend, if this is to succeed, is the use of physical force. The educational ideal represented in these texts seems to encourage parents to employ corporal punishment to a greater extent than was suggested by the Greco-Roman ideal of the *bonus paterfamilias* (good father). The most obvious explanation is that Christians believed that nothing less than eternal salvation was at stake here. Apart from the question of educational methods, Christianity also entailed substantial changes in what was taught. We do not know to what extent the ideas of a John Chrysostom about upbringing corresponded to the de facto praxis of Christian parents, but it is reasonable to suppose that the religious and moral formation of Christian children differed from that given to children in pagan households.

Another element worth noting is that the Christian texts that discuss upbringing mainly assign the responsibility for the practical aspects of this task to the parents, implying the ideal of a greater involvement in upbringing than was generally the case in pagan families in antiquity, where (at least in wealthy households) the daily care and upbringing of children were primarily the duties of nurses and other servants. If the ideals our texts present on this point did, in fact, win acceptance in social life, this would have meant that Christian children had more contact with their parents than was customary in antiquity.

The sketch of children and childhood we can reconstruct on the basis of the sources I have examined in this book shows that in certain areas,

Christianity introduced new anthropological viewpoints, a new ethical evaluation, and new ideals for upbringing. All of this had effects on the societal life of children.

Using a broad approach, I have attempted to reconstruct a holistic picture of the way early Christians thought about children. The limitation of this approach is that it is not possible to study the material in depth at those points where the source material invites us to take a closer look. Much work remains to be done in this area, both in investigating specific topics in greater depth and in examining other aspects relevant to children, for example, children in the monastic tradition. And it would certainly be fruitful to spread the nets wider, taking in inscriptions and perhaps also iconographic material. Research into children in early Christianity is only just beginning. It is my modest hope that this book may stimulate others to do further work on questions related to children and childhood in early Christianity.

NOTES

1. Introduction

1. See for example Aristotle, *Pol.* 1336b, and Karl Olav Sandnes, *Med Homer i Sekken* (Oslo, 2003).

2. For a review of the increasing focus on children in a number of disciplines, see Scott Heller, "The Meaning of Children Becomes a Focal Point of Scholars," *Chronicle of Higher Education* 7 (August 1998): A14–16; Marcia J. Bunge, "Introduction," in *The Child in Christian Thought* (Grand Rapids, Mich.: Eerdmans, 2001), 1–3.

3. See for example, Gareth Matthews, *Philosophy and the Young Child* (Cambridge, Mass.: Harvard University Press, 1980); Gareth Matthews, *The Philosophy of Childhood* (Cambridge, Mass.: Harvard University Press, 1994); Michael S. Pritchard, *On Becoming Responsible* (Lawrence: University Press of Kansas, 1985).

4. For literature, see Bunge, "Introduction," *The Child in Christian Thought*, 2.

5. For literature, see ibid., 2–3.

6. Philippe Ariès, *L'Enfant et la vie familiale sous l'ancien régime* (1960), English translation by R. Baldick, *Centuries of Childhood* (New York: Vintage, 1962).

7. See for example Linda A. Pollock, *Forgotten Children: Parent-Child Relations from 1500 to 1900* (Cambridge: Cambridge University Press, 1983); Shulamith Shahar, *Childhood in the Middle Ages*, trans. Chaya Galai (London: Routledge, 1990); Hugh Cunningham, *Children and Childhood in Western Society since 1500* (London: Longman, 1995); Louis Haas, *The Renaissance Man and His Children: Childbirth and Early Childhood in Florence, 1300–1600* (New York: St. Martin's, 1998).

8. See for examples, M. Bunge, "Introduction," in *The Child in Christian Thought*, 2. See also H. Cunningham, "Histories of Childhood," *The American Historical Review* 103 (1998): 1195–1208.

9. Here I mention some of the major contributions and also some of the most recent. Monograph-size studies include: James Casey, *The History of the Family* (Oxford: Blackwell, 1989); Thomas Wiedemann, *Adults and Children in the Roman Empire* (London: Routledge, 1989); Mark Golden, *Childhood in Classical Athens* (Baltimore: Johns Hopkins University Press, 1990). Children and childhood feature prominently in several studies on family in antiquity; e.g., Keith R. Bradley, *Discovering the Roman Family: Studies in Roman Social History* (New York: Oxford University Press, 1991); Beryl Rawson, *The Family in Ancient Rome: New Perspectives* (Ithaca, N.Y.: Cornell University Press, 1986); Beryl Rawson, ed., *Marriage, Divorce, and Children in Ancient Rome* (Oxford: Clarendon, 1991), contains several articles in which children and childhood constitute the main theme; Suzanne Dixon, *The Roman Family* (Baltimore: Johns Hopkins University Press, 1992), especially pp. 98–159; Richard P. Saller, *Patriarchy, Property, and Death in the Roman Family* (Cambridge: Cambridge University Press, 1994). A recent and brief review of the evidence, with relatively

many references both to secondary literature and to primary sources, is offered by Judith M. Gundry-Volf, "The Least and the Greatest: Children in the New Testament," in *The Child in Christian Thought*, ed. Marcia J. Bunge, 31–34. See also S. Scott Bartchy, "Families in the Greco-Roman World" in *The Family Handbook*, ed. Herbert Anderson (Louisville, Ky.: Westminster John Knox, 1988), 282–86.

10. Bunge, "Introduction," in *The Child in Christian Thought*, 3–4. Bunge correctly notes that "until very recently, issues related to children have tended to be marginal in almost every area of contemporary theology. For example, systematic theologians and Christian ethicists have said little about children, and they have not regarded serious reflections on children as a high priority. What Todd Whitmore has claimed about the Catholic Church can be applied to Christian theology in general: there is no well-developed social teaching on the nature of children and why we should care about and for them. Although the church has highly developed teachings on other issues, such as abortion, economic justice, and moral conduct in war, theologians have not offered sustained reflection on the nature of children or on the obligations that parents, the state, and church have to nurture children."

11. Simon Légasse, *Jésus et L'Enfant: "Enfant," "Petits" et "Simples" dans la Tradition Synoptique* (Paris: Lecoffre, 1969).

12. H. H. Schroeder, *Eltern und Kinder in der Verkündigung Jesu: Eine hermeneutische und exegetische Untersuchung*. Theologische Forschung 53. (Hamburg: Reich. Evang. Verl., 1972).

13. P. Müller, *In der Mitte der Gemeinde: Kinder im Neuen Testament* (Neukirchen-Vluyn: Neukirchener, 1992).

14. Peter Balla, *The Child-Parent Relationship in the New Testament and Its Environments*, WUNT 155 (Tübingen: Mohr Siebeck, 2003).

15. For example, George R. Beasley-Murray, "Church and Child in the New Testament," *Baptist Quarterly* 21 (1965–66): 206–18; Hans-Ruedi Weber, *Jesus and the Children: Biblical Resources for Study and Preaching* (Atlanta: John Knox, 1979); James Francis, "Children and Childhood in the New Testament," in *The Family in Theological Perspective*, ed. Stephen C. Barton (Edinburgh: T. and T. Clark, 1996); William A. Strange, *Children in the Early Church: Children in the Ancient World, the New Testament and the Early Church* (Carlisle, U.K.: Paternoster, 1996) 1–65; Gundry-Volf, "The Least and the Greatest," 29–60; John T. Carroll, "Children in the Bible," *Interpretation* 55 (2001): 121–34.

16. Dawn DeVries, "Toward a Theology of Childhood," *Interpretation* 55 (2001): 162. Besides a special number of the journal *Theology Today* 56, 4 (January 2000) containing eleven articles discussing Christian understandings of children and childhood, DeVries refers to Bunge, ed., *The Child in Christian Thought*. This collection of fifteen essays has primarily a historical approach, dealing with the understanding of children in the history of Christian thought. Only to a limited degree does this volume discuss how we should think theologically about children today and what consequences a theology of childhood should have for our attitude toward children.

17. Cf. Bunge, *The Child in Christian Thought*, xi.

18. References to these topics will be found in the notes when I deal with the actual topics.

19. English translation: *On Vainglory and the Right Way for Parents to Bring up their Children*, by M. L. Laistner, *Christianity and Pagan Culture in the Later Roman Empire* (Ithaca, N.Y.: Cornell University Press, 1967 [1951]), 85–122.

20. In Wood, *The Church and Childhood*, 1–27.

21. Ibid., 27. This is due to the fact that the hierarchical structure of the household remained intact and that the school continued to teach in the Greco-Roman tradition, following already existing pedagogical methodology. However, Clark points to one area where Christianity made a difference to children. It offers them the radical new option of choosing a single-sex community in a monastery, thereby escaping from the burdens and

obligations of ordinary life. If the child's family opposed this option, the child could get support from the church. Thus the teaching of the church could, in certain circumstances, accept that a child might behave in way contradictory to the will of the parents and in opposition to the traditional household codes. Hence, one can argue that Christianity contributed to a new level of freedom for individuals to follow their own choice. "For some, it [Christianity] offered possibilities which were unimaginable in a pre-Christian world. It offered a radically new option, that of dedicating a life to God and of living it in a single-sex community. It supported children who chose that option despite resistance from their families, and could thus give children an escape-route from their indebtedness to their parents and obedience to family purpose. . . . So children might find at least some of their choices taken seriously; and behaviour which would otherwise have been interpreted as frankly naughty might be acknowledged as prophetic." Clark, "The Fathers and the Children," in *The Church in Childhood,* 26. However, as Clark rightly underscores, it was, of course, only a very small minority of Christian children who chose this radical option.

22. G. Gould, "Childhood in Eastern Patristic Thought: Some Problems of Theology and Theological Anthropology," In *The Church and Childhood,* 39–52.

23. Ibid., 39–40.

24. Strange, *Children in the Early Church,* 2: "To understand the place of children in the New Testament and in the early Church, we need to look at the evidence we have . . . also from non-Christian sources, both Jewish and Gentile, because these will illuminate for us the culture in which the early Christians lived."

25. Sarah Currie, "Childhood and Christianity from Paul to the Council of Chalcedon" (Ph.D. diss., Cambridge University, 1993).

26. Ibid., 225.

27. Blake Leyerle, "Appealing to Children," *Journal of Early Christian Studies* 5 (1997).

28. Ibid., 258–59.

29. Ibid., 265.

30. In Bunge, *The Child in Christian Thought,* 61–77.

31. V. Guroian, "The Ecclesial Family: John Chrysostom on Parenthood and Children" *in The Child in Christian Thought,* 73. Guroian also studies the relationship between Chrysostom's ideas about parenting and his theological anthropology, especially in relation to the doctrine of the *imago dei* (image of God). Chrysostom—in agreement with the common Eastern understanding—argues that the fall of Adam did not affect the essential image of God in man, but "the likeness and capacity to grow in divine similitude has been severely weakened" (p. 68). Through the life and saving work of Jesus Christ, the image of God is purified and brings human beings into community with the divine life. In a manner analogous to the role of Jesus Christ, the divine teacher who instructs all humankind how to grow in the divine likeness, God has intended parents to be natural teachers for their children. According to Chrysostom, parents are assigned the sacred task of the moral and religious formation of their children, thereby helping to restore and refine the image of God in them. An underlying premise for this idea is that Chrysostom "attributes to children complete human status (the image of God). . . . They are God's greatest work, made in his very own image and intended by God to participate in the divine life" (p. 69).

32. In Bunge, *The Child in Christian Thought,* 78–102.

33. M. E. Stortz, "'Where or When Was Your Servant Innocent?'" in *The Child in Christian Thought,* 82.

34. Ibid., 84.

35. Ibid., 85. Stortz summarizes as follows: "The meaning of accountability shifted throughout these three initial stages of the life cycle. While the infant's non-innocence might be judged premoral due to its lack of physical strength, the child's developing language skills conferred both an ability to communicate and increasing accountability for behavior. A child was held accountable if he or she violated a verbal rule—often an

arbitrary one. Adolescence heralded the emergence of reason, and a youth faced even greater accountability for his or her behavior. . . . Greater accountability brought with it a greater sense of guilt. Augustine read into these first three first stages of childhood a certain moral nuance."

36. Ibid., 93.

37. John Chrysostom, *De Inani Gloria et de Educandis Liberis*.

38. On children in the Greco-Roman world, see Chapter 2.

2. Children in the Greco-Roman World

1. See G. Gould, "Childhood in Patristic Thought: Some Problems of Theology and Theological Anthropology" in *The Church and Childhood. Papers read at the 1993 Summer Meeting and the 1994 Winter Meeting of the Ecclesiastical History Society*, ed. Diana Wood (Oxford: Blackwell, 1994), 39.

2. See Thomas Wiedemann, *Adults and Children in the Roman Empire* (London: Routledge, 1989), 21.

3. See ibid., 21–22.

4. Cf. ibid., 22–23.

5. Textual references: Mark Golden, *Childhood in Classical Athens* (Baltimore: Johns Hopkins University Press, 1990), 7.

6. Plato, *Resp.* 4.431C.

7. References: Golden, *Childhood in Classical Athens*, 9.

8. Plato, *Leg.* 2.664E.

9. Ibid., *Leg.* 7.808D.

10. References: Golden, *Childhood in Classical Athens*, 7.

11. Ibid.

12. Ibid.

13. See ibid., 6.

14. Wiedemann, *Adults and Children in the Roman Empire*, 22.

15. Cicero, *Phil.* 13.24, following Wiedemann, *Adults and Children in the Roman Empire*, 22.

16. Wiedemann, *Adults and Children in the Roman Empire*, 22. Wiedemann concludes as follows: "That childishness is foolishness, *pueritia amentia*, is common ground. These are the qualities of non-adults: and we may note that, in both Greece and Rome, 'child' was the standard way of addressing a slave, another individual who could not share in the community of adult citizens."

17. Seneca, *Eps.* 33.7; 118.14. For the idea of children as lacking knowledge, see further Brian C. Daleas, "Children in the Roman World: Status and the Growth of Identity" (PhD dissertation, Indiana University, 1998), 70–72; 126.

18. See Wiedemann, *Adults and Children in the Roman Empire*, 23.

19. I mention only a few examples of such advice: Cato the Elder (second century b.c.e.) recommends that babies be bathed in the warmed-up urine of cabbage eaters, and believes that this will make them stronger. When he gives an account of the properties of spittle, Pliny the Elder advises that a nurse should protect a baby against dangers by spitting on it three times if a stranger enters the room, or if a stranger has looked at the child while it was sleeping. On this, see also Wiedemann, *Adults and Children in the Roman Empire*, 17–18.

20. On this, see Wiedemann, *Adults and Children in the Roman Empire*, 18–20. Wiedemann summarizes as follows: "Consequently the ancient world saw them [i.e. children] not just as examples, but—like women—as symbols of human fear as well as physical frailty" (18).

21. Ibid.

22. Pliny the Elder, *HN* 7.1.2–3.

23. Aristotle, *Eth. Eud.* 2.1219b5; cf. *Pol.* 1.1260a14; 8.1339a30; *Pr.* 10.46.896a19.

24. Cicero, *Rep.* p. 137 ed. Ziegler frag. incert. 5, according to Wiedemann, *Adults and Children in the Roman Empire,* 24. Wiedemann notes: "It was all too well understood that one aspect of children's irrationality was that they were not respecters of social conventions. They would make rude noises at passers-by; they would chase peculiar adults, like Horace's poet, along the streets; they would pluck the beard of a venerable philosopher; and a favourite game would be to stick a coin firmly in the mud, and then wait to see if an adult would try to pick it up." See also Daleas, "Children in the Roman World," 70–72, on the link Cicero makes between children and ignorance, when he criticizes adult behavior as childish.

25. For a discussion and textual references, see Daleas, "Children in the Roman World," 68–70.

26. See ibid., 162–70.

27. We find this subject in literature right up to the fourth century c.e.: see Wiedemann, *Adults and Children in the Roman Empire,* 24. As one example, he quotes Ausonius's congratulation of his grandson on the day he became a *iuvenis* (probably his fifteenth birthday): "This is the time when you are active with the strength of youth, and are able to distinguish brave deeds from weak deeds, and appear as your own adviser in behaviour and speech."

28. Plato, *Leg.* 7.789E, *Resp.* 2.377A–B. Cf. Aristotle, *Pol.*7.1336a10. See also Golden, *Childhood in Classical Athens,* 8–9.

29. Quintilian, *Inst.* 1.1.36.

30. Pseudo-Plutarch, *Mor.* 3E–F.

31. See for example Pseudo-Plutarch, *Mor.* 2B–C, 4C; Lucian, *Anach.* 20; Ps.-Plutarch, 4C. This image is particularly elaborate in the writings of Philo, a Jew who lived in Alexandria in the first half of the first century c.e. See also Theresa Morgan, *Literate Education in the Hellenistic and Roman Worlds* (Cambridge: Cambridge University Press, 1998), 255–61; Karl Olav Sandnes, *Med Homer i Sekken* (Oslo, 2003).

32. Morgan, in *Literate Education in the Hellenistic and Roman Worlds,* 256, says that "the most striking feature of such images, as we have noted, is the largely passive role attributed to the pupil and his consequent lack of self-determination." She points out, however, that "the 'land' has a few independent capacities," and notes that the child's innate cognitive presuppositions play a decisive role in the final result (256–58).

33. Quintilian, *Inst.* 1.3.12; 2.19.1–3.

34. Ibid., 1.12.10. For other terminology in Quintilian implying the idea that the teacher molds his pupils, see Morgan, *Literate Education in the Hellenistic and Roman Worlds,* 259–60.

35. Morgan, *Literate Education in the Hellenistic and Roman Worlds,* 244–61, gives a good introduction to classical thinking about pedagogy.

36. For critical voices, see p. 40.

37. Seneca, *Constant.* 12.3.

38. This is argued by Wiedemann, in *Adults and Children in the Roman Empire,* 27, who also quotes Seneca. How widespread was the use of physical force in education? On this, Wiedemann writes: "The universality of violence in the ancient world, as in most pre-industrial societies, is well attested. . . . It was considered entirely normal for adult Greeks or Romans to beat those whom they could not control through rational discourse, namely children and slaves—slaves, whatever their age, being in a sense children who had not been allowed to grow up."

39. For textual references to Greek antiquity, see Golden, *Childhood in Classical Athens,* 11–12.

40. Sarah Currie, "Childhood and Christianity from Paul to the Council of Chalcedon" (PhD diss., Cambridge University, 1993). Currie notes that "The conception of childhood

as *innocentia* appears to have had a broad-based appeal. Innocence appeared on pagan epitaphs as a positive attribute of deceased children from the second century onwards." For further discussion and reference to the primary sources, see Hans Herter, "Das unschuldige Kind," *Jahrbuch für Antike und Christentum* 4 (1961): 146–58.

41. Wiedemann, *Adults and Children in the Roman Empire*, 19. See also Suzanne Dixon, *The Roman Family* (Baltimore: Johns Hopkins University Press, 1990), 100. Dixon points out that "On the whole, the young child seems to have been of minor interest to the Roman literary class. . . . Childhood is occasionally invoked in a detached and general way by adult authors as a symbol of the uneducated or innocent human, but literary references to children and childhood are relatively few and often vague, revealing little interest in activities of young children for their own sake."

42. In the case of Rome, John E. Stambaugh, in *The Ancient Roman City* (Baltimore: Johns Hopkins University Press, 1988), estimates the population at 302 per acre, while Ramsay MacMullen, in *Roman Social Relations: 50 B.C. to A.D. 284* (New Haven, Conn.: Yale University Press, 1974), reckons on 200 inhabitants per acre. By comparison, fewer than 190 inhabitants per acre live in Mumbai (Bombay) today, and fewer than 130 in Calcutta. See Rodney Stark, *The Rise of Christianity: How the Obscure, Marginal Jesus Movement Became the Dominant Religious Force in the Western World in a Few Centuries* (HarperSanFrancisco: San Francisco, 1997), 150.

43. Jerome Carcopino, in *Daily Life in Ancient Rome* (New Haven, Conn.: Yale University Press, 1940), 42, gives the following description: "There were other poor devils who found their stairs too steep and the road to these dung pits too long, and to save themselves further trouble would empty the contents of their chamber pots from their heights into the streets. So much the worse for the passer-by who happened to intercept the unwelcome gift! Fouled and sometimes even injured, as in Juvenal's satire, he had no redress save to lodge a complaint against the unknown assailant; many passages of the *Digest* indicate that Roman jurists did not disdain to take cognisance of this offense."

44. Stark, *The Rise of Christianity*, 154.

45. Cf. ibid., 155. Stark calls the cities in the Greco-Roman world "a pesthole of infectious disease."

46. Ibid., 155, referring to Arthur E. R. Boak, *Manpower Shortage and the Fall of the Roman Empire in the West* (Ann Arbor: University of Michigan Press, 1955), 14.

47. Stark, *The Rise of Christianity*, 155, with many references to secondary literature.

48. Stambaugh, *The Ancient Roman City*, 137. He emphasizes that, in comparison with modern cities, sickness was much more visibly part of life in the Greco-Roman cities: "Swollen eyes, skin rashes, and lost limbs are mentioned over and over again in the sources as part of the urban scene."

49. On this, see Wiedemann, *Adult and Children in the Roman Empire*, 11–16.

50. Ibid., 16. Wiedemann mentions that, according to Pliny, only three of Cornelia's twelve children survived into adulthood, that three of Agrippina's nine children died, and that some children in the imperial family died so young that they have left no trace in the literary sources. On this last point, see R. Syme, "Neglected Children on the *Ara Pacis*," *American Journal of Archaeology* 88 (1984).

51. See Geoffrey Nathan, *The Family in Late Antiquity: The Rise of Christianity and the Endurance of Tradition* (London: Routledge, 2000), 24.

52. Ibid., 27.

53. See Dixon, *The Roman Family*, 111.

54. See Wiedemann, *Adults and Children in the Roman Empire*, 39–42, for examples of inscriptions and literary sources. See also Dixon, *The Roman Family*, 108.

55. Euripides, *Med.* 1032.

56. This investment perspective is emphasized by Wiedemann, *Adults and Children in the Roman Empire*. He argues, among other things, that "As individuals as well as a community,

classical Romans saw their children primarily as an investment in future security. . . . Two ideas were paramount: that children had the function of looking after their parents in old age in return for the sustenance that their parents had given them as infants; and that the child (normally the son) would bury his parents just as his parents had brought him to life. The idea of reciprocity or repayment can already be found in Homer" (39).

57. See also Dixon, *The Roman Family*, who questions the view of Alan Macfarlane, *Marriage and Love in England: Modes of Reproduction 1300–1800* (1986), with which Wiedemann, in *Adults and Children in the Roman Empire* agrees—that in market societies such as modern England, there is no need to take care of one's own future by having children, since those who live in a market society purchase their own security. This entails a different attitude toward children: they are individuals who receive love and care for their own sake, not because they will later repay a debt. Unlike the majority of parents in antiquity, today's parents need not regard their child as a costly necessity; they tend to see children more as "pets" whom they themselves wish to have.

58. Dio Cassius 56.3.

59. See also Dixon, *The Roman Family*, 111.

60. On this, see Beryl Rawson, "The Roman Family" in *The Family in Ancient Rome: New Perspectives* (Ithaca, N.Y.: Cornell University Press, 1986), 9–11. Augustus issued laws that gave political advantages to men who fathered three or more children, and imposed political and economic sanctions on childless couples; these sanctions applied also to unmarried women over twenty, and unmarried men over twenty-five years of age. Similar legislation had already been issued by Julius Caesar in 59 B.C.E., and most of Augustus's successors made use of these laws in order to promote a higher birthrate. As early as 131 B.C.E., the Roman censor Quintus Caecilius Metellus Macedonicus proposed that the senate should make marriage obligatory, since many men—especially from the higher social groups—preferred to live unmarried. Although these men held that "we cannot have a really harmonious life with our wives," this senator insisted that they must take responsibility for producing future citizens, for the good of the Roman empire. Rawson writes, "One theme that recurs in Latin literature is that wives are difficult and therefore men do not care much for marriage" (11).

61. On this, see Wiedemann, *Adults and Children in the Roman Empire,* 32–33: "Children were also 'successors' in a communal sense: as a new generation of citizens, capable of taking over responsibility for protecting the community in warfare. 'It is good that you have given the country and the Roman people a citizen, if you make sure that he is suitable material for the country, useful in the fields, useful in all the activities of war and peace' [Juvenal, *Satire* 14.70–2]. Analysis of the Latin vocabulary found in republican literature suggests that this was indeed largely how Romans—rich and poor alike—of the second and first centuries perceived their children."

62. Dixon, *The Roman Family*, 111–12.

63. On abortion in pagan antiquity, see for example Gillian Clark, *Women in Late Antiquity: Pagan and Christian Life-Styles* (Oxford: Clarendon, 1993), 46–47; Andreas Lindemann, "'Do Not Let a Woman Destroy the Unborn Babe in her Belly': Abortion in Ancient Judaism and Christianity," *Studia Theologica* 49 (1995): 253–71, esp. 253–57.

64. Michael J. Gorman, *Abortion and the Early Church: Christian, Jewish and Pagan Attitudes in the Greco-Roman World* (Downers Grove, Ill.: InterVarsity, 1982); Stark, *The Rise of Christianity*, 119–21.

65. Suzanne Dixon, *Reading Roman Women: Sources, Genres and Real Life* (London: Duckworth, 2001), 56–65.

66. After referring to a number of literary sources, Dixon draws this conclusion: "These literary references, though taken for centuries as evidence of the moral decline of Roman society, are useless as historical information. Rather, they express masculine fears about secret female practices, on a par with fears of poisoning (of husbands or stepchildren)" (61).

67. Celsus, *Med.* 7.29. I believe that it is misleading to speak, as Dixon does in *Reading Roman Women,* 62–63, of "the lack of hard information in 'masculine' medical and scientific works." Celsus's instructions about how available medical equipment is to be used when performing an abortion is surely "hard information." See Stark, *The Rise of Christianity,* who speaks of "the very high rates of abortion in the Greco-Roman world" and identifies this as one cause of "the very low fertility rates" (120).

68. Justinian, *Dig.* 47.11.4. According to Ulpian, this penalty was also imposed as an application of Augustus's *Lex Cornelia* (on murderers and poisoners). The jurist Tryphoninus upheld the view that exile was the appropriate penalty in cases where a woman had an abortion after divorce "to avoid giving a son to her husband who is now hateful," referring to the rescript of the two emperors mentioned above: see Justinian, *Dig.* 48.8.8 and 48.19.39.

69. Justinian, *Dig.* 48.19.38.5.

70. See Gorman, *Abortion and the Early Church,* 30–32.

71. One example of an older study is Leopoldo Armaroli, *Ricerche storiche sulla esposizione degli infanti presso gli antichi popoli e specialmente presso i Romani* (Venice, 1838). Newer works are: Donald Engels, "The Problem of Female Infanticide in the Greco-Roman World," *Classical Philology* 75 (1980): 112–20; Donald Engels, "The Use of Historical Demography in Ancient History," *Classical Quarterly* 34 (1984): 386–93; Emil Eyben, "Family Planning in Graeco-Roman Antiquity," *Ancient Society* 11–12 (1980–81): 5–82; Mark Golden, "Demography and the Exposure of Girls at Athens," *Phoenix* 35 (1981): 316–31; Sarah B. Pomeroy, "Copronyms and the exposure of infants in Egypt," in *Studies in Roman Law in Memory of A. Arthur Schiller,* ed. A. Arthur Schiller et al. (Leiden: Brill, 1986), 147–62; John Boswell, *The Kindness of Strangers. The Abandonment of Children in Western Europe from Late Antiquity to the Renaissance* (New York: Pantheon, 1988); Ryoji Motomura, "The Practice of Exposing Infants and Its Effects on the Development of Slavery in the Ancient World," in *Forms of Control and Subordination in Antiquity,* ed. T. Yuge and M. Doi (Tokyo: Society for Studies on Resistance Movements in Antiquity, 1988), 410–15; Friedolf Kudlien, "Kindesaussetzung im antiken Rom," *Groningen Colloquia on the Ancient Novel* 11 (1989): 25–44; A. Huys, "*Ekthesis* and *Apothesis*: the Terminology of Infant Exposure in Greek Antiquity," *L'Antiquité Classique* 58 (1989): 190–97; William V. Harris, "Child-Exposure in the Roman Empire," *Journal of Roman Studies* 84 (1994): 1–22; Mireille Corbier, "Child Exposure and Abandonment," in *Childhood, Class and Kin in the Roman World,* ed. Suzanne Dixon (London: Routledge, 2001), 52–73.

72. This is correctly emphasized by Corbier, "Child Exposure and Abandonment," 52–53.

73. As will become clear from the notes, I build here to a large extent on Harris, "Child-Exposure in the Roman Empire" (1994), who discusses a wide spectrum of sources in a consistently sober and convincing manner.

74 See Harris, "Child-Exposure in the Roman Empire," 4–5.

75. Ibid., 7–8: "The evidence from the Greeks of Egypt eventually becomes plentiful. By the end of the first century B.C.E. exposing an infant was a familiar practice which could be ordained by a husband without much ado."

76. Ibid., 6. Harris notes: "the incidence of exposure in this period (Late Republic) and almost everything else about it will remain obscure."

77. Ibid.

78. Ibid., 7.

79. Corbier, "Child Exposure and Abandonment," 66.

80. After noting that Tacitus found it worthy of remark that neither the Germans (*Germ.* 19.5) nor the Jews (*Hist.* 5.5) exposed their children, Dixon, in *Reading Roman Women* (2001), 178, n. 26, comments: "Tacitus' apparent surprise that the Jews did not practise infant exposure may imply that it was the Mediterranean norm." Harris, in "Child-Exposure

in the Roman Empire," 8, sums up as follows: "the plethora of Greek evidence may give the impression that exposure was particularly characteristic of the Greek part of the Empire. However, Tacitus and Tertullian, among others, make it plain that the practice was also common in some areas of the West."

81. On childbirth and the first weeks of a baby's life in the Roman context, see Beryl Rawson, "Adult-Child Relationships in Roman Society," in *Marriage, Divorce and Children in Ancient Rome*, ed. Beryl Rawson (Oxford: Clarendon, 1991), 10–15.

82. Corbier, "Child Exposure and Abandonment," 53–58.

83. Ibid., 56, shows, among other things, that children who had not yet received a name— i.e., who were younger than eight days—had a lower status and enjoyed less legal protection than others, according to the Salic law, which punished the murder of infants who had not yet received a name less severely than the murder of children who had been named.

84. Plutarch, *Mor.* 288 C.

85. Corbier, in "Child Exposure and Abandonment," 71, concludes: "The practice of exposure can crystallise the attitudes of romanised and Roman societies towards newborn babies. The rejection of the child by exposure takes place before it is regarded as having attained full human status and integration in the family. We cannot overemphasise this intermediate phase, so foreign to our own conceptions."

86. See Harris, "Child-Exposure in the Roman Empire," 11: "A range of texts from Greek and Roman sources, including a description of an Ephesian law aimed at ensuring that only those who were literally starving could expose their children, indicate that poverty was assumed to be the usual cause of child-exposure."

87. Ibid., 13.

88. Hierocles, *Stob.* 4.24.14. See also Keith Hopkins, *Death and Renewal* (Cambridge: Cambridge University Press, 1983), 225; Golden, *Childhood in Classical Athens,* 87.

89. Suetonius, *Aug.* 94.3. For further textual examples and discussion, see Harris, "Child-Exposure in the Roman Empire," 14.

90. Suetonius, *Calig.* 5.

91. On this phenomenon, see Corbier, "Child Exposure and Abandonment," 61.

92. Harris, "Child-Exposure in the Roman Empire," 14.

93. Ibid., 12 notes: "The criteria that Soranus . . . gives for judging whether an infant is healthy enough to be reared were so extensive and strict that if anything like them was really applied an enormous number of rejections must have resulted."

94. This view is also held by Wiedemann, *Adults and Children in the Roman Empire,* 36; Golden, *Childhood in Classical Athens,* 87; and Harris, "Child-Exposure in the Roman Empire," 11: "Indeed one of the reasons why the Romans relied heavily on child-exposure to control population was that, unlike contraception or abortion, it permitted them to choose the sex of their children."

95. Papyrus Oxyrhynchus 744.

96. See Jack Lindsay, *The Ancient World: Manners and Morals* (London: Weidenfeld & Nicolson, 1968), 168. Lindsay goes so far as to say that in large families, "more than one daughter was practically never reared."

97. On the question of where children were exposed, see Beryl Rawson, "Children in the Roman *Familia,*" in *The Family in Ancient Rome: New Perspectives,* 172; Harris, "Child-Exposure in the Roman Empire," 9–10; and Corbier, "Child Exposure and Abandonment," 61–64.

98. For sources and discussion, see Harris, "Child-Exposure in the Roman Empire," 9–10; Corbier, "Child Exposure and Abandonment," 66–67.

99. See Harris, "Child-Exposure in the Roman Empire," 9; Corbier, "Child Exposure and Abandonment," 67–68.

100. Rawson, "Children in the Roman *Familia,*" 196.

101. This is the view of Motomura, "The Practice of Exposing Infants and its Effects on the Development of Slavery in the Ancient World," 410–15; Boswell, *The Kindness of Strangers*, 42, 128–31. Corbier, "Child Exposure and Abandonment," 60–70, also inclines to this view.

102. This is the view of Harris, "Child-Exposure in the Roman Empire," 10.

103. Ibid., 8–11.

104. Lawrence E. Stager, "Eroticism and Infanticide at Ashkelon," *Biblical Archaeology Review* 17 (1991): 34–53. When I say that this "may be" evidence of infanticide, I take into account the element of uncertainty about whether these babies were killed or died a natural death; there was in fact a tradition of burying (or perhaps one should say: disposing of) the corpses of dead bodies by placing them under the house. On the question of infanticide, see also Harris, "The Theoretical Possibility of Extensive Infanticide in the Graeco-Roman World," *Classical Quarterly* 32 (1982): 114–16.

105. Greek and English text in Cora E. Lutz, *Musonius Rufus: "The Roman Socrates."* (New Haven, Conn.: Yale University Press, 1947), 15.

106. Epictetus, *Discourses* 1.23; Hierocles, *Stob.* 4.24.14.

107. Tacitus, *Germ.* 19.

108. On the emergence and intention of the *alimenta*, see Rawson, "Children as Cultural Symbols: Imperial Ideology in the Second Century," in *Childhood, Class and Kin in the Roman World*, 21–42, with references to secondary literature.

109. Harris, "Child-Exposure in the Roman Empire," 16.

110. For discussions of the terms and of the various groups who could make up a part of "the family," see Moses I. Finley, *The Ancient Economy*, updated ed. (Berkeley: University of California Press, 1973), 17–21; Rawson, "The Roman Family," 7–15; Dixon, *The Roman Mother*, 13–21; Dixon, *The Roman Family*, 1–11.

111. Dixon, in *The Roman Family*, 11, says that the household "would often have included slaves."

112. Halvor Moxnes, "What Is Family? Problems in Constructing Early Christian Families," in *Constructing Early Christian Families: Family as Social Reality and Metaphor*, ed. Halvor Moxnes (London: Routledge, 1997), 32–33. Moxnes notes: "In the discussion of kinship, we have mentioned the paramount importance of honour and shame as cultural values in the ancient Mediterranean world, especially in the area of sexuality and gender relations within the family. The distinction between men's honour and women's shame does not result only in a dual pattern, but in a hierarchical system in which the husband has the most powerful role, closer to God." For further characteristics of "shame/honor" cultures, and ancient Mediterranean culture as a "shame/honor" culture, see Bruce J. Malina, *The New Testament World: Insights from Cultural Anthropology* (Louisville, Ky.: John Knox, 1981); H. Moxnes, "Honor and Shame: Readers Guide," *Biblical Theology Bulletin* 23 (1993): 167–76.

113. Moxnes, "What Is Family?" 11. Moxnes also describes the Roman family as "above all a flexible and pragmatic institution."

114. Nathan, *The Family in Late Antiquity*, 28.

115. Rawson, "The Roman Family," 8. Part of the explanation of this phenomenon is the high rate of infant mortality; another factor is the conscious decision to limit the number of children (contraception, abortion, *expositio*).

116. This is the view of Dixon, *The Roman Family*, 11.

117. For texts and secondary literature, see Dixon, *The Roman Mother*, 137, nn. 16–17.

118. Keith R. Bradley, "Wet-nursing at Rome: A Study in Social Relations," in *The Family in Ancient Rome. New Perspectives*, 201–29; Dixon, *The Roman Mother*, 120–28.

119. See Susan Treggiari, "Jobs for Women," *American Journal of Ancient History* 1 (1976): 88; Bradley, "Wet-nursing at Rome," 208–10; Dixon, *The Roman Mother*, 145–54.

120. Quintilian, *Inst.* 6. pr. 8.

121. Ibid., pr. 8–12.

122. Favorinus, *NA* 12.1.23: "And what is more, once the foundations of natural feeling have been entirely eradicated, any sign of affection which children reared in this way might show their father or mother is primarily an acquired piece of etiquette, not natural love," quoted in Dixon, *The Roman Mother,* 124.

123. Nathan, *The Family in Late Antiquity,* 25, referring to Soranus, *Gynaikeia* 2, and Galen, *De Hyg.*

124. See Tacitus, *Dial.* 28; Quintilian, *Inst.* 1.1.5; Cicero, *Brut.* 210–12, and the discussion in Dixon, *The Roman Mother,* 109–11.

125. Dixon, *The Roman Mother,* 111.

126. Ibid., 110.

127. See for example Plato, *Resp.* 467D; *Polit.* 308D–E; Pseudo-Plutarch, *Mor.* 4A–B.

128. Keith R. Bradley, "Child Care at Rome: The Role of Men," *Historical Reflections* 12 (1985): 485–523; Dixon, *The Roman Mother,* 110.

129. Dixon, *The Roman Mother,* 129.

130. Ibid., 210. Dixon writes: "There is reason to believe that Roman girls did indeed learn from their mothers what was expected of women in their particular social position, but it is important to recognise the limitations of the sources. Balsdon's assertion . . . that, 'In general a mother's relationship was more intimate with her daughter than with her son,' is intrinsically plausible, but difficult to authenticate with hard evidence."

131. Ibid., 215–17.

132. Rawson, "Children in the Roman *Familia,*" 40.

133. Dixon, *The Roman Mother,* 202; see also pp.168–209 on the relationship between a mother and her teenage and adult children.

134. Ibid., 121–22.

135. Plautus, *Mostell.* 118–21; Juvenal 14; Tacitus, *Dial.* 28–29; Horace, *Serm.* 1.6.71–92 (see also Horace, *Carm.* 3.6.37–41), according to Dixon, *The Roman Family,* 118.

136. Cicero, *Att.* 10.4.6. For biographies, see Wiedemann, *Adults and Children in the Roman Empire,* 49–83.

137. For a good and fruitful study of the *paterfamilias,* see John A. Crook, "Patria Potestas," *Classical Quarterly* 17 (1967): 113–22. See also D. Volterra, "Quelques observations sur le mariage des *filiifamilias,*" *Revue Internationale des Droits de l Antiquité* 1 (1948): 213–42; David Daube, *Roman Law: Linguistic, Social and Philosophical Aspects* (Edinburgh: Edinburgh University Press, 1969); W. K. Lacey, "Patria Potestas," in *The Family in Ancient Rome: New Perspectives,* 121–44; Rawson, "The Roman Family," 1–57, esp. 15–31.

138. See J. Evans Grubbs, *Law and Family in Late Antiquity: The Emperor Constantine's Marriage Legislation* (Oxford: Oxford University Press, 1955); Antti Arjava, *Women and Law in Late Antiquity* (Oxford: Clarendon, 1996); Antti Arjava, "Paternal Power in Late Antiquity," *Journal of Roman Studies* 88 (1988): 147–65. See also the brief but informative discussion of "The decline of *patria potestas*" in Matthew Kuefler, *The Manly Eunuch: Masculinity, Gender Ambiguity, and Christian Ideology in Late Antiquity* (Chicago: University of Chicago Press, 2001), 70–76.

139. Nathan, *The Family in Late Antiquity,* 27–28.

140. See Reidar Aasgaard, *"My Beloved Brothers and Sisters!": Christian Siblingship in Paul"* (London: T. and T. Clark, 1998), 59–61, with references to secondary literature.

141. Nathan, *The Family in Late Antiquity,* 27: "The *paterfamilias'* decision may have been final, but even the most conservative and ancient supporters of his power looked ill upon a father who ignored the opinion of various family members."

142. Ibid., 27.: "In sum, a son or daughter of any class was expected to fulfill whatever order a *paterfamilias* gave, provided, of course, it was legal."

143. Richard P. Saller, "Corporal Punishment, Authority, and Obedience in the Roman Household," in *Marriage, Divorce and Children in Ancient Rome,* 144–65.

144. Publilius Syrus, *Max.* 108.

145. For example Seneca, *Ira* 2.21.1–6.

146. See Dixon, *The Roman Family,* 118; Nathan, *The Family in Late Antiquity,* 33–34.

147. This is also the view of Dixon, *The Roman Family,* 118; and Nathan, *The Family in Late Antiquity,* 33–34, who concludes: "the tendency to hit one's offspring was frequently reactive and immediate. Unless a son had done something outrageous, he was unlikely to be punished unless he misbehaved in front of his father." For the view that parents employed corporal punishment on a wide scale, see Lloyd de Mause, "The Evolution of Childhood," in *The History of Childhood,* ed. Lloyd de Mause (London: Souvenir Press, 1976), 39–41; Wiedemann, *Adults and Children in the Roman Empire,* 28–30, 104–6.

148. Wiedemann, *Adults and Children in the Roman Empire,* 28–29, with many references to primary sources.

149. See Augustine, *Conf.* 1.9.15.

150. Quintilian, *Inst.* 1.3.13.

151. Plutarch, *Cat. Mai.* 20.4.

152. For a discussion of the age of these children and the various kinds of work they did, see Wiedemann, *Adults and Children in the Roman Empire,* 154–56.

153. Nathan, *The Family in Late Antiquity,* 26.

154. Ibid., 31, notes: "Slavery was so ubiquitous that frequently free citizens even of humble means possessed a slave or two."

155. Ibid., 35.

156. On this, see for example, Beryl Rawson, "Family Life among the Lower Classes at Rome in the First Two Centuries of the Empire," *Classical Philology* 61 (1966): 71–83; Rawson, "Children in the Roman *Familia,*" in *The Family in Ancient Rome: New Perspectives,* 186–97; Keith R. Bradley, *Slaves and Masters in the Roman Empire: A Study in Social Control* (New York: Oxford University Press, 1987). Dixon, in *The Roman Family,* also offers a valuable discussion of the children of slaves.

157. See Rawson, "Children in the Roman *Familia,*" 186–197 on the definition and use of this term.

158. Ibid., 186.

159. Dixon, *The Roman Family,* 10.

160. Nathan, *The Family in Late Antiquity,* 35.

161. De Mause, "The Evolution of Childhood," in *The History of Childhood,* 43.

162. Kenneth J. Dover, *Greek Homosexuality* (London: Duckworth, 1978).

163. On this, see for example David Halperin, *One Hundred Years of Homosexuality and Other Essays on Greek Love* (New York: Routledge, 1990); Bernadette J. Brooten, *Love between Women: Early Christian Responses to Female Homoeroticism* (Chicago: University of Chicago Press, 1996), with many references to secondary literature. Jorunn Økland, "Intet nytt under Kristus. En Dialog med Bernadette Brooten om kvinners 'unaturlige' begjær i antikken," in *Naturlig Sex? Seksualitet og Kjønn i den Kristne Antikken,* ed. Halvor Moxnes et al. (Oslo: Gyldendal, 2002), 129–73. Økland gives a detailed presentation and evaluation of Brooten's book, arguing that "she shows more clearly than earlier authors how fundamental the antithesis between active and passive was in the way people in late antiquity thought about sexual relations. It was impossible to think about sex without this antithesis: sex was something one person did with another. Accordingly, 'penetration' was the primary image used when people wished to describe what sex consisted of. It was also customary to employ the active/passive antithesis to give meaning to terms such as 'masculine' and 'feminine': the masculine was associated with the active, the feminine with the passive. When male, female, active, and passive were joined together in the bodies of individual human persons in this specific manner, the result was good health" (ET: B. McNeil).

164. Øyvind Norderval, "Holdninger til seksualitet og homoseksualitet i antikken og i oldkirken," *Norsk Teologisk Tidsskrift* 94 (1993): 195.

165. In addition to the literature in n. 204, see Craig A. Williams, *Roman Homosexuality: Ideologies of Masculinity in Classical Antiquity* (New York: Oxford University Press, 1999).

166. Williams, *Roman Homosexuality,* 62. He presents extensive source material and demonstrates that "it is not *homosexuality* but specifically *pederasty* in the Greek sense of publicly acknowledged romantic and sexual relationships between adult and citizen males and freeborn adolescent males (future citizens) that constituted what from a Roman perspective was peculiarly Greek in matters erotic" (63).

167. John Boswell, *Christianity, Social Tolerance and Homosexuality: Gay People in Western Europe from the Beginning of the Christian Era to the Fourteenth Century* (Chicago/London: University of Chicago Press, 1980), 81; Norderval, "Holdninger til seksualitet og homoseksualitet i antikken og i oldkirken," 196–98. Norderval refers to the *Lex Scantinia,* a law that scholars believe was promulgated in the 220s of the Common Era. It is not entirely clear what this law dealt with. Some sources indicate that it was a prohibition of homosexuality, which was seldom enforced. Other sources seem to consider it a prohibition of the sexual exploitation of small children.

168. Pseudo-Plutarch, *Mor.* 11D. Here I presuppose that what Pseudo-Plutarch says is related not only to the situation in Greece, but also to the practice in Rome.

169. According to de Mause, "The Evolution of Childhood," 43.

170. De Mause, "The Evolution of Childhood," 46. He mentions the praise bestowed by Martial on Domitian when he promulgated a law forbidding the castration of babies so that they could work in brothels later on: "Boys loved thee before . . . but now infants, too, love thee, Caesar." He also quotes Paulus Aegineta's description of "the standard method" of castrating small boys: "Since we are sometimes compelled against our will by persons of high rank to perform the operation . . . by compression (it) is thus performed: children, still of a tender age, are placed in a vessel of hot water, and then when the parts are softened in the bath, the testicles are to be squeezed with the fingers until they disappear."

171. Greek and English text in Lutz, *Musonius Rufus,* 16, 103.

172. Justin Martyr, *I Apol.* 27.

173. Clement of Alexandria, *Paed.* 3.3.

174. One of the leading authorities on the Roman family, Suzanne Dixon, goes so far as to claim that children were "routinely . . . sexually exploited." *The Roman Family,* 131.

175. Philippe Ariès, *Centuries of Childhood* (New York: Vintage, 1962).

176. For an overview of the various positions, see Mark Golden, "Did the Ancients Care When Their Children Died?" *Greece and Rome* 35 (1988). For other studies, see Hanne S. Nielsen, "Interpreting Epithets in Roman Epitaphs," in *The Roman Family in Italy: Status, Sentiment, Space,* ed. Beryl Rawson and Paul Weaver (Oxford: Clarendon, 1977), 169–204; Dixon, *The Roman Mother,* 104–14; Dixon, *The Roman Family,* 102–4.

177. Cicero, *Tusc.* 1.93–94.

178. Cf. Ibid., *Att.* 10.18, *quod est natum.*

179. Seneca, *Ep. Mor.* 99. He argues that there is no reason for the father to grieve, pointing out, among other things, that other fathers have had the same experience: "There are countless cases of men who have without tears buried sons in the prime of manhood—men who have returned from the funeral pyre to the Senate chamber, or to any other official duties, and have straightway busied themselves with something else" (99.6).

180. See Nielsen, "Interpreting Epithets in Roman Epitaphs," 173–74.

181. This is also the view of Nielsen, "Interpreting Epithets in Roman Epitaphs," 174. Naturally, these funeral inscriptions are a specific genre where we can expect to find the same conventional elements: social pressures led people to employ particular expressions, and perhaps even to dedicate a funeral inscription to a person whom they had not liked or cared for while that person was alive. It is also possible that social conventions prevented parents from describing feelings linked to the loss of small children.

182. Dixon, *The Roman Mother,* 4, 201, 212, has shown that people commonly thought women displayed more grief than men when older children died.

183. Plutarch, *Mor.* 608 C–D.

184. This is why I believe that Nielsen, in "Interpreting Epithets in Roman Epitaphs," is too cautious and careful when she writes: "it seems to be pointless to concentrate the discussion—as far as mourning is concerned—on the death of infants, since the Romans were not interested in giving any information on infant mortality" (200).

185. See Brent D. Shaw and Richard P. Saller, "Tombstones and Roman Family Relations in the Principate: Civilians, Soldiers and Slaves," *The Journal of Roman Studies* 74 (1984): 124–56. Saller, in "Slavery and the Roman family," discusses funeral inscriptions of children younger than ten years of age. See also Nielsen, "Interpreting Epithets in Roman Epitaphs," 198–202.

186. Dixon, *The Roman Family,* 100.

187. Nielsen, "Interpreting Epithets in Roman Epitaphs," 198. She also notes that "premature death" in literary texts refers usually not to small children, but to "young adults who had not yet accomplished what they had intended to do or ought to have done" (200–201).

188. See for example Michel Manson, "The Emergence of the Small Child at Rome (Third Century B.C.–First Century A.D.)," *History of Education* 12 (1 983): 149–59; S. Dixon, "The Sentimental Ideal of the Roman Family," in *Marriage, Divorce, and Children in Ancient Rome,* 109–11.

189. On this, see esp. Michel Manson, "*Puer Bimulus* (Catulle, 17,12–13) et l'image du petit enfant chez Catulle et ses prédécesseurs," *Mélanges d'archéologie et d'histoire de l'école française de Rome* 90 (1978): 258–59; Manson, "The Emergence of the Small Child at Rome," 154; Nielsen, "Interpreting Epithets in Roman Epitaphs," 185–93.

190. Dixon, *The Roman Family,* 103. Cf. Dixon, "The Sentimental Ideal of the Roman Family," 99–113.

191. Lucretius, 3.894–96, quoted by Dixon, *The Roman Family,* 103.

192. Cicero, *Att.* 1.18.1. Daleas, in *Children in the Roman World,* 75, concludes on the basis of this text that "Cicero clearly implies that the *domus* includes the family as a unit, and there are happy associations with this unit (*fructum domesticum*)."

193. To mention only two examples, children are depicted on several friezes on the Ara Pacis and on coins as propaganda for the *alimenta* program discussed above. Janet Huskinson, in "Iconography: Another Perspective," in *The Roman Family in Italy,* 233–38, is correct to say that "developments in the representation of the child should be set firmly in the historical context of society, that initially—certainly in the earlier Empire—they were stimulated by the needs and policies of the state, through dynastic art, legislation, literary treatment, and so forth, and that they came to be taken up by individual families, particularly by those whose future or upward mobility depended on investment in the child" (234). She also observes that because "Roman art is generally more interested in suggesting status rather than emotion, it can provide only quite limited evidence for changes in sentiment towards children" (321). See also Daleas, *Children in the Roman World,* 140–44.

194. Here I base my remarks to a large extent on Wiedemann, *Adults and Children in the Roman Empire,* 176–208.

195. D. G. Orr, "Roman Domestic Religion: A Study of the Roman Household Deities and their Shrines at Pompeii and Herculaneum." (PhD diss., University of Maryland, 1978); John R. Clarke, *The Houses of Roman Italy, 100 B.C.–A.D. 250: Ritual, Space and Decoration* (Berkeley: University of California Press, 1991), 6–12.

196. It is against this background that John M. G. Barclay, in "The Family as the Bearer of Religion in Judaism and Early Christianity," in *Constructing Early Christian Families: Family as Social Reality and Metaphor,* 67, emphasizes that "the domestic cult was intimately linked with the honour and prosperity of the head of the household." See further Clarke, *The Houses of Roman Italy,* 6–12.

197. Barclay, "The Family as the Bearer of Religion in Judaism and Early Christianity," 67–68.

198. See ibid., 68; Daleas, *Children in the Roman World*, 105–98, 136–37.

199. Prudentius, *C. Symm.* 1.197–211.

200. Barclay, in "The Family as the Bearer of Religion in Judaism and Early Christianity," 68, points out quite correctly that "Infants learnt very early which powers to propitiate in the home, and the demands of *pietas* to one's forebears, living or deceased, made it unthinkable that a child would wish to break the time-honoured traditions or show less than full respect for the *paterfamilias*."

201. Servius, *Aen.* 1.730. See Wiedemann, *Adults and Children in the Roman Empire*, 181.

202. Columella, *Rust.* 12.4.3, quoted by Wiedemann, *Adults and Children in the Roman Empire*, 181.

203. Quoted by ibid., 182.

204. Ibid., 182.

205. Dionysius of Halicarnassus, *Ant. Rom.* 2.22.1.

206. Wiedemann, *Adults and Children in the Roman Empire*, 184.

207. On this, see ibid., 177–79.

208. Ibid., 176–86. The following words sum up Wiedemann's argumentation: "in general, the presence of children at the pagan religious ceremonies of Roman families and of the Roman communities was not a sign of the equality of child and adult, but a sign that the child only marginally belonged to the human community. It was because the child 'did not count', was in a sense 'not there' as a citizen, that the child could be used to assist at ceremonies, and that the child's words could be taken as ominous, mediating between the divine world and the human" (186).

209. Dixon, *The Roman Family*, 130–31.

3. Patristic Teaching about the Nature of Children and Their Characteristics

1. So also G. Gould, "Childhood in Patristic Thought: Some Problems of Theology and Theological Anthropology," in *The Church and Childhood: Papers Read at the 1993 Summer Meeting and the 1994 Winter Meeting of the Ecclesiastical History Society*, ed. Diana Wood (Oxford: Blackwell, 1994), 40: "In explaining what these metaphors convey, patristic authors reveal something about their understanding of what it is that is distinctive, in moral or religious terms, about the condition of childhood as opposed to maturity."

2. What Blake Leyerle, in "Appealing to Children," *Journal of Early Christian Studies* 5 (1997): 244, states with respect to the use of analogy in John Chrysostom is true for other church fathers as well: "For analogies to be persuasive, the fit between the situation portrayed and the perceived realities of daily life must cohere, at least in broad measure."

3. The occurrence of this metaphor reflects the author's intensive use of the metaphors of procreation and kinship. Denise Kimber Buell, in *Making Christians: Clement of Alexandria and the Rhetoric of Legitimacy* (Princeton: Princeton University Press, 1999), demonstrates how the use of these metaphors in theological struggles functions to legitimate Clement's own position and to marginalize others as false.

4. Greek edition SC 70, 108, 158. ET: FC 23. I use the reference system of this English edition.

5. Buell, *Making Christians*, 108.

6. "Etymologically, *Paidagogos* means 'leader of Children', and this is the sense Clement sometimes confines himself to." S. P. Wood, trans., *Christ the Educator* (New York: Fathers of the Church, 1954), xiv.

7. Buell, *Making Christians*, 108.

8. Cf. Matt 19:14.

9. Cf. Matt 18:3.

10. Clement of Alexandria, *Paed.* 1.5.12.

11. Ibid., 1.5.15.

12. Ibid., 1.5.14.

13. Ibid., *Paed.* 1.5.19. I have changed the translation of the term *epios* from "children" to "gentle."

14. Ibid., *Paed.* 1.5.19. Buell, in *Making Christians,* 112, correctly notes Clement's remarkable use of 1 Thess 2:7: "He interprets *epios* in light of the concept of childhood although in this verse *epios* properly qualifies the behavior of the apostles (who are here depicted as nurses in contrast to the Thessalonian 'children')."

15. When discussing the argumentative function of Clement's references to the behavior of animals, Buell, in *Making Christians,* 113, notes: "Clement and his contemporaries also frequently used animals as ciphers for human behavior for one of two opposing purposes: either to distinguish humans positively from animals (animals as 'other') or to recommend certain forms of behavior for humans as 'natural' (using animals to 'think with'). . . . Anecdotes about parent-child relations among animals offer Clement a repository of positive examples for prescribing what is 'natural' about this relationship."

16. Clement of Alexandria, *Paed.* 1.5.15.

17. Buell, in *Making Christians,* 114, rightly pays attention to the fact "that Clement specifies that newly born foals bound toward their *father* rather than their mother. This counter-intuitive description (one would expect a newborn to head toward the mother as its source of food) suggests that Clement employs it here to naturalize a paternal loyalty not necessarily found among animals."

18. Clement of Alexandria, *Paed.* 1.15.

19. Buell, in *Making Christians,* 114 n. 22, comments: "One possible subtext that Clement does not spell out here lends itself to an ascetic reading; it suggests that sexual relations pose a danger for salvation and that childhood constitutes a state in which sexual desire is not an issue."

20. So also Lloyd de Mause, "Evolution of Childhood," in *The History of Childhood,* ed. Lloyd de Mause (London: Souvenir, 1976), 47.

21. See for example, Clement of Alexandria *Str.* 3.6.50. Greek edition in O. Stählin (Berlin: Akademie Verlag, 1960). All references and quotations in English are from the translation in FC 85.

22. It appears that Buell holds this view. *Making Christians,* 111.

23. Clement of Alexandria, *Str.* 3.9.67.1. For Clement's view on marriage, see *Str.* 3.97.5–98.5 and the brief discussion in Buell, *Making Christians,* 81–83.

24. Clement of Alexandria, *Str.* 3.10.68.1–70.4.

25. Ibid., 3.10.68.4.

26. Ibid., 2.23.137.1–147.5.

27. Ibid., *Str.* 2.23.142. A. Oepke, "*pais, paidion ktl,*" in *TDNT* 5:651, rightly notes: "He [Clement] says . . . that childlessness or the loss of children is a heavy burden and the possession of children a great blessing. . . . The pessimism of antiquity . . . is a sin against the Creator."

28. Cf. Eusebius, *H. E.* 3.30.1.

29. Cf. Gould, "Childhood in Eastern Patristic Thought," 40: "Childhood, the beginning of biological life, is thus a symbol, applied to Christians, of the beginning of a new religious life of discipleship in a condition of childlike (*paidikos*) simplicity, freshness, and purity."

30. Clement's positive attitude toward children is also noted by Buell, *Making Christians,* 117, who summarizes: "Clement favors a positive valuation of infants and children in chapter five [of *Paidagogos* 3], consistently exhorting his readers to imagine themselves as children in relation to God."

31. Origen, *Comm. in Mt.* 13.16 (GCS 40 pp. 219–22, ET: *ANF* 9).

32. Cf. Elizabeth A. Clark, *Reading Renunciation: Asceticism and Scripture in Early Christianity* (Princeton: Princeton University Press, 1999), 144–45; 265–66.

33. Origen, *Comm. in Mt.* 13.16.

34. Ibid.

35. Ibid.

36. Ibid.

37. Ibid.

38. Gould, in "Childhood in Patristic Thought," 42, rightly observes that "Both the passions and the rational power of deliberation and choice to resist them are thus seen as developing concomitantly in children with increasing age."

39. Ibid., 42. For an introduction to Origen's anthropology, see for example Peter C. Phan, *Grace and the Human Condition,* Message of the Fathers of the Church 15 (Wilmington: Michael Glazier, 1988), 78–97.

40. Gould, "Childhood in Patristic Thought," 43: "Origen probably associates the development of reason and the passions in children with the development of speech—the term logos is of course appropriate to both."

41. Hermas, *Man.* 2:1. ET: LCL.

42. Hermas, *Sim.* 9.3.

43. Carolyn Osiek, *The Shepherd of Hermas,* Hermeneia (Minneapolis: Fortress Press, 1999), 252.

44. For the use of this word field in *Hermas,* see Heinrich Bacht, "Einfalt," *Reallexikon für Antike und Christentum,* ed. Theodore Klauser et al. (Stuttgart: Hiersemann, 1959), 4:831–34; Norbert Brox, *Der Hirt des Hermas,* Kommentar zu den Apostolischen Vätern 7 (Göttingen: Vandenhoeck & Ruprecht, 1991), 500–502.

45. Cf. Brox, *Der Hirt des Hermas,* 500.

46. Cf. Bacht, "Einfalt," 831. For occurrences and its use in LXX and other Jewish writings, see ibid., 824–28, and Ceslas Spicq, "*haplotes,*" in *Theological Lexicon of the New Testament,* trans. and ed. J. D. Ernest (Peabody, Mass.: Hendrickson, 1994), 1:169–71. The latter notes that "in the first century B.C.E., *haplotes,* so exalted in the Wisdom writings, is considered the supreme virtue of the patriarchs," and refers to several passages in the *Testaments of the Twelve Patriarchs* (170).

47. Osiek, in *The Shepherd of Hermas,* 104, rightly notes, when she comments on the meaning of simplicity in *Mandates* 2, that "It is worth repeating that the command to keep simplicity and innocence focuses not on chastity but on charity in both speech and deed."

48. *Barnabas* 6.11 (ET: LCL).

49. Cf. Ferdinand R. Prostmeier, *Der Barnabasbrief,* Kommentar zu den Apostolischen Vätern 8 (Göttingen: Vandenhoeck & Ruprecht, 1999), 272.

50. For a discussion of the date of composition, see Richard Valantasis, *The Gospel of Thomas* (London: Routledge, 1997), 12–21.

51. *Gospel of Thomas* 37. ET: *The Nag Hammadi Library in English,* rev. ed., ed. James M. Robinson (San Francisco: Harper & Row, 1988), 37.

52. So Jonathan Z. Smith, "The Garments of Shame," *History of Religions* 5 (1966): 234. Smith argues that this experience of transformation is connected with the rite of baptism or the prebaptismal exorcism. For other discussions, see for example Howard Clark Kee, "'Becoming a Child' in the Gospel of Thomas," *Journal of Biblical Literature* 82 (1963): 307–14; Valantasis, *The Gospel of Thomas,* 112–13; T. Zöckler, *Jesu Lehren im Thomasevangelium* (Leiden: Brill, 1999), 235–36.

53. Kee, "'Becoming a Child' in the Gospel of Thomas," 310: "The child, who is thought of as free from sexual urges, demonstrates his innocence by removing his clothing without shame." D. G. Hunter, in "Children," *Encyclopedia of Early Christianity,* 2nd ed., ed. Everett Ferguson (New York: Garland, 1998), 236, also maintains that sexual innocence is implied here.

54. Scholars have long recognized the ascetic nature of the Gospel of Thomas. See for example, Valantasis, *The Gospel of Thomas*, 21–24.

55. Kee, "'Becoming a Child' in the Gospel of Thomas," 311.

56. The text in its entirety is preserved only in a Syriac translation; a few parts of the original Greek text have been preserved in some papyrus fragments, cf. Edgar J. Goodspeed, *Die ältesten Apologeten. Texte mit kurzen Einleitungen* (Göttingen: Vandenhoeck & Ruprecht, 1914). Goodspeed gives the Latin version of the text where the Greek is missing.

57. Aristides, *Apol.* 15 (ET: *ANF* 9, p. 277).

58. So in Joachim Jeremias, *Infant Baptism in the First Four Centuries* (Philadelphia: Westminster, 1964), 71.

59. For example, Aristides, *Apol.* 9, *ANF* 9, p. 270: "much evil has arisen among men, who to this day are imitators of their gods, and practise adultery and defile themselves with their mothers and their sisters, and by lying with males, and some make bold to slay even their parents."

60. K. Aland, in *Did the Early Church Baptize Infants?* trans. G. R. Beasley-Murray (London: SCM, 1963), 56, reaches the same conclusion on the basis of another line of argumentation: "the deduction must be drawn that here a real sinlessness of the child is presupposed in contrast to the sinfulness of the Christian who, despite his baptism (!) does not die in his advanced age in the purity demanded of Christians."

61. Athenagoras, *Res.* 14 (ET: *ANF* 2).

62. Irenaeus, *Dem.* 14 (ET: ACW 16).

63. CSEL 20, 201–18 (ET: *ANF* 3).

64. J. N. D. Kelly, *Early Christian Doctrines*, 5th rev. ed. (London: A and C Black, 1977), 176.

65. Tertullian, *De Anima* 40.1.

66. David F. Wright, "How Controversial Was the Development of Infant Baptism in the Early Church?" *Scottish Journal of Theology* 40 (1987): 4.

67. Latin edition in F. Oehler, ed. (Cambridge: Cambridge University Press, 1853), 761–87, ET: ACW 13.

68. Tertullian, *De Monog.* 8.

69. So W. P. Le Saint in the notes to ACW 13, n. 113, p. 161.

70. So also Gould, "Childhood in Patristic Thought," 46.

71. Cyprian, *Ep.* 64 (Latin text CSEL 3.2, ET: FC 51).

72. He refers to the narrative in 2 Kings 4:32-35.

73. Cyprian, *Ep.* 64.3.2.

74. Wright, in "How Controversial Was the Development of Infant Baptism in the Early Church?" 52, comments that Cyprian "seems ready to kiss and baptize even the baby still wet and unwashed from the womb."

75. Ibid., 51–52.

76. So ibid., 52: "Arguing *a maiori ad minus*, Cyprian reasons that, if an adult convert's erstwhile flagrant wickedness is no bar to his baptism, nothing can possibly stand in the way of the baptism of the newborn innocent." Wright correctly notes that the "contrast to Tertullian's viewpoint could hardly be more marked. . . . The difference between them is attributable in large measure to the conjunction Cyprian makes between infant baptism and original sin. Although the sins needing remission are not the baby's own, they necessitate his baptism."

77. Ibid., 54: "There is in fact not much evidence that churchmen were unduly concerned about infant baptism at all, and the considerable body of fourth-century Christian literature in the east yields remarkably few references to it. . . . Indeed, it is difficult to point to a single eastern father in the fourth century who links infant baptism with sin or original sin."

78. Ed. H. Hörner, *Gregorii Nysseni Opera* 3, I, 67–97. ET: *NPNF* 2nd series, 5. All references and quotations are from the English translation.

79. Gregory of Nyssa, *Infant.,* 373.

80. Ibid.

81. Ibid., 376. On this theme, cf. David L. Balás, *Metousia Theou—Man's Participation in God: Perfections according to Saint Gregory of Nyssa* (Rome: Herder, 1966).

82. Gregory of Nyssa, *Infant.,* 375.

83. "But no one can force us to give the family history of this ignorance, asking whence and from what father it is," *Infant.,* 376. Gould, in "Childhood in Patristic Thought," 49–50, n. 46, summarizes: "Ignorance of God is a defect or privation in the human relationship with God whose origin is difficult to account for (p. 80, 11–20 [*Gregorii Nysseni Opera*, 3, 1]). Gregory's reluctance to attempt to explain the origin of evil in general is apparent here, though he clearly believes that the partly material nature of human beings, however essential to their role in creation as a bond between the material and spiritual worlds, is also what interferes with their spiritual capacity for knowledge of the creator. . . . What we experience as evil is not a substance or positive quality but an absence of knowledge, goodness, and being, an inevitable consequence of our existence at a greater distance from God, and hence at a lower level of being, than that of the purely spiritual world."

84. Gregory of Nyssa, *Infant.,* 376.

85. Ibid., 374.

86. See for example, *Catechetical Oration* 5, in which Gregory of Nyssa writes about the "most excellent and precious of all goods; I mean the gift implied in being his own master, and having a free will. For if necessity in any way was the master of the life of man, the 'image' would have been falsified in that particular part, by being estranged owing to this unlikeness to its archetype," *NPNF* 2nd series, 5, p. 479. Cf. further James Herbert Srawley, ed., *The Catechetical Oration of Gregory of Nyssa* (Cambridge: Cambridge University Press, 1956), xxii–xxiii; Anthony Meredith, *Gregory of Nyssa* (London: Routledge, 1999), 21–22.

87. Gregory of Nyssa, *Infant.,* 376.

88. Cf. *Infant.,* 377 where the author depicts a baby as innocent.

89. Ibid., 374.

90. Ibid.

91. Gould, "Childhood in Patristic Thought," 50.

92. Gregory of Nyssa, *Infant.,* 378.

93. Ibid. Cf. also 377. Johannes Quasten, in *Patrology,* vol. 3 (Allen, Tex.: Christian Classics, 1986), 289–90, summarizes: "Although he [Gregory] speaks repeatedly of 'the inextinguishable fire' and the immortality of the 'worm', of an 'eternal sanction' (*Orat. Cat.* 40), although he threatens the sinner with eternal suffering and eternal punishment, he could not imagine an eternal estrangement from God of his intellectual creatures and explains elsewhere these expressions as referring only 'to long periods of time' (ibid., 26). He believes with Origen in the universal restoration at the end of time, and in the complete victory of good over evil. . . . Gregory sees in the Apokatastasis the magnificent and harmonious conclusion of the entire history of salvation, when every creature shall intone a chant of thanksgiving to the Saviour and even 'the inventor of evil' shall be healed." Quasten goes on to quote *Orat. Cat.* 26. Cf. also Gould, "Childhood in Patristic Thought," 50, n. 50. Gould notes that "The use of this phrase may indicate an equivocation between the idea of eternal punishment and that of purgation as the experience of the wicked after death; generally Gregory seems to favour purgation (e.g. p. 73, 15–17 [*Gregorii Nysseni Opera*, 3, 1])."

94. The following statement sheds light on his thinking: "If nothing in this world happens without God, but all is linked to the Divine will, and if the Deity is skilful and prudential, then it follows necessarily that there is some plan in these things bearing the mark of his wisdom, and at the same time of His providential care. A blind unmeaning occurrence

can never be the work of God: for it is the property of God, as the Scripture says, 'to make all things in wisdom,'" Gregory of Nyssa, *Infant.*, 373.

95. Ibid., 381.

96. Ibid., 380.

97. Ibid. Another reason why God lets infants with particularly strong dispositions to evil grow up is that when the good see God's harsh punishment they will more completely realize the extent of the rewards for virtue (380–81).

98. Ibid.

99. So also Gould, "Childhood in Patristic Thought," 51.

100. Vigen Guroian, "The Ecclesial Family: John Chrysostom on Parenthood and Children," in *The Child in Christian Thought*, ed. Marcia J. Bunge (Grand Rapids, Mich.: Eerdmans, 2001), 63.

101. Greek edition in SC 188. All quotations in English are from the translation in M. L. W. Laistner, *Christianity and Pagan Culture in the Later Roman Empire* (Ithaca, N.Y.: Cornell University Press, 1967). I also follow the reference system of the English translation.

102. Greek edition Migne, PG 47, 319–86, ET by D. G. Hunter, *A Comparison between a King and a Monk—Against the Opponents of the Monastic Life, Two Treatises,* Studies in the Bible and Early Christianity 13 (New York: Edwin Mellen, 1988). In the following I use the reference system of the English translation.

103. John Chrysostom, *Hom. in Mt.* 62.4 (PG 58, ET: *NPNF* 10).

104. Here I change the translation in *NPNF* from "limit" to "height." For the allegorical use of the term *oros* with a similar meaning, cf. G. W. H. Lampe, ed., *A Patristic Greek Lexicon* (Oxford: Clarendon, 1961), 974. Gillian Clark, in "The Fathers and the Children," in *The Church and Childhood: Papers Read at the 1993 Summer Meeting and the 1994 Winter Meeting of the Ecclesiastical History Society*, ed. Diana Wood (Oxford: Blackwell, 1994) 22, also translates *oros* with "height."

105. John Chrysostom, *De Inani* 1; *Oppugn.* 3.6. As the title of the treatise *An Address On Vainglory and the Right Way for Parents to Bring Up Their Children* indicates, its main purpose is to encourage parents to bring up their children in a way that prevents the emergence of vainglory.

106. Clark, in "The Fathers and the Children," 23, states that "John Chrysostom is thinking of little children, those in the category of the *nêpios* or *infants*, and ranges from babes in arms to toddlers."

107. John Chrysostom, *Bapt. Catech.* 3.6 (ET: ACW 31 p. 57).

108. Cf. ACW 31 n. 12, pp. 232–33; Phan, *Grace and the Human Condition*, 201–2.

109. Cf. ACW 31 n. 12, pp. 232–33; Phan, *Grace and the Human Condition*, 202.

110. John Chrysostom, *Hom. in Mt.* 28.3. ET: *NPNF* 1.10.

111. John Meyendorff, *Byzantine Theology: Historical Trends and Doctrinal Themes* (New York: Fordham University Press, 1974), 145. Meyendorff says that this view represents a consensus among the Greek patristic writers.

112. Ibid., 144. Meyendorff, who quotes this text, comments: "In this passage there is a major issue of translation. The last four Greek words were translated in Latin as *in quo omnes peccaverunt* ('in whom [i.e., in Adam] all men have sinned'), and this translation was used in the West to justify the doctrine of guilt inherited from Adam and spread to his descendants. But such a meaning cannot be drawn from the original Greek."

113. Ibid., 144–45. When explaining the understanding of death, Meyendorff says: "Mortality, or 'corruption,' or simply death (understood in a personalized sense), has indeed been viewed, since Christian antiquity, as a cosmic disease which holds humanity under its sway, both spiritually and physically, and is controlled by the one who is 'the murderer from the beginning' (Jn 8:44). It is this death which makes sin inevitable, and in this sense 'corrupts' nature."

114. Ibid., 144. Cf. also Guroian, "The Ecclesial Family," 68. Referring to *Bapt. Catech.* 3.21; *Hom. in Rom.* 10. 2; 3; 4, Phan, in *Grace and the Human Condition,* 203–4, focuses on elements that suggest that Chrysostom's position is not fundamentally different from that of Augustine's. Phan summarizes: "In brief, then, though falling short of Augustinianism, there was here an outline of a doctrine of original sin which would be elaborated in greater detail by Augustine."

115. Clark, "The Fathers and the Children," 23.

116. Cf. Leyerle, "Appealing to Children," 258–59. I am in debt to Leyerle for many of the texts used in the subsequent discussion, as well as to her observations.

117. John Chrysostom, *Hom. in Col.* 4.4, PG 62.330, ET: *NPNF* 13, p. 278.

118. John Chrysostom, *Hom in Heb.* 22.4, PG 63.160, ET: *NPNF* 14, p. 468. In this passage, Chrysostom is encouraging his hearers to be long-suffering. His reference to children's anger functions as a negative paradigm in his argumentative strategy. Laughter is the proper reaction to their anger, and should be employed to reprove and correct the child. If the adult becomes furious he has made himself a child. "For the angry are more senseless than children." Cf. also Chrysostom, *Oppugn.* 1.3, and the comments by Leyerle, "Appealing to Children," 259.

119. John Chrysostom, *Hom. in Col.* 4.4 (ET: *NPNF* 13, p. 278). Cf. also *De Inani* 20, and Leyerle, "Appealing to Children," 260.

120. Leyerle, in "Appealing to Children," 261, argues that according to Chrysostom, children display strong desire and attachment to anything they regard as their own property. The first manifestation of this desire is seen in the infant's desire for the breast, although he or she is physiologically ready for other nutrition. The fact that it could be hard to wean a child is taken by Leyerle as evidence that Chrysostom holds that small children show a strong attachment for things they regarded as their own. It is indeed true that he reflects a great deal of knowledge about weaning techniques, and he was aware that the desire for the breast was strong and difficult to overcome, but I do not agree that Chrysostom links the desire for the breast with a belief that children are driven by greed. Leyerle refers to *Hom. in. Mt.* 17.5 (PG 57.261–62), n. 37 p. 250. Furthermore, her reference to *Hom. in 2 Thess.* 4.4 (PG 62.492) as evidence for a strong appetitive desire in children is not relevant. The point here is not that children have overcome this desire by waiting for "the eldest to serve himself before stretching out their hands," but that the gifts of the table are equal for all. I have not been able to find any explicit evidence that Chrysostom associates children with "a strong appetitive desire and a tenacious attachment to anything they considered their own."

121. John Chrysostom, *Hom in Col.* 4.4 (PG 62.330, ET: *NPNF* 13 p. 279).

122. Cf. Leyerle, "Appealing to Children," 258: "he saw exhibited in children the 'natural' state of every person unimproved by virtuous restraint."

123. Leyerle, "Appealing to Children," 266.

124. Hence, I question Leyerle's view that Chrysostom operates with two contradictory opinions regarding the condition of children. Her reading of *Hom. in Mt.* 17.1 may supply an important premise for her understanding. She uses this passage as evidence for the view that "Of all the passions, human beings are most moved by anger and desire, *and by these from birth*" (259; my italics). However, the construction *tôn genikotatôn en hêmin pathôn* does not imply that the actual passions take root from birth, but rather affirms that human beings in general are moved by desire. The context indicates that it is adult human beings that the author has in mind. For the meaning of *genikos*, see Lampe, *A Patristic Greek Lexicon,* 311.

125. John Chrysostom, *De Inani* 90.

126. John Chrysostom, *Hom. in Eph.* 21. PG 62; ET in *On Marriage and Family Life,* trans. Catharine P. Roth and David Anderson (New York: St. Vladimir's Seminary Press, 2000). All references and quotations are from the English translation.

127. Ibid., *Hom. in Eph.* 21 (*On Marriage and Family Life* 65).

128. Ibid.

129. Cf. also Gould, "Childhood in Patristic Thought," 45: "If young children can desire a long life, Chrysostom must think that they can understand the notion of a reward that goes beyond purely immediate gratification, and therefore that they are capable, though in an immature way, of the use of reason, even if the idea of eternal life is beyond them."

130. John Chrysostom, *De Inani* 52 and 41 respectively.

131. Ibid., *De Inani* 39.

132. Ibid.

133. Ibid.

134. Ibid., *De Inani* 44.

135. Cf. Ibid., *De Inani* 80.

136. This is correctly underscored by Leyerle, "Appealing to Children," 265.

137. John Chrysostom, *De Inani* 22. Cf. also *Hom. in Eph.* 21 (*On Marriage and Family Life* 71); *Oppugn.* 3.19 (p. 171).

138. John Chrysostom, *De Inani* 25–30.

139. Ibid., *De Inani* 29.

140. Cf. for instance John Chrysostom, *Oppugn.* 3.6 (p. 135); *De Inani* 20; 37; 52.

141. John Chrysostom, *De Inani* 20.

142. Ibid.

143. John Chrysostom, *Oppugn.* 3.18 (p. 168).

144. Cf. for example *De Inani* 32; 37.

145. On human beings' ability to learn virtue in general, see the discussion in Antonios Danassis, *Johannes Chrysostomos: Pädagogisch-Psychologische Ideen in seinem Werk* (Bonn: Bouvier Verlag Herbert Grundmann, 1971), 68–71.

146. John Chrysostom, *De Inani* 33.

147. John Chrysostom, *Hom. in Eph.* 21 (*On Family and Marriage Life* 71).

148. V. Guroian, "The Ecclesial Family," 67: "Although he claims that all human beings are made in the image of God, Chrysostom believes that original sin has brought about corruptibility and death and weakened the capacity to grow into God's likeness in virtue and loving communion."

149. Ibid., 68.

150. Cf. Ibid., 66: "These central notions of his vision of parenthood [parents are to reveal the image of God in their children] are best understood in relation to Chrysostom's particular theological anthropology. This anthropology is thoroughly informed by the doctrine of the *imago Dei*: that every human being is created in the image and likeness of God."

151. Jerome, *Ep.* 107 (PL 22, 867–78) and *Ep.* 128 (PL 22, 1095–99). ET: *NPNF* 2nd series, 6.

152. Ibid., *Ep.* 128.1.

153. So also Joan M. Petersen, "The Education of Girls in Fourth-Century Rome," in *The Church and Childhood: Papers Read at the 1993 Summer Meeting and the 1994 Winter Meeting of the Ecclesiastical History Society*, ed. Diana Wood (Oxford: Blackwell, 1994), 29; 35.

154. Jerome, *Ep.* 128.2–3. Gould, in "Childhood in Patristic Thought," 47, summarizes: "Children are not to be permitted any indulgences which they will have to renounce later on, on the specious grounds that it is better for them to have desired them and learnt to renounce them than not to have had them and to carry on desiring them."

155. So also David F. Wright, "How Controversial Was the Development of Infant Baptism in the Early Church?" in *Church, Word, and Spirit: Historical and Theological Essays in Honor of Geoffrey W. Bromiley*, ed. James E. Bradley and Richard A. Mueller (Grand Rapids, Mich.: Eerdmans, 1987), 57.

156. Cf. Ibid. n. 43, p. 57.

157. Cf. John Chrysostom, *Hom. in Eph* 21 (*On Marriage and Family Life* 72).

158. Jerome, *Ep.* 128.1 (PL 22.1095–96).

159. PL 32, 659–868. ET: WSA 1.1. I follow the reference system of this English translation.

160. Maria Boulding in the introduction to Augustine, *The Confessions*, WSA 1.1 (New York: New City, 1997), 10.

161. Mary Ellen Stortz, "'Where or When Was Your Servant Innocent?': Augustine on Childhood," in *The Child in Christian Thought,* 83.

162. The question about the origin of the soul preoccupied Augustine throughout his life. The controversy with the Pelagians offered a particular challenge to reflect on this question. He did not, however, reach a conclusion. See below.

163. Augustine, *Conf.* 1.6.7.

164. Ibid.

165. Colin Starnes, *Augustine's Conversion. A Guide to the Argument of Confessions I–IX* (Waterloo, Ont.: Wilfred Laurier University Press, 1990), 3: "What Augustine implies is that since laughter proper comes only from the sense of a contradiction, then a baby who laughs must be distinguished from a simple animal without rational powers with which to see the contradiction."

166. Augustine, *Conf.* 1.6.8.

167. This is emphasized by Stortz, "'Where or When Was Your Servant Innocent?'" n. 18, p. 82: "'Non-innocence' is my own term to express what I believe to be Augustine's view. He believed that even infants are tainted with original sin, though no opportunity for actual sin has occurred. Thus their only 'innocence' resides in the fact of their physical frailty and their lack of language."

168. Augustine, *De Nup. et Conc.* 1.20.22 (ET: WSA 1.24).

169. Cf. also Starnes, *Augustine's Conversion,* 2.

170. Stortz, "'Where or When Was Your Servant Innocent?'" 84.

171. Augustine, *De Gen. ad Litt.* 10.13.23 (ET: ACW 42): "But who would dare assert that thefts, lies, and false oaths are not sins except one who wishes to commit such sins with impurity? Yet these sins are common in childhood, although it seems that they should not be punished as severely as in adults, because one hopes that with the passing years, as reason begins to take hold, these children will be able to understand better the precepts pertaining to salvation and to give them willing obedience."

172. Cf. *Conf.* 1.18.29.

173. Starnes, *Augustine's Conversion,* 22.

174. Cf. Gillian Clark, ed., *Augustine: The Confessions* (Cambridge: Cambridge University Press, 1995), 115.

175. Starnes, *Augustine's Conversion,* 23.

176. Cf. ibid.: "The meaning is that the kingdom of heaven belongs to the humble, not that children are innocent."

177. Boulding, *The Confessions,* n. 99, p. 60: "That the present triad, *eram . . . vivebam . . . sentiebam* is an intentional reference to the Trinity is evident from the next phrase Augustine uses of himself, *vestigium secretissimae unitatis.* He is made in the image of God, Three in One." Cf. further Starnes, *Augustine's Conversion,* 24.

178. Cf. Starnes, *Augustine's Conversion,* 24.

179. Augustine, *Conf.* 2.3.6: "The thorn-bushes of my lust shot up higher than my head, and no hand was there to root them out. Least of all my father's; for when at the baths one day he saw me with unquiet adolescence my only covering, and noted my ripening sexuality, he began at once to look forward eagerly to grandchildren, and gleefully announced his discovery to my mother. . . . She . . . started up in devout fear and trembling."

180. Starnes, in *Augustine's Conversion,* 34, notes that "It is clear that he was much troubled throughout the period covered in the *Confessions,* both before and after his conversion, by powerful sexual drives."

181. Augustine, *Conf.* 2.2.3; 4.2.2. See further Starnes, *Augustine's Conversion,* 35.

182. Augustine is particularly harsh to his father for being concerned only with Augustine's study for his career in this world, while neglecting his Christian formation (cf. *Conf.* 2.3.5). Although his mother Monica exhorted him not to fornicate and above all not to commit adultery, she did not insist on the point and agreed with her husband not to push him into marriage because they feared that having a wife (a "she-dog") would have negative effects on Augustine's hope for academic success. Now, however, Augustine is of the opinion that she was an instrument for the divine reason which ultimately stood behind the exhortation; at that time, however, he rejected it as "mere woman's talk" (*Conf.* 2.3.7).

183. Sallust, *The War with Catiline.*

184. Ibid., 16. On Catiline, see H. H. Scullard, *From the Gracchi to Nero: A History of Rome from 133 B.C. to A.D. 68* (London: Methuen, 1958), 105–10.

185. O. W. Holmes, quoted by Starnes, *Augustine's Conversion,* 37.

186. Cf. Boulding, *The Confessions,* n. 32, p. 68: "In view of his habitual preoccupation with the opening chapters of Genesis it is not difficult to see the pear tree episode as a parallel to the fall in Gen 3, which was followed by the awakening of disordered sexual concupiscence in Adam and Eve: here we have a symbolic 'fall' in Augustine's life, though his sexual concupiscence is already disordered. The mention of throwing the fruit to pigs evokes the plight of the prodigal son, who is never far from Augustine's mind in these pages (see Lk 15:15-16)."

187. Cf. further Augustine, *Conf.* 2.6.14 : "To do what was wrong simply because it was wrong—could I have found pleasure in that?" and 2.8.16: "What fruit did I ever reap from those things which I now blush to remember, and especially from that theft in which I found nothing to love save the theft itself, wretch that I was? . . . But since my pleasure did not lie in the pears, it must have been in the crime as committed in the company of others who shared in the sin."

188. Augustine, *Conf.* 2.4.9; 2.5.10; 2.7.15.

189. Cf. Stortz, "'Where or When Was Your Servant Innocent?'" 85.

190. Augustine, *Conf.* 2.7.15; 2.10.18.

191. Cf. Elizabeth A. Clark, "From Origenism to Pelagianism: Elusive Issues in an Ancient Debate," *Princeton Seminary Bulletin* 12 (1991): 288–89.

192. Pelagius, *Ep. ad Dem.* (PL 30, 105–16. ET: B. R. Rees, *Pelagius: Life and Letters* [Woodbridge, Suffolk, U.K.: Boydell, 1988]).

193. Pelagius, *Ep. ad Dem.* 16.2–3.

194. Pelagius, *Expos. Xiii Epist. Pauli* (on Rom 5:12): "*Therefore, just as through one person sin came into the world, and through sin death* [*propter ea sicut per unum hominem in hunc mundum peccatum intrauit et per peccatum mors*]. By example or by pattern. Just as through Adam sin came at a time when it did not yet exist, so in the same way through Christ righteousness was recovered at a time when it survived in almost no one. And just as through the former's sin death came in, so also through the latter's righteousness life was regained. *And so death passed on to all people, in that all sinned* [*et ita in omnes homines mors pertransiit in quo omnes peccauerunt*]. As long as they sin the same way, they likewise die. For death did not pass on to Abraham and Isaac and Jacob, concerning whom the Lord says: 'Truly they are all living.' But here he says all are dead because in a multitude of sinners no exception is made for a few righteous." Theodore S. de Bruyn, trans., *Pelagius' Commentary on Romans: A Translation, with Introduction and Notes* (New York: Oxford University Press, 1993), 92–93.

195. Pelagius, *Libellus Fidei* 17 (PL 48, 490).

196. *Libellus Fidei* 17 (PL 48, 490); *Expositio Catholicae* (PLS 1, 1684).

197. Pelagius in Augustine, *De Pec. Org.* 2.15.16: "The reason why infants are not in the same state in which Adam was before the transgression, is because they are not yet able to receive the commandment, whereas he was able; and because they do not yet make use of that choice of a rational will which he certainly made use of, since otherwise no commandment would have been given to him" (ET *NPNF* 5, p. 242).

198. Pelagius, *Ep. ad Dem.* 4. See further *De Lib. Arbit.* in Augustine, *De Grat. Chr.* 1.7.8.

199. Cf. for example, Pelagius, *De Lib. Arbit.* fragments in Augustine, *De Grat. Chr.* 1.3.4; 18.19; *Ep. ad Dem.* 2–3.

200. Pelagius, *De Lib. Arbit.*, frg. 3 (PLS 1, 1543). See further Torgny Bohlin, *Die Theologie des Pelagius und Ihre Genesis* (Uppsala: A.-B. Lundequistska Bokhandeln; Wiesbaden: Otto Harrassowitz, 1957), 31–36; Clark, "From Origenism to Pelagianism," n. 32, p. 289.

201. At the Council of Carthage in 411, Caelestius argues that the question whether or not sin is transmitted is not yet settled in the church. He himself opposed the idea that inherited sin was transmitted to infants, and referred to certain holy men, among them Rufinus the Syrian, who held the same position. At the Synod of Diospolis in 415, the following points were put forward as a summary of Caelestius's teaching: (1) that Adam was created mortal, and would have died whether or not he had sinned; (2) that Adam's sin injured only himself and not the human race; (3) that the law no less than the Gospel leads us to the kingdom; (4) that there were sinless men previous to the coming of Christ; (5) that newborn infants are in the same condition as Adam before the fall; (6) that the whole human race does not die through Adam's death or transgression, nor does the whole human race rise again through the resurrection of Christ, cited by Augustine, *De Gestis Pelagii* 23. Cf. further Gerald Bonner, *Augustine and Modern Research on Pelagianism* (Villanova, Pa.: Villanova University Press, 1972), 36; Peter Brown, *Augustine of Hippo: A Biography* (Berkeley: University of California Press, 1969), 344–45; Clark, "From Origenism to Pelagianism," 290.

202. Clark, "From Origenism to Pelagianism," 290.

203. For other aspects of the teaching of Julian's opponents that were condemned as Manichaean, see Elizabeth A. Clark, *The Origenist Controversy: The Cultural Construction of an Early Christian Debate* (Princeton, N.J.: Princeton University Press, 1992), 217–18.

204. Cf. Julian, *Ad Florum* in Augustine, *Op. Imp.* 1.6; 2.178.2. Tertullian is perhaps the most prolific adherent of this theory, cf. *De Anima* 27. He argues that all souls "were contained in Adam, since they must all be ultimately detached portions of the original soul breathed into him by God." Phan, *Grace and the Human Condition,* 109–10.

205. E. A. Clark notes that "this identification of traducians and Manicheans is explicitly noted by Julian at least seven times in *To Florus.*" Clark, "From Origenism to Pelagianism," 292.

206. Julian, *ad Florum* in Augustine, *Op. Imp* 2.24.1: "But how does this sin come to be in the little one? But God gave this. Through the soul's entrance into the body? But the soul which is newly created by God owes nothing to the bodily seed," (ET: WSA I/25, p. 171). All the following quotations in English are from this edition. See also 4.90.

207. Julian, *Ad Turbantium* in Augustine, *Op. imp.* 2.1.2.

208. Julian, *Ad Florum* in Augustine, *Op. Imp.* 1.48.3.

209. Quoted in Augustine, *De Grat. Chr.* 2.21.23.

210. Cf. further Julian, *Ad Florum* in Augustine, *Op. Imp.* 1.62; 5.23.

211. "The voice of all nature cries out in such agreement that justice belongs inseparably to God that it would be easier to find someone who denies his substance than someone who denies his justice." Julian, *ad Florum* in Augustine, *Op. Imp.* 3. 9.

212. Augustine, *Contra Duas Epistolas Pelagianorum* 4.4.7 (ET: WSA 1/24).

213. Augustine, *De Pecc. Mer. et Rem.* 1.35.65 (ET: *NPNF* 5; all the following quotations of this work are from this edition). Cf. also *De Nup. et Conc.* 2.27.45.

214. See for example Augustine, *De Pecc. Mer. et Rem.* 1.26.39.

215. Cf. Clark, "From Origenism to Pelagianism," 295.

216. Augustine, *De Pecc. Mer. et Rem.* 3.10.18.

217. Augustine, *Contra Iulianum* 3.3.8–9. (ET: WSA 1.24. All the following quotations in English of this writing are from this edition).

218. Augustine, *Contra Iulianum* 3.4.10.

219. Augustine, *Contra Iulianum* 3.6.13: "in creating human nature he [God] certainly did not inflict defects upon a nature that did not deserve them. . . . In the case of some little ones who have already been reborn, the evils with which they were born remain, or such evils befall them, and heaven forbid that we should say that these evils are not deserved." See also 2.1.3; *Contra Iulianum Op. Imp.* 2.236.2.

220. Augustine, *Contra Iulianum Op. Imp.* 2.236.2. Cf. also Augustine, *Ep.* 166.10.

221. Augustine, *Contra Iulianum* 5.10.43.

222. Cf. for example ibid., 6.4.8; 5.13–14.

223. Augustine, *De Nup. et Conc.* 2.33.56.

224. Cf. William Harmless S.J., "Baptism," in *Augustine through the Ages. An Encyclopedia,* ed. A. D. Fitzgerald (Grand Rapids, Mich.: Eerdmans 1999), 90: "What deeply offended him [Augustine] in Pelagian claims about infants' sinlessness was that such claims implicitly denied that Jesus had saved infants, for if they were truly sinless, then there would be nothing for him to save them from."

225. Augustine, *Contra Iulianum* 3.12.25.

226. Augustine, *De Nup. et Conc.* 2.35.60.

227. Augustine, *Serm.* 293.10 (ET: WSA 3/8).

228. Augustine, *De Pecc. Mer. et Rem.* 1.16.21 (ET: *NPNF* 5).

229. Augustine, *Serm.* 294.

230. Augustine, *Ep.*, 166.10 (ET: FC 30).

231. Augustine, *De Pecc. Mer. et Rem.* 1.34.63. Cf. also *De Catech. Rudibus* 1.2; *De Nup. et Conc.* 2.29.50.

232. This argumentation implies that Augustine's theology of inherited sin worked, to some extent, from the principle of *lex orandi, lex credendi* (the church prays what she believes); cf. Harmless, "Baptism," 89.

233. Augustine, *De Gra. et Lib. Arbit.* 22.44. Cf. also *Serm.* 293.10: "Finally, the baby itself bears witness to its wretchedness by crying. As best it can, feeble nature, understanding practically nothing, gives its testimony; it does not begin with laughter, it begins with a wail."

234. Stortz, in "'Where or When Was Your Servant Innocent?'" 100, comments: "We take the narcissism of an infant more lightly, hopeful that the child will grow out of it. Augustine found in it seeds of selfishness that he discovered in adults on a larger, more sinister scale."

235. This is stressed by Stortz, "'Where or When Was Your Servant Innocent?'" 100.

236. S. Currie, in "Children and Christianity from Paul to the Council of Chalcedon" (PhD diss., Cambridge University, 1993), 109, maintains that "Antique Christianity marked a break from the pagan past in its ability to conceive of children as moral actors in their own moral drama." She is right to emphasize the moral accountability of children in Christianity, but in my opinion she exaggerates the difference between the Greco-Roman tradition and the early Christians. Though the Christian tradition appears to put more stress on the moral responsibility of children than the pagan tradition, pagans too viewed children as moral agents who ought to lead virtuous lives.

4. Abortion, Infanticide and *Expositio*, and Sexual Relations between Children and Adults

1. See Michael J. Gorman, *Abortion and the Early Church: Christian, Jewish and Pagan Attitudes in the Greco-Roman World.* (Downers Grove, Ill.: InterVarsity, 1982), 34.

2. One example is Philo, *SpecLeg* 3.108–9: "If a man comes to blows with a pregnant woman and strikes her on the belly and she miscarries, then, if the result of the miscarriage is unshaped and undeveloped, he must be fined both for the outrage and for obstructing the artist Nature in her creative work of bringing into life the fairest of living creatures, man. But, if the offspring is already shaped and all the limbs have their proper qualities and places in the system, he must die, for that which answers to this description is a human being, which he has destroyed in the laboratory of Nature who judges that the hour has not yet come for bringing it out into the light, like a statue lying in a studio requiring nothing more than to be conveyed outside and released from confinement."

3. See Gorman, *Abortion and the Early Church,* 35; Frederick Christian, *Augustinus-Lexikon,* ed. Cornelius Mayer (Basel: Schwabe, 1986), 1; Andreas Lindemann, "'Do Not Let a Woman Destroy the Unborn Babe in Her Belly': Abortion in Ancient Judaism and Christianity," *Studia Theologica* 49 (1995): 253–54, 258–59.

4. Gorman, *Abortion and the Early Church,* 41.

5. Ibid., 38.

6. Philo begins this exposition at *SpecLeg* 3.83.

7. Philo describes the methods employed to kill children in the following harsh words: "with monstrous cruelty and barbarity they stifle and throttle the first breath which the infants draw or throw them into a river or into the depths of the sea, after attaching some heavy substance to make them sink more quickly under its weight." *SpecLeg* 3.114–15.

8. Philo, *SpecLeg* 3.110–16, at 115. The fact that Philo presupposes that many children who were exposed died, argues against one of the main theses of John Boswell, *The Kindness of Strangers: The Abandonment of Children in Western Europe from Late Antiquity to the Renaissance* (New York: Pantheon, 1988), namely, that almost all children who were exposed were in fact rescued. It is indeed clear that Philo is writing polemically, but it is too simple to dismiss him by calling his words "more a rhetorical device than a realistic apprehension" (48).

9. On the date and other general questions, see P. W. van der Horst in the introduction to Pseudo-Phocylides, in *The Old Testament Pseudepigrapha,* vol. 2, ed. James H. Charlesworth (London: Darton, Longman & Todd, 1985), 565–73.

10. Pseudo-Phocylides, 184–85.

11. On the date and other general questions, see the introductions by J. J. Collins to each book of the *Sibylline Oracles,* in *The Old Testament Pseudepigrapha* vol. 1, ed. J. H. Charlesworth.

12. *Sib. Or.* 2.281–83.

13. *Sib. Or.* 3.765–66.

14. Josephus, *Ant.* 4.278. For a discussion of Josephus and of rabbinic material that claims, against the background of Exod 21, that "the fetus does not have the legal status of a person," see Gorman, *Abortion and the Early Church,* 41–42.

15. See Gorman, *Abortion and the Early Church,* 34.

16. See Boswell, *The Kindness of Strangers,* 151, with textual references.

17. Held at Usha in Galilee in the mid-second century C.E.

18. Kethuboth 49b–51a, at 49b. ET: I. Slokti in *The Babylonian Talmud, Nashim* 3, ed. Isidore Epstein (London: Soncino, 1936).

19. Kethuboth 49b; see further Boswell, *The Kindness of Strangers,* 150.

20. Gorman, *Abortion and the Early Church,* 48.

21. On the basis of "internal evidence," many scholars hold that this document was composed at the beginning of the second century, but it is not possible to determine a precise date. On this, see Kurt Niederwimmer, *The Didache: A Commentary,* Hermeneia (Minneapolis: Fortress Press, 1998), 52–54.

22. On the question of the composition of this document, see Niederwimmer, *The Didache,* 1.

23. On the tradition of the "two ways," see, for example, Robert A. Kraft, *Barnabas and the Didache,* The Apostolic Fathers. A New Translation and Commentary, vol 3., ed. Robert M. Grant (New York: Nelson & Sons, 1965), 4–16; Niederwimmer, *The Didache,* 59–63; Willy Rodorf, "An Aspect of the Judeo-Christian Ethic: The Two Ways" in *The Didache in Modern Research,* ed. Jonathan A. Draper (Leiden: Brill, 1996), 148–53.

24. For a discussion of the life setting of the document, see W. Rodorf, "An Aspect of the Judeo-Christian Ethic," 153–59.

25. On this, see the discussion by Niederwimmer, *The Didache,* 30–41.

26. *Did.* 2:2 (ET: AFNTC).

27. See Niederwimmer, *The Didache,* 90: "As in *Did.* 5.2 (and as we find frequently in Jewish and Christian texts) the prohibitions on abortion and exposing of infants are connected. Thus the next command is prohibiting the killing of newborn children and thus implicitly forbidding that they be exposed"; see also Ferdinand R. Prostmeier, *Der Barnabasbrief.* Kommentar zu den Apostolischen Vätern 8 (Göttingen: Vandenhoeck & Ruprecht, 1999), 544.

28. *Did.* 5:2.

29. This is the position also taken by Lindemann, "'Do Not Let a Woman Destroy the Unborn Babe in Her Belly,'" 262.

30. *Did.* 5:2.

31. Lindemann, too, notes that the author provides a theological justification for the stance he takes: "'Do Not Let a Woman Destroy the Unborn Babe in Her Belly,'" 262.

32. See Reider Hvalvik, *The Struggle for Scripture and Covenant: The Purpose of the Epistle of Barnabas and Jewish-Christian Competition in the Second Century,* WUNT 2. Reihe, 82 (Tübingen: Mohr Siebeck, 1996), 17–55; Prostmeier, *Der Barnabasbrief,* 111–34.

33. Kraft, in *Barnabas and the Didache,* 134–60, presents a synoptic overview of the material common to both texts.

34. Here, the obligation to show love to one's neighbor has been intensified, as a comparison with the formulation of this commandment in the synoptic Gospels shows: "as yourself" has become "more than yourself."

35. This is the position taken by Gorman, *Abortion and the Early Church,* 50.

36 See R. McL. Wilson, ed., *New Testament Apocrypha,* vol. 2 (Philadelphia: Westminster, 1965), 664.

37. *Apocalypse of Peter* 8, Ethiopic text.

38. Ibid.

39. Clement of Alexandria, *Ecl.* 41: "The Scripture says that children exposed by parents are *delivered to a protecting (= temelouchos) angel,* by whom they are brought up and nourished. And they shall be, it says, as the faithful of a hundred years old here (cf. Isa 65:20; Wisd Sol 4:16). Wherefore Peter also says in his Apocalypse, "*and a flash of fire, coming from their children and smiting the eyes of the women.*" Cf. also *Ecl.* 48–49: "For example, Peter in the Apocalypse says *that children born abortively receive the better part.* These *are delivered to a care-taking (temelouchos) angel,* so that after they have reached knowledge they may obtain the better abode, as if they had suffered what they would have suffered, had they attained to bodily life. But the others shall obtain salvation only as people who have suffered wrong and experienced mercy, and shall exist without torment, having received this as their reward. [49] *But the milk of the mothers which flows from their breasts and congeals, says Peter in the Apocalypse, shall beget tiny flesh-eating beasts and they shall run over them and devour them*—which teaches that the punishments will come to pass by reason of the sins," following R. McL. Wilson, *New Testament Apocrypha,* vol. 2, 674, n. 2 and 675, n. 1.

40. Methodius, *Symp.* 2.6. For the view that Methodius is employing the *Apocalypse of Peter* here, see F. J. Dölger, "Das Lebensrecht des ungeborenen Kindes und die Fruchtabtreibung in der Bewertung der heidnischen und der christlichen Antike," in *Antike und Christentum* (Münster: Aschendorff, 1933), 4:50ff.

41. Clement of Alexandria, *Paed.* 2.10.96. (ET: FC 23).

42. Clement of Alexandria, *Str.* 2.18 (*ANF* 2, 368). In another passage, he contrasts the Alexandrians' interest in animals and their attitude toward them with their attitude to *expositio*: "they will not even come near an orphaned child, though they feed their parrots and bustards with their own hands. Even worse, they abandon to exposure the children born to them, yet lavish care on their brood of birds. They set a higher value on unreasoning animals than they do on rational men," *Paed.* 3.4.30 (FC 23, 224).

43. Clement of Alexandria, *Paed.* 3.3.21 (FC 23).

44. Ibid.

45. See also William V. Harris, "Child-Exposure in the Roman Empire," *Journal of Roman Studies* 84 (1994): 11.

46. I emphasize this point against Boswell, *The Kindness of Strangers,* 158–59, who broadly asserts that Clement's opposition to *expositio* is conditioned by his view of the place and function of sexuality within marriage.

47. Cf. K. Wengst, "Diognetus, Letter to," in *Dictionary of Early Christian Literature,* ed. Siegmar Döpp and Wilhelm Geerlings (New York: Crossroad, 2000), 176–77.

48. *Diogn.* 5.6.

49. Athenagoras, *Leg.* 35.6. Greek text in Edgar J. Goodspeed, *Die ältesten Apologeten: Texte mit kurzen Einleitungen* (Göttingen: Vandenhoeck & Ruprecht, 1914). ET: W. R. Schoedel, *Athenagoras, Legatio and De Resurrectione,* Oxford Early Christian Texts (Oxford: Clarendon, 1972).

50. 1 *Apol.* 27. Greek text in E. J. Goodspeed (ET: *ANF* 1).

51. 1 *Apol.* 29.

52. See Harris, "Child-Exposure in the Roman Empire," 10.

53. Latin text CSEL 69, ET: FC 10.

54. *Apol.* 9.17.

55. Ibid.

56. Ibid., 9.7.

57. Ibid., 9.8.

58. Tertullian, *De Anima* 23–37, esp. 37.

59. See Tertullian, *De Anima* 25.3; 26.4–5; 37.1–2, and the discussion in Gorman, *Abortion and the Early Church,* 55–58, and Lindemann, "'Do Not Let a Woman Destroy the Unborn Babe in Her Belly,'" 263–65.

60. Papinian, in Justinian, *Digest* 35.2.9.1. See Gorman, *Abortion and the Early Church,* 58.

61. Tertullian, *De Anima* 37 (*ANF* 3, p. 217); cf. Exod 21:22-23.

62. This view is also taken by John T. Noonan Jr., "An Almost Absolute Value in History," in *The Morality of Abortion: Legal and Historical Perspectives,* ed. John T. Noonan Jr. (Cambridge, Mass.: Harvard University Press, 1970), 12.

63. CSEL 2, ET: ACW 39.

64. Municius Felix, *Octav.* 30.1.

65. Ibid., 30.2.

66. Noonan, "An Almost Absolute Value in History," 12.

67. In my view, Boswell, in *The Kindness of Strangers,* 157, plays down the strength and extent of the Christian condemnation of *expositio* when he writes: "A few Christian moralists . . . condemned it, as a few pagan ethical writers had, but they were a minority and almost certainly urging their followers to a higher standard of conduct than the norm." Bearing in mind the amount of words devoted to this matter in the Christian and the pagan traditions respectively, there can be no doubt that the former is the stronger representative of the condemnation of *expositio,* which is rejected by a strikingly large number of early Christian texts. The fact that these were composed in various parts of the Roman empire, that they represent a variety of genres, and that they were written by the most central

church fathers in the period under examination, indicates that the opposition to *expositio* was particularly strong.

68. See Harris, "Child-Exposure in the Roman Empire," 17, n. 149.

69. *Adv. Haer.* 9.7 (*ANF* 5, p. 131).

70. Cyprian, *Ep.* 52.2. Here I follow the interpretation and translation in *ANF* 5, which takes "the fruit of a father's murder" as a reference to the aborted child. FC 51 has an alternative translation: "quickly after a parricide," which would refer to Novatian's father, who (as Cyprian has just mentioned) died of hunger on the street. This probably implies a criticism of Novatian for not looking after his own father; nevertheless, Novatian did not in fact kill him, and this is why I believe that these words refer to the aborted child. See also Gorman, *Abortion and the Early Church,* 111, n. 49.

71. On this, and other elements that may indicate Christian influence, see Gorman, *Abortion and the Early Church,* 61–62.

72. Lactantius *Inst.* 6.20; cf. 5.9 (ET: FC 49).

73. Lactantius *Inst.* 6.20.

74. Ibid.

75. Ibid.

76. For a brief introduction to the council of Elvira, see Michael P. McHugh, "Elvira," in *Encyclopedia of Early Christianity,* 2nd ed., ed. Everett Ferguson (New York: Garland, 1999), 370. Samuel Laeuchli, *Power and Sexuality: The Emergence of Canon Law at the Synod of Elvira* (Philadelphia: Temple University Press, 1972), 3–16, gives a longer presentation.

77. English translation of the conciliar decisions: Laeuchli, *Power and Sexuality,* 126–35.

78. Laeuchli, in *Power and Sexuality,* 99, interprets the decrees as speaking of abortion, and his translation reflects this understanding of the Latin text.

79. Gorman, *Abortion and the Early Church,* 64, referring to Huser, *Canon Law,* p. 17.

80. This position is also taken by Gorman, *Abortion and the Early Church,* 64.

81. The well-known theologian Ephrem the Syrian (c. 306–373) is an exception: according to Gorman, *Abortion and the Early Church,* 65, he argued in *De Timore Dei* 10 that abortion should be punished by death.

82. Canon 21; ET in Charles Joseph Hefele, *A History of the Christian Councils, from the Original Documents,* vol. 1: *To the Close of the Council of Nicaea, A.D. 325,* trans. William R. Clark (Edinburgh: T. and T. Clark, 1883).

83. See Hefele, *A History of the Councils,* 220; Gorman, *Abortion and the Early Church,* 65.

84. Cf. canons 20; 23; and 22. See also Gorman, *Abortion and the Early Church,* 65–66.

85. We know little about Amphilochius. He was appointed bishop in 374 and took part in the council of Constantinople in 381, as pastor of the most important church in Lycaonia and first in rank among twelve other bishops. He also played an active role in persuading emperor Theodosius to publish edicts against the Eunomians, the Arians, the Macedonians, and the Apollinarians: see *Saint Basil: The Letters,* vol. 3, trans. R. J. Deferrari (New York: Putnam, 1934), 5–6, n. 5.

86. Basil, *Ep.* 188.2, written in 374. Greek and English texts: LCL 215.

87. Greek text SC 320, 329, 336; ET: *ANF* 7. For a brief introduction, see George Dion Dragas, "Apostolic Constitutions," in *Encyclopedia of Early Christianity,* 92–93.

88. *Apost. Con.* 7.3.

89. See also Gorman, *Abortion and the Early Church,* 69.

90. John Chrysostom, *Hom. in Rom.* 24 (ET: *NPNF* 11, p. 520).

91. Augustine, *Ep.* 22.13.

92. Augustine, *Ep.* 121. See further Gorman, *Abortion and the Early Church,* 69.

93. Augustine, *De Nup. et Conc.* 1.17; cf. *Qu.* 2.80. This distinction underlies Augustine's discussion in the *Enchiridion* (a treatise on the faith that he wrote for laypeople toward the end of his life) about whether an aborted fetus shares in the resurrection: cf. 23.85–86.

94. Otto Wermelinger, "Abortus," in *Augustinus-Lexikon*, vol 1., ed. Cornelius Mayer (Basel: Schwabe, 1986), 8. Wermelinger is correct to note: "The evaluation of abortion depends on the point in time at which it is assumed . . . that the fetus receives its soul in the womb, and when the fetus which has been conceived is to be classified as a human person" (ET: B. McNeil).

95. Augustine, *Quaest. in Heptat.* 2.

96. *Contra Iulianum* 6.43, and Wermelinger, "Abortus," 8.

97. See for example Augustine, *De Nup. et Conc.* 1.17: "It is, nonetheless, one thing to have intercourse only out of the desire to have children; that involves no sin. It is something else to seek the pleasure of the flesh by having intercourse—though not with someone other than one's spouse: that involves a pardonable sin" (WSA I/24).

98. Cf. p. 108 in the present study. Gorman, in *Abortion and the Early Church*, 72, attempts to show that Augustine's opposition to abortion is ultimately rooted in the idea of God as creator, but I find this inaccurate. Gorman's reference to *De Nup. et Conc.* 1.1, where Augustine writes that all human life is "God's own work," is irrelevant, since Augustine does not relate this affirmation to abortion.

99. Page 132.

100. See William L. Langer, "Infanticide: A Historical Survey," *History of Childhood Quarterly* 1 (1974): 353–65.

101. C.Th. 5.9.1, cf. also C.Th. 5.10.1. This represents a fundamentally new line of thought: see J. Evans Grubbs, "Constantine and Imperial Legislation on the Family," in *The Theodosian Code: Studies in the Imperial Law of Late Antiquity*, ed. Jill Harries and Ian Wood (London: Duckworth, 1993), 134: "This law [C.Th. 5.9.1] is indeed innovative, because although earlier emperors had felt that those who brought up abandoned children ought to be compensated for their trouble, they had always respected the claims of paternal power."

102. On this, see Grubbs, "Constantine and Imperial Legislation on the Family."

103. See Geoffrey S. Nathan, *The Family in Late Antiquity: The Rise of Christianity and the Endurance of Tradition* (London: Routledge, 2000), 67: "Constantine was therefore probably trying to discourage exposure by legalizing the finality of the act. Once a child was abandoned, it was gone for good."

104. C.Th. 11.27.1.

105. C.Th. 11.27.2.

106. Grubbs, "Constantine and Imperial Legislation on the Family," 135.

107. See Timothy D. Barnes, "Lactantius and Constantine," *Journal of Roman Studies* 63 (1973): 29–46; Grubbs, "Constantine and Imperial Legislation on the Family," 135. However, Grubbs is correct to point out that although Constantine's legislation "probably discouraged parents from exposing their newborn children," it was not fully in accord with Christian thinking. The emperor did not forbid *expositio* by law, and he allowed those who rescued children to use them as slaves (135–36). Nevertheless, this does not prevent Grubbs from concluding that C.Th. 5.9.1 and 11.27.1 and 2 are "primarily 'Christian' in intent." Of all the Constantinian laws related to marriage and family, this legislation and the law on divorce (C.Th. 3.16.1) are the only decrees that she describes in these terms.

108. C.J. 8.51.2, following Harris, "Child-Exposure in the Roman Empire," 21.

109. C.Th. 9.14.1.

110. This is the view of H. Bennet, "The Exposure of Infants in Ancient Rome," *Classical Journal* 18 (1923): 351. Harris, "Child-Exposure in the Roman Empire," 22, holds that the words *quae constituta est* "probably" refer to C.Th. 9.14.1, and adds: "It should not surprise anyone who considers the history of punishment in the fourth century that the penalty for exposure was capital."

111. Thus Boswell, *The Kindness of Strangers*, 163.

112. Ibid.

113. See ibid.; Harris, "Child-Exposure in the Roman Empire," 22.

114. See Harris, "Child-Exposure in the Roman Empire," 22.

115. For examples, see Boswell, *The Kindness of Strangers*, 160–74. I am indebted to him for the texts on which I draw here.

116. Basil of Caesarea, *Ep.* 217.52; cf. *Ep.* 199.3 (ET: FC 28).

117. Basil of Caesarea, *Ep.* 217.52 (ET: FC 28).

118. Basil of Caesarea, *Hex.* 8.6. Such parents are compared to the eagle, which displays a complete lack of justice when it takes care of one eaglet and kicks another one out of the nest.

119. Immediately after this criticism of *expositio,* Basil invokes the injustice of the eagle to rebuke parents who make unfair distinctions among their children when dividing their inheritance among them; this is another indication that he has in mind parents who are fairly well-off.

120. *Hom. in Illud Lucae, Destruam* 4, following Boswell, *The Kindness of Strangers,* 165.

121. *Hex.* 18.58 (ET: FC 42).

122. In his attempt to minimalize this father's critical attitude to *expositio,* Boswell, in *The Kindness of Strangers,* 167–68, overlooks this point, or else waters it down. He is correct to emphasize Ambrose's condemnation of the rich, but he misinterprets the text when he writes that Ambrose "simply notes" that poor people expose their children. In context, the reference to this practice functions as a negative counterpart to the care that the birds show for their children.

123. Basil of Caesarea, *Hex.* 18.61 (ET: FC 42).

124. Ambrose, *De Nab. Hist.* 5.19–25.

125. Augustine, *De Nup. et Conc.* 1.17 (15): "This infliction of cruelty on their offspring so reluctantly begotten, unmasks the sin which they had practiced in darkness, and drags it clearly into the light of day. The open cruelty reproves the concealed sin" (*NPNF* 5). Cf. also *Ep.* 98.

126. Augustine, *Ep.* 98.6 (*NPNF* 1).

127. Aristides, *Apol.* 15 (*ANF* 9, Syriac version, p. 277).

128. Cyprian, *Ep.* 64.

129. Clement of Alexandria, *Str.* 2.23. On Clement's attitude to children, see Chapter 3 of the present study.

130. Ambrose, *Exp. in Luc.* 1.30: *diuinum igitur munus fecunditas est parentis.*

131. Augustine, *De Nup. et Conc.* 1.5.4; 1.16.14; 1.17.15. See also Justin Martyr, 1 *Apol.* 29; Athenagoras, *Leg.* 33; Clement of Alexandria, *Paed.* 2.10; *Str.* 3.7.58; 3.12.79.

132. Augustine, *Serm.* 346C 2 (ET: WSA III/10).

133. *Did.* 2:2; *Barn.* 19:4.

134. Theophilus of Antioch, *Autol.* 1.2 (ET: *ANF* 1).

135. Athenagoras, *Leg.* 34 (ET: *ANF* 2).

136. Clement of Alexandria, *Paed.* 3.8 (ET: *ANF* 2).

137. Clement of Alexandria, *Paed.* 2.10. See also Øyvind Norderval, "Holdninger til Seksualitet og Homoseksualitet i Antikken og i Oldkirken," *Norsk Teologisk Tidsskrift* 94 (1993): 208–9. For a wider discussion, with the main focus on Clement's rejection of sex beween women, see Bernadette J. Brooten, *Love between Women: Early Christian Responses to Female Homoeroticism* (Chicago: University of Chicago Press, 1996), 320–36.

138. Elizabeth A. Clark, "Sexuality," in *Encyclopedia of Early Christianity,* 1054.

139. Gregory of Nyssa, *Ep. Can.* 4.

140. Norderval, "Holdninger til Seksualitet og Homoseksualitet i Antikken og i Oldkirken," 199–201.

141. Rom 1:25-27; 1 Cor 6:9-10; 1 Tim 1:9-11.

142. See for example the appendix "Select Annotated Bibliography on Romans 1:26f. and the New Testament and Homosexuality Generally," in Brooten, *Love between Women,* 363–72.

143. Although Jesus presupposes and confirms marriage as an institution (Matt 5:27-32; 19:1-9), it appears that he presents celibacy as something good (Matt 19:10-12). Paul sees no need to change existing societal structures and one's own civil status, because he expects Jesus to return soon; but if one is unable to remain in celibacy, one should get married. In any case, because desire is a powerful instinct that can lead one to sin, it must be kept in check. Paul also points to his own sexual abstinence as an ideal for those who live in marriage (1 Cor 7:1-40). In the later epistles, however, marriage is seen as a normal and permanent order of things (1 Tim 3:2-4, 12; 5:9-10, 14; Titus 1:6; 2:3-5). On the view taken of marriage in the New Testament, see for example, Willy Rodorf, "Marriage in the New Testament and in the Early Church," *Journal of Ecclesiastical History* 20 (1969); Will Deming, *Paul on Marriage and Celibacy: The Hellenistic Background of 1 Corinthians 7* (Cambridge: Cambridge University Press, 1995); Dale B. Martin, "Paul without Passion: On Paul's Rejection of Desire in Sex and Marriage," in *Constructing Early Christian Families*, ed. Halvor Moxnes (London: Routledge, 1997).

144. Another early father who expresses the same idea is Justin Martyr: "Either we marry to have children, or, refusing to marry, we live in continence for the rest of our lives" (1 *Apol.* 29).

145. See Clement of Alexandria, *Paed.* 2.10.91; *Str.* 3.5.42–44; 3.7.57; 3.11.71; 3.12.87.

146. Norderval, "Holdninger til Seksualitet og Homoseksualitet i Antikken og i Oldkirken," 205.

147. Jostein Børtnes, "Sex og Vennskap mellom Menn i Antikken og den Tidlige Kirke," in *Naturlig Sex? Seksualitet og Kjønn i den kristne Antikken*, ed. Halvor Moxnes et al. (Oslo: Gyldendal, 2002), 202 (ET: B. McNeil).

148. Ibid. J. Børtnes observes: "It would have been more than surprising, had it been allowed within such an ethic for men to have sex with other men, and when we turn to the church fathers of the fourth century, we find a completely unambiguous condemnation of such activities. This is clearest in John Chrysostom" (ET: B. McNeil).

149. Børtnes, "Sex og Vennskap mellom Menn i Antikken og den Tidlige Kirke," 203–4 (ET: B. McNeil). For a more thorough discussion of John Chrysostom's reading of Rom 1:26-27, see Brooten, *Love between Women*, 344–48. I believe that Brooten argues convincingly in support of the main thesis in her book, namely, that the condemnation of sex between women that we find in Paul and in the early church in general was not different from the negative attitude to this form of sexual intercourse that existed elsewhere in the culture within which Christianity emerged.

150. John Chrysostom, *Oppugn.* 3.8. ET: D. G. Hunter, *A Comparison between a King and a Monk.*

151. Against John Boswell, *Christianity, Social Tolerance, and Homosexuality: Gay People in Western Europe from the Beginning of the Christian Era to the Fourteenth Century* (Chicago: University of Chicago Press, 1980), 132.

152. Thus Boswell, *Christianity, Social Tolerance, and Homosexuality*, 131; Norderval, "Holdninger til Seksualitet og Homoseksualitet i Antikken og i Oldkirken," 210.

153. See Johannes Quasten, *Patrology*, vol. 3, P Allen: Christian Classics (Utrecht: Spectrum, 1950), 463.

154. See D. G. Hunter, *A Comparison between a King and a Monk*, 140, n. 45. Hunter refers to *De sancto Babyla* 49, where Chrysostom "criticizes Plato and Socrates for teaching that pederasty is 'respectable and a part of philosophy.'"

155. This view is also taken by D. G. Hunter, *A Comparison between a King and a Monk*, 140, n. 45.

156. John Chrysostom, *Hom. in Mat.* 73.3.

157. Athanasius, *Life of Antony* 6; ET: R. C. Gregg, *Athanasius* (1980).

158. Basil, *Renunt.* 6 (PG 31, 640) and *Sermo asceticus* 323 (PG 32, 880). ET: J. Boswell, *Christianity, Social Tolerance, and Homosexuality*, 159–60.

159. See Aline Rousselle, *Porneia: On Desire and the Body in Antiquity* (Oxford: Blackwell, 1988), 134–35, for texts that indicate that children were sexually abused in monasteries.

5. Making "Athletes of Christ": Upbringing and Education of Children

1. See Michael Gärtner, *Die Familienerziehung in der alten Kirche: Eine Untersuchung über die ersten vier Jahrhunderte des Christentums mit einer Übersetzung und einem Kommentar zu der Schrift des Johannes Chrysostomus über Geltungssucht und Kindererziehung* (Köln-Wien: Böhlau Verlag, 1985), who has collected and systematically presented a number of Christian texts from the first four centuries. My discussion of this period is based largely on this textual material.

2. Walter Bauer, *A Greek-English Lexicon of the New Testament and Other Early Christian Literature*, 2nd ed., trans. and rev. William F. Arnt, F. Wilbur Gingrich, and Frederick W. Danker (Chicago: University of Chicago Press, 1979), 603; Henry George Liddell and Robert Scott, *A Greek-English Lexicon*, 9th ed. (Oxford: Clarendon, 1973), 1286–87, G. W. H. Lampe, *A Patristic Greek Lexicon* (Oxford: Clarendon, 1961), 995–96.

3. In our present context, it is not necessary to give an account of the wide-ranging scholarly discussions of the background to the household codes; I note only that the most convincing view holds that the household codes in the New Testament and in other early Christian writings must be seen against the background of what Xenophon and Aristotle say about the various groups in the household and their relationships to one another. For textual references and an introduction to the *status quaestionis* (state of the question), see Peter Balla, *The Child-Parent Relationship in the New Testament and Its Environments*, WUNT 155 (Tübingen: Mohr Siebeck, 2003), 165–73.

4. On the relationship between Eph 6:1-4 and Col 3:20-21, see for example Andrew T. Lincoln, *Ephesians*, Word Biblical Commentary 42 (Dallas: Word, 1990), 395–97; Jürgen Becker and Ulrich Luz, *Die Briefe an die Galater, Epheser und Kolosser* (Göttingen: Vandenhoeck & Ruprecht, 1998), 174; and Ernest Best, *A Critical and Exegetical Commentary on Ephesians* (Edinburgh: T. and T. Clark, 1998), 523. Best holds that we cannot say with certainty whether the author of Ephesians makes use of the household code in Colossians: he "is as likely to have drawn it directly from the tradition as from Colossians."

5. It is possible to argue that the exhortation to "children" is in fact addressing persons who have reached adulthood, but when one considers all aspects of the texts, I believe it most probable that these were children who had not yet become adults. This view is also taken by Peter T. O'Brien, *Understanding the Basic Themes of Colossians, Philemon* (Dallas: Word, 1982), 224, and Lincoln, *Ephesians*, 403. Best, in *A Critical and Exegetical Commentary on Ephesians*, 563, concludes that the children addressed by the author "must have been old enough to understand what is said, but they could have been small, subteenagers, or older teenagers and young adults." For the contrary view, that Colossians is referring to adult "children," see Gärtner, *Die Familienerziehung in der alten Kirche*, 36–37.

6. Many inscriptions that speak of a good housewife include the exhortation to women to love their husbands and their children: see Adolf Deissmann, *Bible Studies: Contributions, Chiefly from Papyri and Inscriptions, to the History of Language, the Literature, and the Religion of Hellenistic Judaism and Primitive Christianity*, 2nd ed., trans. Alexander J. Grieve (Edinburgh: T. and T. Clark, 1901), 225; Martin Dibelius and Hans Conzelmann, *The Pastoral Epistles*, Hermeneia (Philadelphia: Fortress Press, 1972), 140.

7. This is also the view of Dieter Lührmann, "Neutestamentliche Haustafeln und antike Ökonomie," *New Testament Studies* 27 (1981): 91–97; William A. Strange, *Children in the Early Church: Children in the Ancient World, the New Testament and the Early Church* (Carlisle: Paternoster, 1996), 75; Balla, *The Child-Parent Relationship in the New Testament and its Environments*, 181.

8. Dibelius and Conzelmann, *The Pastoral Epistles*, 53.

9. See Gärtner, *Die Familienerziehung in der alten Kirche*, 39.

10. For an overview of the most important works in the field of social anthropology on this subject and the discussion among scholars about whether it is appropriate to call the Mediterranean culture an "honor/shame culture," see Halvor Moxnes, "Honor and Shame: Readers Guide," *Biblical Theology Bulletin* 23 (1993): 168–69. Moxnes concludes that "it is fair to say that the thesis of a specific Mediterranean honor and shame culture holds, even if many aspects have been modified" (169). Another premise for the development of the honor/shame model is that Mediterranean societies have undergone lesser changes in their societal structures in the last 2500 years than many Western societies. One example of this stability is the patron/client relationships with their accent on honor: see S. N. Eisenstadt and Luis Roniger, *Patrons, Clients, and Friends: Interpersonal Relations and the Structure of Trust in Society* (Cambridge: Cambridge University Press, 1984), 50–81.

11. See Julian A. Pitt-Rivers, "Honour and Social Status," in *Honour and Shame: The Values of Mediterranean Society*, ed. J. G. Peristiany (London: Weidenfeld & Nicolson, 1965), 21–23; Moxnes, "Honor and Shame," 168.

12. Bruce J. Malina, *The New Testament World: Insights from Cultural Anthropology* (Louisville, Ky.: John Knox, 1981), 47, summarizes as follows: "Honor can be ascribed or acquired. Ascribed honor befalls or happens to a person passively through birth, family connections, or endowment by notable persons of power. Acquired honor is honor actively sought and garnered most often at the expense of one's equals in the social contest of challenge and response." See also Philip F. Esler, *The First Christians in their Social Worlds: Social-Scientific Approaches to New Testament Interpretation* (London: Routledge, 1994), 25–29.

13. Halvor Moxnes, "Honour and Righteousness in Romans," *Journal for the Study of the New Testament* 32 (1988): 63. See also Moxnes, "Honor and Shame," 168, and Malina, *The New Testament World*, 27–48.

14. Bruce J. Malina and Jerome H. Neyrey, "Honor and Shame in Luke-Acts: Pivotal Values of the Mediterranean World," in *The Social World of Luke-Acts: Models for Interpretation*, ed. Jerome H. Neyrey (Peabody, Mass.: Hendrickson, 1991), 26.

15. Malina, *The New Testament World*, 27–28.

16. See Rodney Stark, *The Rise of Christianity: How the Obscure, Marginal Jesus Movement Became the Dominant Religious Force in the Western World in a Few Centuries* (San Francisco: HarperSanFrancisco, 1997), 149–151.

17. Balla, in *The Child-Parent Relationship in the New Testament and Its Environments*, 181, takes substantially the same view, though without employing the categories of shame and honor, when he affirms that the aim of the household codes and other exhortations in the Pastoral Letters is to demonstrate to "the environment that Christians share their basic expectations concerning the ethical conduct in the household, the kernel of the wider society."

18. See Gärtner, *Die Familienerziehung in der alten Kirche*, 41.

19. See pp. 169–71 of the present chapter.

20. *Did.* 4:9; *Barn.* 19:5.

21. Polycarp, *Phil* 4:2.

22. Clement of Alexandria, *1 Clem.* 21:8.

23. Hermas, *Vis.* 1.3.1; cf. 2.2.2.

24. On this question, see for example Carolyn Osiek, *The Shepherd of Hermas*, Hermeneia (Minneapolis: Fortress Press, 1999), 49, 54.

25. *Didasc.* 22.

26. ET: R. H. Connolly, *Didascalia Apostolorum: The Syriac Version Translated and Accompanied by the Verona Latin Fragments* (Oxford: Clarendon, 1929).

27. Cf. Gärtner, *Die Familienerziehung in der alten Kirche*, 51, who points out correctly that "parents bear responsibility for the eternal salvation of their children, and that they put their own salvation at risk when they know that their children are sinning" (ET: B. McNeil).

28. *Didasc.* 14.

29. *Didasc.* 17.

30. *Didasc.* 14.

31. Greek text SC 320, 329, 336 (ET: *ANF* 7).

32. *Apost. Con.* 4.11.1–2.

33. *Apost. Con.* 4.11.24–29.

34. G. W. H. Lampe, *Greek Patristic Lexicon*, 85.

35. Jerome, *Ep.* 107.3.

36. Ibid., 107.13.

37. Ibid., 107.6.

38. Pythagoras employs the Greek letter upsilon to symbolize the different directions taken by the path to good and evil; cf. Persius 3.56. "Pythagoras depicted the Choice of Life under the form of the Greek letter u, which was originally made with one straight stroke on the right, and half-way up a curved branch on the left. The lower part represents the period of childhood; the branching ways the time when the choice has to be made between good and evil. This steep path to the right is the path of virtue" (F. A. Wright, *Select Letters of St. Jerome* [New York: Putnam, 1933], 354, n. 2).

39. On this, see John Chrysostom, *De Virginitate*. See also J. N. D. Kelly, *The Golden Mouth: The Story of John Chrysostom—Ascetic, Preacher, Bishop* (Grand Rapids, Mich.: Baker, 1995), 45–46.

40. John Chrysostom, *De Inani* 19: "Raise up an athlete for Christ! I do not mean by this, hold him back from wedlock and send him to desert regions and prepare him to assume the monastic life. It is not this that I mean. I wish for this and used to pray that all might embrace it; but as it seems to be too heavy a burden, I do not insist upon it. Raise up an athlete for Christ and teach him though he is living in the world to be reverent from his earliest youth."

41. See Kelly, *The Golden Mouth*, 98.

42. John Chrysostom, *Hom. in Eph.* 20; ET: *On Marriage and Family Life* 57, trans. Catharine P. Roth and David Anderson (New York: St. Vladimir's Seminary Press, 2000): "If we regulate our households (properly) . . . we will also be fit to oversee the Church, for indeed the household is a little Church. Therefore, it is possible for us to surpass all others in virtue by becoming good husbands and wives." See also Chrysostom's *Homily on Acts* (*NPNF* 11, p. 277), and Vigen Guroian, "The Ecclesial Family: John Chrysostom on Parenthood and Children," in *The Child in Christian Thought*, ed. Marcia J. Bunge (Grand Rapids, Mich.: Eerdmans, 2001), 65.

43. John Chrysostom, *Hom. in Eph.* 21. Greek text MPG 62, pp. 149–156; ET: *On Marriage and Family Life*, 65–72. My page references are to this English translation.

44. John Chrysostom, *Hom. in Eph.* 21, *On Marriage and Family Life* 68–69.

45. Antonios Danassis, in *John Chrysostomos: Pädagogisch-Psychologische Ideen in seinem Werk* (Bonn: Bouvier Verlag Herbert Grundmann, 1971), 55, summarizes this fundamental aspect of Chrysostom's thinking as follows: "John Chrysostom's views about the earthly and the heavenly life are fundamentally important for the differentiation he makes in the goal of education. For him, the earthly life is a preparation for the heavenly life. Holding fast to worldly things makes the individual fearful and prevents him from being open to higher goals. Hence he is unworthy of his great mission" (ET: B. McNeil). See also Danassis's discussion of the goal of upbringing in Chrysostom (55–61).

46. John Chrysostom, *De Inani* 19; 39; 63; 90.

47. Ibid., *De Inani* 39.

48. John Chrysostom, *Hom. in Eph.* 21, *On Marriage and Family Life* 68. See also ibid. 67, 71.

49. See for example, John Chrysostom, *De Inani* 22 and *Hom. in Eph.* 21, *On Marriage and Family Life* 71.

50. See for example, John Chrysostom, *De Inani* 16; 19; 25; 49; 50; 69; 70; 81; 88.

51. Liddell and Scott, *A Greek-English Lexicon,* 1576.

52. Gärtner, in *Die Familienerziehung in der alten Kirche,* 446, summarizes as follows: "Education means bringing the child's life into the desired order. And this educational ideal is a religious, moral-ethical ideal" (ET: B. McNeil). Gärtner observes that this primary focus on the ethical and moral formation of the child links Chrysostom's concern with a fundamental aspect of non-Christian upbringing in classical antiquity, but he points out correctly that this moral-ethical formation has a specific content in Chrysostom's eyes, namely the formation of children in keeping with the fact that they are made in God's image.

53. John Chrysostom, *Hom. in Eph.* 21, *On Marriage and Family Life,* 71–72.

54. John Chrysostom *Hom. in Eph.* 21, *On Marriage and Family Life,* 69.

55. John Chrysostom *Hom. in Eph.* 21, *On Marriage and Family Life,* 71.

56. John Chrysostom, *Oppugn.* 3.3 (p. 126); page references to the English translation by D. G. Hunter.

57. Ibid., 3.4 (p. 133).

58. Ibid., 3.3 (pp. 128–29).

59. Ibid., 3.3 (p. 129).

60. Cf. Titus 1:6.

61. Chrysostom, *Hom. in Eph* 21, *On Marriage and Family Life* 71–72.

62. John Chrysostom, *Oppugn.* 3.2 (pp. 124–25). He refers to 1 Cor 5:1-5; 10:24; Gal 6:1; 1 Thess 5:11, 14; Rom 15:17.

63. Ibid., 3.4.

64. John Chrysostom, *Hom. in Eph.* 21, *On Marriage and Family Life* 71.

65. See p. 86.

66. John Chrysostom, *De Inani* 22.

67. On the idea of participation in God as the definitive destiny of the human person according to Eastern Christian theology, see David L. Balás, *Metousia Theou—Man's Participation in God: Perfections according to Saint Gregory of Nyssa* (Rome: Herder, 1966), and John Meyendorff, *Byzantine Theology: Historical Trends and Doctrinal Themes* (New York: Fordham University Press, 1974), 138–41, 163–64, 171–75.

68. Guroian, in "The Ecclesial Family," 69, notes correctly that "Parenthood is right in the thick of a web of human relations, obligations, and the synergy of human and divine wills that contributes to salvation. Thus parents hold not only an ecclesial office but also a soteriological one, a salvific one. God has put parents in care of their children's soul, and whether a child inherits the kingdom of heaven relies upon the care he or she receives from parents." Guroian also points out the implicit parallel between Christ and the parents' role as educators: "Chrysostom argues that when parents educate their children in virtue, they assume a role comparable to Christ's action for all of humanity. . . . Parents are not the saviors of their children, but they are, according to God's will and design, their natural teachers, as Christ is the divine teacher for all of humankind" (68).

69. For some examples of the use made of "shame/honor" in Chrysostom's commentary on Matthew, see Hendrick F. Stander, "The Concept of Honour/Shame in Chrysostom's Commentary on Matthew," paper delivered at the Fourteenth International Conference on Patristic Studies, Oxford 2003 (forthcoming in *Studia Patristica*).

70. John Chrysostom, *Hom. in Eph.* 21, *On Marriage and Family Life* 71–72.

71. John Chrysostom, *De Inani* 15; *Hom. in Eph.* 21, *On Marriage and Family Life* 69.

72. John Chrysostom, *Hom. in Eph.* 21, *On Marriage and Family Life* 69.

73. John Chrysostom, *Hom. in 1 Tim.* 10 (*NPNF* 13, p. 440).

74. Ambrose, *De bono mortis* 8.35 (ET: FC 65).

75. Cf. Ambrose, *De Iacob* 2.7; *De Ioseph* 2.5.

76. Augustine, *Conf.* 2.3.5 (WSA I/1).

77. Augustine, *Serm.* 323.1.

78. Ibid., 13.9 (WSA III.1).

79. Ibid., 15A 3. Geoffrey Nathan, in *The Family in Late Antiquity: The Rise of Christianity and the Endurance of Tradition* (London: Routledge, 2000), 147, asks what was Augustine's "greatest concern" with regard to the education parents were to give their son, and answers his own question as follows: "Odd as it may seem, his great fear, expressed weekly to his flock, was that young men, so untrained and wanton, would squander their inheritance. In several sermons, Augustine railed against the danger of using one's wealth to indulge his desires." Nathan cites in support of this interpretation the same texts to which I refer here. He is correct to observe that Augustine here reflects general attitudes in classical society, where one sign of maturity and a sense of responsibility in a son was to be concerned with the inheritance from his father and to look after this well; but Nathan sees Augustine's focus on property and money in a wider theological and ethical framework. Augustine regarded money as an instrument that allowed people to satisfy various desires that tied human beings to this earth, and such a use of money was seen in negative terms. Money could and should, however, be used for something positive, namely for alms to the poor and for other good causes administered by the church. This, however, does not permit us to draw the conclusion that the obligation to give alms to the poor is the real concern behind his admonition that parents must bring up their children to be responsible heirs. It is of course possible that Augustine was motivated in this way, but the texts do not say this explicitly. It is true that he reproaches fathers for accumulating property in view of a future inheritance, when the heir is in fact already dead (*Serm.* 9.20–21), but this passage does not bear the weight Nathan places upon it, when he employs it as an argument for his view.

80. Eph 6:4 and Col 3:20.

81. *Epictetus*, 2.10.7. See also Balla, *The Child-Parent Relationship in the New Testament and its Environments*, 74, 175.

82. On the father's authority and position in the household, see Chapter 2 of the present study, pp. 38–40.

83. On this, see Andrew T. Lincoln, *Ephesians*, 399–402.

84. Philo, *SpecLeg* 2.22ff.; cf. also *Decal* 119–20.

85. Lev 20:9; Deut 21:18-21.

86. Philo, *SpecLeg* 2.232: "And therefore the fathers have the right to upbraid their children and admonish them severely and if they do not submit to threats conveyed in words to beat and degrade them and put them in bonds. And further if in face of this they continue to rebel . . . the law permits the parents to extend the punishment to death." Cf. also Josephus, *Ap* 2.27.206.

87. Ps.-Phocylides, *Sent.* 207–209.

88. Lincoln, *Ephesians*, 400–401.

89. Deut 6:4-7.

90. Josephus, *Ap.* 1.12.60.

91. See for example, Prov 13:24; 19:18; Sir 7:23-25; 22:3-6; 30:1-13. For other types of texts, cf. for example 4 Macc 18:10-19; Josephus, *Ap* 2.173–74; 2.178; 2.204; Philo, *LegGai* 115; 210; *Praem* 162; *SpecLeg* 1.314; 2.88; 4.149–50. See also John M. G. Barclay, "The Family as the Bearer of Religion in Judaism and Early Christianity," in *Constructing Early Christian Families: Family as Social Reality and Metaphor*, ed. Halvor Moxnes (New York: Routledge, 1997), 69–72.

92. Barclay, "The Family as the Bearer of Religion in Judaism and Early Christianity," 70.

93. Col 3:21.

94. Eph 6:4.

95. This is the view of Kurt Niederwimmer, *Didache: A Commentary,* Hermeneia (Minneapolis: Fortress Press, 1998), 110. For the use of this term in Hellenistic material, see H. R. Balz, "*Phobeô ktl,*" in *TDNT* 9:193–92.

96. On this, see J. Wanke, "*Phobeô ktl,*" in *TDNT* 9:202–3.

97. See ibid.

98. Gärtner, *Die Familienerziehung in der alten Kirche,* 44, with references to secondary literature.

99. Clement of Alexandria, *1 Clem.* 21:8.

100. My interpretation of this passage assumes that *en auto* at 21:8 refers to *phobos* (not to *theos*). See the discussion in Horatio E. Lona, *Der erste Clemensbrief,* Kommentar zu den Apostolischen Vätern 2 (Göttingen: Vandenhoeck & Ruprecht, 1998), 284.

101. See Odd M. Bakke, *"Concord and Peace": A Rhetorical Analysis of the First Letter of Clement with an Emphasis on the Language of Unity and Sedition,* WUNT 2. Reihe 143 (Tübingen: Mohr Siebeck, 2001), 126–36, 191–96.

102. *Did.* 4:9; *Barn.* 19:5.

103. See Niederwimmer, *Didache,* 141–42; Ferdinand R. Prostmeier, *Der Barnabasbrief,* Kommentar zu den Apostolischen Vätern 8 (Göttingen: Vandenhoeck & Ruprecht, 1999), 544–45.

104. *Didasko* (*Did.* 4:9; *Barn.* 19:5); *paideuo* (*1 Clem.* 21:5, about the young; Polycarp, *Phil.* 4:2); *manthano* (*1 Clem.* 21:8); *noutheteo* (Hermas, *Vis.* 1.3.1–2.).

105. *Didasc.* 22 (ET: Connolly, *Didascalia Apostolorum*).

106. Ibid.

107. Hippolytus, *Apostolic Tradition* 6. Tertullian and Cyprian likewise hold that it is impossible for Christians to exercise certain professions: cf. Tertullian, *De Idol.* 9–11, and Cyprian, *Ep.* 2.1.

108. *Didasc.* 22.1–3 (ET: Connolly, *Didascalia Apostolorum*).

109. Cf. Gärtner, *Die Familienerziehung in der alten Kirche,* 176. I draw on the same texts as Gärtner.

110. Proverbs 6:6-11.

111. 2 Thessalonians 3:10.

112. *Didasc.* 13 (ET: Connolly, *Didascalia Apostolorum,* 128–29).

113. "And let those who are young in the Church be ministering diligently, without sloth, in all things that are needful, with much reverence and modesty": *Didasc.* 13 (ET: Connolly, *Didascalia Apostolorum,* 128). See also Gärtner, *Die Familienerziehung in der alten Kirche,* 176.

114. See Gärtner, *Die Familienerziehung in der alten Kirche,* 181.

115. *Didasc.* 22 (ET: Connolly, *Didascalia Apostolorum,* 194).

116. Ibid. 22 (ET: Connolly, *Didascalia Apostolorum,* 193).

117. Ibid.

118. Cf. Gärtner, *Die Familienerziehung in der alten Kirche,* 179–80, who correctly observes: "With regard to corporal discipline, he relies heavily on the educational praxis reflected in the Book of Proverbs" (ET: B. McNeil).

119. Cf. Gärtner, *Die Familienerziehung in der alten Kirche,* 180.

120. The admonition to beat one's children to make them obedient is preceded by an exhortation to teach them the Word of the Lord, and is followed by an exhortation to teach them sacred scripture. It is possible that the words: "bring them [i.e., their children] under with cutting stripes and make them submissive" should be read as a concretization of the preceding sentence. In this case, these words are to be interpreted metaphorically: the author is speaking of the "blows" inflicted by the Word of God. Such a reading would envisage a milder form of discipline, and would be in keeping with the text as we have it in the *Didascalia.* However, if the words about "stripes" did in fact function as a concretization of the

preceding exhortation to teach children the Word of God, we would have expected to find participial forms of the verbs. The imperative forms that the author employs make this an independent sentence. Besides this, the prominent position that he gives to his quotations from Proverbs and Sirach indicate that his words about "stripes" are to be taken literally. Gärtner, does not discuss the possibility of interpreting *stuphete de auta kai darmois kai poi- eite hupotaktika* metaphorically, but is content to note that we do not find in the *Apostolic Constitutions* the same toning down of corporal punishment that we find in our text of the *Didascalia*. Gärtner, *Die Familienerziehung in der alten Kirche*, 306.

121. Jerome, *Ep.* 107.4. As we have seen in Chapter 2, pp. 19–20, this awareness that a child can be formed while it is still small is not confined to Jerome.

122. Jerome, *Ep.* 107.8.

123. Ibid., 107.4.

124. Ibid., 128.3a.

125. Ibid., 107.9.

126. Ibid., 128.3a.

127. Ibid.

128. Ibid.

129. Ibid., 107.9. It is unthinkable that Paula should go out alone: "At no time let her go abroad, lest the watchmen find her that go about the city, and lest they smite and wound her and take away from her the veil of her chastity, and leave her naked in her blood. Nay rather when one knocks at her door, let her say: 'I am a wall and my breasts like towers'" (*Ep.* 107.9; quotation from *Cant.* 8.10).

130. Jerome, *Ep.* 107.7.

131. Ibid., 107.11.

132. Ibid., 107.5.

133. Joan M. Petersen, in "The Education of Girls in Fourth-Century Rome," in *The Church and Childhood: Papers Read at the 1993 Summer Meeting and the 1994 Winter Meet- ing of the Ecclesiastical History Society,* ed. Diana Wood (Oxford: Blackwell, 1994), 35, notes: "The advice about personal adornment seems a little premature for girls of four or five years old. It seems as though Jerome used his letters often as vehicles for his own thoughts and opinions, without always paying attention to the needs of the recipient."

134. Jerome, *Ep.* 107.10.

135. Ibid., 107.11.

136. Ibid., 128.3a.

137. Ibid., 107.10.

138. Jerome, *Ad Jov.*

139. Ibid. 2.12. Unlike those who lead an ascetic life, persons whose god is the belly have no control over their lusts. Lusts and desires are nourished by every form of luxury: "Take away the luxurious feasting and the gratification of lust, and no one will want riches to be used either in the belly, or beneath it" (*Ad Jov.* 2.11; *NPNF* 6). Food stimulates sexual desire. See further K. O. Sandnes, *Belly and Body in the Pauline Epistles* (Cambridge: Cambridge University Press, 2002), 238–244. Sandnes, p. 240, n. 53, quotes Teresa M. Shaw, *The Burden of the Flesh: Fasting and Sexuality in Early Christianity* (Minneapolis: Fortress Press, 1988): "'underlying Jerome's defence of fasting is his understanding of the connection between pleasure of eating and sexual desire' (p. 101). How according to many writers in the Early Church repletion in food entices toward sexual intercourse, has been worked out in detail by Shaw."

140. Jerome, *Ep.* 107.10: "I strongly disapprove—especially for those of tender years—of long and immoderate fasts in which week is added to week and even oil and apples are forbidden as food."

141. Jerome, *Ep.* 107.9.

142. See Chapter 3, p. 87.
143. Jerome, *Ep.* 107.12.
144. Ibid., *Ep.* 107.4.
145. Ibid.: "Above all you must take care not to make her lessons distasteful to her lest a dislike for them conceived in childhood may continue into her maturer years."
146. Cf. Quintilian, *Inst.* 1.1.26–27; and further, J. M. Petersen, "The Education of Girls in Fourth-Century Rome," 34.
147. Jerome, *Ep.* 128.3a.
148. On this, see Jerome, *Ep.* 107.4.
149. Ibid., *Ep.* 107.9.
150. Ibid.
151. John Chrysostom, *De Inani* 27.
152. Ibid., *De Inani* 28.
153. Gärtner, in *Die Familienerziehung in der alten Kirche,* 280, observes that this shows that "when he makes this comparison, he is interested not so much in the stability of the lock, as in its character. It is not only important *that* the gate of speech is closed: it also matters *how* it is closed" (ET: B. McNeil).
154. The description of the appearance of the city of the soul seems inspired by the description of the heavenly city in Revelation: cf. Gärtner, *Die Familienerziehung in der alten Kirche,* 280. Gärtner cites other passages in which Chrysostom says that God dwells in the human person (280–81).
155. John Chrysostom, *De Inani* 28. This applies to adults as well: they too must always have God's Word on their lips. See Gärtner, *Die Familienerziehung in der alten Kirche,* 283, with reference to *Hom. in Jo.* 32 (31) (OPG 59, 186). On the private reading of scripture by the members of Chrysostom's congregation, see Reiner Kaczynski, *Das Wort Gottes in Liturgie und Alltag der Gemeinden des Johannes Chrysostomus* (Freiburg: Herder, 1974), 310, 398. Gärtner, p. 283, summarizes as follows: "The child is to speak the words of God not superficially and seldom, but in a thorough manner" (ET B. McNeil).
156. John Chrysostom, *De Inani* 28.
157. We find a similar use of this term in Eusebius of Caesarea and the Cappadocian fathers. See Gärtner, *Die Familienerziehung in der alten Kirche,* 287.
158. In addition to John Chrysostom, *De Inani* 28, cf. 34 and 60.
159. John Chrysostom, MPG 62, 362–364 (ET: *NPNF* 13).
160. John Chrysostom, *NPNF* 13, p. 301.
161. See Kaczynski, *Das Wort Gottes in Liturgie und Alltag der Gemeinden des Johannes Chrysostomus,* 340, 343. One clear indication that the psalms and other Christian hymns were commonly sung in Christian families in the fourth century is that Emperor Julian's attempt to restore the pagan religion and culture included a decree that pagan religious songs were to be sung in people's homes. Cf. Julian, *Ep.* 56; Johannes Quasten, *Musik und Gesang in den Kulten der heidnischen Antike und christlichen Früzeit* (Münster: Verlag der aschendorffschen Verlagsbuchhandlung, 1930), 136; Gärtner, *Die Familienerziehung in der alten Kirche,* 290.
162. Here, and in my following remarks about spiritual songs, I rely chiefly on the excursus on "Das Lied in der christlichen Familienerziehung" in Gärtner, *Die Familienerziehung in der alten Kirche,* 287–93.
163. Cf. John Chrysostom, *Hom. in Col.* 9, where he lists various aspects of Christian morality that children learn by singing psalms.
164. Cf. John Chrysostom, *De Inani* 60.
165. Ibid., *De Inani* 80.
166. Ibid., *De Inani* 30.
167. John Chrysostom, *Oppugn.* 3.3 (p. 128).

168. John Chrysostom, *De Inani* 30. On Chrysostom's views about the employment of punishment and rewards in upbringing, see J. Seidlmayer, *Die Pädagogik des Johannes Chrysostomus* (Münster: Münsterverlag, 1926), 45–58; Danassis, *Johannes Chrysostomus,* 178–90.

169. John Chrysostom, *Hom. in Col.* 4.3 (*NPNF* 13, p. 277).

170. John Chrysostom, *De Inani* 41.

171. On this, see Danassis, *John Chrysostomos,* 188–90.

172. Danassis, *John Chrysostomos,* 190.

173. Blake Leyerle, in "Appealing to Children," *Journal of Early Christian Studies* 5 (1997): 257, claims that, in comparison with verbal punishment and threats of corporal punishment, "a program of inducement" is preferable, but I do not believe that our texts justify this interpretation. In my view, it is clear that punishment—or the threat of punishment—is the most important element in Chrysostom's writings and occupies most space in our texts. This is certainly the case, if we limit "reward" to something parents give their children (whether material objects or a positive affirmation in the form of caresses or praise, etc.), prescinding from the rewards they receive from others in the form of acknowledgement and the satisfaction they feel at mastering a task or possessing knowledge about something.

174. John Chrysostom, *De Inani* 67.

175. See Gärtner, *Die Familienerziehung in der alten Kirche,* 310.

176. See ibid., 310–11.

177. John Chrysostom, *De Inani* 36: "he that hears no base or wicked words does not utter base words either."

178. In chapter 37, Chrysostom compares the child to a little plant. Just as one must give a sprout a great deal of attention and care, so parents too must ensure that their child receives the correct care from its earliest years. This is why he exhorts them to "take thought for good nurses," so that "a fair foundation from the ground up be laid for the young and that from the beginning they may receive nought that is evil." As we have seen, John Chrysostom is not the only writer who is aware that the influences to which children are exposed while they are small have great significance for the formation of their personality. This was a widespread view in antiquity: cf. 22–23.

179. Chrysostom, *Hom. in Eph.* 21, *On Marriage and Family Life* 67. M. Gärtner, in *Die Familienerziehung in der alten Kirche,* 282, sums up as follows the importance and the place the Bible is to have in education and in life: "The entire course of a person's life should be accompanied by the Word of God, which must be continually on one's lips. Chrysostom aims at a total permeation of life by the Christian principles, which are to give this life its structure. The biblical writings should be recited not only continuously, but also in a serious manner" (ET B. McNeil).

180. Chrysostom, *Hom. in Eph.* 21, *On Marriage and Family Life* 69: "A man who never travels by sea doesn't need to know how to equip a ship, or where to find a pilot or a crew, but a sailor has to know all these things. The same applies to the monk and the man of this world. The monk lives an untroubled life in a calm harbor, removed from every storm, while the worldly man is always sailing the ocean, battling innumerable tempests."

181. John Chrysostom's writings attack greed relatively often. This vice shows that a person prefers to satisfy his stomach rather than to satisfy the demands made by God. We see this vice in the narrative of Cain and Abel, where Cain chooses to reserve the best portions for his own stomach rather than to give them to the one to whom they rightly belong, namely, God. For scriptural references and discussion, see Gärtner, *Die Familienerziehung in der alten Kirche,* 40.

182. When Chrysostom uses this particular narrative as the starting point for a warning against jealousy, he reflects a long tradition going back to the intertestamental literature: *T. Benj.* 7 in the Testaments of the Twelve Patriarchs. Christian sources include *1 Clem* 4:1-7;

Theophilus, *Autol.* 2.29; Jerome, *Ep.* 125. Other examples in Chrysostom are *Hom. in Gen.* 46.3 (MPG 54, 425); *Hom. in Rom.* 7.6 (MPG 60, 449).

183. Philo employs the narrative of Jacob and Esau in a similar manner: Esau acted as he did because he was the slave of his belly, and lacked self-control, and he serves as a cautionary example, one who failed to demonstrate or practice *enkrateia*. Philo sometimes speaks of earthly desire as a synonym for the delights of the stomach. For textual references and discussion, see Sandnes, *Belly and Body in the Pauline Epistles,* 117–21.

184. This has been convincingly demonstrated by Sandnes, *Belly and Body in the Pauline Epistles*; for textual references to Chrysostom, see ibid. 244–52.

185. John Chrysostom, *De Inani* 64–87.

186. G. W. H. Lampe, *A Patristic Greek Lexicon,* 657.

187. Gärtner, *Die Familienerziehung in der alten Kirche,* 65 (ET: B. McNeil). He suggests the German translation "Durchsetzungskraft."

188. Lampe, *A Patristic Greek Lexicon,* 806.

189. See M. L. W. Laistner, *Christianity and Pagan Culture in the later Roman Empire* (New York: Cornell University Press, 1967), 139, n. 36; Gärtner, *Die Familienerziehung in der alten Kirche,* 387–89.

190. John Chrysostom, *De Inani* 65.

191. A nonviolent treatment of slaves is also an element in the educational program in chapter 10 of Ps.-Plutarch's treatise on upbringing.

192. Chrysostom returns at a later point in his treatise (ch. 79) to the moral danger posed by the theater. He writes that the father must take his son with him and stand outside the theater exit at the end of the play. There they are to observe the members of the audience as they emerge, and are to laugh at the young men because they are "inflamed with desire." While they stand there, the father is to ask his son what the audience gained by being in the theater—and he himself is to reply: "Nothing but shame, reproach, and damnation." Chrysostom concludes that "abstention from all these spectacles and songs conduces not a little to virtue."

193. In another context, Chrysostom mentions Diogenes, Aristides, and Archelaus (the teacher of Socrates) as persons worth imitating: see Laistner, *Christianity and Pagan Culture in the later Roman Empire,* 53.

194. John Chrysostom held that a person with a full stomach would yield more easily when tempted by the devil, as we see in his interpretation of the temptations of Jesus (Matt 4:1ff.) in *Hom. in Matt.* 13. Fasting "is a most powerful shield against the devil." Fasting belongs typically to the Christian life; luxury, drunkenness, and elaborate meals belong to life before baptism. On this, with further textual references to Chrysostom, see Sandnes, *Belly and Body in the Pauline Epistles,* 244–52.

195. On this, see Gärtner, *Die Familienerziehung in der alten Kirche,* 433. Gärtner describes Chrysostom's thinking on this point as "the typical expression of ethical intellectualism" (ET: B. McNeil).

196. Gärtner, in *Die Familienerziehung in der alten Kirche,* 432, notes that Chrysostom elsewhere lists those things a Christian must know about: "about the soul, the body, immortality, the kingdom of heaven, punishment, hell, the patience of God, forgiveness, penitence, baptism, the forgiveness of sins, the heavenly and the earthly creation, the angels, the wickedness of the demons, the tricks of the devil, life, the religious commandments, the true faith, and the sects which have wandered away from the right path" (MPG 49, 364G).

197. John Chrysostom, *Hom. in Eph., On Marriage and Family Life* 67. See also Gärtner, *Die Familienerziehung in der alten Kirche,* 312–13.

198. John Chrysostom, *Hom. in Eph.* 21, *On Marriage and Family Life* 68.

199. John Chrysostom, *De Inani* 39–40.

200. Ibid., 32.

201. John Chrysostom, *Hom. in 1 Tim.* 10 (*NPNF* 13, p. 439).

202. John Chrysostom, *Hom. in Col.* 10 (*NPNF* 9, p. 301).

203. John Chrysostom, *De Inani* 32.

204. John Chrysostom, *Hom. in Eph.* 21, *On Marriage and Family Life* 65.

205. Ibid., *Hom. in Eph.* 21, *On Marriage and Family Life* 69–70.

206. John Chrysostom, *De Inani* 47–49.

207. John Chrysostom, *Hom. in Eph.* 21, *On Marriage and Family Life* 69.

208. See p. 196 in the present chapter.

209. On this, see O. M. Bakke, *"Concord and Peace,"* 54–57, with many references to texts and to secondary literature.

210. Augustine, *Conf.* 1.9.15.

211. Augustine, *Conf.* 1.9.14 (WSA I/1): "All the same, I would be beaten whenever I was lazy about learning. This punishment was taken for granted by grown-up people and many people had undergone it before we did, laying down those rough roadways along which we were now being driven, as we bore our part in the heavy labor and pain allotted to the sons of Adam."

212. See Chapter 3 of the present study, pp. 91–92.

213. Augustine, *Conf.* 1.9.15.

214. Augustine, *Serm.* 13.9; 149B 4.

215. Augustine, *Serm.* 13.9, WSA III/1: "The father . . . considers what is good for him. . . . If he [the son] goes on living in a way that leads to his ruin, and if the father is afraid of offending his wastrel son with harshness of discipline—isn't he then cruel by sparing him?" Cf. also Augustine, *Serm.* 159B 4.

216. Augustine's strict attitude may be a response to his own early years. He had experienced what happened when a father neglected discipline: the result was that Augustine took the path of sin.

217. See p. 174 of the present chapter.

218. See Chapter 3 of the present study, p. 92.

219. Augustine, *Serm.* 159B 4 (WSA III/11). See also *Serm.* 349.2; 385.2; 387.2.

220. For a general introduction to the school and teaching in antiquity, see Henri Irenee Marrou, *A History of Education in Antiquity,* trans. George Lamb (New York: Sheed and Ward, 1956); James Bowen, *A History of Western Education,* vol. 1: *The Ancient World: Orient and Mediterranean, 2000 B.C.–A.D. 1054* (New York: St. Martins, 1972) 43–216; Stanley F. Bonner, *Education in Ancient Rome: From the Elder Cato to the Younger Pliny* (London: Methuen, 1977); Teresa Morgan, *Literate Education in the Hellenistic and Roman Worlds* (Cambridge: Cambridge University Press, 1998).

221. Morgan, in *Literate Education in the Hellenistic and Roman Worlds,* has demonstrated this on the basis of papyrus discoveries. The papyri basically confirm what the literary sources tell us (50). Her conclusion is that the school "is one of the places where it is possible to see how strongly, despite all local variations of politics, bureaucracy, culture and social structure, a sector of the ancient world regarded itself as an entity" (24).

222. The status of Homer's works, the *Iliad* and the *Odyssey,* in Hellenistic culture can be compared with the status the scriptural canon was to enjoy in the Christian tradition. Scholars have often compared the authority and function of Homer's writings with those of the Bible; see for example J. F. Procope, "Greek Philosophy, Hermeneutics and Alexandrian Understanding of the Old Testament," in *Hebrew Bible/Old Testament: The History of its Interpretation,* vol. 1., ed. M. Sæbø (Göttingen: Vandenhoeck & Ruprecht, 1996), 462.

223. For a more extensive list, and tables showing the distribution of classical authors in the educational process, see Morgan, *Literate Education in the Hellenistic and Roman Worlds,* 313, 316–19.

224. See for example Quintilian, *Inst.* 1.1.36; Plato, *Resp.* 377B; Seneca, *Ep. Mor.* 88.1–4, 8, 20; Plutarch, *Mor.* 3E–F; *Mor.* 7C-D; and discussion in Sandnes, *Med Homer i Sekken* (Oslo, 2003).

225. Plato, *Resp.* 377C; 378B; 378D–E; 381D–382A; 383A–C; 386A–397B. See also Lucian, *Menippus* 3–4.

226. See, for example, Heraclitus, *Homerika Problemata (Quaestiones Homericae)* 1–3. This author, whom many scholars date to the first century c.e., disagrees with Plato's critical approach to Homer, and says that the problem is that people have not understood the philosophical (i.e., allegorical) meaning in Homer's words.

227. Cf. Tertullian, *De Idol.* 10.1. See Marrou, *A History of Education in Antiquity,* 321. John T. Townsend, in "Ancient Education in the time of the Early Roman Empire," in *The Catacombs and the Colosseum: The Roman Empire as the Setting of Primitive Christianity*, ed. Steven Benko and John J. O'Rourke (Valley Forge, Pa.: Judson, 1971), 149, sums up: "Hellenistic schools as the educational institutions of a pagan society were inseparably associated with pagan religion. Not only did the curriculum center around the pagan classics, which were taught in classrooms decorated with representations of pagan gods; but also the students were often expected, and even compelled, to take part in pagan religious festivals."

228. See Morgan, *Literate Education in the Hellenistic and Roman Worlds,* 19.

229. See ibid., 25–32.

230. See ibid., 33–39 for a discussion with many references to the sources. Øivind Andersen, in the "Forord" of *Dannelse, Humanitas, Paideia*, ed. Øivind Andersen (Oslo: Sypress Forlag, 1999), 11, writes: "In reality, the plan often included other subjects as well, such as history, law, medicine, and architecture. But the idea was that there existed a particular group of subjects which the educated person ought to master in order to be fully qualified as a man, a citizen, and a human being" (ET: B. McNeil).

231. See for example Plutarch, *Mor.* 7C–D, and Seneca, *Ep.* 88. Seneca writes that the encyclical education prepares the mind to receive virtue (20). Hence, the element that comes *after* this educational program is the most important.

232. On this, see Sandnes, *Med Homer i Sekken.*

233. Greek text: Edgar J. Goodspeed, *Die ältesten Apologeten. Texte mit kurzen Einleitungen* (Göttingen: Vandenhoeck & Ruprecht, 1984); ET: *ANF* 2.

234. *Didasc.* Latin text and ET: R. H. Connolly, *Didascalia Apostolorum,* 12–13. In the ET the quoted text is part of chapter 2. I have changed the last sentence of Connolly's translation.

235. Clement of Alexandria, *Strom.* 1.2.20.1–2; 1.9.43.1; 6.10.80.5–81.1.

236. Ibid., 1.9.43.1. Clement also says at 1.16.80.5 that some Christians believe that the devil is the author of Greek philosophy and education.

237. On the basis of Clement of Alexandria's *Strom.* 6.10.80.5–81.1, Sandnes finds this not improbable (*Med Homer i Sekken*).

238. Tertullian, *De Praescriptione Haereticorum* (ET: *ANF* 3). Tertullian expresses the same ideas in his *Apologeticum* 46.18.

239. Tertullian, *De test. Anim.* 1. In *De Spectaculis* 17, Tertullian says: "we despise the teaching of secular literature as being foolishness in God's eyes" (ET: *ANF* 3).

240. Tertullian, *De Idololatria* 10 (ET *ANF* 3).

241. Tertullian: "But when a believer *learns* these things, if he is already capable of understanding what idolatry is, he neither receives nor allows them; much more if he is not yet capable. Or, when he *begins* to understand, it behooves him first to understand what he has previously learned, that is, touching God and the faith. Therefore he will reject those things, and will not receive them; and will be as safe as one who from one who knows it not, knowingly *accepts* poison, but does not *drink* it" (ch. 10).

242. Hippolytus, *Apost. Trad.* 16.5.

243. Canons of Hippolytus 12. ET: Paul F. Bradshaw et al., *The Apostolic Tradition*, Hermeneia (Minneapolis: Fortress Press, 2002), 89.

244. See Werner Jaeger, *Early Christianity and Greek Paideia* (Cambridge, Mass.: Belknap, 1961), 60: Clement and Origen "claim that their faith fulfils this paideutic mission of mankind to a higher degree than had been achieved before."

245. Clement of Alexandria, *Strom.* 1.5 (ET: *ANF* 2).
246. Most of Philo's *De Congressu* is an exegesis of Genesis 16.
247. B. Schlager, in "Saints Basil and John Chrysostom on the Education of Christian Children," *The Greek Orthodox Theological Review* 36 (1991): 45, correctly points out that Chrysostom nowhere in this treatise condemns pagan education per se.
248. John Chrysostom, *De Inani* 81.
249. Ibid., 79.
250. Schlager, in "Saints Basil and John Chrysostom on the Education of Christian Children," 51, concludes: "This reference clearly permits the inclusion of suitable pagan characters, and presumably pagan literature in general, in the stories told to children by their parents." In view of Chrysostom's affirmative attitude to classical education, Schlager writes that he has a generally open attitude to classical culture (47).
251. I differ on this question from G. Af Hällström, "Klassisk Bildning enligt Johannes Khrysostomos," in *Dannelse, Humanitas, Paideia*, who argues that Chrysostom consciously seeks to replace the encyclical studies by a corresponding Christian educational program. He is right to observe that Chrysostom's youthful treatise *Comparatio Regis et Monachi* exhorts parents to send their children to the monasteries, so that they may receive instruction and moral education; but we must remember that when he wrote these words, he was a radical adherent of the ascetic ideals, and thought that all Christian children should go to school in monasteries. Later, he moderated his views, and sought to plant the Christian faith and life more deeply among those who lived ordinary lives in the cities. Hällström is of course right to say that parents should use the Bible in Christian formation at home, and should replace the pagan models with Christian ones (though, as we have pointed out, without completing rejecting the former). This, however, does not mean that Chrysostom argued that Christian children should not undertake the encyclical studies. His point was to ensure the correct equilibrium between these studies and a Christian upbringing.
252. On the dating, see for example the secondary literature cited by Schlager, "Saints Basil and John Chrysostom on the Education of Christian Children," 39, n. 7.
253. See ibid., 39.
254. Basil, *Leg. Lib. Gent.* 2.1–3 (Greek text and ET: LCL).
255. Basil, *Leg. Lib. Gent.* 2.5–8. In ch. 8, Basil returns to his introductory remarks about the usefulness of Greek literature. Here, too, he underscores its propaedeutic role.
256. The ethical perspective, which supplies the criterion for what one should learn for one's own life from pagan literature, is also set out in ch. 9.
257. See for example, Basil, *Leg. Lib. Gent.* 4.4–5.
258. See for example, Bowen, *A History of Western Education,* vol. 1, 264–65; Jaeger, *Early Christianity and Greek Paideia,* 80–81; H. Fuchs, "Die frühe christliche Kirche und die antike Bildung," in *Das frühe Christentum im Römischen Staat,* ed. R. Klein (Darmstadt: Wissenschaftliche Buchgesellschaft, 1971), 41; Sandnes, *Med Homer i Sekken.*
259. See Sandnes, *Med Homer i Sekken.*
260. On the catechumenate in the patristic age, see for example, Michael Dujarier, *A History of the Catechumenate: The First Six Centuries* (New York: Sadlier, 1979); Thomas M. Finn, *Early Christian Baptism and the Catechumenate,* 2 vols. (Collegeville, Minn.: Liturgical, 1992); William Harmless, *Augustine and the Catechumenate* (Collegeville, Minn.: Liturgical, 1995).
261. See Marrou, *A History of Education in Antiquity,* 431–32; William Barclay, *Train Up a Child: Educational Ideals in the Ancient World* (Philadelphia: Westminster, 1959), 250–51. However, Marrou's observation that "none of the Christians ever suggested that children should be brought up differently, away from the pagan schools" (428) is an oversimplification.
262. See Everett Ferguson, "Education," in *Encyclopedia of Early Christianity,* 2nd ed., ed. Everett Ferguson (New York: Garland, 1998), 361: "Christians not only studied in the

traditional schools but in the third and fourth centuries were increasingly filling the ranks of their teachers, even the state-supported professorships."

263. On this, see Marrou, *A History of Education in Antiquity,* 427–34; Ferguson, "Education."

264. See Chapter 3, pp. 91–92.

265. 1 Sam 2:12-36.

266. John Chrysostom, *Hom. in Eph.* 21, *On Marriage and Family Life* 65.

267. See Chapter 2, p. 35–36.

6. Children's Participation in Worship

1. Sources from the third century onward reflect an awareness that various groups are to have their own specific places in church during worship, and lay down regulations about this. Mostly, they speak of the places for men and women, but some prescribe where the children are to have their place, or simply mention this place in passing. For example, when the *Apostolic Constitutions* regulates the tasks of the deacons with regard to the exchange of the kiss of peace among the various groups in the congregation, we read: "And let the children stand at the reading desk; and let another deacon stand by them, that they may not be disorderly." This church order also says that, immediately before the offertory procession, the deacon is to tell the children to join their mothers (*Apost. Con.* 8.11.10 [ET: *ANF* 7, p. 486] and 8.12.2). See Maria-Regina Bottermann, *Die Beteiligung des Kindes an der Liturgie von den Anfängen der Kirche bis heute* (Frankfurt: Peter Lang, 1982), 47–51.

2. A. Oepke, *Zur Frage nach dem Ursprung der Kindertaufe* (1928), 84ff.

3. J. Leipold, *Die urchristliche Taufe im Licht der Religionsgeschichte* (Leipzig: Dörffling & Franke, 1928).

4. Joachim Jeremias, *Die Kindertaufe in den ersten vier Jahrhunderten* (1958); ET: *Infant Baptism in the First Four Centuries* (Philadelphia: Westminster, 1964).

5. Oscar Cullmann, *Die Tauflehre des Neuen Testaments* (1948); ET: *Baptism in the New Testament,* trans. J. K. S. Reid (London: SCM, 1950).

6. Kurt Aland, *Die Säuglingstaufe im Neuen Testament und in der alten Kirche* (1961); ET: *Did the Early Church Baptize Infants?* trans. G. R. Beasley-Murray (Philadelphia: Westminster, 1963).

7. Joachim Jeremias, *Nochmals: Die Anfänge der Kindertaufe* (1962); ET: *The Origins of Infant Baptism: A Further Study in Reply to Kurt Aland* (London: SCM, 1963).

8. On the debate after Aland and Jeremias, see for example Paul King Jewett, *Infant Baptism and the Covenant of Grace: An Appraisal of the Argument That as Infants Were Once Circumcised, So They Should Now be Baptized* (Grand Rapids, Mich.: Eerdmans, 1978), 47–71; Neil Dixon, *Troubled Waters* (London: Epworth, 1979), 29–34; Everett Ferguson, "Inscriptions and the Origin of Infant Baptism," *Journal of Theological Studies* 30 (1979); Colin Buchanan, *A Case for Infant Baptism,* 3rd ed. (Nottingham, U.K.: Grove, 1984); David F. Wright, "The Origins of Infant Baptism—Child Believers' Baptism," *Scottish Journal of Theology* 40 (1987); David F. Wright, "How Controversial Was the Development of Infant Baptism in the Early Church?" in *Church, Word, and Spirit: Historical and Theological Essays in Honor of Geoffrey W. Bromiley,* ed. James E. Bradley and Richard A. Mueller (Grand Rapids, Mich.: Eerdmans, 1987); Gerhard Barth, *Die Taufe in frühchristlicher Zeit* (Neukirchen-Vluyn: Neukirchener, 2002), 128–38.

9. Aland, *Did the Early Church Baptize Infants?* 90.

10. Philemon 10, 16; Aristides, *Apol.* 15.6. See also Jeremias, *The Origins of Infant Baptism,* 13.

11. Aland, *Did the Early Church Baptize Infants?* 90.

12. Jeremias, *The Origins of Infant Baptism,* 13.

13. Aland, *Did the Early Church Baptize Infants?* 89–90.

14. See Jeremias, *The Origins of Infant Baptism,* 15.

15. Ibid., 14–16.

16. Cf. my remarks above about "shame/honor" cultures in Chapter 5.

17. Jeremias, *Infant Baptism in the First Four Centuries,* 22–24. The example of the prison warder in Philippi is taken from this passage.

18. Ibid., 23 shows that the same collective thinking underlies the narrative of the businesswoman Lydia, who governed her own household (probably because she was a widow). When she embraced the faith, she was baptized with all her family. Jeremias points out that the narrative is highly compressed; Luke does not say that the gospel was proclaimed to the members of Lydia's family as well. It is, nevertheless, striking that Luke could compose his narrative in this way, "For by so doing he gives expression to the fact that '*the solidarity of the family in baptism* and not the decision of the single member' was the decisive consideration" (Jeremias quotes here from Cullmann, *Baptism in the New Testament,* 45).

19. Pseudo-Clementines, *Hom.* 13.4.4, par. *Recogn.* 7.29; and *Hom.* 15.1.2, par. *Recogn.* 10.1–4. See further discussion in Jeremias, *Infant Baptism in the First Four Centuries,* 68–69.

20. Jeremias also argues along these lines, but his presentation of the evidence in support of his hypothesis does not give this factor the weight I believe it deserves. Besides this, his position is based on the view that Paul and Luke reflect the same family solidarity he discerns in the Old Testament use of the term "house" in secular and cultic contexts. Jeremias follows E. Stauffer, "Zur Kindertaufe in der Urkirche," *Deutsches Pfarrerblatt* 49 (1949): 152–54, in claiming that the New Testament usage has its roots in a specific Old Testament usage, to which it corresponds completely: Jeremias, *Infant Baptism in the First Four Centuries,* 20–21; Jeremias, *The Origins of Infant Baptism,* 20–25. The noun *bêth* (house) is frequently used in the sense of "family" in the Old Testament, where we frequently hear of a person's "whole" (*kôl*) house: Gen 7:1; 12:17; 14:26; 18:19; 34:30; 36:6; 45:11; Deut 14:26; Josh 24:15. In some cases, this does not include the children, but this is expressly stated: Gen 50:8; 1 Sam 1:21-22; cf. Exod 12:37. On the basis of the Old Testament material, Stauffer concludes that this phrase in the relevant passages not only *includes* the children, but actually refers primarily to them. More recent scholarship questions the existence of a specific usage of the concept or formula of *oikos* in the Old Testament in this sense: see Aland, *Did the Early Church Baptize Infants?* 87–94. Initially, Jeremias followed Stauffer's view that "NN and his house" appeared to be a formulaic phrase borrowed from the ritual vocabulary of the Old Testament, especially in connection with the terminology of circumcision: *Infant Baptism in the First Four Centuries,* 20–21. Subsequently, Jeremias accepted much of Aland's criticism of the hypothesis that this is a ritual formula, though continuing to view it as a specific phrase used both in secular and in cultic contexts: *The Origins of Infant Baptism.* 20. For further discussion of the so-called *oikos* formula, see for example P. Weigandt, "Zur sogenannten 'Oikosformel,'" *Novum Testamentum* 6 (1963): 49–74; Gerhard Delling, "Zur Taufe von 'Häusern' im Urchristentum," *Novum Testamentum* 7 (1964): 285–311; A. Strobel, "Der Begriff des 'Hauses' im griechischen und römischen Privatrecht," *Zeitschrift für die neutestamentliche Wissenschaft* 56 (1965): 91–100. An overview of the debate is provided by L. Schenke, "Zur sogenannten 'Oikosformel' im Neuen Testament," *Kairos* 8 (1971): 226–43.

Even if the Old Testament does operate with a specific concept of *oikos,* we may still ask whether this influenced Paul and Luke to any real extent. There appears to be significant support in recent scholarship for the view that the New Testament phrase "NN and his/her house" does not permit any precise conclusions about whether or not children were baptized. In addition to the articles just mentioned, see for example Edmund Schlink, *Die Lehre von der Taufe* (1969), ET: *The Doctrine of Baptism,* trans. H. J. A. Bouman (St. Louis: Concordia, 1972), 135; Dixon, *Troubled Waters,* 32–33; Jewett, *Infant Baptism and the Covenant of Grace,* 47–54; E. Glenn Hinson, "Infant Baptism," in *Encyclopedia of Early Christianity,* 2nd ed., ed. Everett Ferguson (New York: Garland, 1998), 572. In my own argumentation,

I do not necessarily posit a correspondence between the Old Testament use of the concept of *oikos* and the usage in Paul and Luke, although I do not wish to exclude this possibility altogether. My point is that the general family structure in Greco-Roman antiquity would tend to suggest that children were baptized along with their parents when the latter converted to Christianity.

21. Cullmann, for example, underscores that "the understanding of Christian Baptism as a fulfilment, and thus a repeal, of Jewish circumcision is not just a theological foundling, appearing only at a late date after the Apologist Justin; nor is it just a supplement designed to support Christian Baptism. This conception is already present explicitly in Col 2:11, and implicit especially in Rom 2:25ff.; 4:1ff.; Gal 3:6ff.; and Eph 2:11ff. A fundamental kinship between circumcision and Christian Baptism is thus apparent." Cullmann, *Baptism in the New Testament*, 56–69, at 56–57. It is interesting to note that we find a similar viewpoint in Jewett, a scholar who has sharply criticized all historical and theological arguments in favor of the practice of infant baptism. He concludes that his analysis confirms "the claim of the Paedobaptists that there is a fundamental affinity of meaning between circumcision in the Old Testament and the baptism in the New. . . . Thus circumcision may fairly be said to be the Old Testament counterpart of Christian baptism." Jewett, *Infant Baptism and the Covenant of Grace*, 87, 89. Nevertheless, he criticizes Cullmann for a one-sided emphasis on the affinities between circumcision and baptism, which leads him not to take seriously what Jewett calls the "temporal and earthly" aspects of circumcision; on this, see Jewett's chapter "A Critical Evaluation of the Argument from the Covenant," 89–138. The analogy between circumcision and baptism leads Cullmann, Jeremias, and a number of other scholars to maintain that Jewish-Christian parents would have seen the baptism of their children as something normal: see Cullmann, *Baptism in the New Testament*, 56–69; Pierre Charles Marcel, *The Biblical Doctrine of Baptism: Sacrament of the Covenant of Grace* (London: J. Clarke, 1953); John Murray, *Christian Baptism* (Philadelphia: Presbyterian and Reformed, 1972), 52–53; Buchanan, *A Case for Infant Baptism*, 9–12.

22. See J. P. T. Hunt, "Colossians 2:11-12, the Circumcision/Baptism Analogy, and Infant Baptism," *Tyndale Bulletin* 41 (1990): 227–44.

23. Cyprian, *Ep.* 64.

24. Hunt, "Colossians 2:11-12, the Circumcision/Baptism Analogy, and Infant Baptism," 231–32.

25. Jeremias, *Infant Baptism in the First Four Centuries*, 31: "To these contacts between primitive Christian baptism and proselyte baptism in the matter of terminology, of baptismal instruction and the baptismal rite must be added in conclusion the following correspondences in the doctrine of baptism and its illustrative material."

26. Ibid., 39.

27. *Sib. Or.* 4.62ff.; Epictetus, *Diss.* 2.9.9–21.

28. See for example Rudolf Bultmann, *Theologie des Neuen Testaments* 5, durch einen Nachtrag erw. Aufl. (Tübingen: Mohr Siebeck, 1965), 42; Schlink, *The Doctrine of Baptism*, 135.

29. Jewett, in *Infant Baptism and the Covenant of Grace*, 64, notes that "for the present, at least, the majority of scholars suppose a pre-Christian origin of the practice" of proselyte baptism. Roughly twenty years earlier, Jeremias had observed: "In fact, nearly all scholars who in the last sixty years have concerned themselves with the date of the introduction of proselyte baptism have come to the conclusion that it came into practice in pre-Christian times." Jeremias, *Infant Baptism in the First Four Centuries*, 29.

30. See Jewett, *Infant Baptism and the Covenant of Grace*, 64. If proselyte baptism really did have its roots in Christian baptism, this would be a strong indicator that children were baptized in the earliest Christian communities. The oldest rabbinic sources, the Tannaitic traditions, contain a number of explicit references to children who were baptized when their parents converted to Judaism: references in Jeremias, *Infant Baptism in the First Four Centuries*.

31. See for example Barth, *Die Taufe in frühchristlicher Zeit,* 132.

32. Cullmann, *Baptism in the New Testament,* 78. Jeremias, *Infant Baptism in the First Four Centuries,* 48–55, presents detailed arguments in support of the interpretation of *koluein* in Mark 10:13-16 as a technical term.

33. The baptismal candidate (Mark 10:14 and parallels; Acts 8:36); water (Acts 10:47); the one who baptizes (Matt 3:14); and God himself (Acts 11:17). See also A. W. Argyle, "O. Cullmann's Theory concerning *kôluein,*" *Expository Times* 67 (1955–56): 17.

34. See Aland, *Did the Early Church Baptize Infants?* 96.

35. Tertullian, *De Bapt.* 18.4–5. Latin text and ET: E. Evans, *Tertullian's Homily on Baptism* (London: SPCK, 1964), 39.

36. Ibid., 18.4.

37. This view is also taken by Wright, "How Controversial Was the Development of Infant Baptism in the Early Church?" 47.

38. Tertullian, *De Bapt.* 18.6.

39. Ibid.

40. Wright, "How Controversial Was the Development of Infant Baptism in the Early Church?" 49.

41. On the role of godparents in the early church, see Joseph H. Lynch, *Godparents and Kinship in Early Medieval Europe* (Princeton, N.J.: Princeton University Press, 1986), 117–42.

42. Tertullian, *De Bapt.* 18.4.

43. Lynch, in *Godparents and Kinship in Early Medieval Europe* (1986), 126, is somewhat more cautious: "Instead, the parent/sponsor spoke and acted for the child during the ceremonies and accepted the obligation to foster religious and moral development as the child matured."

44. See Wright, "How Controversial Was the Development of Infant Baptism in the Early Church?" 47.

45. Tertullian, *De Anima* 40.1.

46. Ibid., 41.1: "*malum igitur animae . . . ex originis uitio antecedit, naturale quodammodo. Nam, ut diximus, naturae corruptio alia natura est.*" J. H. Waszink, ed., *Quinti Septimi Florentis Tertulliani De Anima* (Amsterdam: Meulenhoff, 1947).

47. Wright, "How Controversial Was the Development of Infant Baptism in the Early Church?" 48. On Tertullian's position with regard to the doctrine of original sin, see for example Norman Powell Williams, *The Ideas of the Fall and Original Sin: A Historical and Critical Study* (London: Longman, Green, 1927), 231ff.; Kelly, *Early Christian Doctrines,* 175–77.

48. In agreement with Williams, Jeremias writes: "Tertullian is acquainted . . . with the idea of Adam's 'original sin' with all its depraving consequences for each of his offspring; but he has not yet developed an explicit doctrine of the 'original guilt' of Adam's descendants. Had he already known the idea of a hereditary responsibility for Adam's fall, it would of necessity have led him to assent the baptism of the *parvuli.*" Jeremias, *The Origins of Infant Baptism,* 69.

49. Aland, in *Did the Early Church Baptize Infants?* 62, speaks of Tertullian's "rather tortuous argumentation" on this point.

50. I wholly agree with the analysis of Jeremias, *The Origins of Infant Baptism,* 65: "Tertullian when opposing the necessity for infant baptism is evidently at a loss for a good case, as we see from his 'rather tortuous argumentation' [K. Aland] that the godparents are burdened with a responsibility which they cannot be expected to bear. Would he have let slip the chance of pointing out that he was defending against attempts to introduce innovations to the Church's good old custom of baptizing children only at the stage of puberty, if this completely effective argument had been at his disposal?"

51. Cyprian, *Ep.* 64.

52. On the dating of these textual witnesses, see Alistair Stewart-Sykes, *Hippolytus: On The Apostolic Tradition. An English Version with Introduction and Commentary* (New York: St. Vladimir's Seminary Press, 2001), 45–47.

53. Paul F. Bradshaw et al., in *The Apostolic Tradition*, Hermeneia (Minneapolis: Fortress Press, 2002), 124, argue that chapter 20 consists of at least three strata, with 21.1–5 (the remarks about infant baptism) as the "original core." See also Jeremias, *Infant Baptism in the First Four Centuries*, 73–74.

54. See Jeremias, *The Origins of Infant Baptism*, 28–32.

55. Francis Xavier Funk, *Didascalia et Constitutiones Apostolorum*, vol. 2 (Paderborn: Schoeningh, 1906, 109; ET: Bradshaw et al., *The Apostolic Tradition*, 112.

56. Bradshaw et al., *The Apostolic Tradition*, 130.

57. Aland, *Did the Early Church Baptize Infants?* 51.

58. See also Jeremias, *The Origins of Infant Baptism*, 31.

59. Bradshaw et al., *The Apostolic Tradition*, 124.

60. Aland, *Did the Early Church Baptize Infants?* 47.

61. On this, see the detailed discussion by Jeremias, *The Origins of Infant Baptism*, 69–75. See also Wright, "How Controversial Was the Development of Infant Baptism in the Early Church?" 53–54.

62. My remarks here are based largely on Jeremias, *The Origins of Infant Baptism*, 69–75.

63. Origen, *Hom. in Luc.* 14.3 (GCS 49, 87.18–19; ET: FC 94).

64. Ibid.

65. Ibid., 14.4.

66. Ibid., 14.5.

67. Origen, *Hom. in Lev.* 8 (GCS 29 [VI], ET: FC 83).

68. Ibid., 8.3.1.

69. Ibid., 8.3.5.

70. Wright, "How Controversial Was the Development of Infant Baptism in the Early Church?" 54.

71. Origen, *Hom. in Lev.* 8.3.5.

72. See Jeremias, *The Origins of Infant Baptism*, 72.

73. Ibid., 72. Jeremias observes correctly that the reference to infant baptism "has no importance for its own sake," but when he goes on to say that it "is added quite incidentally . . . as an appendix to a train of reasoning complete in itself," he does not grasp its function in Origen's argumentation. It is not by chance that Origen refers here to baptismal practice. His point is that this will strengthen and confirm his understanding of the scriptural texts.

74. Greek text: MPG 14, 1047; ET: FC 103.

75. Ps 51:5.

76. Phil 3:21; Rom 6:6; 7:24.

77. Origen, *Com. in Rom.* 5.9.11 (on Rom 6:6).

78. Ibid. The last part of the quotation is an allusion to Job 14:4-5.

79. Origen, *Com. in Rom.* 5.9.11.

80. Aland, *Did the Early Church Baptize Infants?* 48.

81. For sources (literary texts and inscriptions) and a discussion, see Jeremias, *Infant Baptism in the First Four Centuries*, 59–80; Jeremias, *The Origins of Infant Baptism*, 33–63; and Aland, *Did the Early Church Baptize Infants?*

82. Irenaeus, *Adv. Haer.* 2.22.4 (MPG 7, 784).

83. On this, see Jeremias, *Infant Baptism in the First Four Centuries*, 72–73; Jeremias, *The Origins of Infant Baptism*, 62–63. For a different interpretation, see Aland, *Did the Early Church Baptize Infants?* 58–59.

84. Wright, "How Controversial Was the Development of Infant Baptism in the Early Church?" 51: "In the west, if not so obviously in the east, it found the theological justification it needed in the dogma of original sin. If there is a persisting controversy about infant

baptism in the patristic age, it concerns primarily the question 'why?' rather than 'whether,' although the absence of confident answers to the former must to some extent have diverted pressure onto the latter."

85. I argue here against Aland, in *Did the Early Church Baptize Infants?* 106, who holds that the converse is true: "From the moment that the taint of original sin was believed to apply to the newborn child, its baptism became a necessity under the new presuppositions."

86. Wright, "How Controversial Was the Development of Infant Baptism in the Early Church?" 51. See also Williams, *The Ideas of the Fall and Original Sin,* 223; Jaroslav Pelikan, *The Emergence of the Catholic Tradition (100–600)* (Chicago: University of Chicago Press, 1971), 290–92; Tatha Wiley, *Original Sin: Origins, Developments, Contemporary Meanings* (New York: Paulist, 2002), 60.

87. The data presented here are given by Jeremias, *Infant Baptism in the First Four Centuries,* 88.

88. This means that Ambrose did not receive baptism until after he was elected bishop.

89. For references to these inscriptions, see Jeremias, *Infant Baptism in the First Four Centuries,* 89–90.

90. Gregory Nazianzen, *Or.* 40 (MPG 36; ET: *NPNF* 2nd series, 7).

91. By this age, children are old enough that "they may be able to listen and to answer something about the Sacrament; that, even though they do not perfectly understand it, yet at any rate they may know the outlines; and then to sanctify them in soul and body with the great sacrament of our consecration. For this is how the matter stands; at that time they begin to be responsible for their lives, when reason is matured, and they learn the mystery of life (for of signs of ignorance owing to their tender years they have no account to give), and it is far more profitable on all accounts to be fortified by the Font, because of the sudden assaults of danger that befall us, stronger than our helpers." Gregory Nazianzen, *Or.* 40.28.

92. John Chrysostom, *Baptismal Catecheses* 3.6 (SC 50, pp. 153–54; ET: ACW 31).

93. Siricius, *Ep.* 1.2.3 (MPL 13, 1134–1136).

94. Optatus, *Adversus Parmenianum* 5.10, quoted from Jeremias, *Infant Baptism in the First Four Centuries,* 94.

95. Jeremias, *Infant Baptism in the First Four Centuries,* 93–94. Pages 91–92 refer to texts from both Arian and Donatist groups that indicate that they practiced infant baptism, and to a number of church orders based on Hippolytus's *Apostolic Tradition,* which envisage infant baptism as normal ecclesiastical praxis. However, since these church orders are dated to between the 370s and c. 500—that is, the period in which other material shows that infant baptism was once more becoming the norm—we must be cautious in using them as evidence that "the custom of baptizing infants (*infantes, infantes parvi, nêpia*) continued *unbroken.*" One premise in Jeremias's argumentation is that these church orders reflect an older established practice. He may be right to some extent, but the totality of available material shows very clearly that for five or six decades in the fourth century, the church did not normally practice infant baptism.

96. Augustine, *Conf.* 1.11.17–18.

97. Many of those mentioned in our table became central leaders in the early church. Wright, in "Infant Dedication in the Early Church," in *Baptism, the New Testament, and the Church: Historical and Contemporary Studies in Honour of R. E. O. White,* ed. Stanley E. Porter and Anthony R. Cross (Sheffield: Sheffield Academic, 1999), 353, observes: "Almost everyone born in these baptism-deprived generations who has left us his or her story seems to turn out remarkably well. From their ranks came that distinguished bevy of theologians, bishops, Church statesmen, monastic leaders, biblical scholars and preachers who constituted 'the golden age of church Fathers,' as early Church historians once had no qualms in calling it."

98. Ibid., 153.

99. Augustine, *Conf.* 1.11.17.

100. Wright, "Infant Dedication in the Early Church," 354.

101. This is the view of Wright, "Infant Dedication in the Early Church," 353.

102. Augustine, *Conf.* 5.14.25; 6.11.18.

103. Wright, "Infant Dedication in the Early Church," 354.

104. Jerome, *Preface to Job* (ET: *NPNF* 2nd series, 6, p. 492); *Ep.* 82.2 (ET: *NPNF* 2nd series, 6). See also J. N. D. Kelly, *Jerome: His Life, Writings, and Controversies,* 7; Wright, "Infant Dedication in the Early Church," 355–56.

105. Gregory Nazianzen, *Or.* 18.11 (ET: FC 22).

106. Gregory Nazianzen, *De Vita Sua* 85–92 (ET: FC 75). Gregory's mother had a vision in a dream in which he was likened to Samuel: "As soon as I made my appearance, straightway in the noblest of contracts, I became Another's. Like some lamb, some pleasing calf, but a victim of high quality endowed with reason I was offered to God (I hesitate to say it) like a young Samuel." Cf. also his *Epitaphia* 27, 79, 80, where we also find the idea that he, like a second Samuel, was dedicated to God immediately after his birth (LCL, *The Greek Anthology* 2, pp. 412, 434).

107. Gregory Nazianzen, *Or.* 43.73 (FC 22).

108. For texts and discussion, see Wright, "Infant Dedication in the Early Church," 358–60.

109. This is because the final redaction of the most important textual witness to such a ritual, namely the *Life of Porphyry,* which relates, among other things, that Emperor Theodosius I (born 346/347) was marked with the sign of the cross by a bishop when he was seven days old (chs. 44–45), was probably not completed before the seventh century. Furthermore, part of the textual material in John Chrysostom, *Hom. in 1 Cor.* 12.7 (12.14, *NPNF*) to which Wright refers makes it completely clear that it is within the framework of the family that a child is to be marked with the sign of the cross; the rest of the relevant material in Chrysostom, which presupposes that a priest is to perform this ritual, need not be understood as speaking of a dedication of the child to the church and its enrollment among the catechumens, but can perfectly well reflect the practice of marking with the sign of the cross small children who accompanied their parents to worship. This is indicated by the fact (as we have just seen) that Chrysostom states that small children receive baptism.

110. Wright, "Infant Dedication in the Early Church," 360: "Although the texts that speak explicitly of admission to the catechumenate soon after birth are not numerous, the practice must have been extremely common. Very many in the crowds of catechumens urged incessantly by bishops in their sermons to overcome their lethargy or reluctance and commit themselves to baptism must first have been registered as catechumens at birth." Wright refers to A. Laurentin and M. Dujarier, *Catéchuménat* (1969), 63–65; Michael Dujarier, *A History of the Catechumenate: The First Six Centuries* (New York: Sadlier, 1979), 81–84, 92.

111. Gregory Nazianzen, *De Vita Sua* 92–94 (ET: FC 75).

112. Wright, "Infant Dedication in the Early Church," 353. In my view, Wright takes too little account of the gap between text and reality. We must remember that the *De Inani Gloria* is an argumentative text that exhorts parents to put into practice the ideals proposed by Chrysostom. The very fact that he reproaches them for neglecting the Christian dimension of upbringing is itself evidence that many parents did not bring up their children in keeping with his ideals.

113. See Wright, "Infant Dedication in the Early Church," 358–61, with references to secondary literature.

114. See Chapter 5 of the present study.

115. Studies that discuss this subject directly and aim to give an overview of children's participation in the Eucharist in the early church include: P. Zorn, *Historia Eucharistiae Infantum* (1936); David Holeton, *Infant Communion—Then and Now,* Grove Liturgical Study 27 (Bramcote: Grove, 1981), 4–7; William A. Strange, *Children in the Early Church:*

Children in the Ancient World, the New Testament and the Early Church (Carlisle: Paternoster, 1996), 103–7. See also Jewett, *Infant Baptism and the Covenant of Grace*, 41–43.

116. On the similarities between the Eucharist and the Jewish Passover meal, see for example Joachim Jeremias, "*Pascha*," in *TDNT* 5:897–904; A. J. B. Higgins, *The Lord's Supper in the New Testament* (London: SCM, 1952); I. M. Marshall, *Last Supper and Lord's Supper* (Exeter: Paternoster, 1980), 57–75; Leon Morris, *The Gospel according to John* (London: Marshall, Morgan and Scott, 1971), 774–86; Robin Routledge, "Passover and Last Supper," *Tyndale Bulletin* 53 (2002): 203–21.

117. Jewett, in *Infant Baptism and the Covenant of Grace*, 201–207, underscores "The basic similarity between passover and eucharist." I believe he is correct to point out the inconsistency on the part of supporters of infant baptism, who have often made a great point out of the analogy between circumcision and baptism, but refuse to draw a corresponding conclusion for church practice in the case of the analogy between the Passover and the Lord's Supper.

118. Justin Martyr, 1 *Apol.* 61.10–12; *Apost. Trad.* 21.23–28.

119. Cyprian, *De Lapsis* 25 (ET: *ANF* 5).

120. Ibid., 26.

121. Ibid., 9.

122. Cyprian, *Ep.* 64.3.

123. Ibid., 64.2.

124. Cyprian, *Ad Quirinum* 3.25 (ET: *ANF* 5).

125. See Holeton, *Infant Communion*, 5.

126. SC 336 (ET: *ANF* 7).

127. E. Diehl, ILCV 1.1549.

128. This interpretation assumes that the words *ita ut consueta repeterit*, which are not entirely clear, refer to the sacrament.

129. See for example Augustine, *De Pecc. Mer. et Rem.* 1.20.27; 1.24.34; *Ep.* 106.

130. Augustine, *De Pecc. Mer. et Rem.* 1.20.27 (ET: WSA 1/23).

131. See the Letter of the Milvetan Council to Innocent 2.3 (PL 33, 673) and Innocent I, *Ep.* 182.5, following Holeton, *Infant Communion*, 7.

132. Cf. *Apost. Con.* 8.22; Cyprian, *Ep.* 39.1, 4; Origen, *Hom. in Num.* 15.1; *Didasc.* 9. On the tasks of the lector and the emergence of this ministry, see Adolf von Harnack, *Sources of the Apostolic Canons with a Treatise on the Origin of the Readership and the Lower Orders* (London: Norgate, 1895); J. G. Davies, "Deacons, Deaconesses and the Minor Orders in the Patristic Period," *Journal of Ecclesiastical History* 14 (1963): 10–14; Robert Martineau, *The Office and the Work of a Reader* (Oxford: Mowbray, 1970).

133. Graeme W. Clarke, "An illiterate lector?" *Zeitschrift fur Papyrologie and Epigraphik* 57 (1984): 103.

134. Cyprian, *Ep.* 38.2; 39.4; *Apostolic Constitutions* 2.57; Jerome, *Ep.* 147.6.

135. *Quaestiones veteris et novi testamenti* 101, following Thomas Wiedemann, *Adults and Children in the Roman Empire* (London: Routledge, 1989), 187.

136. Cyprian, *Ep.* 38.

137. Ibid., 38.1.1. For a brief introduction to the role and function of the laity in the appointment of persons to clerical offices, including references to texts and secondary literature, see Graeme W. Clarke, *The Letters of St Cyprian of Carthage*, vol. 2 (New York: Newman, 1984), 178–79, n. 1.

138. Johannes Quasten, *Musik und Gesang in den Kulten der heidnischen Antike und christlichen Frühzeit* (Münster: Verlag der aschendorffschen, 1930), 138.

139. Ibid., 90.

140. Augustine, *Serm.* 352.1.

141. Victor of Vita, *De Persecutione Vandalorum* 3.34, following Wiedemann, *Adults and Children in the Roman Empire*, 187.

142. See Wiedemann, 187.

143. ILCV 1280; 1283; 1273; cf. Wiedemann, *Adults and Children in the Roman Empire*, 187–88.

144. Ennodius, *Vita Epiphanii* 8, cf. Wiedemann, *Adults and Children in the Roman Empire*, 187.

145. CIL XI 1709 (Florence = ILCV 1277A) and CIL VIII 453 (Ammaedare = ILCV 1285), cf. Clarke, "An illiterate lector?" 103.

146. Papyrus Oxyrhynchus 33:2673.

147. Cyprian, *Ep.* 27.1.2.

148. Ibid., 38.2.2.

149. Clarke, "An illiterate lector?" 104.

150. Clarke, *The Letters of St. Cyprian*, vol. 1, 358, n. 11.

151. Ibid. 359, n. 11.

152. This is attested in an epitaph from Lyons that calls a certain Stephanus leader of the school for lectors: CIL XIII 2385–86. See also Quasten, *Musik und Gesang in den Kulten der heidnischen Antike und christlichen Frühzeit*, 139; Bottermann, *Die Beteiligung des Kindes an der Liturgie von den Anfängen der Kirche bis heute*, 55.

153. Cf. A. de Waal, *Sänger und Gesang auf altchristlichen Inschriften Roms vom 4. bis 9. Jahrhundert* (1895), 300; Quasten, *Musik und Gesang in den Kulten der heidnischen Antike und christlichen Frühzeit* (Mainz, 1930), 138.

154. F. J. Dölger, *Sol Salutis: Gebet und Gesang im Christlichen Altertum: Mit besonderer Rücksicht auf die Ostung in Gebet un Liturgie*, 3. um Hinweise vermehrte Auflage (Münster: Aschendorff, 1972), 88.

155. O. Braun, *Buch der Synhados* (1900), 341: cf. Bottermann, *Die Beteiligung des Kindes an der Liturgie von den Anfängen der Kirche bis heute,* 43 (ET: B. McNeil).

156. Quasten, *Music and Worship in Pagan and Christian Antiquity,* trans. B. Ramsey (Washington, D.C.: National Association of Pastoral Musicians, 1983), 91.

157. *Peregrinatio Aetheriae* 24.5 (CSEL 39, 72). See also Dölger, *Sol Salutis,* 64.

158. Quasten, *Music and Worship in Pagan and Christian Antiquity,* 89–90, with references to *Testamentum Domini* 2.22; 2.4; 1.26; 2.11.

159. *Apost. Con.* 8.6: *Porro in singulis horum, quae diaconus proloquitur, ut iam diximus, populus respondeat: Kyrie eleison, et ante cunctos pueri.*

160. John Chrysostom, *Hom. in Mt.* 71.4 (PG 58, 666; ET: *NPNF* 10, p. 435).

161. Basil of Caesarea, *In Fam. et Siccit. Hom.* 3 (PG 31, 309).

162. Gregory Nazianzen, *Or.* 16.13 (PG 35, 952B).

163. ET: B. McNeil, from Simon K. Landersdorfer, ed., *Ausgewählte Schriften der syrischen Dichter Cyrillonas, Balâus, Isaak von Antiochien und Jakob von Sarug* (Kempten: Kösel, 1913), 20.

164. This argument is put forward by scholars such as Josef A. Jungmann, *Missarum Sollemnia: Eine genetische Erklärung der römischen Messe*, 1. 5., verb. Aufl. (Vienna: Herder, 1962), 525; Dölger, *Sol salutis,* 87–88; Bottermann, *Die Beteiligung des Kindes an der Liturgie von den Anfängen der Kirche bis heute,* 55.

165. See Quasten, *Musik und Gesang in den Kulten der heidnischen Antike und christlichen Frühzeit,* 133.

166. This view is also taken by Bottermann, *Die Beteiligung des Kindes an der Liturgie von den Anfängen der Kirche bis heute,* 55.

7. Children and a Life of Religious Perfection

1. Tertullian, *Ad Uxorem* (CSEL 70, 96–124; ET: *ANF* 4).

2. Ibid., 1.5.

3. Ibid.

4. Ibid.

5. CSEL 70, 125–132; ET: *ANF* 4.

6. Tertullian, *De Exhort. Cast.* 12.

7. See Michael Gärtner, *Die Familienerziehung in der alten Kirche: Eine Untersuchung über die ersten vier Jahrhunderte des Christentums mit einer Übersetzung und einem Kommentar zu der Schrift des Johannes Chrysostomus über Geltungssucht und Kindererziehung* (Köln-Wien: Böhlau Verlag, 1985), 164.

8. See ibid., 164: Tertullian's "polemic against children is wholly intended as propaganda for sexual abstinence. One cannot say that he lacks understanding of what it means to love children. But he certainly has no understanding of a love for children that is stronger than the desire for abstinence" (ET: B. McNeil).

9. *Passio Sanctarum Perpetuae et Felicitatis*. Latin text and ET: Herbert Musurillo, *The Acts of the Christian Martyrs. Introduction, Texts and Translations* (Oxford: Clarendon, 1972). For an introduction to this *passio*, see ibid.; Ross S. Kraemer and Shira L. Lander, "Perpetua and Felicitas," in *The Early Christian World*, vol. 2, ed. Philip F. Esler (London: Routledge, 2000).

10. Herbert Musurillo, *The Acts of the Christian Martyrs*, xxvii. One argument in favor of the authenticity of the first-person narrative of Perpetua is that "the style of the framework passages is quite different from the narrations in the first person" (ibid.). Stuart G. Hall, in "Women among the Early Martyrs," in *Martyrs and Martyrologies: Papers Read at the 1993 Summer Meeting and the 1993 Winter Meeting of the Ecclesiastical History Society*, ed. Diana Wood (Oxford: Blackwell, 1993), holds that Perpetua herself wrote chs. 3–10. Kraemer and Lander, in "Perpetua and Felicitas," 1058, note: "recent scholarship generally considers the prison account of Perpetua to be authentic and accurate, and the *Passio* as a whole to be a reasonably trustworthy representation of the martyrdom of Perpetua, Felicitas, and their male associates." They themselves take a more critical attitude on these questions.

11. *Passio Perp. et Felic.* 1.

12. This is also the position of Hall, "Women among the Early Martyrs," 16.

13. Musurillo, *The Acts of the Christian Martyrs*, xxvi.

14. *Passio Perp. et Felic.* 3.

15. Ibid., 6.

16. See Mary T. Malone, *Women and Christianity*, vol. 1: *The First Thousand Years* (Maryknoll, N.Y.: Orbis, 2001), 109. Malone comments on this scene: "This is a very vivid description of how the old Roman system of being *in patria potestate*—in the father's power—could, and did, break down for a daughter. As Perpetua had tried to explain to her father, the power of God had now taken over in her life and earthly systems of power were irrelevant."

17. *Passio Perp. et Felic.* 6.

18. Ibid.

19. Ibid.

20. Ibid., 15.

21. Ibid., 15.

22. Ibid., 18.

23. Ibid., 20.

24. *Passio Perp. et Felic.* 21.

25. Tertullian, *De Anima* 55.4.

26. Greek and Latin texts, with ET: Musurillo, *The Acts of the Christian Martyrs*.

27. Eusebius, *Historia Ecclesiastica* 4.15.48.

28. See Musurillo, *The Acts of the Christian Martyrs*, xv–xvi.

29. *Martyrdom of Saints Carpus, Papylus, and Agathonicê* 42.

30. Ibid., 44.

31. Ibid., 46.

32. Hall, in "Women among the Early Martyrs" (1993) 8, notes: "Most striking is the voluntary suicidal martyrdom, resembling a death by suttee." He also notes that Agathonicê was not the only such martyr: "During the local Egyptian persecution which anticipated the formal decrees of Decius in 248–9, one victim was an elderly virgin called Apollonia. They 'broke out all her teeth with blows on her jaws, and piling up a pyre before the city threatened to burn her alive, if she refused to recite along with them their blasphemous sayings. But she asked for a brief space, and, being released, without flinching she leaped into the fire and was consumed' [Eusebius, *H.E.* 6.41.7]. This comes nearer the case of Agathonicê than some other examples, such as the unnamed Roman matron who stabbed herself to death rather than be procured by Maxentius [Eusebius, *H.E.* 8.14.17]." Eusebius does not tell us whether this Roman matron had children.

33. Eusebius, *H.E.* 6.43.11 (ET: *NPNF* 2nd series, 1).

34. *Martyrdom of Saints Carpus, Papylus, and Agathonicê* 6.

35. A. S. Lewis, *Select Narratives of Holy Women* (1900), 170.

36. Ibid., 175.

37. Ibid., 177.

38. Agnes Smith Lewis, in *Select Narratives of Holy Women: From the Syro-Antiochene or Sinai Palimpsest as Written above the Old Syriac Gospels* (London: Clay and Sons, 1900), xxiv, suggests that this *passio* "may possibly have become intended for an allegory of the manner in which the Divine Wisdom, or in other words Christianity, with her three daughters, Faith, Hope, and Love, were received in the capital of the Roman Empire; how their beauty was acknowledged, while they themselves were derided, tortured, and slain; how the death of the body had no real power over them. . . . Two grains of truth may be found in the legend: Hadrian's cruelty to the Christians, and the painful nature of his mortal sickness."

39. Latin text and ET: LCL 398.

40. Prudentius, *Peristephanon* 10.661–64.

41. Ibid., 10.665–95.

42. Ibid., 10.711–15.

43. Ibid., 10.721–25.

44. Ibid., 10.736–37.

45. Ibid., 10.741–45.

46. Ibid., 10.746–50.

47. Ibid., 10.751–80.

48. Ibid., 10.781–90.

49. Ibid., 10.830–40; quotation from Ps 116:15-16 (Vulgate: 115:6-7).

50. *Peristephanon* 10.841–45.

51. Eusebius, *H.E.* 6.2.3–7 (*NPNF* 2nd series, 1).

52. Here, I am indebted to Gillian Clark, "The Fathers and the Children," in *The Church and Childhood: Papers Read at the 1993 Summer Meeting and the 1994 Winter Meeting of the Ecclesiastical History Society*, ed. Diana Wood (Oxford: Blackwell, 1994), 1–4, whose article begins with references to patristic authors who praise parents who abandon their children in order to lead a life of devotion.

53. *Sisoes* 10, quoted from Clark, "The Fathers and the Children," 1.

54. This is also the view of Clark, "The Fathers and the Children."

55. On this event, see Susan Ashbrook Harvey, *Asceticism and Society in Crisis: John of Ephesus and the Lives of the Eastern Saints* (Berkeley: University of California Press, 1990), 96–97.

56. This is also the view of Clark, "The Fathers and the Children," 1.

57. Malone, *Women and Christianity*, vol. 1, 136.

58. *Ep.* 45.2 (*NPNF* 2nd series, 6). Note that the words "intercourse" and "intimacy" have no sexual connotations here.

59. For a short but instructive introduction to this remarkable milieu, see Malone, *Women and Christianity,* vol. 1, 134–145. More detailed studies: J. N. D. Kelly, *Jerome: His Life, Writings, and Controversies.* (London: Duckworth, 1975); Elizabeth A. Clark, *Jerome, Chrysostom and Friends: Essays and Translations.* Studies in Women and Religion 2 (New York: Edwin Mellen, 1979); Elizabeth A. Clark, *The Life of Melania the Younger: Introduction, Translation, and Commentary* (Lewiston: Edwin Mellen, 1984).

60. Jerome, *Ep.* 29.9 (ET ACW 36).

61. See Clark, "The Fathers and the Children," 2, with reference to Clark, *The Life of Melania the Younger,* 86–90, on the problems posed by the traditions about Publicola.

62. In *Ep.* 39.6, Jerome reflects the criticism to which he had been exposed.

63. Ibid.

64. See Malone, *Women and Christianity,* vol. 1, 137.

65. Jerome, *Ep.* 108.6.

66. The departure scene is part of a letter Jerome sent to Eustochium to console her, shortly after Paula's death.

67. After briefly presenting some of the texts to which I have referred here, Clark, in "The Fathers and the Children," 3, comments: "There must have been reasons why committed Christians thought it right to behave like this to children, and why others were expected to admire them for it. What was it about their theology, or about their society, which made them do so?"

68. For a brief introduction to the ideology of martyrdom, see Everett Ferguson, ed., "Martyr, Martyrdom," in *Encyclopedia of Early Christianity,* 2nd ed. (New York: Garland, 1998), 724–27.

69. This is hinted at by Clark, "The Fathers and the Children," 4.

INDEX OF BIBLICAL REFERENCES

INDEX OF ANCIENT AUTHORS